Reprint Publishing

For People Who Go For Originals.

www.reprintpublishing.com

Mrs. Lina Meier,
Teacher of Cookery, German Cooking School,
Milwaukee, Wis.

THE ART

OF

GERMAN COOKING AND BAKING

Revised and Enlarged Edition.

Compiled and Published by

Mrs. LINA MEIER,

German Cooking Teacher.

MILWAUKEE, U. S. A.
1922.

COPYRIGHT 1922.
By Mrs. LINA MEIER, Milwaukee, Wis.

PREFACE TO REVISED EDITION.

This cook-book consists of about 1,250 recipes which have been tested and prepared. It is divided into 26 Chapters, as follows:

Chapter	Recipes
1 Soups	68
2 Beef	36
3 Veal	42
4 Mutton	32
5 Pork	35
6 Poultry and Game Birds	56
7 Game	25
8 Fish	61
9 Headcheese and Gelatines	12
10 Dressings or Gravies	58
11 Potatoes	26
12 Vegetables	74
13 Salads	47
14 Eggs	15
15 Omelets, Pancakes, Waffles Noodles and Pies	58
16 Jams and Sauces	23
17 Desserts	128
18 Beverages	29
19 Wheat and Rye Bread, Yeast Cakes, Baking Powder Cakes and Tarts	111
20 Fillings and Frostings	27
21 Cookies	53
22 Confectionery	20
23 Preserves	115
24 Menu	5
Sandwiches	8
25 Cookery for Invalids	63
26 Miscellaneous	12

In giving to the public this second edition I am glad to be able to offer a revised and improved cook book. It has been my aim to improve it in every way and to make it as clear, practical and helpful as possible.

The previous material has been carefully revised and changes made in the wording where it was believed that the language could be improved upon to make the author's meaning more clear and comprehensible. A radical change has also been made in the construction and arrangement of the pages, which I trust will be an advantage.

In recognition of the friendly attitude of the great public toward my first book, I wish to say that the entire edition of about 5,000 copies is scattered all over the country and many assurances of appreciation have come to me. I therefore feel encouraged to send this new edition out upon the world, knowing that it is the same excellent cook book, only improved and augmented, and I hope that the book will contribute materially to the happiness and attractiveness of many homes and help to solve many problems, especially for brides and beginners.

Respectfully,

MRS. LINA MEIER,

Author.

Milwaukee, Wis., U. S. A.

Reliable Weights and Measures as used in this Book.

		Are equal to
Flour	1 quart or 4 teacups	1 lb.
Flour (sifted)	3 coffee cups, level	1 lb.
Flour	2 tablesps., well-rounded	1 oz.
Flour	1 teaspoonful. heaped	½ oz.
Sugar, granulated	2 measuring cups, level	1 lb.
Sugar, "A" coffee	1¾ coffee cups, level	1 lb.
Sugar, powdered	2½ coffee cups, level	1 lb.
Sugar, powdered	2 tablesps., well-rounded	1 oz.
Sugar, best Brown	2 coffee cups, level	1 lb.
Sugar, granulated, "A" or brown	1 tablesp., well-heaped	1 oz.
Butter, soft	2 full cups, well-pressed	1 lb.
Butter, soft	1 tablesp., well-rounded	2 ozs.
Butter, soft	Piece size of an egg	1 oz.
Lard	2 cups	1 lb.
Eggs	10, but if quite large 9	1 lb.
Cornstarch	3 cups	1 lb.
Indian Meal	2¾ coffee cups, level	1 qt.
Coffee, ground	4 cups	1 lb.
Chocolate, sweet	3 grated tablespoons	1 oz.
Rice	2 cups, heaped	1 lb.
Rice	2 tablespoons	1 oz.
Sago	2 cups, heaped	1 lb.
Barley	4 cups	1 lb.
Bread crumbs	1 cup, grated	2 ozs.
Chopped meat	2 cups, heaped	1 lb.
Suet	1 pint	1 lb.
Nutmeg	2 cups	1 lb.
Almonds	5 medium-sized	1 oz.
Figs	2 cups	1 lb.
Dates	2 cups	1 lb.
Raisins	2 cups	1 lb.
Prunes	2 cups	1 lb.
Citron	2 cups, heaped	1 lb.
1 cup		4 ozs.
2 rounded tablespoons		1 oz.

CHAPTER 1.
SOUPS.

No. 1—BOUILLON.

4 lbs. ox-bones
6 qts. water
⅛ of an onion
½ of a carrot

1 small piece celery
1 small piece kohlrabi
1 small piece parsley-root
1 tomato, salt

Preparation: The soupbone is put over the fire in 6 qts. of cold water after it has been washed in cold water. Soupgreens and salt are added and the whole is boiled slowly 4 hours until it is boiled down to 2 or 3 quarts. Before using pour the bouillon through a fine sieve. If you like the bouillon very strong and of a good color add ½ teaspoonful of beef extract.

No. 2—BOUILLON.

The soupbone and the soupgreens are fried lightbrown with a piece of butter or lard. Water is then added and salt. Boil 4 hours as in the preceding recipe and strain before using.

No. 3—OX-TAIL BOUILLON.

3 lbs. ox-tail
1 tbsp. butter

5 qts. cold water
Salt
Soupgreens

Preparation: Cut the ox-tail into small pieces and together with the soupgreens, fry them in butter lightbrown. Add 5 qts. of water and salt. Let it boil 4 or 5 hours slowly down to 2 qts. This bouillon will be very strong and may be served in cups, and bread or cheese-sticks may be served with it.

No. 4—BOUILLON OF MEAT EXTRACT.

Soupgreens
1 tbsp. butter or lard

1 tsp. extract of meat
Salt, 1 qt. water

Preparation: Stew the soupgreens in butter or lard a little while, then add water and salt and boil slowly for 20 minutes. Add the meat extract and strain. The yolk of one egg may be stirred into it.

No. 5—BOUILLON OF BEEF.

3 lbs. of beef
1 lb. of soupbone

Salt
4 qts. water
Soupgreens

Preparation: Soupbone, soupgreens, and salt and water are put over the fire to boil one hour, then the beef is added and the whole is boiled slowly for another 2 or 2½ hours. Strain after boiling. This soup is very strong. Boiled in this way the meat is tender and nourishing.

No. 6—BOUILLON.
Made of Roastbones or Meat Remnants.

2 lbs. of roastbones Salt
Soupgreens 2 qts. water

Preparation: Chop the bones and put over the fire with soupgreens, salt and water; boil 2 hours, then strain. If the bouillon is not strong enough, add a little meat-extract.

No. 7—DUMPLINGS FOR BOUILLON.
Marrow Dumpling Soup.
Quantity for 6 Persons.

3 tbsps. of melted beef marrow ½ tsp. chopped parsley
2 eggs 1 pinch nutmeg
¾ pt. grated rolls 1 tbsp. cold water
  ½ tsp. salt

Preparation: Boil or cook the marrow until it is melted, strain it through a fine sieve. Put 3 tablespoonfuls into a dish and let it cool off. Then beat it to foam and add the yolks of the eggs, salt, parsley, nutmeg, the grated rolls and water. Finally beat the whites of 2 eggs to stiff froth and stir into the mass.

Form small dumplings, let bouillon come to a boil, put the dumplings in and boil slowly ¼ hour.

It is best to try one dumpling first; in case it does not hold together, add some more grated roll.

The soup must be served at once. A little chopped parsley put into it is a pleasing and palatable addition.

No. 8—BUTTER-DUMPLING SOUP.
Quantity for 6 Persons.

2 tbsps. of butter, 2 eggs ½ tsp. parsley
¾ pt. grated rolls 1 pinch nutmeg
¼ tsp. of salt 1 tbsp. of cold water

Preparation of butter-dumplings is the same as the marrow-dumplings in No. 7.

The butter is beaten to a cream at once and less salt is added, because the butter is already salted.

No. 9—LIVER-DUMPLING SOUP.
Quantity for 6 Persons.

¼ lb. of chopped calf's liver
1 tsp. butter
A little grated onion
1 tsp. finely chopped parsley
5 tbsps. grated rolls
2 eggs
1 tsp. salt, (scant)
1 pinch nutmeg

Preparation: The butter is stirred and liver, yolk of eggs, salt, parsley, onion, nutmeg and roll crumbs added. The whites of eggs are beaten to a froth and stirred into the mass, then small dumplings are formed. When the bouillon comes to a boil, put the dumplings in and boil ¼ hour.

The soup should be served at once.

No. 10—MEAT-DUMPLING SOUP.
Quantity for 6 Persons.

¼ lb. of finely chopped veal or poultry
2 eggs
¼ pt. grated rolls
1 tsp. of butter
½ tsp. finely chopped parsley
1 tsp. salt
1 pinch nutmeg

Preparation: The butter is stirred, then meat, yolk of eggs, parsley, salt, nutmeg added and well mixed. The whites of eggs beaten to a froth and added to the mass. Small dumplings are formed and when bouillon boils, let the dumplings boil in it 10 minutes. A little parsley may be put into the soup, which must be served at once.

No. 11—SPONGE-DUMPLING SOUP.
Quantity for 6 Persons.

3 eggs
¼ tsp. of salt
½ pt. milk or bouillon

Preparation: Eggs and milk or bouillon are well stirred or beaten, salt is added and the mass boiled in double-boiler for 20 minutes. If you have no double-boiler put your soup into a small pot and place this into a larger one with boiling water.

The bouillon is put into the souptureen and the dumplings are cut with a teaspoon and put into the bouillon. A little finely chopped parsley is added.

No. 12—FARINA-DUMPLING SOUP.
Quantity for 6 Persons.

½ pt. milk
4 tbsps. fine farina
1 egg
1 tsp. of butter
¼ tsp. of salt
1 pinch of nutmeg

Preparation: The milk is brought to a boil, stir in the farina and butter and salt, then boil 2 or 3 minutes, stirring constantly until the mass loosens from the pot. Take from the stove, stir into it the yolk of egg. Beat the white of the egg to a froth and add to the mass. When it is cool make small dumplings, or you may also cut into sponges with teaspoon. Let the bouillon boil 5 minutes with the dumplings. Some chopped parsley in the soup is very good.

No. 13—STIRRED SPONGE DUMPLINGS.
Quantity for 6 Persons.

2 tbsps. of butter
6 tbsps. of flour
2 tbsps. of milk
2 eggs
¼ tsp. of salt
½ tsp. finely chopped parsley
1 pinch of nutmeg

Preparation: The butter is beaten to a cream, add yolks of 2 eggs, salt, parsley, nutmeg, flour and milk.

The whites of 2 eggs are beaten to a froth and stirred in. When the bouillon boils cut out small sponges with teaspoon and boil 5 minutes.

If the dumplings are too soft, add some more flour. The soup must be served at once.

No. 14—CURDLE SOUP.
Quantity for 6 Persons.

¾ pt. milk
2—3 eggs
3 tbsps. of flour
½ tsp. of salt
1 pinch of nutmeg
1 tsp. of finely chopped parsley

Preparation: The milk, eggs, flour, salt and nutmeg are well mixed.

When the bouillon boils the mass is slowly poured into it and boiled 5 minutes. The soup must be stirred constantly while boiling, lest it should burn. When served the parsley is added.

No. 15—MARROWSTRIPS FOR SOUP.
Quantity for 6 Persons.

⅛ lb. beef marrow, 2 rolls
⅛ lb. butter, (scant)
1 pinch of salt
1 pinch of white pepper

Preparation: The rolls are cut into equal strips and baked light brown in the butter. They are then placed on a platter. Soak the marrow in water, cut into layers and place on the hot bread. Sprinkle with salt and pepper and place the pan or platter into a hot oven. Leave it in the oven until the marrow is transparent and serve with the bouillon.

No. 16—BREADSTICKS FOR BOUILLON.
Quantity for 6 Persons.

½ pt. warm milk
½ cake yeast
1 tbsp. of milk
1 pinch of salt

Preparation: The warm milk and flour is beaten to a thin dough. The yeast is dissolved in a tablespoonful of warm milk and added to the dough. The whole is placed near a warm stove for rising which requires about ½ hour.

When this is done, work the dough with flour thick enough to roll out in ½ inch layer. Cut this dough into narrow strips 4 inches long and set aside for rising again, then bake them in a tin until of a yellow color. Serve them fresh and warm with a strong bouillon.

No. 17—CHEESESTICKS FOR BOUILLON.
Quantity for 12 Persons.

⅛ lb. Swiss cheese
⅛ lb. Parmesan cheese
¼ lb. butter
¼ lb. flour
1 pinch salt
1 pinch paprika (red pepper)

Preparation: The butter is beaten to foam, the cheese is grated fine and added, also salt and paprika. Then the flour is kneaded into it to make a smooth dough and rolled out to ½ inch thickness. Cut in ½ inch strips and 5 inches long. Now bake in a medium hot oven to a light yellow color. If too dark the sticks will taste bitter.

They are served fresh and warm with strong bouillon.

No. 18—CHEESE PASTRY.
Quantity for 12—15 Persons.

¼ lb. flour
¼ lb. (scant) Parmesan cheese
⅛ lb. fresh, good butter
6 tbsps. thick, sour cream
1 pinch salt
1 pinch sugar
A little nutmeg
A little paprika (red pepper)

Preparation: The butter is beaten to a cream, and the finely grated cheese added. The cream, sugar, salt, nutmeg, paprika and flour added, made into a fine paste and rolled out into ½ inch thickness. Cut out with a small glass and bake in a medium hot oven to a light yellow color.

Remarks: It is better to put the paste on ice for a while and then roll it out. They are served hot with bouillon; or this pastry, as also the cheesesticks in No. 17 may be served as dessert instead of bread, butter and cheese.

No. 19—FLOUR DUMPLINGS.
Quantity for 6 Persons.

1 cup of flour
1½ cups of boiling water
1 tbsp. of butter
1 tsp. of salt, 1 egg

Preparation: The flour and salt are mixed and the boiling water, in which the butter is melted, poured on and the mass stirred briskly, after which the egg is mixed in.

The bouillon should be boiling, and the dumplings are formed or cut out with a teaspoon, put into the bouillon, and boiled 8 minutes.

Remarks: These dumplings may be made large, boiled in salt water 10 minutes and served with stewed fruit.

No. 20—RICE SOUP WITH BOUILLON.
Quantity for 6 Persons.

½ cup of rice
3 qts. of bouillon
2 cups of cold water

Preparation: The rice is washed and put on with 2 cups of cold water to boil 5 minutes; then pour off the water. Now add 3 qts. bouillon and cook slowly for 1 hour.

No. 21—BOUILLON RICE SOUP WITH TOMATOES.
Quantity for 6 Persons.

½ cup rice
2 cups water
½ qt. canned tomatoes or 1½ lbs. fresh tomatoes.
3 qts. bouillon

Preparation: After the bouillon boils as in No. 1, add instead of one tomato the quantity mentioned in this recipe. Proceed as in No. 20, strain the bouillon and boil the rice in it for 1 hour.

No. 22—RICE SOUP WITH MILK.
Quantity for 6 Persons.

1 cup of rice
3 cups of water
2 qts. of milk
½ tsp. of salt

Preparation: The rice is washed in water, and boiled for 5 minutes. Pour off the water and gradually add milk. It takes the rice about 1½ to 2 hours to get soft. Serve with sugar and cinnamon or cooked prunes.

In the summer time rice is palatable and refreshing, served cold with milk.

No. 23—COLD RICE SOUP WITH APPLES.
Quantity for 6 Persons.

¾ cup of rice
2 qts. water
2 lbs. sweet-sour apples
½ lemon
¼ tsp. of salt
½ cup sugar

Preparation: The rice is washed and boiled in 2 cups of water for 5 minutes, then this water is poured off and 2 qts. added to boil 1 hour. In the meantime peel the apples and remove the core, cut them up in ⅛ths and put into rice, also cut up the ½ lemon in slices and add to the soup. Boil all this 20 minutes after adding salt and sugar as stated above.

If the soup is too thick, add some more water. It can be served warm, but it tastes better when cold.

Remarks: You can improve the soup by adding ½ pt. of white wine and more sugar.

No. 24—BARLEY SOUP WITH BOUILLON.
Quantity for 6 Persons.

¾ cup of pearl barley
2 cups of water,
3 qts. bouillon
Some finely cut asparagus

Preparations: The barley is washed in cold water and then brought to boiling in cold water. The water is poured off and the bouillon poured on and with this it is boiled slowly for 1½ hours. During the last ¾ of an hour the asparagus is put in and boiled until soft. If you wish, you may leave out the asparagus.

If the soup looks too white you may add some meat extract or stir into it the yolk of one egg.

No. 25—BARLEY GRUEL SOUP WITH BOUILLON.
Quantity for 6 Persons.

1 cup of pearl barley
1 tbsp. of butter
Some pieces of asparagus if you like
3 qts. strong bouillon

Preparation: The barley is washed and boiling water poured on and off twice. Heat the butter and cook the barley in it for a while. Then the bouillon is poured on and the soup is boiled slowly for 2½ hours. Now the soup is strained through a fine hairsieve and heated again.

If you wish some asparagus in it, which gives it a nice flavor, cook the asparagus pieces separately in bouillon until soft and add it to the soup, or stir the yolk of one egg into the soup.

This soup is very good for sick persons, but for this purpose the asparagus is left out.

No. 26—BARLEY GRUEL SOUP.
Quantity for 6 Persons.

1 cup of pearl barley
1 tbsp. of butter
3 qts. of water
Salt according to taste
1 pinch of nutmeg
2 tsps. of chopped parsley

Preparation: The barley is washed and put over the fire in some cold water. Let it get hot and pour off the water. Put the barley into the butter and let it steep a while, then add more water and boil for one hour. Add salt and nutmeg and at last add the parsley. You can also add a piece of fresh butter.

No. 27—SWEET BARLEY GRUEL SOUP.
Quantity for 6 Persons.

This soup is the same as No. 26 with the exception of parsley and nutmeg which are left out. ½ cup of sugar and some cinnamon are added. The soup is then strained through a fine hairsieve and the yolk of one egg is stirred into it.

No. 28—SAGO SOUP WITH BOUILLON.
Quantity for 6 Persons.

1 cup of sago
3 qts. of bouillon
1 qt. of water

Preparation: The sago is soaked for 1 hour in cold water. Pour off the water and add boiling hot bouillon, and in this the sago is left to boil until it is transparent.

No. 29—SAGO SOUP WITH RED WINE OR RASPBERRY JUICE.
Quantity for 2 Persons.

¼ cup of sago
3 cups of water
½ cup of sugar
2 slices of lemon
1½ cups red wine or raspberry juice

Preparation: The sago is soaked in cold water for one hour. This water is then poured off and 3 cups of fresh water added in which the sago is boiled until soft and transparent. Add the quantity of red wine or juice, sugar and lemon and let it boil 5 minutes longer. Remove the lemon slices.

Serve this soup with zwieback or with small slices of toast.

No. 30—FARINA SOUP WITH BOUILLON.
Quantity for 6 Persons.

¾ cup of farina   2 qts. of bouillon

Preparation: Let the already strained bouillon boil, then pour the farina into it slowly while stirring it, and leave it to boil 10 minutes.

No. 31—GREEN CORN SOUP WITH BOUILLON.
Quantity for 6 Persons.

1½ cups of green corn   1 or 2 yolks of eggs
1 tbsp. of butter   1 milk roll cut into small cubes
3 qts. of bouillon   ½ tbsp. of butter

Preparation: The green corn is steeped in the tablespoonful of butter, then the bouillon is added and this boiled slowly for 2 hours. This is then strained through a hairsieve and the yolk of one egg stirred in.

The milk roll is cut into cubes and fried in the ½ tablespoonful of butter until light yellow. When serving the soup put these bread cubes into it or serve them with the soup.

No. 32—OATMEAL SOUP.
Quantity for 6 Persons.

2 cups of oatmeal   Some salt
2 tbsps. of butter   ½ tsp. of meat extract
              2½ qts. of water

Preparation: The oatmeal is put on with the water and salt and boiled slowly for ½ hour, then the soup is strained or pressed through a hairsieve. Now add butter and meat extract and let this all come to a boil. If the soup is too thick add some more boiling water.

Remarks: Instead of water you may also take milk and leave out the meat extract. You may add some sugar. Small pieces of rolls fried in butter are good with this soup. It is very good for invalids.

No. 33—BEAN SOUP WITH BOUILLON.
Quantity for 6 Persons.

1 cup of nice white beans   ½ lb. of ham bones
            3 qts. of good bouillon

Preparation: The beans are soaked in water for some hours, pour off the water, put on fresh water and bring to boil. After boiling for 10 minutes, pour off this water and boil again. Now pour it off for the last time, add the bouillon and boil the beans in this until soft. The ham bone is boiled in the bouillon. It requires 3 hours to cook this soup.

No. 34—BEAN-PUREE SOUP WITH CRAB OR LOBSTER BUTTER.
Quantity for 4 Persons.

¾ cup of white beans
1½ qts. of water
1 tbsp. of butter
1 tbsp. of crab or lobster-butter
1½ qts. of bouillon
Some white pepper
3 tbsps. of cream

Preparation: The beans are soaked, drained and boiled until soft in 1½ qts. of water. When they are soft the water must be all boiled down. Strain the beans through a fine sieve. This puree or mass is stewed in the butter and the crab or lobster-butter and then the bouillon is added, also the white pepper. The cream is put into the soup dish and the soup is poured over it.

Begin preparation of this soup about 3 hours before time to serve.

No. 35—PEA SOUP WITH BOUILLON.
Quantity for 6 Persons.

1½ cups of peas
3 qts. of bouillon
1 roll
½ tbsp. of butter
½ lb. ham or bones

Preparation: The peas are prepared just like the beans in No. 33, then they are boiled until soft in bouillon for 3 hours. The soup is then strained. If it is ham that is being boiled in the bouillon, cut same into small pieces and put them into the strained peas.

Cut the roll into small cubes, fry them in butter until light yellow and serve with the soup.

No. 36—LENTIL SOUP.
Quantity for 6 Persons.

2 cups of lentils
3 qts. of bouillon
½ tbsp. of butter
1 tbsp. of flour
1 lb. of Wiener sausage

Preparation: The lentils are soaked in water for one hour, then this water is poured off and the lentils brought to boil in cold water. They must boil for 10 minutes. This water is again poured off and the bouillon added; in this the lentils are boiled until soft which requires 2½ to 3 hours. When the lentils are done, the butter is heated and the flour stirred into it; this is then poured into the soup. Ten minutes before serving put the Wieners into the soup, let come to a boil and then merely steep. The Wieners are served with the soup.

Remarks: Put very little salt into the soup, because the Wieners are already seasoned.

No. 37—FRESH VEGETABLE SOUP WITH BOUILLON.
Quantity for 6 Persons.

3 small carrots
2 small kohlrabis
¼ head of celery
¼ head of cauliflower
30 pods of shelled peas

6 asparagus stalks
2 potatoes if you like
½ tbsp. of butter
1 tbsp. of flour
3 qts. bouillon

Preparation: The butter is heated and flour put into it to stew, then the bouillon is added; all vegetables and potatoes cut into small pieces, and put into the boiling bouillon and cooked for one hour until soft. If you cannot get all of these vegetables you may put less of it into the soup. Instead you may put small meat dumplings of veal or chicken into it. These dumplings are prepared as in recipe No. 10.

No. 38—ASPARAGUS SOUP WITH BOUILLON.
Quantity for 6 Persons.

2 lbs. of asparagus
3 qts. of bouillon

1 tbsp. of butter
2½ tbsps. of flour

Preparation: The butter is heated and the flour stewed in it, then the bouillon is added and let come to a boil. The asparagus is peeled, cut into small pieces, 1½ inches long, and boiled in the bouillon for ¾ of an hour.

If the asparagus is tender it will be done after ½ hour cooking.

No. 39—CAULIFLOWER SOUP WITH BOUILLON.
Quantity for 6 Persons.

1 head of cauliflower
3 qts. bouillon

1 tbsp. of butter
2½ tbsps. of flour

Preparation: The preparation of this soup is the same as No. 38. The cauliflower is broken into small roses and boiled in the prepared bouillon about 20 minutes.

No. 40—SORREL SOUP WITH BOUILLON.
Quantity for 6 Persons.

¼ lb. of sorrel
½ lb. lettuce leaves
¼ lb. butter
3 tbsps. of flour
2½ qts. bouillon
5 tbsps. of cream
Some sugar
1 pinch of pepper
1 roll cut into small cubes
½ tbsp. of butter
2 yolks of eggs

Preparation: The sorrel and lettuce leaves are put into boiling water for a minute and placed in a sieve to drain. It is then put into ¼ lb. of butter and stewed for 10 minutes. After this the mass is pressed through a sieve and stirred with the yolks of eggs and cream. The bouillon should be prepared and heated beforehand; the butter should be heated and the flour stirred in, and to this the bouillon is gradually added. The cubes of roll are fried light yellow in the ½ tablespoonful of butter. When the puree is done it is poured into the boiling bouillon and sugar and pepper put in to suit taste. The fried roll cubes are served with the soup.

No. 41—CELERY SOUP WITH MILK.
Quantity for 6 Persons.

2 small bundles of fresh celery or
1½ head of celery
2 tbsps. of butter
3 tbsps. of flour
1½—2 qts. of milk and ½ qt. cream
1—2 yolks of eggs
1 pinch of pepper
1 pinch of salt

Preparation: The celery is cut into small pieces, and boiled in water until soft, then strained through a hairsieve. The butter is heated with the flour in it and the milk is now added. The boiled and strained celery is added, let come to a boil, stirring constantly. Add enough salt and pepper to suit your taste, stir in the yolks and serve at once. If you leave the soup standing it will get thick.

No. 42—TOMATO SOUP.
Quantity for 6 Persons.

1 qt. canned tomatoes, or
4 lbs. of fresh tomatoes
1 qt. of water
1 tbsp. of butter
½ tsp. of sliced onions
1 pinch of pepper
Salt, some sugar
2 tbsps. of flour
1 roll cut into cubes
½ tbsp. of butter
1 tsp. of chopped parsley

Preparation: The tomatoes are boiled in water for a few minutes. If you have taken fresh tomatoes let them cook ½ hour in 1¼ qts. of water. Butter and finely cut onions are steeped so that the onions remain light yellow, add the flour and cook a little more. Butter, flour and onions are now put into the boiling tomatoes, and boiled with them. Then the mass is strained, sugar, salt, pepper added, the whole heated, the chopped parsley put in, and the soup served. The roll cubes are fried light yellow and put into the soup or if you wish you can serve them with the soup.

No. 43—TOMATO SOUP WITH MILK.
Quantity for 6 Persons.

1 qt. canned tomatoes or	1 pinch of salt
4 lbs. fresh tomatoes	1 pinch of sugar
1 qt. of milk	1 pinch of pepper
½ tbsp. of butter	1 tsp. of baking soda

Preparation. The can of tomatoes is heated, the fresh tomatoes must be boiled until soft in ½ qt. of water, then pressed through a fine sieve.

The milk and butter are brought to boil in a double boiler and the tomatoes are put into it. Salt, pepper and sugar put in, then the soda stirred in and the soup served at once.

No. 44—MOCK-TURTLE SOUP.
Quantity for 8 Persons.

½ calf's head without the brains	⅛ qt. red wine
1 calf's tongue or 2 feet	Salt and pepper
⅛ lb. of raw ham, (scant)	⅛ lb. of butter
1 carrot	⅛ lb. of flour
1 piece of parsley-root	1/16 qt. of Madeira wine
½ of a celery-root	4 eggs
2 small onions	2½ qts. of water

Preparation: The finely cut ham, soupgreens and onions are fried and the calf's head and tongue or chopped feet are then put in and the quantity of water added. The feet must be scalded before using.

The whole is cooked until tender and salt and pepper added. Then it is strained. The skin of the calf's head is cut into small pieces (also the tongue and feet) a little salt is strewn over the meat and the red wine poured over it.

Butter and flour are browned and the bouillon, from which the fat has been removed is poured on, also the Madeira wine.

The soup is now slowly boiled for one hour. The scum and fat must be taken off.

Now the meat with the red wine are put in.

—18—

The eggs are boiled hard and the whole yolks put into the soup. You can also cut the yolks in halves and put one-half into each soup dish.

It requires 3 hours to cook this soup.

No. 45—POTATO SOUP WITH BOUILLON.
Quantity for 6 Persons.

2 lbs. of raw or unboiled peeled potatoes
2 qts. bouillon of oxbones, (soup-bones)
or bouillon of rabbitroast bones,
or bouillon of poultryroast bones
1 roll cut into small cubes
½ tbsp. of butter

Preparation: The potatoes are pared, cut into small pieces and cooked until soft in the bouillon, then pressed through a sieve. If you wish you may leave the pieces of potatoes whole.

The roll cubes are toasted light yellow and put into the soup or served with it.

Remarks: Potato-soup of rabbitroast bones or fowl bones is very good. If there is some meat left on these bones, cut it in small pieces and put it into the soup.

No. 46—POTATO SOUP.
Quantity for 6 Persons.

2 lbs. of raw potatoes
2 qts. of water
1½ tbsps. of fresh butter
Salt
1 roll cut into cubes
½ tbsp. of butter
½ tsp. of meat extract

Preparation: The potatoes are pared, cut into small pieces, and cooked until soft in the 2 qts. of water, then pressed through a sieve and cooked again. Salt, butter, meat extract are now added.

The roll cubes are fried light yellow in the ½ tablespoonful of butter and put into the soup before serving.

No. 47—WHITE WINE SOUP.
Quantity for 6 Persons.

1 qt. light white wine
1 qt. water
1 stick of cinnamon
2 cloves
2 tsps. of lemon sugar or
4 slices of lemon
¼ lb. of sugar
3 tbsps. of corn starch or flour
1 pinch of salt
3 eggs

Preparation: The water with the spices is boiled for 2 minutes before the wine is added and let come to a boil again.

The yolks of the 3 eggs are stirred with flour and a little water and then stirred into the soup. Let it come to a boil once more, stirring constantly. Then it is taken from the stove. The whites of the eggs are beaten to a stiff froth and put into the soup when served.

Cloves, lemon slices, and cinnamon are taken out. Zwieback or toasted slices of rolls are served with this soup.

No. 48—RED WINE SOUP.
Quantity for 6 Persons.

1 qt. light red wine	1 stick of cinnamon
1 qt. of water	¼ lb. of sugar
1 small piece of lemon peel	3 tbsps. of cornstarch or common flour
3 cloves	

Preparation: Boil the water, sugar and spices for 10 minutes. The flour mixed with some water is stirred in and let come to a boil, stirring constantly.

Heat the red wine and put it into the soup but do not boil any longer. Serve at once. Serve zwieback or small soup macaroons with it.

No. 49—BEER SOUP.
Quantity for 6 Persons.

1½ qts. of beer	1 pinch of salt
½ qt. water	3 tbsps. of flour or cornstarch
1 stick of cinnamon	3 slices of lemon or lemon sugar
2 cloves	3 eggs
	¼ lb. sugar

Preparation: Water, beer, sugar and spices are brought to a boil. The flour and yolks of eggs are mixed with water and stirred into the soup and brought to a boil again. The whites of eggs are beaten to a stiff froth and put into the soup when served.

Zwieback or toasted slices of rolls are served with the soup.

No. 50—APPLE SOUP.
Quantity for 6 Persons.

2 lbs. of apples	2 tbsps. of cornstarch
2 qts. of water	⅛ lb. of currants
¼ lb. of sugar	Juice of ½ lemon and a small piece of rind
1 stick of cinnamon	

Preparation: The apples with their peelings on are cut into pieces and the core removed, and then boiled in the water with the spices until soft. The flour is mixed with a little water and put into the apples while boiling. Then the whole is strained or pressed through a sieve. Now the washed currants are added and a cup of red wine or white wine and cooked again.

Remarks: All fruit soups may be prepared this way, i. e., plum, cherry, apricots, strawberries, raspberries, currants, grapes, gooseberries or rhubarb soups are made this way but some need more sugar than others, or the wine is left out.

Dried fruit may also be used.

No. 51—RYE BREAD SOUP.
Quantity for 6 Persons.

2 lbs. of rye bread
2 qts. of water
Salt
1 tumbler full of white wine
Some sugar, about 1 tbsp.
1 tbsp. of fresh butter
½ cup of currants

Preparation: The rye bread which may be stale is put on with 2 qts. of cold water and boiled a little, then pressed through a hairsieve.

If it should be too thick, leave out some bread. It is then boiled with the salt, sugar, currants and butter for a little while. The white wine is poured into the soup dish and the soup added to it while boiling hot.

No. 52—FLOUR SOUP, (WHEAT).
Quantity for 6 Persons.

⅛ lb. of butter
⅛ lb. of flour
½ qt. of water
1 pinch of salt
1½ qts. of milk

Preparation: The butter is browned, flour stirred in, milk, water and salt added. The soup must be boiled 20 minutes, constantly stirring it. You may stir into it the yolk of one egg.

No. 53—RYE FLOUR SOUP.
Quantity for 6 Persons.

⅛ lb. of rye flour
2 tbsps. of butter
½ qt. of water
1 qt. of milk
1 pinch of salt
2 yolks of eggs

Preparation: The rye flour is stirred into the cold water, butter and salt added and cooked for 20 minutes while stirring constantly. Add the milk and boil again; then stir in the yolks.

No. 54—MILK SOUP.
Quantity for 6 Persons.

2 qts. of milk
1 small stick of cinnamon
1 tbsp. of lemon sugar
⅛ lb. of sugar
1 pinch of salt
⅛ lb. cornstarch

Preparation: 1½ qts. milk, sugar, spices and salt, let come to a boil. The flour is mixed with ½ qt. of milk and stirred into the boiling milk, then boiled for ¼ hour. Stir in one egg yolk, then serve.

No. 55—CHOCOLATE SOUP.
Quantity for 6 Persons.

2 qts. of milk
½ lb. of sweet chocolate or
⅛ lb. of cocoa
1 tbsp. of lemon sugar
¼ lb. of sugar
1 small stick of cinnamon
1 pinch of salt
⅛ lb. of cornstarch

Preparation: Prepare the chocolate soup just the same as the milk soup No. 54. Grate the chocolate and stir it into the flour or cornstarch and milk. If it gets too thick add more milk.

No. 56—FISH SOUP WITH FISH-DUMPLINGS.
Quantity for 6 Persons.

2½ lbs. of pickerel or other fish
1½ qts. of water
½ of an onion, salt
⅛ lb. of flour
⅛ lb. of butter
1 qt. of bouillon
8 oysters
15 shrimps or crabs
⅛ qt. white wine
2 tbsps. of butter
2 yolks of eggs
12 small fish dumplings

Preparation: The fish is scaled, drawn and washed. The meat is cut from the bones, the liver and gall removed. The bones are chopped up and with water, onions, salt and spices slowly stewed for a fish bouillon.

Melt ⅛ lb. butter, stir in the flour, simmer to a light yellow, pour the fish bouillon in, let it simmer slowly for ¾ of an hour.

The crawfish or crabs are boiled in the meantime. The meat is taken out of the shells. The oysters and the fish liver, which is cut into pieces, are heated in the white wine, but not boiled. The meat of the pickerel is also cut into small pieces and stewed in 2 tablespoonfuls of butter until tender.

The fish dumplings are also cooked 10 minutes in the white wine. When done, put the dumplings into the soup tureen. All the meat, liver, crabs and oysters are put into the soup tureen, the gravy is strained and the yolks of 2 eggs stirred in and then poured into the tureen. Salt to taste. It is a very fine soup.

The fish dumplings are made the same way as the meat dumplings in No. 10, only instead of meat take fish, and take half the quantities given in No. 10. Leave out the nutmeg.

No. 57—CRAWFISH OR CRAB SOUP WITH MARROW-DUMPLINGS OR LIVER-DUMPLINGS.

Quantity for 6—8 Persons.

24 small crabs
¼ lb. of butter
2½ qts. of bouillon
1 pinch of white pepper

Preparation: The crabs are washed carefully and thrown into boiling salt water, but taken out again immediately. Mash the crabmeat and stew it ¼ of an hour in the ¼ lb. of butter. After this stir in the bouillon, cover and cook slowly 1 hour.

Marrow dumplings or liver dumplings are cooked in the soup which has been strained. The marrow dumplings are prepared as directed in No. 7 and the liver dumplings as in No. 9. Take the same quantities. Serve at once when the dumplings are done.

No. 58—OYSTER SOUP.

Quantity for 6 Persons.

1 qt. oysters
1 qt. milk
1 pinch of salt
1 pinch of pepper
2 tbsps. of fresh butter

Preparation: The milk is boiled and butter, salt, and pepper added. The oysters with their juice are put into the boiling milk; stir constantly while doing this, let come to boiling; stirring continually; then serve at once. Serve crackers with the soup.

No. 59—CHICKEN BOUILLON TO DRINK.

Quantity for 4 Persons.

1 chicken
1 egg
1½ qts. of water
Some salt

Preparation: The chicken is cleaned well and all fat removed. The meat is removed from the bones and chopped fine, the bones cracked or split, the egg is stirred in and with water and salt put into a covered pot and cooked slowly for 3 hours. Strain through a sieve and serve. This soup is very good for invalids and convalescents.

No. 60—PIGEON BOUILLON TO DRINK.
Quantity for 3 Persons.

2 pigeons
1 egg
1¼ qts. of water
Some salt

Preparation: The pigeons are cleaned well and washed. The meat is removed from the bones and chopped fine, the bones split or cracked and the egg stirred in. Put on the fire with the water and salt and cook in a covered pot for 3 hours. Strain and serve. This soup is also good for sick people.

No. 61—PIGEON SOUP.
Quantity for 6—8 Persons.

2 old pigeons
2 lbs. of soupbone, or better
1 lb. of beef
Some soupgreens
3 qts. of water
Scarcely ¼ lb. of fine barley
2 tbsps. of butter
2 yolks of eggs
4 asparagus stalks

Preparation: The pigeons are cleaned well and the breast and clubs or legs cut off and left whole. The other meat is chopped, also the beef, and all is boiled until soft in the quantity of water with salt and soupgreens. In the meantime the barley is soaked. Drain well and stew the barley in butter for a little while, then gradually pour on the strained bouillon.

Peel the asparagus and cut it into inch lengths and add to the barley and bouillon. Boil for 1 hour. The meat from the breast and legs is cut fine and put into the soup when served. If you have used beef for the soup you may make hash or salad of it.

No. 62—CHICKEN SOUP.
Quantity for 6 Persons.

1 chicken
2½ qts. of water
Some soupgreens
Salt
6 asparagus stalks, a few pieces of cauliflower
¼ cup of good rice, good measure
¼ tsp. of meat extract

Preparation: The chicken is cleaned well, washed and cooked until soft with soupgreens, salt and water which requires 1½ hours. If it is an old chicken it will require 2 to 3 hours. The rice is washed and put on with some cold water to get partly done. When the water is all boiled down add the strained bouillon.

The asparagus and cauliflower are cleaned and cut into

small pieces and cooked until soft with the rice in the bouillon. When the soup is done the meat extract is added.

The chicken breast is cut into small pieces and put into the soup. You can also carve the whole chicken and serve it with the soup.

No. 63—PARTRIDGE SOUP.
Quantity for 6 Persons.

2 old partridges	2 tbsps. of butter
4 potatoes cut in cubes	Salt
2 carrots cut in pieces	2 qts. of water
3 tbsps. of flour	1½ tbsps. of butter

Preparation: The partridges are cleaned well and fried in the 2 tablespoonfus of butter to a light brown. The flour is browned in the 1½ tablespoonfus of butter and the water added, also potatoes, carrots and salt and the fried partridges; all of this is boiled until tender in a covered pot. This will require 2 to 2½ hours. The partridge breast is cut in pieces and served in the soup.

The remaining partridge meat may be utilized in hash or dumplings.

No. 64—WILD GAME OR POULTRY SOUP.
Quantity for 4—6 Persons.

You can make soups from all kinds of wild or tame birds. Follow directions given for chicken, pigeon or partridge soup. If the soup is made of bones and remnants and not rich enough you may add meat extract.

No. 65—RED WINE SOUP WITH SAGO.
Quantity for 6 Persons.

¾ bottle of red wine	1 stick of cinnamon
1 qt. of water	¼ lb. of sugar
¼ lb. of sago	2 slices of lemon
	½ cup raisins

Preparation: The sago and raisins are boiled until soft in the water. Then the red wine is added, also cinnamon, sugar and lemon slices, and the soup is brought to boil again. Zwieback or toasted rolls are served with it.

No. 66—TOMATO SOUP WITH SMALL MEAT OR POTATO DUMPLINGS.

Quantity for 6 Persons.

1 qt. can of tomatoes	¼ tbsp. of sliced onions
1 qt. of water	Salt to suit taste
1½ tbsps. of butter	1 pinch of pepper
2 heaping tbsps. of flour	1 tbsp. of sugar

Meat Dumplings.

¼ lb. beef	1 egg
¼ lb. pork	Salt and pepper to suit taste
	1 tbsp. of butter

Potato Dumplings.

½ cup grated potatoes	2 tbsps. of flour
½ egg	Salt and pepper to suit taste

Preparation: Tomatoes are cooked in the water for 10 minutes. The butter is melted and the onions put in and stewed a little, then the flour is stirred in and the whole is put into the soup. Salt, pepper and sugar are added and after a few minutes boiling the whole is strained.

The meat dumplings contain beef, pork, 1 egg, butter, salt and pepper, which is all mixed and small dumplings are formed.

The potato dumplings are made of mashed or grated boiled potatoes which are mixed with 1 egg, flour, salt and pepper. Small dumplings are formed and rolled in flour.

The tomato soup must be boiling when the dumplings are put in, and boil 10 minutes. Serve the soup at once with the dumplings in it.

A teaspoonful of finely chopped parsley may be put in the soup.

No. 67—BUTTERMILK SOUP OR SOUR MILK SOUP.

Quantity for 6 Persons.

1½ qts. of buttermilk or sour milk	1 small stick of cinnamon
½ qt. sweet milk	3 slices of lemon
¼ lb. of sago	1 pinch of salt
	1 cup of sugar

Preparation: Buttermilk and sweet milk are brought to a boil with the sago. Cinnamon and lemon added. Cook slowly for one hour, stirring frequently. Add salt and a little sugar. The soup may be served hot or cold.

No. 68—OYSTERPLANT SOUP.
Quantity for 6 Persons.

2 bundles of oysterplants	1 pinch of pepper
2½ tbsps. of butter	Salt to suit your taste
2 tbsps. of flour	2 yolks of eggs
	1½ qts. of milk

Preparation: The oysterplants are scraped and cut into small pieces. Put the clean oysterplants immediately into water mixed with vinegar and flour so that they will not get black.

When they are well cleaned they are stewed with the butter and a little water until tender; then stir in the flour and cook a few minutes. Then the milk is gradually added while stirring the soup constantly. Now the soup is left to cook a little, stirring occasionally and then salt and pepper are added.

At last the yolks of 2 eggs are stirred in.

CHAPTER 2.
BEEF.

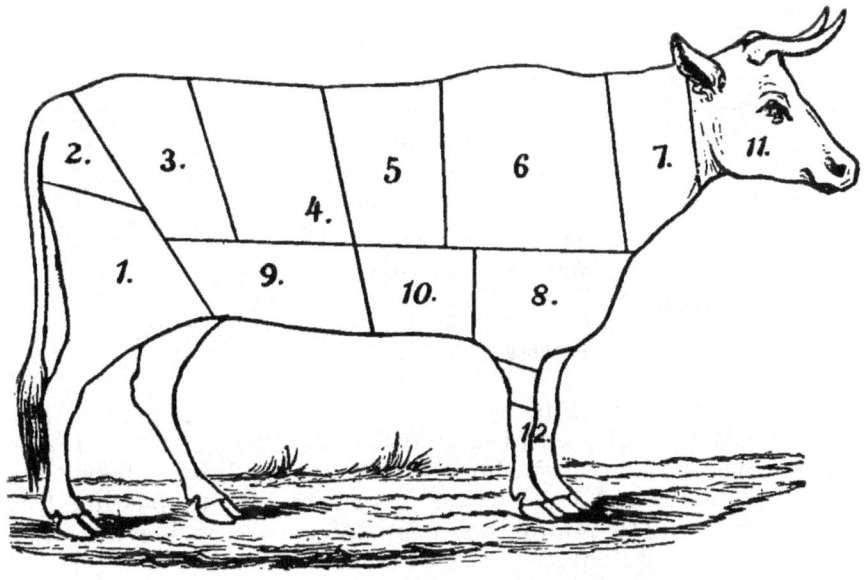

1. Beef Round.
2. Rump.
3. Sirloin.
4. Loin and Porterhouse with Fillet.
5-6. Rib Roast.
6. Chuck of Beef.
7. Neck.
8. Round Shoulder.
9. Beef Flank.
10. Beef Brisket.
11. Head.
12. Shank.
13. Tail.

Preparation of All Kinds of Beef Dishes. Boiled, Roasted and Salted Beef. How Remnants of Beef May be Utilized.

The best quality of beef has a nice red color and white suet. The meat of young cows is more pale and tender.

Old cows have dark, brownish red meat and yellow suet. Young beef makes a good roast, but a poor bouillon. Old beef makes a tough roast, but a good bouillon.

The best Pieces for Roasting.

The fillet, roastbeef, and the inner part of the forerib.

The best Pieces for braising or Pot Roast.

The rump, the sirloin, the fillet, roastbeef, (well-hung), also the chuck and round shoulder, (well-hung).

The best Pieces for Bouillon.

The meat from the round, the rump, the chuck, in fact all lean meat and bones.

Meat for Salting and Pickling.

The meat from the round, also from the brisket, but without bones.

Best Pieces for Boiling.

The rump, the brisket and chuck.

No. 1—ROAST BEEF.
Quantity for 6—8 Persons.

6 lbs. of roastbeef	½ cup of water
2—3 tbsps. of butter	1 cup of water for gravy
½ of an onion, to suit taste	¾ tbsp. of flour

Salt, pepper

Preparation: The roastbeef is salted and peppered, put into a roasting-pan with the quantity of water given and roasted in the oven. After ½ hour's roasting add 2 to 3 tablespoonfuls of butter and let it roast for another hour, basting frequently. In 1½ hours the roastbeef is rare inside and in 2 hours it is well done.

If the roast is small, it will require 15 minutes less per pound, and if larger 15 minutes longer for roasting. When the roast is done, put it on a platter and make the gravy.

Take ¾ tablespoonful of flour, put it into the pan, stir it well and let it boil 3 minutes, then pour in the 1 cup of water, boil a few minutes, strain and serve.

Remarks: Be careful that the butter does not turn too dark during the roasting. Should this be the case add a little water, so that the gravy may not taste bitter.

No. 2—MEAT-PUDDING.
How to Utilize Roast Beef.
Roastbeef With Rice Covering.
Quantity for 4—6 Persons.

1¼ lbs. left over roast beef	¼ tsp. chopped onions
½ cup of rice	2 tbsps. of butter
2 tbsps. of grated Swiss or Parmesan cheese	2 tbsps. of grated rolls
	½ cup of left over gravy
½ tbsp. of flour	½ qt. of bouillon or water

2 yolks of eggs

Preparation: The roast meat is chopped, but not too fine, and stewed in a pan with the butter and onions. The gravy is mixed with flour, salt and pepper and poured on the meat which is left to cook a few minutes until the gravy gets thick.

The rice is cooked until soft and thick in the water or bouillon, the grated cheese is put in and at last the yolks of 2 eggs. Taste the rice for salt. Butter a pudding-mold and strew in some grated rolls, now put in one layer of rice and one layer of meat and so on until all the meat and rice are in. Close the mold well and set in a steamer over a kettle of boiling water and steam for 2 hours.

After the pudding is done, turn it out and pour over it a Dutch gravy or serve the gravy separately with it.

No. 3—BEEF-FILLET ROAST.
Quantity for 6—8 Persons.

4—6 lbs. of fillet
¼ lb. of butter
Salt and pepper
½ cup sweet or sour cream
½ cup of water
For larding take ⅛ lb. of bacon
½ tbsp. of flour

Preparation: The fillet roast is freed from fat and skin. The bacon is cut in narrow strips and the fillet larded with it.

The butter is put into the frying-pan and heated and then the fillet browned in it on both sides and sprinkled with salt and pepper. It is roasted in the oven for ¾ of an hour, basting frequently with the gravy or water; the cream is put on 1 spoonful at a time. The roast must be of a nice pink color. It is placed on a platter.

The gravy: The given quantity of flour is put into the pan and browned, the water poured over and cooked for a few minutes; then strain and serve.

You can also put champignons into the gravy, which makes it richer.

No. 4—BEEF-FILLET BEEFSTEAK.
Quantity for 6 Persons.

2½ lbs. of fillet
¼ lb. of butter
Salt and pepper
¼ cup of water

Preparation: Cut the 2½ lbs. of fillet into 6 pieces, trim off the fat and skin and pound slightly. They are then formed into round beefsteaks and sprinkled with salt and pepper.

The butter is put into a frying-pan and heated and the steaks quickly browned on both sides, which requires about 5 minutes. Fry for 5 minutes more, basting and turning occasionally. The steaks are then taken out and put on a platter. The water poured into the butter and boiled a little while; this gravy is put over the steak. Beefsteak is fried in an open frying-pan on the top of the stove.

No. 5—BEEF-FILLET STEAKS WITH CHAMPIGNONS AND FRIED GOOSELIVER.

Quantity for 6 Persons.

2½ lbs. of fillet	½ lb. champignons
¼ lb. of butter	½ tbsp. of butter
Salt and pepper	¼ tsp. of flour
¼ cup of water	2 tbsps. of sweet cream
½ lb. gooseliver and	⅛ tsp. of meat extract
⅛ lb. of butter with it	

Preparation: The fillet is prepared just the same as in No. 4, and also fried the same way. The gooseliver is salted and peppered and sprinkled with flour, then fried light yellow in ⅛ lb. of butter; add 1 tablespoonful of water, cover the pan and stew ¼ hour longer.

The water having been drained off the champignons, add ½ tablespoonful of butter, ¼ teaspoonful of flour and a little salt and then cook a little. The cream and meat extract are added and simmered a while longer.

The ready fried beefsteaks are put on a hot platter. The gooseliver is cut into as many pieces as there are steaks, and one piece put in the center of each steak. The prepared champignons are placed around each piece of gooseliver on top of each steak.

The gravy is put on the platter too. You can garnish the platter with scallops of puff paste. This dish is nice between courses.

No. 6—BROILED STEAK OF ROAST BEEF.

Quantity for 6 Persons.

3 lbs. of roastbeef	Salt, pepper
	¼ lb. of butter (scant)

Preparation: The roastbeef is cut into 1½ inch thick slices and pounded well. A broiler is put on the open medium hot fire and the slices laid on to broil for 20 minutes, turning frequently. Put them on a hot platter, sprinkle with pepper and salt, cut the butter into small pieces and place them on the hot meat. Serve at once.

No. 7—STEAK FROM THE BEEF ROUND.

Quantity for 6 Persons.

3—4 lbs. round steak	Salt, pepper
¼ lb. of butter	¼ cup of water
	1 onion

Preparation: The meat is cut into slices ¾ inch thick and pounded slightly.

The butter is heated; the onion is sliced and fried till light yellow in the butter, then taken out and the meat put into this hot onion butter after it has been salted and peppered. Fry for 5 to 8 minutes to a light brown, turning it once or twice.

The meat is put on a hot platter and the onions on top. A little water is put into the pan with butter and boiled a little. This gravy is poured over the meat. Serve at once.

Remarks: If you do not like onions, omit them.

No. 8—CHOPPED GERMAN STEAK OR HAMBURG STEAK.

Quantity for 6 Persons.

2½ lbs. chopped steak	Salt, pepper
1 tbsp. of butter	1 tsp. of grated onion
2—3 eggs	1/6 lb. of butter

Preparation: The lean meat from the round is chopped fine or ground fine by putting it twice or three times through the grinder, then salted, peppered and mixed with the eggs, a tablespoonful of butter and onion if you like. If you do not like onions, omit them.

After mixing well, scant ¼ lb. dumplings are formed and flattened to 1½ inches in thickness. The butter or lard heated, the steaks put in and fried about 10 minutes, turning and basting frequently.

Serve the steaks on a hot platter, and for gravy pour a little water into the frying-pan with the butter, let come to a boil, and pour over the steaks.

Remarks: You may serve mustard gravy with this steak by adding 2 teaspoonfuls of mustard to the steak-butter and 1 teaspoonful of flour and bouillon or water, boiled for 2 minutes and strained.

No. 9 RAW BEEFSTEAK A LA TARTARE.
Quantity for 6 Persons.

2 lbs. of chopped meat
Salt, some pepper
6 yolks of eggs
2 tsps. of chopped onions

2 pepper-pickles
2 salt-pickles
1/8 lb. sardines
1½ tbsps. of capers

Preparation: The beef which must be very fresh and free from sinews, is chopped or ground twice in the grinder. Mix with salt and pepper and form into 6 equal 1¼ inch thick steaks. With a knife, score or mark squares on the surface. Make a depression in the middle of each steak and put into this carefully one raw yolk of egg. Garnish each steak with a small heap of onions, chopped small pieces of pickles, sardines from which the bones have been removed. Capers and mustard mixed with oil and vinegar may be served with it. The steaks must be served fresh.

No. 10—FILLET BEEFSTEAK FOR BREAKFAST.
Quantity for 2 Persons.

1 lb. of fillet meat
1/8 lb. of butter
½ onion

Some salt
1 pinch of pepper
6 tbsps. of gravy
4 potatoes peeled

Preparation: The pan which must have a cover is buttered. The potatoes and onions are cut into cubes, salted and peppered and put into the pan.

The pounded meat, cut into slices is browned on both sides in 1 tablespoonful of butter from the 1/8 lb. This must be done quickly in about one minute. The browned meat is then put on the raw potatoes. The gravy is poured into the beefsteak butter, or if you have no gravy, take water and boil it for one minute with a little meat extract, pour it over the potatoes and meat, cover well, and cook it 5 minutes over a hot fire; then set it aside and cook it slowly for 20 minutes more. Serve it at once in the covered pan. The pan must be small for such a small portion.

Remarks: Instead of potatoes and onions you can take fresh or canned champignons, morels or mushrooms. This dish is good for sick persons if you omit the onions and mushrooms and take potatoes only.

No. 11—BEEF POT ROAST.
Quantity for 6 Persons.

4 lbs. of meat
1 piece of fat bacon
Salt
6 pepper-corns
1 bay-leaf
1 clove
2 tbsps. of suet
3 tbsps. of flour
1 tbsp. of red wine or Madeira
½ of an onion

Preparation: The meat—from rump, chuck or sirloin—is pounded. The bacon cut in small thick pieces is stuck into the meat, heat the suet, add onions and brown meat slightly on both sides. When this is done it is placed on a platter. Flour is browned in the suet to which water and the spices are added, and cooked. The browned meat is put into the gravy, which should cover it. Cover the pot well. The best thing for a pot roast is an iron pot. Put the covered roast into the moderately hot oven for 2½ to 3 hours, basting frequently. One-half hour before done, pour the wine over it. When done, take the roast out and prepare the gravy. Take off all fat; if too thick add more water and strain.

No. 12—BRAISED BEEF SLICES.
Quantity for 6 Persons.

3 slices of meat, 3 lbs.
Salt, pepper
⅛ lb. of butter
½ qt. of bouillon
10 small peeled onions
3 carrots cut into cubes
1½ tbsps. of flour
1½ tbsps. of vinegar

Preparation: The meat slices are salted, pounded, browned in hot butter and put into a pot. The carrots and onions are added and the bouillon is poured over. Cook slowly until tender.

The meat, carrots and onions are taken out with a big skimmer. The flour is browned in the butter in which the meat was first browned, the gravy of the meat added and the vinegar; boil and strain. The onions and carrots are arranged around the roast slices and a few tablespoonfuls of the gravy put on the meat. You can also add for garnishing some nice cuts of boiled potatoes or small potato dumplings.

No. 13—ROASTED RIB-PIECE.
Quantity for 6 Persons.

4 lbs.—2 ribs
Some fine spices, salt
¾ qts. good vinegar
⅛ lb. of butter
2 kohlrabis cut in cubes
¼ celery-root cut in cubes
½ parsley-root cut in cubes
2 onions, cut up small
3 carrots cut in cubes

Preparation: The bones and tendons are taken out, the

meat is then rubbed with salt and the spices and put into vinegar for ½ hour. The vegetables, which have been cut into small pieces, are stewed in the given quantity of butter until soft. Add salt, and a little water from time to time to prevent the vegetables from becoming brown. The meat is fried in a pan with butter or lard for ½ hour, turning occasionally. One-half of this fried meat is put into a flat pan, the stewed vegetables are put on top and the other half of the meat is placed on top of this and the whole is thus baked ¾ hour in a medium hot oven. From time to time drop on a little butter.

When serving, be careful to place the roast on the platter without dropping some of the vegetables. The gravy may be served with it.

Remarks: When the roast is ready for baking you can roll it in a piece of oiled paper and bake it in that.

No. 14—SOUR ROAST.
Quantity for 6 Persons.

4 lbs. of meat	3 cloves
2 qts. of vinegar	Some salt
1 onion cut in slices	2½ tbsps. of flour
10 pepper-corns	2 tbsps. of drippings
3 bay-leaves	½ glass red wine
	⅛ lb. of bacon

Preparation: For the sour roast take the same kind of meat as in No. 11, pound it, put it into vinegar with the spices and leave it in that for 4 days, turning it over once in a while. After this time take it out and lard it with bacon cut into pieces one-third inch thick and 2½ inches long. Pierce the meat with a pointed knife and insert the bacon.

Heat the lard and fry the meat light brown on both sides and place it on a platter. Brown the flour in the lard and pour on the vinegar with the spices, water and salt. Put in a piece of honeycake (Pfeffer Kuchen) if on hand, and ½ tablespoonful of sugar, boil all and put the roasted meat into this gravy. Cover the roast and bake in the oven for 2½ to 3 hours, turning and basting frequently with the gravy. One-half hour before done, pour in the red wine.

When the roast is tender, finish the gravy. Put the roast on a platter, take all grease off the gravy and strain it. If it is too thick, add more water, if not sour enough, add more vinegar.

Potato dumplings or noodles are good with this roast.

No. 15—BEEF-ROULADE.
Quantity for 6 Persons.

2—2½ lbs. of beef cut into ½ inch thick slices
¼ lb. bacon cut into thin slices
1 onion chopped fine
Salt, pepper
1½ tbsps. of flour
⅛ lb. of butter or lard
1½ cups of bouillon or water

Preparation: The best meat for this is from the round. The meat slices are pounded and cut into squares, then sprinkled with salt and pepper, covered with bacon and onions, rolled up and fastened with twine or toothpicks.

Heat the butter or lard and brown the roulades in it, sprinkle flour over and stew, adding some salt and the bouillon or water. Then stew slowly for 1 hour in a covered pan or pot. If the roulades are small it requires less time, if large it requires from 2 to 2½ hours. The roulades are served with the gravy after the twine or toothpicks have been removed.

No. 16—BEEF-GULASH.
Quantity for 6 Persons.

2 lbs. of meat
2 small onions in cubes
1 tbsp. of lard
Salt
1 pinch of paprika
1 cup of water
1 tbsp. of flour

Preparation: The onions are stewed in the lard. The meat is cut into pieces 1½ inches thick and 1½ inches square and added to the stewed onions, stewed 10 minutes, flour, salt and pepper added, and stewed 10 minutes longer, and then 1 cup of water poured over. In a covered pot or pan it is now stewed for 2 to 2½ hours, stirring often. If it gets too dry, pour on more water. Gulash must not be too juicy. A little red wine may be added.

Remarks: From leavings of roastbeef fillets or pot roast you can prepare gulash in ½ hour. Instead of water you may use the left-over gravy.

No. 17—STEAMED BEEF-BRISKET.
Quantity for 6—8 Persons.

6 lbs. of beef brisket
Salt
Soupgreens
1 small onion
8 pepper-corns
2 cloves
2 yolks of eggs
1½ tbsps. of Parmesan cheese, grated
2 tbsps. grated rolls
1½ tbsps. of butter
6 qts. water
1 bay-leaf

Preparation: The beef is pounded and tied into a white

cloth in a good shape. The water is heated with salt, soupgreens and spices to the boiling point, then the meat added which must boil 1 hour so little that you hardly notice it. The pot must be well covered. If there are bones in the meat, they should be removed and put into the stock.

When the meat is tender, take it out, cover it with fricassee gravy which is first stirred with 2 yolks of eggs. Strew the Parmesan cheese and roll crumbs over it and baste with some melted butter. Now set it into the oven and bake for 20 minutes. You can garnish the roast with fried cut potatoes or macaroni.

Cucumber-salad, mixed pickles or salt- or pepper pickles go nicely with this meat.

Remarks: The bouillon may be boiled down and used for soup.

No. 18—BEEF CUTLETS OF ROASTBEEF.
Quantity for 6 Persons.

3 lbs. roastbeef   Salt, pepper
               ¼ lb. butter

Preparation: The meat is cut into 3 slices and bones, tendons, fat and skin removed from it. It is then pounded well. It must be 1½ inches thick. The butter is heated, the meat fried 20 minutes, turning it over several times. The last 5 minutes you put it off the hot fire and let it simmer. Sprinkle with salt and pepper, then baste with the butter. Serve on a hot platter and garnish with parsley. The remnants may be used for gulash.

No. 19—BOILED BEEF.
Quantity for 6 Persons.

4 lbs. of meat   1 lb. of bones
Soupgreens   4—5 qts. of water
               Salt

Preparation: The meat which may be from the rump, thick rib-piece or breast, is washed. The water with the bones, all soupgreens and salt is boiled for 1 hour, then put in the meat and boil slowly 2½ hours. With this meat serve onion, mustard, horse-radish or leek-gravy.

Remarks: This meat may be utilized for hash, salad, meat pudding or beef with onions and eggs.

No. 20—BEEF HASH.

1 lb. remnants of meat	½ wine glass of white wine
¼ of an onion	1 cup bouillon
1 tbsp. of butter	Salt, pepper
1 tsp. of flour	

Preparation: The meat is chopped fine and may be of soup-meat, roast or steak. The onions are cut fine and stewed in butter, then the chopped meat put in, the flour strewn over it, simmered a little while longer, salt and pepper added and bouillon. If you take water add ¼ tablespoonful of meat extract and wine. Let it cook ¼ hour and serve. Fresh boiled, peeled potatoes are nice to serve with it.

No. 21—HASH WITH POTATOES.
Quantity for 4—6 Persons.

1—1½ lbs. of meat	A little pepper
Boiled or roasted beef	Salt
¼ onion	1 cup of bouillon or water
1 tbsp. of butter	4 peeled, boiled potatoes

Preparation: The meat is chopped fine. The onions are cut fine and steeped in the butter, then the meat put in and cooked 5 minutes. Salt and pepper are added, the potatoes are also chopped fine and added and water or bouillon poured on. The whole is cooked for ¼ of an hour, then served. served.

No. 22—BEEF WITH ONIONS.
Quantity for 6 Persons.

1½ lbs. boiled beef	1 tbsp. of vinegar
1 onion	1 pinch of pepper
2 tbsps. of butter or suet	Salt
2 tbsps. of flour	½ tsp. of meat extract
½ qt. of bouillon	

Preparation: The onion is cut fine and simmered in the butter or suet until soft; then add flour, simmer until brown; pour on the bouillon, vinegar, salt, pepper and meat extract and let come to a boil.

The meat is cut in slices and put into the gravy and heated.

No. 23—BOILED BEEF SLICES FRIED WITH EGGS AND ONIONS.
Quantity for 6 Persons.

1½ lbs. boiled beef	6 eggs
1 onion	Salt
2 tbsps. of butter or good drippings	1 pinch of pepper

Preparation: Meat and onions are cut into inch thick slices. Sprinkle with salt and pepper and fry in the butter or lard until light brown. Put the meat and onions on a hot platter. Fry the eggs in butter, strew salt over and lay them on each slice of meat. Be careful to keep the yolk whole.

Potato salad is good served with this meat.

No. 24—BEEF SALAD.
Quantity for 6 Persons.

1 lb. of boiled beef	1½ tbsps. of oil
2 yolks of eggs	½ tsp. of grated onions
Vinegar to taste	2 tsps. of capers
Salt	½ cup of cold bouillon
1 pinch of pepper	3 tbsps. of cream
	½ tsp. of mustard

Preparation: The meat is cut in cubes and mixed with the egg yolks and cream. Now vinegar, bouillon, mustard and all the other ingredients except the oil are mixed in well. After the salad has stood for 1 to 2 hours, covered up well, the oil is stirred in. The salad is served in mound-shape, garnished with hard boiled eggs and pepper-pickles cut into nice slices.

No. 25—CROQUETTES.
Quantity for 6 Persons.

1 lb. boiled beef	Salt
½ lb. raw or boiled chopped pork	1 pinch of pepper
¼ onion, grated	1 tsp. of capers
2 rolls soaked in water	Juice of ½ lemon
	2½ tbsps. of butter or lard
2—3 eggs	

Preparation: The meat is chopped fine or ground twice and mixed well with all the given spices and the soaked rolls. Make oblong dumplings of this mass, roll them in roll crumbs and fry to a light brown in the butter or lard. For gravy serve one of sardines or prepare one of the croquette drippings as follows: When the croquettes are done put ½ tablespoonful of flour into the drippings and let it stew a while, then add ½ cup of bouillon or water, ½ teaspoonful of meat extract and salt according to taste. Let it boil a while and pour the gravy over the croquettes.

No. 26—MEAT PUDDING No. 2.
Quantity for 6 Persons.

1 lb. boiled beef or roast beef	1 tsp. ground capers
⅛ lb. bacon	1 roll soaked and the water pressed out
2 yolks of eggs	
2 whites of eggs beaten to foam	Salt, pepper
4 tbsps. of gravy	½ tbsp. of butter
½ tsp. of grated onions	1 tbsp. of roll crumbs
	3 chopped sardines

Preparation: Meat and bacon are chopped fine and mixed well with yolks of 2 eggs, gravy, chopped sardines, onion, salt, capers, pepper and the roll. Add the beaten whites of eggs; put into a pudding-mold which has been buttered and strewn with roll crumbs. Set it in a steamer over a kettle of boiling water and let it steam 1½ hours, or bake in the oven for 1 hour.

No. 27—KÖNIGSBERGER KLOPS.
Meat Balls.
Quantity for 6 Persons.

1½ lbs. finely chopped raw beef	3 eggs
¼ lb. fat pork, chopped	1 pinch of pepper
⅛ lb. of butter	Salt
1½ roll—the crust cut off	The juice of ¼ of a lemon
1 tsp. of grated onion	Some flour to roll them in

Preparation: The beef and pork are mixed well with the butter; add the roll which has been soaked and the water pressed out, and all other things mentioned above, and mix well. Then small dumplings are made, rolled in flour, and boiled slowly in bouillon or salt water for 15 or 20 minutes. Put them into a deep dish and pour white fricassee gravy over them. Sauerkraut is nice with this meat. You can also fry the Klops instead of boiling them.

No. 28—FRIED BEEF LIVER WITH BREAKFAST BACON.
Quantity for 6 Persons.

2 lbs. of liver cut into thin slices	Salt, pepper, flour
¾ lb. of bacon cut into thin slices	

Preparation: The bacon must be lean and is fried light yellow, then placed on a platter on the stove. The liver slices are salted and peppered, dipped into flour and fried in the bacon dripping, quite crisp. It is put on the platter with the bacon. One-half cup of water or bouillon is poured into the lard in which the bacon and liver were fried and left to boil. This gravy may be served separately or on the meat. It requires only a few minutes to fry the liver.

No. 29—COW-UDDER.
Quantity for 6 Persons.

1½ lbs. cow-udder	2 bay-leaves
1 onion,	1 clove
Salt	2 qts. of water
	6 pepper-corns

Preparation: The cow-udder is washed well and placed over the fire with much cold water. As soon as it comes to a boil the water is poured off and the 2 qts. of fresh water poured on and all the spices named added, then boiled until soft which requires 4 or 5 hours. Then it is cut in pieces, and these are rolled in roll crumbs and fried in butter until light yellow. Or a nice brown gravy is made by taking 2 tablespoonfuls of butter and in it brown 2 tablespoonfuls of flour, then add some of the bouillon, 1 tablespoonful of vinegar, ½ glass red wine, 1 teaspoonful of sugar—all this well cooked.

Now the udder is put into this gravy, stewed a little while and served. The gravy must not be too thick.

No. 30—CORNED BEEF.

30 lbs. of beef	6 tbsps. of sugar
2 lbs. of salt	10 qts. of water
	Scant ⅛ lb. of saltpetre

Preparation: Water, saltpetre, sugar and salt are boiled until an egg will float on the mixture. Then this mixture is poured, while hot, on to the fresh meat. The liquid must be 1½ inches above the meat after a stone or something heavy is placed on it. The meat may remain in this mixture for 3 to 4 weeks and should be turned once in a while. Smaller pieces need only 8 to 10 days.

No. 31—CORNED BEEF FOR COOKING.
Quantity for 6 Persons.

3 lbs. of pickled beef	4 qts. of water
	Some soupgreens

Preparation:. When the beef is very salty, soak it in water for a few hours. Put it to boil with the 4 qts. of water and soupgreens and boil for 2½ to 3 hours slowly. Larger pieces need more time.

Cabbage goes nicely with this beef. In carving, cut against the grain.

No. 32—SMOKED CORNED BEEF.

When the meat is taken out of the brine, hang it in a cool, airy place for one day and then smoke it.

No. 33—PICKLED BEEF TONGUE.

2 tongues	1 tsp. of saltpetre
¼ lb. of salt	1 tbsp. of sugar

Preparation: The throat end is cut off and the skin of the tongue is cut with a sharp knife at several places. Salt, sugar and saltpetre are heated and the tongues rubbed well with the mixture. They are then packed into a jar and weighted with a stone. They must be turned every day. It takes 10 to 14 days to pickle the tongues.

No. 34—SMOKED, PICKLED OR FRESH BEEF TONGUE FOR COOKING AND FRYING.

Quantity for 6 Persons.

For Cooking.

1 fresh, smoked or pickled beef tongue	2 cloves
	Some soupgreens
1 bay-leaf	½ onion
6 pepper-corns	3 qts. of water

For Frying.

2 tbsps. of butter	½ wine glass of red wine
1 tbsp. of flour	½ tsp. of sugar
½ cup of bouillon or water	Juice of ¼ lemon

Preparation: Cut off the throat end and if the pickled tongue is too salty, leave it in water for a few hours, the same with fresh tongue to remove the slime or mucous. The smoked tongue is left in water over night. After this is done the tongue is cooked until soft in the 3 qts. of water, adding bay-leaf, pepper-corns, cloves, soupgreens and onion. If it is a fresh tongue, add some salt. It requires 3 hours to cook a tongue.

When the tongue is soft, take it out of the water and skin it. You can serve the tongue in this manner or cold and sliced. If you wish to serve the tongue warm and whole, it is nicer to fry it. Put it into a low frying pan, add the given quantity of butter and fry it 10 minutes on both sides, add 1 tablespoonful of flour and let it simmer a few minutes. Now add the bouillon or water. With the water put in ¼ teaspoonful of meat extract, red wine, sugar, salt and lemon juice, and then cook ¼ of an hour, basting it several times. Then serve. The gravy must be strained.

Boiled, warm tongue is nice with vegetables. Cut the tongue into slices and place it around the vegetables like scales.

No. 35—RAGOUT OF OX-TONGUE.
Quantity for 6 Persons.

For Cooking.
1 tongue, smoked, pickled or fresh
3 qts. of water
2 cloves
6 pepper-corns
¼ onion
1 bay-leaf

Sauce.
3 tbsps. of butter
3 tbsps. of flour
½ qt. bouillon or water
½ cup Madeira or red wine
1 pt. of champignons
6 truffles
Juice of ½ lemon
1 tsp. of sugar
Salt
3 pepper-corns
1 clove
½ bay-leaf
¼ tsp. of meat extract
1 slice of lemon

Preparation: The tongue is cooked the same as in No. 34. For ragouts the smoked tongue is preferable. When the tongue is soft, skin it and cut it into thin slices.

Gravy: Brown the butter and flour, add the bouillon, salt, sugar, pepper, 1 clove, ½ bay-leaf, one slice of lemon and the juice of ½ lemon, Madeira or red wine and the water from the champignons. Let it boil for ½ hour and strain.

Peel the truffles, chop them fine and put them into the strained gravy and if the champignons are large cut them into quarters and put them also in the gravy and finally the slices of tongue. The gravy must not be too spicy if it is a smoked or pickled tongue. After the ragout has been thus prepared it may stew on the stove for ¼ hour. The gravy must not be too thin and watery.

The ragout is placed on a platter and garnished with warm scallops of puff-paste or meat dumplings.

Meat Dumplings.

¼ lb. finely chopped veal
¼ lb. finely chopped pork
1 roll, soaked and the water pressed out
1 egg
Some grated onion, salt, pepper
1 tbsp. of finely chopped champignons
1 tsp. of finely chopped truffles.

Mix this all very well and form small dumplings, then put them into boiling hot salt water or bouillon and cook for 10 minutes slowly, or fry in butter light brown and place them around the tongue ragout.

The plates and the platter on which they are served must be hot.

Remarks: This is a fine dish for parties.

No. 36—CHOP SUEY.
For About 6 Persons.

½ lb. veal
½ lb. pork
1 lb. beef
2 tsps. molasses
1 large stalk celery
3 large onions
1 tbsp. lard
1 tbsp. flour

Preparation: Cut the meat in cubes; put the lard and flour in pan and brown; add meat and put enough water on to cover it; add the molasses and cook slowly for 1 hour.

Cut the stalk of celery in small pieces and add them to the meat. Cut the onions fine and fry them light brown in a little butter; add to the rest and boil slowly another half hour. Serve with plain Chinese sauce.

CHAPTER 3.

VEAL.

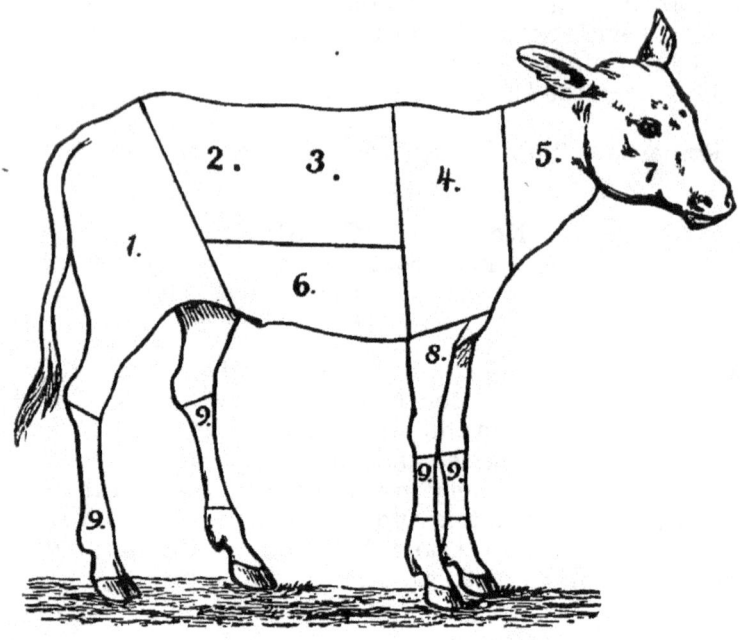

1. Leg.
2-3. Kidney roast and small chops.
4. Shoulder.
5. Neck.
6. Breast.
7. Head.
8. Shank Leg.
9. Four Legs.

Preparation of Veal.

Appearance of Good Veal.

It must be of a white color, a fine firm grain and have plenty of fat.

Do not buy very young veal because those calves are as a rule not healthy. Cheap meat is never economical. Veal is quickly prepared because it does not require long boiling. The bouillon is good for invalids because it contains much gluten.

Best Pieces for Roast.
(Leg or Loin.)

The leg with the fricandeau, the fillet, loin and kidney roast.

Small Pieces for Frying.

The chump end of loin for chops, veal-cutlets from rib-piece, fillet.

Pieces for Pot Roast.

The breast, neck, shoulder.

Pieces for Boiling.

The thick rib-piece, neck.

Pieces for Bouillon.

The calves' feet, calf-bones, calf-tail, also lean meat.

Parts for Fricassee.

Lungs, brain, sweetbreads, breast piece.

No. 1—LEG OF VEAL.
Quantity for 8—10 Persons.

6—8 lbs. leg of veal
⅛ lb. of bacon
⅛ lb. of butter
½ cup sweet or sour cream
Salt, pepper
1½ cups of water
2 tbsps. of flour

Preparation: The meat is pounded, boiling water poured over, i. e., scalded, which makes the meat white; let the water run off immediately. Sprinkle with salt and pepper and put into pan. Cut the bacon into thin slices and put it on the meat, add the butter and place into oven. Roast for 2 hours, basting frequently. About ½ hour before done, put the flour into the gravy and stew 5 minutes, then add water and put the cream on the leg in spoonfuls. When the roast is tender, put on platter and strain the gravy which must not be too thin.

Remarks: If the roast has much stock, pour some off before adding flour, stand cold and let it jelly. Now cut it into slices and serve with slices of tenderloin. Veal roast may be utilized in various ways.

No. 2—WARMED UP VEAL ROAST.
Quantity for 6 Persons.

1½ lbs. of veal roast
⅛ lb. of butter
⅛ lb. of sardines
1 tbsp. of capers
Some salt
Juice of ½ lemon
Left-over gravy
For the gravy, 1 tsp. of flour

Preparation: Put the roast into an earthen dish, heat the gravy, pour it over the roast, cover up the dish, place it into a covered pot with boiling water, let it boil slowly for one hour and baste the roast several times.

The gravy is usually thin, therefore add the flour and serve with the roast; the contents of the dish must not boil, otherwise the roast will become dry. Cut the roast into slices, place them into a buttered mold, put the sardines, capers and bits of butter between them and drip the lemon juice on. Cover the mold, put it into the dish with boiling water and boil for ¾ hours. The meat is served in the mold, the gravy heated and served with it.

No. 3—VEAL ROAST WITH POTATOES.
Quantity for 6 Persons.

1 lb. of veal roast
Salt
1 pinch of pepper
4 big, raw potatoes, peeled and cut into thin slices
¼ onion
Left-over gravy

Preparation: The meat is cut into small pieces, placed in 2 or 3 layers alternately with sliced potatoes into an earthenware buttered dish so that the top layer will be potatoes. Season each layer with salt, pepper and a little onion.

The meat gravy which may be diluted with bouillon or water is poured over the whole until level with the potatoes; then put small pieces of butter on top and bake in the oven for 1½ hours.

If you have no left-over gravy then take 1 tablespoonful of butter, brown it, stir in 1½ tablespoonfuls of flour, add water or bouillon, ½ teaspoonful of meat extract, 3 tablespoonfuls of cream (if on hand), boil and pour over the potatoes and meat and bake. Serve in the earthen dish.

No. 4—VEAL ROAST RAGOUT—BROWN.
Quantity for 6 Persons.

1½ lbs. of veal roast
½ pt. brown gravy
1½ tsps. sugar
1¼ tbsps. vinegar, (preferably wine vinegar)
1 tbsp. butter
2 gherkins or
4 sweet-sour pickles
1½ tbsps. of small pearl onions; pickled ones preferred

Preparation: If you have no left-over gravy then make a false gravy by directions given in No. 3. Add sugar and vinegar according to taste, cut pickles into small pieces and put into the gravy with the onions. Cut the meat into pieces and put it into the hot gravy; it must not boil, otherwise the meat will be tough; put another piece of butter on top and serve.

No. 5—SHELLS FILLED WITH VEAL ROAST.
Quantity for 6 Persons.

½ lb. veal roast
1½ tbsps. of butter
2 tbsps. of flour
Salt, pinch of pepper
3 tbsps. of white wine
Juice of ½ lemon

½ cup of cream
1 cup of bouillon or water and
¼ tsp. meat extract
½ tbsp. of Parmesan cheese, grated
1 tbsp. of rolls, grated

Preparation: The butter is melted and flour stirred in. Stew it and add water or bouillon (if you take water, use ¼ teaspoonful of meat extract), cream, white wine, salt, pepper, lemon juice. The gravy must boil. Taste it to make sure that it may not be either too salty, too sweet, or too sour.

Chop the veal roast and put it into the gravy. The mixture should be pretty thick; fill it into the shells, sprinkle with the Parmesan cheese and roll crumbs and place small pieces of butter on top. Then bake them in the oven to a light yellow color which requires 10 minutes. Serve at once.

No. 6—VEAL ROAST PUDDING.
Quantity for 6 Persons.

1 lb. veal roast
⅛ part of an onion chopped fine
3 tsps. of parsley, chopped fine
⅛ lb. of butter, good measure
3 eggs

Salt
1 pinch of pepper
¼ cup of sweet cream
1 roll, grated
½ pt. of tomato or sardine gravy
1 tsp. of Parmesan cheese

Preparation: The veal roast is chopped fine. Three-fourths of the butter is creamed, and the 3 yolks stirred in, meat, salt, pepper, Parmesan cheese, roll crumbs, cream, parsley, all well mixed. The chopped onion is cooked in butter for a little while and then stirred in.

The white of egg is beaten stiff and also added to the mass. A tin pudding-mold is buttered and strewn with roll crumbs, the mixture put in, and the closed mold set in a steamer over boiling water and steamed for one hour.

Dump the pudding on a hot platter and pour over it tomato or sardine gravy.

No. 7—VEAL ROAST SALAD.
Quantity for 6 Persons.

1 lb. veal roast	1 tsp. of mustard
3 yolks of eggs	¼ qt. of milk
1 tbsp. of flour	½ tbsp. of butter
2 tsps. of salt	4 mustard pickles
Some pepper	2 tbsps. of pearl onions
3 tbsps. of wine vinegar	

Preparation: Milk, flour, yolks of eggs, salt, pepper, vinegar, and butter are stirred to a gravy and brought to boil. It requires 10 minutes time till the gravy is thick and smooth. Veal roast and pickles are cut into thin slices. Meat, pickles and onions are put into layers in a dish and between each two layers a few spoonfuls of gravy, concluding with gravy over the top.

Three hard boiled eggs quartered and placed on or around the salad makes it look nice.

No. 8—SADDLE OF VEAL.
Quantity for 10 Persons.

6—7 lbs. of veal saddle	¼ lb. of bacon
Some salt	1 cup of cream
1 pinch of pepper	2½ tbsps. of flour
¼ cup of butter, or good roast drippings	

Preparation: The saddle of veal is well prepared by the butcher so it will lie flat in the pan. Skin and scald the veal and lard it with bacon, then sprinkle with salt and pepper and put into the pan. Heat the butter, pour it over the meat and set it into a medium hot oven. Pour a little water over once in a while so the butter does not get too brown; the roast must be basted every 10 minutes to make it juicy. It requires 1 or 1½ hours roasting to make it tender. One-quarter of an hour before done put in the flour and cream. The gravy must be strained before serving. The kidneys may be removed, cut into thin slices, arranged around the roast with the pieces overlapping each other like scales.

Remarks: The gravy may be prepared in various ways. Instead of cream take ¼ cup of Madeira or red wine and cut truffles into thin slices and put into the gravy.

Another way is to take cream and champignons and lemon juice.

The left-over roast may be utilized for ragout, gulash, fricassee, meat dumplings or in a pudding made of roast and potatoes. The bones are split and used to make bouillon.

No. 9—ROAST VEAL LOIN WITH KIDNEY.
Quantity for 6 Persons.

3 lbs. of veal loin with the kidney
Salt
1 pinch of pepper
⅛ lb. of butter or lard
1 tbsp. of flour
¼ cup of cream
½ cup of water

Preparation: Pound the meat and sprinkle with salt and pepper. Cut the kidney off and if it is very fat, cut some of the fat off and render it to be used for frying or cooking. The roast is then put on and basted with hot butter or lard; the kidney is put in with the roast. Let it roast until well done and baste it frequently. Shortly before it is done, add flour to the gravy and then the cream. If there should be too little gravy, add more water and let it roast ¼ hour longer. Baste with the gravy several times and serve. The gravy must be strained, the kidney cut in slices and arranged around the roast for garnishing.

No. 10—ROASTED FRICANDEAU OF VEAL.
Quantity for 6 Persons.

3 lbs. fricandeau or cushion of veal
1 small piece of bacon for larding
⅛ lb. of butter
½ cup of cream
1 cup of water
1 tbsp. of flour

Preparation: The fricandeau, which is a choice piece of lean meat cut from the thickest part of the leg, is nicely trimmed, pounded and larded with bacon. It requires 1 to 1¼ hours to roast it. Prepare it just the same as directed in No. 9.

No. 11—STUFFED BREAST OF VEAL.
Quantity for 6 Persons.

3½ lbs. of breast of veal
Salt, 1 pinch of pepper
⅛ lb. of butter for roasting

The Filling.

½ lb. of chopped beef or veal
½ lb. of chopped pork
1½ soaked rolls
1 tbsp. of butter
¼ tsp. of grated onion
2 eggs
Salt, 1 pinch of pepper
2 tsps. of finely chopped parsley
Juice of ¼ lemon

Preparation: The meat is pounded a little, washed, an incision is made between meat and bone and ¼ teaspoonful of salt rubbed in. The ingredients for the filling are mixed well and put into the cavity formed by the cut, then sewed up. The ⅛ lb. of butter is heated, the stuffed breast put in and roasted a little; then add 2 tablespoonfuls of flour, sprinkle with salt and pepper, let it cook 10 minutes.

Now pour in 1 cup of water, roast for 1½ hours, basting frequently. Strain the gravy and serve.

No. 12—BREAST OF VEAL WITH BEER.
Quantity for 6 Persons.

5 lbs. of breast of veal	½ small onion
Salt	3 thin slices of lemon
4 pepper-corns	3 tbsps. of flour
2 cloves	⅛ lb. of good butter, heaped
1 bay-leaf	1 bottle of beer

Preparation: This breast of veal should be from the brisket end as the meat is thicker and it does not have as much bone and skin as a piece from the middle breast. It must be pounded and tied with a white string into a good shape. Then it is roasted in the butter to a nice brown color on all sides. When this is done, put the meat into another dish. Put the flour and sliced onion into the butter, cook them brown and add the beer; then add all the spices, put in the meat, cover, and bake in oven slowly for 2 hours, turn over occasionally and baste with gravy. If you do not like beer, use water. The gravy must not be too thin; if it gets too thick, add more water or beer; strain it. Garnish the roast with slices of lemon.

No. 13—CALF'S HEAD RAGOUT.
Quantity for 6—8 Persons.

1 calf's head with brain and tongue	½ of tomato
½ lb. of beef	Salt
½ lb. of veal	½ pt. red wine
¼ lb. of raw ham	⅛ lb. of butter
6 pepper-corns	1 onion
2 bay-leaves	⅛ lb. of flour
1 piece of tarragon	1 pinch of paprika
1 piece of carrot	¼ pt. of Madeira
1 piece of celery	Juice of ¼ lemon
1 piece of kohlrabi	1 tsp. of sugar
	4 hard boiled eggs cut into ⅛ths
1 piece of parsley root	

Preparation: The calf's head is split in half, the brain and the tongue taken out and soaked in water. Take the skin off the calf's head, brush the skin in water until it is white, then boil it with the tongue until tender. Put in the split head bones, all the soupgreens, salt, pepper-corns, bay-leaf, tarragon and boil for 2 hours. The bouillon must be boiled down to 1½ or 2 qts.

When the skin is done, cut it into squares. The tongue is skinned and cut into slices. Both are put into a dish and red wine, salt and pepper added.

Beef, veal, ham and onion are cut into pieces and fried brown in ⅛ lb. of butter. Add ⅛ lb. of flour, cook a little and add the calf's head bouillon and Madeira and cook slowly for 2 hours. The gravy must be strained, the fat taken off and then seasoned. Put into it the pieces of skin and tongue, some lemon juice and sugar. Serve the ragout on a hot platter. Fry the brains to a light yellow, cut it in pieces and garnish the ragout with them; also with scallops of pastry and the ⅛ths of eggs. It is a fine side dish.

No. 14—CALF'S TONGUE.
Quantity for 6 Persons.

3 calves' tongues	1 bay-leaf
Salt	2 cloves
2 qts. of water	1 slice of lemon
6 pepper-corns	¼ onion

The Gravy.

½ cup of sour cream	2 tbsps. of capers
⅛ lb. of butter	¼ tsp. of sugar
3 tbsps. of flour	2 yolks of eggs
2 tbsps. of lemon juice	Salt, 1 pinch of pepper

Preparation: The tongues must be fresh and washed well, cooked until tender in 2 qts. of water with all the given ingredients, then skinned and cut into slices.

The Gravy: Butter is heated, flour stirred in, bouillon added and cooked well with lemon juice, cream, sugar and capers.

The slices of tongue are put in the gravy and heated, the yolks of eggs stirred in and then served. The gravy must not be too thin. The slices of tongue may be salted, dipped into yolks of eggs and roll crumbs and fried in butter.

No. 15—CALF'S BRAINS.
Quantity for 6 Persons.

3 calves' brains	1 egg
Some salt	½ cup of grated rolls
1 pinch of pepper	1 qt. of water

Preparation: The brains are soaked in water. One quart of water is brought to boil, the brains put in and boiled for 5 minutes, then taken out and the small veins and skin removed, then salted and peppered. Beat the egg well, dip the brains in and then in roll crumbs and fry in hot butter to a golden yellow.

Remarks: When the brains have been thus prepared, drip a few drops of lemon juice on and then bake, or, it may be served with lemon slices.

No. 16—VEAL FRICASSEE.
Quantity for 6 Persons.

2½ lbs. breast of veal (brisket) 4 pepper-corns
2 qts. of water 2 cloves
¼ onion ½ bay-leaf
Salt

Gravy.

3 tbsps. of butter 2 yolks of eggs
2 tbsps. of flour and bouillon 1 wineglassful of white wine

Preparation: The meat is cut into nice pieces and the cartilage left on. Scald it for ½ minute and drain well. With the 2 qts. of water, onion, salt and spices, it is boiled until tender. Boil down the bouillon to ¾ of a quart so it is very strong. It requires 1 hour to cook the meat done.

The Gravy.

Heat the butter, put in the flour and stew a little. Butter and flour must remain white, stir in the veal bouillon gradually that the gravy may become smooth. Then add the white wine and cook 1 minute, stir in the yolks of eggs and stop cooking. The meat, which has been kept hot, is put into the gravy and served. Rice cooked in water and bouillon is nice served with this. Place the meat in the middle of the platter and garnish with the rice.

No. 17—VEAL GULASH.
Quantity for 6 Persons.

2¼ lbs. of veal 1 pinch of pepper
1 small onion 1 tbsp. of flour
1 tbsp. of butter 1 cup of water
Salt

Preparation: The meat is cut into 1½ inch squares. The onion is cut into small cubes and fried slightly in the butter, the meat is then added and stewed 10 minutes. Add the flour, salt and pepper and stew 5 minutes more. The water is then poured in and covered up. Stir it once in a while and let it cook until done, which will require about 1½ hours. Gulash must not be too juicy.

No. 18—UNBREADED VEAL CUTLETS.
(Chops).
Quantity for 6 Persons.

3 lbs. veal chops	Juice of ¼ lemon
⅛ lb. of butter	½ tbsp. of capers
Salt	½ tbsp. of meat extract if necessary
1 pinch of pepper	1 cup of water
½ cup of cream	

Preparation: The cutlets are cut from the back, each one containing a bone. It is pounded, shaped neatly and sprinkled with salt and pepper. The butter is heated, the cutlets put in and fried brown on both sides, then put on platter. Put into the butter the ½ tablespoonful of flour and brown it. Should there be too much butter, take some out before putting in the flour, then pour into the butter and flour one cup of water, salt if necessary, lemon juice and cream. Press the capers through a sieve and stir into the gravy. Put the cutlets into this gravy, cover the pan and stew 10 minutes, then serve. If the gravy is too light brown, add the ½ teaspoonful of meat extract.

Remarks: Anyone who does not like the taste of capers and lemon juice may leave them out, also the cream. If you wish the gravy very fine, leave off the above and add champignons and finely chopped or cut truffles and 2 tablespoonfuls of Maderia.

No. 19—BREADED VEAL CUTLETS.
Quantity for 6 Persons.

3 lbs. of veal cutlets	Salt, pepper
1 egg	Roll crumbs or cracker crumbs
1 tbsp. of milk	⅛ lb. of butter

Preparation: The cutlets are pounded, shaped neatly and sprinkled with salt and pepper. The egg is mixed well with the milk; in case you have some white of egg left over, use that with milk, dip the cutlets into it, then into the roll or cracker crumbs and place them into the hot butter to brown on both sides. Put the fried cutlets on a platter.

The Gravy: Put ¼ tablespoonful of flour into the hot cutlet butter and stew, add a half cupful of water, cook a little while, pour it over the cutlets, garnish with lemon slices and serve.

No. 20—VEAL CUTLETS AF A FINE SIDE-DISH.
Quantity for 6—8 Persons.

3 lbs. of veal cutlets
1 lb. of sweetbreads
½ lb. of boiled calf's tongue
1 pt. can of champignons

Salt, pepper
⅛ lb. of butter
1 tbsp. of Parmesan cheese
1 tbsp. of crab butter

1 small can of truffles

Preparation: The cutlets are pounded, salted and peppered and fried to a light brown on both sides in ⅛ lb. of butter.

The tongue is cooked well done in water with salt, a piece of onion, 4 pepper-corns, 2 cloves, 1 bay-leaf; ¼ hour before done, put in the sweetbreads. When both are done, skin them and chop them or cut them into cubes.

The gravy: Put 2 tablespoonfuls of flour into the cutlet butter, stew a little while, then add bouillon in which the tongue and sweet-breads were cooked, add some of the champignon juice, a wine glass of red wine, 1 tablespoonful of lemon juice, 1 teaspoonful of sugar and cook for ¼ hour, strain and put champignons, finely chopped truffles, sweetbreads and tongue in the sauce and heat.

Put the cutlets into an oblong or round casserole, strew with Parmesan cheese, drip some crab butter over. The ragout is poured over them and the whole is baked in the oven for ¼ hour and when served in the casserole, it is a very fine dish.

No. 21—CHOPPED VEAL CUTLETS.
Quantity for 6 Persons.

3 lbs. of veal cutlets
Salt, pepper

Some flour
⅛ lb. of butter

1—2 eggs

Preparation: The cutlets are chopped and cut off the rib-bone. Remove all tendons and skin, and shape the chopped meat round and press it against the bone. Beat the egg well. Salt and pepper the cutlets, dip carefully into the egg and then into the flour. Now heat the butter and fry the cutlets in it to a light brown on both sides. Handle them carefully so they will not fall apart, then take them out and place them on a hot platter. Put ½ cup of water into cutlet butter, salt if necessary and cook, pour over cutlets, garnish with lemon slices and serve.

No. 22—BREADED VEAL CHOPS.
Quantity for 6 Persons.

2¼ lbs. of veal
Salt, pepper
½ tbsp. of flour
1 or 2 whites of egg
1 tbsp. of milk
1 cup of roll or cracker crumbs
⅛ lb. of butter or half butter and half lard
¾ cup of water

Preparation: The meat for this must be from the loin or leg. It is cut into ¾ inch slices, pounded, salted and peppered. Beat the white of egg well or take egg and milk, dip the pieces of veal in and then into the roll or cracker crumbs. Fry them brown in the hot butter or lard, this will require 10 minutes. They must not be rare inside. For the gravy, put ½ tablespoonful of flour into the lard or butter, brown and add ¾ cup of water; add a little salt if necessary, cook well, then pour it over the meat, garnish with lemon slices and serve.

No. 23—VIENNA VEAL-SCHNITZEL, (VEAL CUTLETS).
Quantity for 6 Persons.

2¼ lbs. of veal from the leg
Salt, pepper
2 eggs
Juice of ½ lemon
⅛ lb. of butter
6 eggs
Flour

Preparation: The veal is cut into six ¾ inch thick slices, pounded, salted, peppered. Beat the eggs well, dip the meat into it and then sprinkle with flour. Heat the butter and fry the slices to a light brown on both sides. While they are frying, drip the lemon juice on. When well done, put them on a hot platter. Make the gravy with ½ cup of water poured into frying butter and salt if necessary, cook and pour over the cutlets. The eggs are fried and placed on each cutlet carefully so the yolk does not run out.

No. 24—VEAL CUTLET OR SCHNITZEL A LA HOLSTEIN.
Quantity for 6 Persons.

2¼ lbs. of veal from the leg
2 eggs
Salt
1 pinch of paprika
⅛ lb. of butter
4 hard boiled eggs
2 tbsps. of pickled beets, chopped
1 tbsp. of capers
1 small pickle
6 sardines
6 slices or six-eighths of a lemon
¼ tbsp. of flour.
¾ cup of water
½ tsp. of meat extract
1 tbsp. of onions

Preparation: The meat is cut into six ½ inch thick slices, sprinkled with salt and paprika and dipped into well beaten egg. The butter is heated and the meat fried brown on both sides, then put on a hot platter. The ¼ tablespoonful of flour stirred into the butter and ¾ cup of water added with ½ teaspoonful of meat extract and salt, if necessary, then boiled and poured over the meat.

The hard boiled eggs are chopped fine, the whites separate from the yolks. The sardines are drained and cut into halves lengthwise, then rolled up. Now arrange your dish neatly, little heaps of beets, onions, pickle, white and yolk of egg, lemon slices on each cutlet. The rolled sardines in the middle of the lemon slice, heaps of the rest around each and the capers singly in between. Should be prepared quickly but appetizingly.

No. 25—VEAL CUTLETS IN WHITE WINE.
Quantity for 6 Persons.

2½ lbs. of veal from the leg
⅛ lb. of butter
Salt, pepper
1 kohlrabi, cut into dainty pieces
½ carrot, cut into dainty pieces
½ parsley root, cut into dainty pieces
⅛ celery root, cut into dainty pieces
10 small pieces of cauliflower
½ pt. of white wine.
1 cup of water
2 tbsps. of flour.

Preparation: The meat is cut into slices ¾ inch thick, salted and peppered, then fried light brown on both sides in the heated butter and placed on a platter.

For the gravy stir 2 tablespoonfuls of flour into the butter and brown, then add water and wine, the vegetables and salt. The vegetables must be cooked very tender, then put in the veal schnitzel or cutlets and cook slowly for 20 minutes. The whole, schnitzel, gravy, and vegetables, is served in one dish. It makes a fine dish. The gravy must not be thick.

No. 26—VEAL STEAK FROM THE LEG.
Quantity for 6 Persons.

2½ lbs. of veal
⅛ lb. of butter
Salt
1 pinch of white pepper
¼ cup of water

Preparation: The steak must not be cut too thick. Remove the skin from the steak and pound it well, then fry it in the butter on medium fire for ½ hour, turning and basting it several times. Serve it on a hot platter and sprinkle with salt and pepper and put a little fresh butter over the whole.

For the gravy, pour into the frying butter ¼ cup of water, cook well and strain, then serve separately. Garnish the steak with lemon slices.

No. 27—SWEETBREADS.
Quantity for 6 Persons.

2 lbs. of sweetbreads	Roll crumbs or cracker crumbs
Salt, pepper	⅛ lb. of butter
	1—2 eggs

Preparation: The sweetbreads are cooked in salt water for 10 minutes, then taken out and skinned. It is then cut lengthwise if it is very thick and sprinkled with salt and pepper. The egg is beaten well and the sweetbreads dipped into that and then into the roll or cracker crumbs. Then it is fried to a golden yellow in the butter. For the gravy, pour a little water into the hot butter and boil, then pour over the sweetbreads. This is a good dish with vegetables.

No. 28—SWEETBREADS IN SHELLS OR OTHER SMALL MOLDS.
Quantity for 6 Persons.

1¼ lbs. of sweetbreads	2 tbsps. of butter
½ pt. of champignons, scant	2 tbsps. of flour
3 truffles	Some bouillon
½ wine glass of white wine	½ tbsp. of Parmesan cheese
Salt	½ tbsp. of roll crumbs
1 pinch of pepper	½ cup of cream
	¼ tsp. of meat extract

Preparation: The sweetbreads are boiled in ¾ qts. of salt water until tender, which requires ¼ hour. Take them out, skin them well and cut them into very small pieces. Boil down the bouillon of it to 1½ cups.

The Gravy: Heat the butter and stir in the flour and stew but do not brown it, then add the bouillon, cream, wine, lemon juice and juice of the champignons, salt and pepper and cook until it thickens.

The champignons and truffles are chopped fine and put into the gravy with the sweetbreads. Heat and fill into shells or other small molds, sprinkle with a little Parmesan cheese, a few roll crumbs and a little piece of butter and bake in oven light brown, which requires 10 minutes. This makes a fine side-dish.

No. 29—PUFF-PASTE PATTIES FILLED WITH SWEETBREAD RAGOUT.

Quantity for 6 Persons.

½ lb. fresh and very cold butter
½ lb. good flour
1 white of egg
¼ pt. of cold water
1 tbsp. of strong brandy
This makes 6 small patties.

The Filling.

¾ lbs. of sweetbreads
¼ pt. of champignons
3 truffles
1/3 wine glass of white wine
Juice of ¼ lemon
1½ tbsps. of flour
1 cup bouillon
½ cup of cream
¼ tsp. of meat extract
Salt and 1 pinch of pepper.
1½ tbsps. of butter

The Paste.

Preparation: The flour is made into a smooth paste with water, ½ of the egg and brandy, then rolled out. The butter, which must be very hard, is placed on the paste in a chunk, the paste folded around it and then rolled out again. The board and rolling pin must be well covered with flour. This is repeated 4 or 5 times. The last time roll out the paste ¼ inch thick, cut out with a tumbler or cake cutter, then cut narrow strips and fasten them to the edge of the disk by brushing them first with the egg. Set the strips one on top of another until the edge is 1½ inch high, put a small mold in the opening. With a smaller tumbler, cut out the covers. Bake them both light brown or yellow. After cooling off, carefully remove the small mold, fill the patties with the ragout, cover with the baked covers and bake the patties 10 minutes in medium hot oven. Serve at once.

The filling is made like the one in No. 28. For 6 patties cut out 6 bottoms and six covers and use the other paste for strips.

No. 30—CROQUETTES OF SWEETBREADS.

Quantity for 4 Persons.

1 lb. of sweetbreads
½ pt. can champignons
1½ tbsps. of lemon juice
2 yolks of eggs
2 tbsps. of white wine
Salt, pepper
1 egg
Roll crumbs for breading
2 tbsps. of butter
3 tbsps. of flour
1 cup bouillon
¼ cup champignon juice
¼ cup of cream
Good lard for baking

Preparation: The sweetbreads are boiled in salt water until almost done, then skinned and cut into cubes.

The Gravy: Heat the butter and stir in the flour, add 1

cup of bouillon, white wine, lemon juice, cream, champignon juice, salt and pepper, then boil. It must be savory and thick.

The champignons are cut into small pieces and put into the gravy, also the sweetbread cubes. Then stir in the yolks of 2 eggs. Cool it and shape into oblong croquettes. Beat the egg well, dip in the croquettes and then into the roll crumbs. Bake in deep lard to a golden yellow color. If the croquettes are too soft, add more flour. If you want them as a side-dish, take only half the quantity given.

Remarks: You can make croquettes from remnants of veal and prepare them much more simply. See No. 31.

No. 31—CROQUETTES FROM VEAL REMNANTS.
Quantity for 6 Persons.

1 lb. of veal
Salt, pepper
1½ tbsps. of lemon juice
2 yolks of eggs
2 tbsps. of butter or drippings
3 tbsps. of flour
1 cup of bouillon or
1 cup of water mixed with
¼ tsp. of meat extract
½ cup of cream
1 egg and roll crumbs for breading
Good lard for baking

Preparation: The meat is cut very fine. The preparation is the same as in No. 30, Sweetbread Croquettes.

No. 32—MEAT BALLS FROM VEAL REMNANTS.
Quantity for 6 Persons.

1½ lbs. of veal
2 eggs
1½ tbsp. of butter
1 tbsp. of lemon juice
1 pinch of nutmeg
1 tsp. of capers
Salt, pepper
Roll crumbs for breading

Preparation: The meat is chopped fine or ground twice and mixed well with the eggs, salt, pepper, lemon juice, capers and nutmeg. It is then formed into oblong shapes, dipped in roll crumbs and baked or fried to a light brown in hot butter or lard, then placed on a platter.

For the gravy put ½ tablespoonful of flour into the butter or drippings, steep and add ¾ cup of water or bouillon or left-over gravy. Strain and pour over the meat balls and serve. They are also good served cold.

No. 33—VEAL HASH FROM REMNANTS.
Quantity for 6 Persons.

1 lb. of veal	½ tbsp. of flour
1 tsp. of chopped onions	½ cup of cream
Salt, pepper	Some water if necessary
1½ tbsps. of butter	2 tbsps. of white wine

Preparation: The meat is chopped and put into hot butter with onions. Cook and then add ½ tablespoonful of flour, salt, pepper and cream and boil slowly for 5 minutes. If it gets too thick, add more water or cream and the wine, if you wish. Serve on fresh wheat bread toast. This is a fine breakfast dish.

No. 34—LIVER DUMPLINGS.
Quantity for 6 Persons.

1¼ lbs. of calf liver	Salt, pepper
¼ lb. of bacon	1 pinch of nutmeg
3 rolls	½ onion
⅛ lb. of butter, good measure	3 qts. of salt water or broth for
4 eggs	cooking
2 cups of flour	

Preparation: The liver and bacon are chopped very fine or ground twice. The rolls are grated and browned in butter. The onions are cut fine and cooked or fried to a light yellow in ½ tablespoonful of butter.

Mix well the crumbs, onion, eggs, salt, pepper, nutmeg, flour, liver and bacon, then cut out dumplings with a floured round wooden ladle as large as a medium sized potato. The salt water must boil, then put in the dumplings and cook for 10 minutes. Put them in a dish or platter and baste with browned butter in which some roll crumbs or onions are fried.

Try one dumpling first and if it does not stay whole, add more flour.

Sauerkraut will go well with this dish.

No. 35—VEAL OR CALF'S LIVER WITH BREAKFAST BACON.
Quantity for 6 Persons.

2½ lbs. of calf's liver	1 tbsp. of flour
½ lb. of bacon	1 onion
Salt	1 cup of water
1 pinch of pepper	Flour for dipping
1 oz. of butter	

Preparation: Liver is cut into ¼ inch strips and bacon in 3x4 inch slices. The bacon is fried light yellow, then put on a platter and kept hot. The liver is sprinkled with salt and pepper, dipped in flour and baked to a light brown in butter or the bacon drippings. Then placed on the same platter with the bacon and served. Stir into the bacon drippings or butter 1 tablespoonful of flour and the sliced onions, boil and add water or bouillon. Strain the gravy and serve.

No. 36—LARDED AND BAKED CALF'S LIVER.
Quantity for 6 Persons.

2½ lbs. of calf's liver in one whole piece	1 carrot
Salt, pepper	1 onion
⅛ lb. of bacon for larding	1 small piece of celery
¼ lb. of butter	5 pepper-corns
½ pt. of cream	2 cloves
1 tbsp. of flour	1 bay-leaf
	1 pt. light white wine

Preparation: The white wine, carrot, onion, celery, pepper-corns, cloves, bay-leaf, 1 pinch of salt are covered and boiled slowly for ½ hour.

The liver is skinned, larded, salted and peppered and the cooked wine with contents poured over. Let stand for 10 hours. After that, roast the liver in hot butter in the oven for 30 minutes and baste frequently. During the last 10 minutes, pour the wine in which the liver had been lying over it and boil. Stir in 1 tablespoonful of flour and cream and boil again. The liver is served on a hot platter. The gravy is strained and served separately. Garnish the dish with lemon slices and parsley.

No. 37—LARDED BRAISED CALF'S LIVER.
Quantity for 6 Persons.

2½ lbs. calf's liver, whole	1 bay-leaf
Salt, pepper	3 cloves
⅛ lb. of bacon for larding	6 pepper-corns
1 carrot cut in pieces	1 pinch of nutmeg blossom
1 piece of parsley root	½ pt. red wine or white beer,
1 onion, sliced	(weiss beer)
⅛ lb. butter	1¼ tbsps. of flour

Preparation: The liver is skinned and larded and sprinkled with salt and pepper, fried quickly until light brown in ⅛ lb. of butter. Flour, onion, carrot and parsley root and all the spices are added and all fried in the liver butter a while. Then pour in the red wine or beer and enough bouillon to cover the liver. Cover and bake in the oven 1½ hours. Serve on a hot platter and strain the gravy.

Remarks: You can fry the larded liver without wine or beer, using only bouillon and ½ cup of cream.

No. 38—VEAL KIDNEYS.
Quantity for 6 Persons.

2 veal kidneys
½ lb. raw ham
⅛ lb. butter
½ onion
1 cup veal roast gravy

1 tbsp. of flour
3 tbsps. of champignons
　or mushrooms
1½ tbsps. of lemon juice
½ tsp. of sugar

4 tbsps. of red wine or Madeira

Preparation: The veal kidneys are fried, some fat cut off, then they are cut in thick slices, sprinkled with salt and pepper, fried one minute in the ⅛ lb. of butter until light brown and put on a hot platter. The ham is sliced and fried in the same butter rapidly about 2 minutes on both sides and placed on the platter with the kidney slices. In the same butter, fry the sliced onions, flour and the sliced champignons. Pour in the veal gravy, Madeira or red wine, lemon juice and sugar, boil and taste. Put in the meat slices and heat again but do not cook; serve at once. Toasted wheat bread served with this dish or placed around the edge of the platter is very nice.

No. 39—VEAL KIDNEY ON BREAD OR ROLLS.
Quantity for 6 Persons.

¼ lb. of veal kidneys or remnants of same
1 tbsp. of roll crumbs
1 tbsp. of capers
1 tbsp. of chopped parsley

1 yolk of egg
1 tbsp. of butter
3 rolls or wheat bread
Parmesan cheese and a little
　butter

1 tsp. of chopped onions

Preparation: The calf kidney must be cooked tender and chopped fine, then mixed well with the roll crumbs, capers, parsley, onions, yolk of egg, butter, salt and pepper. Cut the rolls or the wheat bread in slices, cover each thickly with the mixture and sprinkle with Parmesan cheese. Put on a few drops of melted butter and bake in a medium hot oven for 5 minutes. Serve this dish with asparagus, cauliflower or spinage.

If you do not like the taste of cheese, leave it out.

No. 40—VEAL OR CALF'S TRIPE.
Quantity for 6 Persons.

2 calves' tripes
⅛ lb. of butter
3 or 4 tbsps. of flour
Bouillon
2 yolks of eggs

Salt
8 pepper-corns
1 onion
1 bay-leaf
2 cloves

Water

Preparation: The calf's tripe must be fresh. It is cleaned well and scalded several times, then rubbed down with salt and left in water for ¼ day. After that it is cut into 3 inch squares and cooked until tender. Now add salt, pepper-corns, bayleaf, cloves and onion. Heat the butter and flour, take some of the bouillon when the tripe is done and pour it into the butter to make the gravy thick and stir in 2 yolks of eggs.

Put the tripe and gravy on one platter and serve. The bouillon may boil down to leave just enough for the gravy, making it pretty strong.

No. 41—STEWED VEAL OR CALF'S TONGUE WITH RAISINS.
Quantity for 6 Persons.

2 calf tongues
¼ lb. washed raisins
1 slice of lemon peel
½ pt. of white wine
2½ tbsps. of butter
2½ tbsps. of flour
3 qts. of water
Salt
6 pepper-corns
½ onion
1 bay-leaf
2 cloves
Juice of ½ lemon

Preparation: Soak the calf tongues in water. Cover and cook slowly in 3 qts. of water with salt, lemon peel, bay-leaf, cloves, onion and pepper; when tender, skin and slice. Brown the butter and flour and add the tongue bouillon, white wine, raisins and lemon juice. Cook ½ hour and season with sugar, salt or lemon juice. Put the tongues into the gravy and heat but do not boil. The gravy must be thick. Serve. Potato dumplings are nice with this meat.

No. 42—STUFFED VEAL CROWN ROAST.
Quantity for 8—10 Persons.

1 saddle of veal
½ lb. chopped veal
1 qt. fresh champignons or
1 pt. canned champignons
2 eggs
Salt according to taste
1 pinch of pepper
1 piece of butter
½ soaked roll
Small peeled potatoes

Preparation: The saddle of veal is freed from all fat and the rib-bones are freed from meat 2 inches from the end. The prepared saddle of veal is tied together so it looks like a crown.

The fresh champignons are cooked until tender in butter and some bouillon or water. Add the 2 eggs, the chopped veal, pepper, salt and roll and mix well. This stuffing may or may not be stewed a little with butter and then put into the crown of veal. On the small ribs stick some potatoes so that they will not get too brown.

Roast the stuffed crown of veal 2 or 2½ hours, same as veal roast.

CHAPTER 4.
MUTTON.

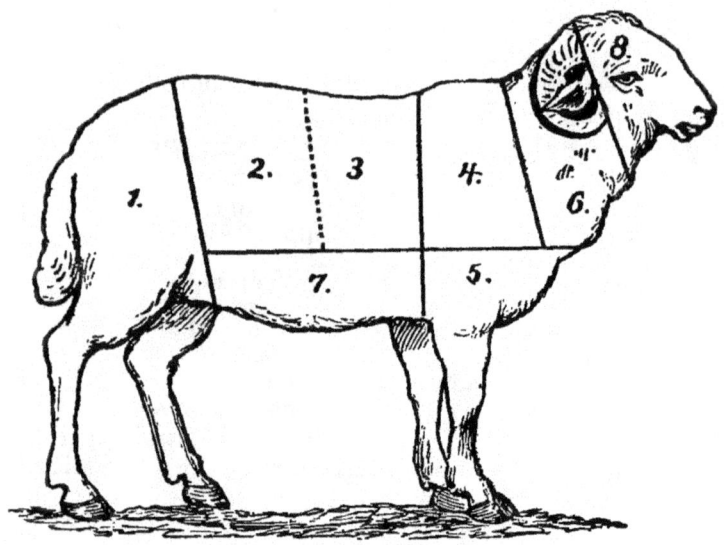

1. Leg.
2-3. Loin and small Ribs, or Loin Chops and Rib Chops.
4-5. Shoulder and Round Shoulder.
6. Neck.
7. Breast.
8. Head

LAMB OR MUTTON.
Boiled and roasted mutton.

How scraps of mutton may be utilized.

The best time for lambs is from beginning of December to the end of April. Good lamb meat is hard or firm and white and the fat also. Avoid buying soft, reddish meat of lamb or mutton. The forequarter is the most tender part of lamb.

The wether furnishes the best meat when he is 2 to 3 years old. Up to one year it is called lamb meat or lamb, older than that it is called mutton. Good mutton must be juicy, red and covered with a layer of white fat.

Best parts for roasts are leg and loin.

Best pieces for braising and stews are leg, loin and breast.

Small pieces for frying, cutlets and steaks from leg.

Best meat to make bouillon is all lean meat, the feet, scraps of cutlets and bones.

Mutton is less nourishing than beef. It may be kept fresh in vinegar, buttermilk or sweet milk.

Especially old mutton will be more palatable after being kept in vinegar or milk for a while.

No. 1—LEG OF MUTTON, ENGLISH STYLE.
Quantity for 6—8 Persons.

6 lbs. of leg of mutton	1 tbsp. of butter
Salt	1 small bunch of peppermint
1 pinch of pepper	Some vinegar and sugar

Preparation: Remove some fat from the leg of mutton, wash it well, pound it, salt and pepper it, and put into oven with ½ pint of boiling water. Add 1 tablespoonful of butter and roast 1½ hours, basting frequently; the roast will be quite rare inside. If you wish it well done, roast 2 to 2¼ hours.

Wash the peppermint well and chop it very fine, stir it with vinegar and sugar and serve with the meat. If you do not like peppermint sauce, pour off all fat from the roast, add 1½ tablespoonfuls of flour, brown it and pour in 1 cup of water, ¼ cup of cream and let this boil; then season with salt, strain the gravy and serve it with the meat.

No. 2—LEG OF MUTTON IN MILK.
Quantity for 6—8 Persons.

6 lbs. of leg of mutton	½ bay-leaf
2—3 qts. of milk	⅛ lb. of butter
⅛ lb. of bacon for larding	2 tbsps. of flour
Salt, pepper	½ cup of sweet or sour cream
2 cloves	A few drops of lemon juice
½ onion	1 cup of water

Preparation: The membrane and fat are removed from the leg of mutton and it is then well pounded and put into sweet milk for 2 or 3 days, turning it twice every day. The milk should cover the roast. In winter leave it in the milk for 3 days, in summer only 2. After this wash it off, lard it, salt and pepper it, put into oven with water, the spices and onion. After roasting it for ½ hour, add the butter, roast for 2 hours, basting frequently.

During the last ½ hour take off some fat, stir in 2 tablespoonfuls of flour and add 1 cup of water, gradually, also the cream and a few drops of lemon juice; now leave it in the oven a little longer. If the gravy has boiled down too much in the last ½ hour, add some more water. The gravy must be smooth and strained before serving with the roast. This is a very good dish.

No. 3—LEG OF MUTTON WITH RED WINE.

Quantity for 6—8 Persons.

6 lbs. of leg of mutton	10 pepper-corns
⅛ lb. of bacon	⅛ lb. of butter
10 sardines	Salt
1 qt. of thin vinegar	1½ tbsps. of flour
2 small onions	½ pt. of red wine
3 cloves	½ pt. of water
1 bay-leaf	

Preparation: The leg of mutton is cleared from all membrane and fat, pounded and larded. The sardines are drained and cut lengthwise into halves and the leg of mutton larded with them. The thus prepared leg of mutton is covered with 1 qt. of vinegar, onion slices, cloves, pepper-corns and bay-leaf and left in the vinegar for 24 hours, turning it over once in a while.

After this time the leg of mutton is fried with the butter and after ½ hour the flour is stirred in, add salt and pepper, the ½ pint of water and gradually the red wine. The roast is cooked slowly for 2 or 2½ hours and turned and basted several times until well done. The gravy is strained and served with the roast.

Remarks: If you do not like the taste of sardines, lard with bacon only.

No. 4—ROASTED LEG OF MUTTON WITH CHAMPIGNONS.

Quantity for 6—8 Persons.

6 lbs. leg of mutton	8 pepper-corns
⅛ lb. of butter	Juice of one lemon
2 tbsps. of flour	2 cloves
2 wine glasses of Madeira	½ bay-leaf
½ pt. champignons	Water or bouillon
Salt	

Preparation: The leg of mutton is freed from all fat and membrane, salted and fried in the ⅛ lb. of butter to a nice brown on both sides, and placed on a platter. Brown the flour in the same butter, add ⅛ onion and water or bouillon, salt and spices. Put the meat back into this gravy, it must be half way covered with it, cover it up and roast in oven 2½ hours. Then take meat out again, strain the gravy, take off all fat, pour the gravy back into the roaster, add Madeira and lemon juice, place the meat into it, cover, and cook it ½ hour longer. Finally cut up the champignons and put them into the gravy. Leg of mutton and gravy may be served on the same platter or separately. The gravy must be smooth, not thick.

No. 5—STUFFED ROASTED LEG OF MUTTON.
Quantity for 6—8 Persons.

The preparation and contents are the same as No. 4.

The bone is taken out, the cavity is filled with a stuffing as described in No. 11, of the previous chapter, Stuffed Veal Breast, and is cooked just the same as No. 4, of this chapter. You may omit the champignons.

No. 6—MUTTON STEW.
Quantity for 8 Persons.

5 lbs. of leg of mutton	½ carrot
½ tbsp. of caraway seeds	¼ parsley root
Salt	Water
1 large onion sliced	A thin white cloth

Preparation: The leg of mutton must be of a good quality. It is pounded, washed and tied into a thin white cloth; then put into boiling water; salt, onion, carrot, parsley root, caraway seeds added and cooked slowly for 2½ hours. The leg of mutton must be white outside and pink inside and juicy. Garnish with parsley and serve. A mustard or caper gravy is served with this meat.

No. 7—LARDED SADDLE OF MUTTON, MOCK VENISON.
Quantity for 6 Persons.

6 lbs. of saddle of mutton.	½ pt. sweet or sour cream
⅛ lb. of butter	A few drops of lemon juice
⅛ lb. of bacon for larding	1 tbsp. of flour
Salt, pepper	

Preparation: The ribs of the saddle of mutton are chopped off, the outer hard membrane is trimmed off and the bones cut out. Then the meat is pounded and larded, strewn with salt and pepper and put into the pan with the ⅛ lb. of butter with which it is basted very often. Water is added from time to time and cooked one hour. Now the flour is stirred in, ½ cup of water and the cream and lemon juice added and boiled again ½ hour. The meat must be basted very often. The gravy is then strained and served with the meat.

No. 8—SADDLE OF MUTTON A LA ENGLISH STYLE.
Quantity for 6 Persons.

6 lbs. of saddle of mutton   1 pt. of water
Salt, pepper, soupgreens

Preparation: The saddle of mutton is pounded and skinned. The ribs are chopped off a little, the fat is left on. Now the meat is salted and peppered and put into the oven with 1 pint of boiling water, and soupgreens. Let it roast 1 hour, basting frequently. Then serve.

For the gravy, take 1 tablespoonful of flour, stir it into the drippings and add ¼ cup of cream. Skim the gravy. You can also serve a peppermint sauce as in No. 1. A Bearnaise gravy is nice too.

No. 9—MUTTON TENDERLOIN.
Quantity for 4 Persons.

2 mutton fillets   ½ tbsp. of flour
⅛ lb. of bacon   1 cup of water
Salt, pepper   Juice of ½ lemon
3 tbsps. of butter   2 tbsps. of white wine
Bouillon

Preparation: The two fillets are cut from a saddle of mutton, (they are situated below the ribs alongside of the back). Cut the fillets lengthwise and crosswise so they make 8 pieces. Lard each piece nicely with the bacon, salt and pepper it, put the butter into the pan and fry quickly. Then stir in ½ tablespoonful of flour and pour in enough bouillon or water mixed with meat extract so the fillets are almost covered. Cover the pan and cook slowly ½ hour. Finally add the lemon juice and wine. Strain the gravy and pour it on the fillets or serve separately.

No. 10—STEWED RACK OF MUTTON.
Quantity for 6 Persons.

4 lbs. rack or rib piece   ½ onion
½ carrot   ⅛ celery root
½ parsley root   Salt
½ kohlrabi   3 qts. of water

Preparation: The rib-bones are partly chopped through and the whole piece of meat bound with string, then boiled slowly in 3 qts. of boiling water, salt and soupgreens. When done, put on a hot platter. A mustard or morel gravy is nice with it. The remnant of bouillon is used to cook vegetables in or for soup.

No. 11—MUTTON STEW WITH WHITE CABBAGE.
Quantity for 6 Persons.

4 lbs. of lean mutton
1 large head of white cabbage
2 tbsps. of butter
Water
Salt

Preparation: The cabbage is cut into 12 parts and put on the fire with boiling water, then cooked for 10 minutes. The water is then drained off and fresh boiling water put on. The meat is washed and salted, put in and cooked with the cabbage slowly for 2½ hours. Then it is served on a hot platter. The cabbage must not have too much gravy. If it is not rich enough, add more butter. Serve it with the meat and potatoes.

No. 12—MUTTON STEAK.
Quantity for 6 Persons.

4 lbs. of mutton chops or cutlets
1 piece of butter
Salt, pepper

Preparation: The cutlets are pounded well, and the bones all trimmed out. A pan is larded with some mutton fat and heated. The meat is put in and fried on the stove ¼ hour, turning it over often. Serve on a hot platter, salt and pepper, and butter. A peppermint sauce, as in No. 1, is good with this meat.

No. 13—MUTTON CUTLETS OR CHOPS.
Quantity for 6 Persons.

4 lbs. of mutton chops
⅛ lb. of butter
Salt, pepper
½ cup of water

Preparation: The real cutlet piece is the loin with the upper ends of the ribs. Every cutlet must have a rib and be one inch thick. They are pounded, skinned and the fat cut off, salted and peppered. The butter is melted in a pan and the cutlets put in and fried 3 to 5 minutes. Then they are served on a hot platter. For gravy pour some hot water or bouillon into the frying butter and perhaps a little more salt. Pour the gravy over the cutlets and serve hot.

No. 14—MUTTON CUTLETS BROILED.
Quantity for 6 Persons.

4 lbs. of mutton chops
1 piece of fresh butter
Salt, pepper

Preparation: The cutlets are pounded and placed on a broiler 5 minutes, turning them once; placed on a hot platter, seasoned with salt and pepper, buttered and served at once.

No. 15—BROILED BREADED MUTTON CHOPS.
Quantity for 6 Persons.

4 lbs. mutton chops
Salt, pepper

1 cup grated rolls
3 tbsps. of Parmesan cheese
⅛ lb. of butter

Preparation: Trim off the skin and fat, pound, salt and pepper the cutlets. Heat some butter and dip each cutlet into it, then into a mixture of roll crumbs and Parmesan cheese. Now broil to a light brown on a broiler, which requires 5 minutes. Serve on a hot platter and pour the rest of the melted butter over them.

Remarks: You can also fry the cutlets in a pan; then you need an additional ⅛ lb. of butter.

No. 16—MUTTON CHOPS WITH POTATOES.
Quantity for 6 Persons.

3½ lbs. mutton chops
Salt, pepper
1 pt. cream or milk
⅛ grated onion

2 tbsps. of Parmesan or Swiss cheese
⅛ lb. of butter
2 lbs. boiled, chopped potatoes.
3 yolks of eggs

Preparation: There should be 12 pieces of chops; salt and pepper them and fry them brown on both sides in butter. The boiled potatoes are pressed through a potato masher and mixed well with the remainder of the butter, which is creamed with the yolks of 3 eggs, salt, grated onion, cheese, cream and the rest of the butter which is left in the pan. Half of this mixture is placed into a casserole, the fried cutlets are placed on top and the remainder of the mixture put on to cover them. Then strew bread crumbs over the whole and small pieces of butter and bake in a medium hot oven for ½ to ¾ hour. Serve in the casserole.

No. 17—STEWED MUTTON CUTLETS.
Quantity for 6 Persons.

4 lbs. of mutton cutlets
Salt, pepper
Some bacon for larding
½ pt. of champignons
4 truffles
1 small wineglassful of Madeira or red wine

1 tbsp. of flour
Some bouillon or water mixed with ½ tsp. meat extract
2 tbsps. of butter

Preparation: The cutlets must be 2 inches thick. They are pounded and larded with bacon strips after the skin and fat have been removed from them, then peppered and salted and dipped in flour. Now they are quickly fried in butter and placed on a hot platter.

For the gravy, brown the flour in the butter, add bouillon, wine, salt, and the cutlets. Cover and stew until done. ¼ hour before they are done, skim the fat off and add the sliced champignons and chopped truffles. Serve the cutlets and gravy on the same hot platter. It is best to warm the plates with such a dish.

Remarks: You can prepare the cutlets more simply by omitting the champignons and truffles and putting 4 tomatoes into the gravy. Strain the gravy.

No. 18—IRISH STEW.

Mutton Cutlets stewed with all kinds of vegetables and Potatoes.

Quantity for 6 Persons.

3 lbs. of mutton chops	2 lbs. of raw potatoes
1 head of Savoy cabbage	Bouillon or water
5 kohlrabis	¼ lb. of butter
3 small onions	Salt, pepper
	¼ head white cabbage

Preparation: The vegetables and potatoes are cleaned and peeled well and cut into small pieces. In an iron kettle, which has been buttered, the vegetables are placed in layers, then a layer of cutlets, seasoned with salt and pepper; on this a layer of potatoes and onions; repeat this twice, taking care that you do not season too highly with salt. Potatoes must be the last layer. Fill up with hot bouillon or water. Place a piece of butter on top. Stew or boil for 3 hours, well covered.

No. 19—BAKED MUTTON KIDNEYS.

Quantity for 6 Persons.

10 mutton kidneys	Salt, pepper
1 piece of butter	½ tbsp. of mustard
	Grated rye bread

Preparation: The kidneys are cut half way through, skinned and rubbed with salt and pepper. Melted butter mixed with mustard is put over them and then they are dipped in rye bread crumbs, basted with butter and baked 15 minutes.

This dish is very nice garnished with cooked vegetables.

No. 20—MUTTON KIDNEY PUDDING.
Quantity for 6 Persons.

8 raw mutton kidneys	18 champignons
1 small onion	½ cup of rice
Salt, white pepper	Bouillon or water
2 tbsps. of butter	1 tbsp. of butter
Juice of 1 lemon	2 yolks of eggs
1 tbsp. of flour	

½ pt. gravy or broth from the meat

Preparation: The kidneys are sliced ½ inch thick. Butter, onions and sliced champignons are cooked; flour, gravy, salt and pepper are added. The sliced kidneys are put in and cooked slowly 15 minutes. Add lemon juice.

The ½ cup of rice is boiled until soft in bouillon or water to a thick mush, then the butter and finally the 2 yolks of eggs are stirred into it. A pudding-mold is buttered and strewn with roll crumbs, then put in a layer of rice and a layer of meat, alternately, until all is in; the last layer should be rice. Cover and cook in a steamer over a kettle of boiling water, for 2 hours. After it is done, dump it on a hot platter and serve with Dutch gravy.

No. 21—MUTTON RAGOUT.
Quantity for 6 Persons.

2 lbs. of mutton, lean, without bones	Salt, pepper
	2 tbsps. of flour
1 large onion	¾ qt. bouillon or water
⅛ lb. of butter	1 wineglass red wine

Preparation: The meat is cut into 1½ inch pieces. Butter stewed with onion and the pieces of meat are put in to cook 10 minutes. Add the flour and cook another few minutes, then add bouillon or water, salt and pepper and cook until well done. During the last 15 minutes, pour in the red wine and serve with a wreath of boiled rice. (Boil 1 cupful of rice in salt water until tender but retaining its firmness and add a piece of butter).

No. 22—MUTTON WITH POTATOES.
Quantity for 6 Persons.

1½ lbs. left-over mutton roast	Salt, pepper
1 onion, sliced	Left-over gravy
1½ lbs. sliced raw potatoes	1 small piece of butter

Preparation: The meat is cut into small thin slices, also the peeled potatoes. A casserole is buttered and filled with 1 layer of raw potatoes, 1 layer of meat, salt, pepper and sliced onion. Repeat twice, with potatoes for the last layer. Pour the gravy over, (if it is too thick, dilute with cream or milk) put a few small pieces of butter on top, bake in oven for 1½ hours.

If you have no left over gravy, make one of 1 tablespoonful of browned butter, flour, water or bouillon, cream, pepper and salt. Pour over the contents of the casserole and bake it.

No. 23—MUTTON WITH PICKLES.
Quantity for 6 Persons.

1½—2 lbs. of mutton roast or boiled mutton remnants	Salt, pepper
Scant ⅛ lb. of butter	1 clove,
2 tbsps. of flour	½ bay-leaf
¼ small onion, sliced	1 tbsp. of wine vinegar
1 pt. thin gravy or bouillon	3 sweet-sour pickles
½ tsp. of meat extract	3 tbsps. of pickled pearl onions
	1 tsp. of sugar

Preparation: The cold, fried or boiled mutton is cut into small pieces. The butter and onions are browned, then flour stirred in. Add salt, pepper, cloves, bay-leaf, vinegar, sugar and bouillon or thin gravy and boil until quite thick. The pickles, cut into small cubes, and onions, are now put in, stewed a little while; add the pieces of meat, heat, but do not boil, then serve. If the gravy is too light, add some meat extract or sugar coloring. Fresh boiled, peeled potatoes go well with this dish.

No. 24—MUTTONROAST SALAD.
Quantity for 6 Persons.

1 lb. mutton roast	½ pt. cream
2 yolks of eggs	4 mustard pickles
Salt, pepper	1 vinegar pickle
Some wine vinegar	2 tbsps. of pearl onions
1 tsp. of mustard	2 tbsps. of oil

Preparation: Meat, pickles, onions, all this cut into small pieces and mixed well with the other ingredients, then garnished with hard-boiled eggs.

No. 25—MUTTON PIE.
Quantity for 6 Persons.

3—4 lbs. of mutton from the leg	2½ tbsps. of flour
1 qt. water	Juice of one lemon
1/6 part of a small celery root	1 pinch of white pepper
2 small onions	3 doz. oysters
Some salt	½ pt. can of champignons
	2 tbsps. of chopped parsley
2 tbsps. of butter	

The Paste.

½ lb. fresh butter ¾ lb. of flour
¼ lb. lard 2 tbsps. of brandy
1½ glasses water

Preparation: The meat is cut into pieces the size of cutlets, boiled until tender in 1 qt. of water, celery root, 2 small onions, salt. Cook 2 tablespoonfuls of butter and flour and add veal bouillon; then add lemon juice, salt and pepper, if necessary, boil a few minutes, but do not let the gravy get thick.

The Paste: Butter and lard must be very cold. You may omit the lard and use more butter instead if you wish. Both are cut into the flour, the very cold water and brandy poured in and then stirred to a light paste and rolled out on a well floured board. The butter must be visible all through the paste. Do not knead much. Roll out, line a baking-dish with half of the paste, then put in layers of meat, oysters, then sliced champignons, chopped parsley, the gravy poured over the whole and then covered up with the other half of the paste in which make a few cuts, finish off the edge and bake in medium hot oven 1 to 1½ hours.

Remarks: Leave some of the gravy, mix with oyster liquor and the juice of ½ lemon and serve with the pie.

No. 26—MUTTON PIE PREPARED SIMPLY.

The preparation of this pie is just the same as in No. 25, but instead of oysters and champignons, take raw, very thinly sliced potatoes.

No. 27—LAMB ROAST.
Quantity for 6—8 Persons.

6 lbs. of lamb quarter ½ pt. sour or sweet cream
Salt, pepper 2 tbsps. of lemon juice
½ lb. of butter 1 cup of water
1 tbsp. of flour

Preparation: The lamb meat must be two days old. It is pounded, salted, peppered and put into the oven with the cup of water. After 10 minutes the browned butter is poured hot over the meat. Baste frequently, gradually adding the cream and lemon juice, and roast for 1½ to 2 hours.

For the gravy, stir into the butter some flour and a little water and cook (if necessary) a while longer. Serve the gravy with the roast after straining.

No. 28—BREADED LAMB ROAST.

Quantity for 6 Persons.

4 lbs. of lamb quarter	1½ cups of sour cream
Salt, pepper	1 tbsp. of flour
2 eggs	1 tbsp. of lemon juice
Finely sifted roll crumbs	1 cup of water
	½ lb. of butter

Preparation: The meat is pounded, rubbed with salt and pepper, then rolled in beaten egg and bread crumbs. Heat the butter and fry the meat quickly on top of the stove, then put it into the oven, basting it often and adding the cream in spoonfuls, also a little water, if the butter should get too brown. Cook in slow heat 1½ hours until the roast looks golden yellow; then serve.

For the gravy, stir 1 tablespoonful of flour into the butter, add water, cook and strain. You can also add chopped champignons.

No. 29—MUTTON OR LAMB RAGOUT.

Quantity for 6 Persons.

3 lbs. of mutton or lamb	1½ qts. of water
⅛ lb. of butter	3 tbsps. of flour
Salt	Juice of ½ lemon
6 pepper-corns	1 wineglass red wine
2 cloves	½ pt. can champignons
1 bay-leaf	5 truffles, chopped and peeled
¼ carrot	½ tsp. of sugar
	½ onion

Preparation: The mutton or lamb, which should be from the breast, is cut into equal sized pieces, stewed a little in 2 tablespoonfuls of butter, then add 1½ qts. of water, carrot, onion, salt, pepper, cloves, bay-leaf and cook the meat until tender.

For the gravy, take the rest of the butter, brown it with flour, add the strained mutton bouillon, the red wine, lemon juice, some of the champignon juice and boil slowly ½ hour. The gravy should be quite thick. Now put in the meat, champignons, truffles and spices and boil 15 minutes longer. Taste it for salt and spices. Serve on a hot platter, and garnish the rim with crescents of puff paste and small fried meat dumplings. The dumplings are prepared the same way as the Ox-tongue Ragout in No. 35, Chapter 2.

No. 30—LAMB STEW.
Quantity for 6—8 Persons.

Head, liver, lungs and heart	⅛ lb. of butter
Salt	1 egg
8 whole pepper-corns	Roll crumbs
1 onion	2 tbsps. of flour
1 bay-leaf	Some herb vinegar
2 cloves	

Preparation: The head is split in two, brain and tongue taken out and soaked in water. The tongue is boiled until tender in water with salt, pepper, bay-leaf, cloves and onion. In the same water, cook the brain and also the heart, liver, lungs and head until tender.

When the tongue, heart and lungs are well done, cut them into cubes. All the meat is put into a pot. Season with salt, pepper and a piece of butter, pour in some bouillon and stew. Cut the meat off the head, season with salt and pepper, dip in egg and roll crumbs and fry in butter to a golden yellow. The same is done with the brains. The liver is cut into slices, salted, peppered, dipped in flour and also fried.

The hash of tongue, lung and heart is placed in the middle of a hot platter, the liver slices placed in a wreath around it, the meat from the head, which has been cut into neat pieces, and the brains placed on top of the hash.

The gravy should be prepared before dishing out the hash. For the gravy, take one tablespoonful of flour, stir it in the butter in which the meat, brains and liver have been fried, add some of the bouillon and a little vinegar, lemon juice or white wine. Serve the gravy with the meat.

No. 31—PLAIN RAGOUT OF MUTTON OR LAMB.

The preparation is the same as in No. 29. Instead of wine, take wine vinegar or herb vinegar and leave off the champignons and truffles.

No. 32—LAMB CROWN ROAST.

Contents and preparation are the same as No. 42 of previous chapter, Veal Crown Roast.

CHAPTER 5.

PORK.

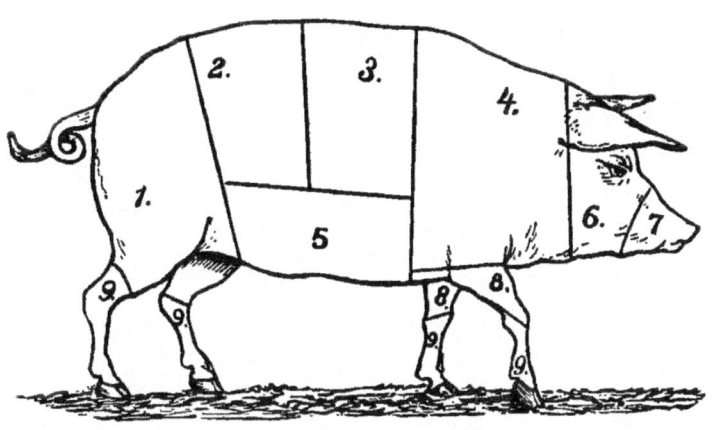

1. Ham.
2. Pork Loin.
3. Pork Chops.
4. Pork Shoulder
5. Belly.
6. Head.
7. Snout.
8. Shanks.
9. Feet.

Boiled, Fried and Salted Pork.

Also recipes for utilizing left-over pork.

Good pork from well fed yearlings is tender, light and not too fat. The fat or lard must be white, the hide light. Inferior pork has a yellow hide, smeary lard and very fat, dark meat.

Suckling pig is considered a delicacy in the kitchen. It is usually 2 or 3 weeks old.

Best Pieces for Roasts.

The leg, the pork loin, the slightly smoked rib piece, the fillets.

Small Pieces for Frying.

The cutlets, the fillets and ham slices.

Best Pieces for Stew.

The pork shoulder and fillets.

Best Pieces for Boiling.

The belly, the hip-bone, head, shoulder and marbled pieces.

Best Pieces for Smoking and Salting.

The hams, pork loins, smoked tenderloin, (called lachsschinken), the belly for lean bacon, the pork loin as fat bacon, tenderloin and shoulder.

For Gelatines.

The hide or skin and bones.

No. 1—PORK ROAST.
Quantity for 6—8 Persons.

4 lbs. rib roast	1 onion
Salt	1½ tbsps. of flour
6 pepper-corns	1 cup of cream
2 cloves	1½ cups of water
	1 bay-leaf

Preparation: The meat is washed and pounded, some fat trimmed off and salted. The roast is put into the oven with 1 cup of boiling water, all spices and onion and roasted 1½ to 2 hours, basting it frequently. The roast must be crisp outside. When it is done, put it on a platter and prepare the gravy. If there is too much fat, skim it off, put the flour into it, stew a little while, add the cream and some water if necessary, cook, strain and serve with the roast.

No. 2—FRESH YOUNG LEG OF PORK FOR ROAST.
Quantity for 10—15 Persons.

8—10 lbs. of leg of pork	1 onion
Salt	2 tbsps. of flour
6 pepper-corns	1 pt. of water
3 cloves	½ wineglass red wine or Madeira
	2 bay-leaves

Preparation: The meat is pounded, skinned, some of the fat cut off, rubbed with salt and put in oven with 1 pt. boiling water, all spices and onion and roasted 2½ to 3 hours, basting it frequently.

For the gravy, skim off the fat, stir in the flour, stew a little while, then add some water, the wine or cream, and cook it well, strain and serve with the meat.

No. 3—BREADED LEG OF PORK.
Quantity for 10—15 Persons.

The meat is prepared the same way as described in No. 2, but ¾ hours before done, 8 cloves are stuck into it, ½ teaspoonful of sugar and 1 cup of rye bread crumbs roasted in butter are strewn over it. Cover it well with the bread crumbs by pressing it down with a knife, baste with drippings and roast ½ to ¾ hour longer.

For the gravy, stir in 1½ tablespoonfuls of flour, 1 glass red wine, 1½ cups of water; cook, strain and serve.

No. 4—BRAISED PORK ROAST.
Quantity for 6 Persons.

4 lbs. of pork	1 small onion
Salt, pepper	2 tbsps. of flour
3 cloves	1½ pts. of water
1 bay-leaf	2 tbsps. of white wine

Preparation: The meat is fried quickly to a light brown in 1 tablespoonful of lard and onion on the open fire, the flour is stirred in and browned a little. Now the water is poured on, salt and spices and wine added and then roasted in oven 2 to 2½ hours, turning and basting frequently.

For the gravy, skim off the fat, strain it and serve with the roast which must be a light brown.

No. 5—SOUR PORK ROAST.
Quantity for 6 Persons.

4 lbs. of pork shoulder	1 handful of salt for pickling
1 qt. vinegar	1½ tbsps. of flour
2 onions	2 cups of water
6 pepper-corns	Salt
3 cloves	1 pinch of pepper
2 bay-leaves	1 wineglass of red wine if you wish

Preparation: The meat is pounded and put into a jar or earthen dish with 1 qt. of vinegar, sliced onion, salt, cloves, peppers and bay-leaves and left in it for 2 days, turning it once or twice. When taken out to roast, put it into the oven with 1 cup of water, salt and pepper, also ½ of the onions that are in the vinegar, then roast 1¼ hours, basting frequently.

For the gravy, stir in the flour, stew a few minutes, add some water, the wine or ½ cup of cream, cook, pour over the roast. When this is done, strain the gravy and serve with the roast.

No. 6—PORK STEW.
Quantity for 6 Persons.

3 lbs. of pork
Salt
4 pepper-corns
½ onion
2 cloves
1 bay-leaf
2½ qts. of water

Preparation: The meat is washed and put on with 2½ qts. of cold water, onion, salt, spices and cooked slowly 2 to 2½ hours, covered. Skim the bouillon several times. Cut the meat in slices and arrange the vegetables around it. The bouillon may be used for boiling all kinds of vegetables, beans, peas and lentils.

No. 7—SALT PORK OR HIP-BONE FOR STEW.
Quantity for 6 Persons.

4 lbs. of salt pork or hip-bone
6 pepper-corns
2 cloves
1 bay-leaf
1 onion
3 qts. of water

Preparation: The salt pork or hip-bone is put on with 3 qts. of cold water, spices and onion, and cooked slowly for 3 hours. The pot must be well covered and ought to be an earthen dish. The broth will be jellied when cold and can be utilized for all kinds of headcheese.

No. 8—SMOKED HAM FOR COOKING.
Quantity for 15—20 Persons.

10 lbs. of ham
2 onions
6 cloves
2 bay-leaves
10 pepper-corns
Sufficient water

Preparation: The ham is soaked in water over night, then put it on the fire with cold water enough to cover it, onions and spices added. Cook it slowly in a large kettle for about 4 to 5 hours. Serve it warm with a Madeira gravy, or cold in slices.

No. 9—SMOKED HAM BOILED, BREADED WITH RYE BREAD CRUMBS.
Quantity for 15—20 Persons.

10 lbs. of ham
Sufficient water
Rye bread crumbs
1 tsp. of brown sugar
Cloves for larding

Preparation: The ham is soaked in water over night, then put on the fire with sufficient cold water to cover it, boil slowly for 4 hours. It will be quite done by this time. Put it on a platter, skin it and lard it where the skin has been removed with 30 to 40 cloves, sprinkle side with the sugar and thickly with the rye bread crumbs, then lay the ham into a pan and bake it in the oven for 1 hour. Serve with a Madeira gravy. This is a fine dish.

No. 10—HAM IN BURGUNDY WINE.
Quantity for 15—20 Persons.

10 lbs. of ham	1 very large pig's bladder
2 bottles of Burgundy wine	2 tbsps. of butter
2 small sliced onions	2½ tbsps. of flour
A leek	¼ pt. of Madeira
1 piece of thyme	½ cup of bouillon
1 piece of marjoram	A cloth to tie up the ham
¼ lb. of truffles	Water to boil in
¼ lb. of champignons	

Preparation: The skin is cut off and the bones are taken out as well as possible. To the wine add the onion, the chopped leek, thyme and marjoram, then leave the ham in it for 24 hours, turning it over often. After that take it out, make a stuffing of truffles, champignons, 1 tablespoonful of butter, salt, pepper and ½ cup of bouillon mixed well and stuff the cavity left after removing the bone with it and sew it up. Clean the bladder well inside and outside, make a cut into it and put the stuffed ham inside, then pour in the wine with all its contents in which the ham has been lying for 24 hours, sew it up carefully. Then tie the whole into a white cloth and put it on the fire in cold water to boil for 4 to 5 hours slowly. After this, take the cloth off, open the suture, pour the fluid into a pot and put the ham into a pan.

Brown the butter and flour, add some of the ham fluid and Madeira, cook it well and add perhaps ½ teaspoonful of sugar, (better taste the gravy first). Fill some of this gravy over the ham and put it into the oven, roast for ¼ hour, then serve it with the gravy. Ham prepared in this way is very fine. If wine cannot be had, use Ginger Ale.

No. 11—FRIED HAM WITH EGGS.
Quantity for 6 Persons.

1 lb. raw ham sliced very thin	12 eggs
1½ pts. milk	1 pinch of salt and white pepper
⅛ lb. butter	

Preparation: The ham is put in milk for 6 hours, then dry off the ham slices and fry them quickly in butter, put them on a platter and pour the butter over. In the meantime the eggs have been fried in butter with salt and pepper and now they are carefully placed on the ham.

Remarks: You need not put the ham into the milk and instead of ham you may take breakfast bacon. (Bacon and Eggs).

No. 12—BOILED HAM WITH NOODLES.
Quantity for 6 Persons.

1 lb. of boiled ham	1 pinch of pepper
Noodles made from 2 eggs	2—3 eggs
1 pt. milk	Some butter
Salt	

Preparation: The ham is chopped fine. The noodles are cooked in salt water for ten minutes, then poured into a colander. Butter a casserole and put in a layer of noodles, then a layer of ham and repeat 2 or 3 times until all is in. The top layer must be noodles. The milk is well mixed with 2 or 3 eggs and very little salt and pepper and poured over the whole mass, a few pieces of butter on top and baked in oven slowly for 1 hour.

No. 13—BOILED HAM WITH MACARONI.
Quantity for 6 Persons.

1 lb. of boiled ham	Juice of 1 lemon
½ lb. of macaroni	2 tbsps. of Parmesan cheese or
1 pt. of milk	Swiss cheese
Very little salt and pepper	2—3 eggs

Preparation: The ham is chopped fine and the macaroni broken in 2-inch pieces, boiled in salt water for ½ hour, then drain. Butter a casserole, put in a layer of macaroni and one of ham, repeat 2 or 3 times, with macaroni for the last layer. The milk is stirred well with eggs, salt, pepper, lemon juice and grated cheese and poured over the mass, then baked in the oven for one hour, after putting a few small pieces of butter on top. Serve in the casserole in which it was baked.

No. 14—BREADED HAM.
Quantity for 6 Persons.

1 lb. raw ham	2 cups of roll crumbs
⅛ lb. of butter or lard, good measure	1 pinch of salt
	1½ pts. of milk
3 whites of eggs	

Preparation: The ham is cut into ¼ inch thick slices and put into milk for 5 hours, then taken out, dried, salted, dipped into white of egg and then into roll crumbs mixed with the flour. Then it is fried in hot butter on both sides. These ham slices are nice to serve with vegetables.

No. 15—ROASTED PORK-FILLET.
Quantity for 6 Persons.

2—2½ lbs. of pork-fillet
⅛ lb. bacon for larding
Salt, pepper
1 tbsp. of flour
½ cup of sweet or sour cream
1 cup of water
2 tbsps. of butter or drippings

Preparation: The pork-fillets are pounded, the skin and most of the fat removed, then larded with bacon, salted and peppered. Put the fat which you cut off into a flat baking tin with some butter; into this heated lard and butter, put your fillets, baste often and let it roast in the oven 45 minutes to 1 hour. This depends on the size of the meat. 15 minutes before done, pour off some of the lard, stir in the flour to brown, then the water and gradually the cream, basting frequently. Strain the gravy and serve with the fillet.

No. 16—STUFFED PORK-FILLET CALLED MOCK-DUCK.
Quantity for 6 Persons.

2 large fillets of 2½ lbs. or 4 small ones
⅛ lb. bacon for larding
Salt, pepper

For Stuffing.

½ lb. chopped pork
½ lb. chopped veal
2 eggs
½ tbsp. of butter
½ tbsp. of lemon juice
1 tbsp. of capers
Salt
1 pinch of pepper
2 tbsps. of butter for frying
½ tbsp. of flour
¼ cup of sweet or sour cream
1 cup of water

Preparation: The skin and fat are removed from the fillets and these pounded flat. Chopped pork and veal, eggs, ½ tablespoonful of butter, lemon juice, capers, salt and pepper are mixed well. This stuffing is placed between two fillets and these are then tied together with string or fastened together with toothpicks. If there are four fillets, put ½ of the stuffing on two and place the other two on top, then put bacon strips on top and fry them like No. 15, 1 to 1½ hours. Strain the gravy and serve with the fillets. This makes a very fine dish.

No. 17—ROASTED PORK CUTLETS.
Quantity for 6 Persons.

3 lbs. of pork cutlets	1 clove
Salt, pepper	½ bay-leaf
1 egg	¼ small onion
1½ cups grated rolls	⅛ lb. of butter or lard
1 tbsp. of flour	1 cup of water

Preparation: The pork cutlets are pounded, salted and peppered. The egg is beaten with a tablespoonful of milk and the cutlets dipped into this and then into the bread crumbs, then fried until light brown in hot butter or lard. This will require 15 minutes if they are ½ inch thick; if they are thicker, fry them for 20 minutes and place them on a hot platter.

If there is much fat in the pan, take some of it out and brown onion slices and flour in the remaining fat; add water, clove and bay-leaf, also salt and pepper, if necessary, and cook for 5 minutes. Strain the gravy and pour over cutlets or serve it separately.

No. 18—CHOPPED PORK CUTLETS.
Quantity for 6 Persons.

Preparation and ingredients are the same as in No. 17. The cutlets are chopped, carefully breaded and fried in butter about 8 to 10 minutes if the cutlets are ½ to ¾ inch thick.

No. 19—STEWED PORK CUTLETS.
Quantity for 6 Persons.

3 lbs. pork cutlets	1 bay-leaf
Salt, pepper	4 pepper-corns
½ cup of flour for dipping	½ sliced onion
1½ pts. of bouillon or water mixed with ½ tsp. of meat extract	1½—2 tbsps. of flour
	1 wineglass Madeira or red wine
	Juice of ¼ lemon
2 cloves	Butter

Preparation: The fat is cut off and the cutlets salted and peppered and dipped in flour, then fried quickly in hot butter on both sides. They are then taken out and put on a hot platter. The sliced onion and flour are browned in the drippings, bouillon, wine, spices, lemon juice, salt, 4 pepper-corns added, and cooked a while. The cutlets are then put into this gravy, covered and placed into the oven to stew one hour. When done, strain the gravy and serve with cutlets on the same platter.

No. 20—PORK KIDNEYS.
Quantity for 6 Persons.

1¾ lbs. pork kidneys	⅛ lb. of butter
Salt, pepper	1 pt. of bouillon
1½ tbsps. of flour	1½ tbsps. of vinegar

Preparation: The kidneys are cut crosswise into ¼ inch slices and fried in the hot butter 1 minute. Salt and pepper, stir in the flour, cook another minute and pour in bouillon and vinegar and cook 1 to 2 minutes more, stirring constantly. Have a good hot fire. The kidneys are tender when they do not look red any longer. If they cook too long, they get hard. Serve at once.

No. 21—PORK RAGOUT OR PORK PEPPER.
Quantity for 6 Persons.

2 lbs. of lean pork	1½ tbsps. of vinegar or
1½ tbsps. of butter or lard	1 wineglassful of red wine
Salt, pepper	3 tbsps. of flour
½ onion	Some water or bouillon
2 cloves	½ cup of pig's blood if you can
1 bay-leaf	get it

Preparation: The meat is cut into 2½ inch squares. The butter and flour is browned, then bouillon or water, onion slices, spices and salt added and cooked a few minutes. Put in the meat and cook slowly ½ hour. Add the vinegar or red wine and continue to cook slowly until done, which will require ½ to 1 hour. Put the ragout in a warm dish and stir the blood into the gravy, strain and pour over the meat.

Remarks: You may omit the blood.

No. 22—MOCK-RABBIT.
Quantity for 6 Persons.

1 lb. chopped pork	1 tbsp. of capers
1 lb. chopped veal	Salt
1 lb. chopped beef	1 pinch of pepper
2 tbsps. of butter	⅛ lb. of butter or lard for frying
3 eggs	½ tbsp. of flour
2 soaked rolls	1 cup of water
Juice of ½ lemon	1 cup of roll crumbs

Preparation: All the meat must be chopped very fine and mixed well with the roll from which the water has been well drained, eggs, 2 tablespoonfuls of butter, lemon juice, capers, salt, pepper, and 1 teaspoonful of grated onion. It is shaped into an oblong loaf and strewn with roll crumbs. The butter or lard is heated, the loaf of meat put in and baked in the oven one hour, basting frequently. Take out the mock-rabbit carefully and put it on a platter. For the gravy, brown ½ tablespoonful of flour in the drippings, add the water, boil, and when done, strain and serve with the mock-rabbit. You may also add ¼ cup of cream and some lemon juice to the gravy.

Remarks: You may also put 2 to 3 peeled, hard boiled eggs into the loaf of meat, whole, before baking it. It is fine for slicing cold.

No. 23—STUFFED HOG'S HEAD.
Quantity for 10 Persons.

1 hog's head with ears	2 small onions
Salt	⅛ of a celery root
6 whole peppers	½ pt. of wine vinegar
7 qts. of water for cooking	4 cloves
1 carrot	2 bay-leaves

The Stuffing.

1 lb. chopped lean pork	3 eggs
1 lb. chopped lean veal	Juice of ½ lemon
Salt, pepper	1 tsp. of grated onion
¼ lb. butter	1 pinch of nutmeg.
2 soaked rolls	

Extra.

1 lb. boiled beef tongue	⅛ lb. truffles, cut in small pieces
½ lb. of boiled veal	½ lb. bacon
½ lb. cooked pork	1 white cloth to tie up

Preparation: The head is cleaned well and split open lengthwise without cutting the skin. The bones are all taken out and the inside of the head is salted and peppered. The bones are split and put over the fire with the 7 qts. of water, the carrot, onion, celery, vinegar, cloves, and bay-leaf.

For the stuffing, mix well the chopped veal, salt, pepper, soaked rolls, ¼ lb. of butter, 3 eggs, grated onion, lemon juice, nutmeg and put the stuffing into the head, 1 inch thick, then make a layer of boiled tongue (½ inch slices), pork and veal. Then a thin layer of truffles. Repeat this, putting in stuffing, sliced meat and truffles alternately until both sides of the head are filled, sew it up, lay a piece of pork skin before the throat opening and sew it on. Tie up the whole head in the white cloth or sew it into the cloth and cook it 4 hours in the same water in which you have boiled the bones. After it is done, leave it in the bouillon and cool it off; when it is nearly cold, place it on a board and weight it down. When it is cold, cut off the cloth and pick out all threads. Cut off a slice from the head so you can see the stuffing. Garnish by pinning a lemon slice into each eye with a toothpick, into the mouth place a bunch of parsley and around the head, green lettuce.

This will make a fine cold supper or lunch. Serve a cold mustard gravy with it.

Remarks: The bouillon, after being boiled down considerably, may be used for aspic or head cheese.

No. 24—PORK RIBS AND SAUERKRAUT.
Quantity for 6 Persons.

3 lbs. salted pork ribs	1 pinch of sugar
1 lb. sauerkraut	6 large, peeled and sliced apples
¼ lb. butter	½ bottle of white wine

For Meat Dumplings.

¼ lb. chopped pork	Salt, pepper
¼ lb. chopped veal	1 tbsp. of butter
1 egg	¼ tbsp. of grated onion

Preparation: The pork ribs which have been salted for several days are cut into pieces, washed, dried and fried on both sides in hot butter, then put into a pot, the sauerkraut on top. (If the sauerkraut is too sour, soak it in water and drain). Add ¼ lb. of butter, apples, white wine and sugar, cover and cook slowly for 2 hours. When it gets too dry, pour in some water.

The Meat Dumplings: The chopped pork and veal, soaked roll, egg, 1 tablespoonful of butter and onion are mixed well. Shape into dumplings and fry well done in the butter in which you fried the ribs.

Arrange the sauerkraut in the middle of the platter, the ribs around it and the dumplings piled on top in a heap. Then serve. If you cannot get wine, omit it.

No. 25—SAUSAGE.
Quantity for 6 Persons.

2½ lbs. marbled pork	½ tsp. of cloves
Salt	½ tsp. of thyme
	½ tsp. of white pepper

Preparation: The meat is ground three times or chopped very fine, then mixed well with the spices, filled into casings made from hog intestines and fried while fresh.

No. 26—FRIED SAUSAGE.

2½ lbs. of sausage	Salt, pepper
2 tbsps. of lard	1 cup of bouillon or water
1 small onion	½ tsp. of meat extract
	1 tbsp. of flour

Preparation: The sausage is fried slowly in the hot lard until brown, then take it out and put the sliced onion into the same lard, add the flour, brown it, add water or bouillon, meat extract, if you have it, salt and pepper and cook. Pour this strained gravy over the sausage and serve.

No. 27—SAUSAGES.
Quantity for 6 Persons.

½ lb. lean pork
½ lb. fat pork from the loin
1 pinch of white pepper
2 casings of sheep intestines
Salt

Preparation: Meat and fat are chopped fine or ground 3 times, salted and peppered, filled into the casings and formed into lengths of sausages. You can improve the sausage by adding chopped truffles.

No. 28—FRIED SAUSAGES.
Quantity for 6 Persons.

1 lb. of sausages
2 whites of eggs
½ cup of flour
1 cup of grated rolls
Salt, drippings or butter

Preparation: The sausages are salted, dipped into white of egg, flour and bread crumbs and fried in hot drippings or butter to a nice brown color. They are nice with vegetables.

Remarks: You can prepare them like No. 26 and omit the bread crumbs.

No. 29—WHITE CABBAGE PIE WITH PORK.
Quantity for 6—8 Persons.

1 head of white cabbage
¾ lb. chopped pork
¾ lb. chopped beef
2 eggs
Salt
1 pinch of peppe
2 tbsps. of butter or drippings

Preparation: Remove the outer leaves and the core of the cabbage and boil until tender in salt water. Mix well the chopped pork and beef, butter, eggs, salt and pepper. Butter a pudding-mold, drain the salt water from the cabbage and put in layers of cabbage and meat; repeat 3 times until all is in, the cabbage being on top, then close the mold, put it in a steamer over a kettle of boiling water and boil for 2 hours. Dump on a dish or platter after draining off the broth.

For the Gravy: Stir 5 rolled crackers with 1 tablespoonful of butter, salt, pepper, add the broth and boil. If it gets too thick, add some bouillon or water; stir in 2 yolks of eggs and serve with the pie.

Remarks: For the filling you may take pork only and for gravy thickening use flour instead of crackers.

No. 30—CABBAGE SAUSAGES.
Quantity for 6 Persons.

1 head of white cabbage	1 onion
¾ lb. chopped pork	Left-over gravy or
Salt, pepper	1 pt. of false gravy
	⅛ lb. of bacon

Preparation: The whole head of cabbage is boiled until half done in salt water. The outer leaves are then carefully taken off and some of the mixture of chopped pork, salt and pepper put on each leaf and the leaf is rolled or wrapped around it and tied with string. The bacon and onions are cut into small pieces and fried, then these little cabbage sausages are fried in it to a nice brown color. The gravy is poured over them, the pan is covered and the sausages stewed for 1½ to 2 hours, the string removed and served.

Remarks: If you have no gravy, make one by browning 1 tablespoonful of butter and 2 tablespoonfuls of flour and adding water or bouillon. Put in 3 tablespoonfuls of cream if you have it; salt, pepper and boil. If you have no bouillon, stir ½ teaspoonful of meat extract with water.

No. 31—SPANFERKEL OR ROAST LITTLE PIG.
Quantity for 8—10 Persons.

1 suckling pig	½ lb. of butter
Salt	¾ pt. of water
	1 pinch of pepper

Preparation: The well washed and dressed pig is soaked in water for a few hours. The eyes are taken out and it is salted inside and outside. The fore and hind legs are bent under the pig and in this way it is placed into a pan with a tray on which it rests. Pour in some water and let it roast for 10 minutes. The butter is melted and the pig is brushed with it every 5 to 10 minutes. Gradually add water and cook it 1½ hours. Prick the skin several times so it will not blister; the butter will make the pig crisp. The drippings will be served as gravy or you can also serve a truffle, caper or tomato gravy with it.

No. 32—STUFFED SPANFERKEL OR ROAST LITTLE PIG.
Quantity for 8—10 Persons.

1 suckling pig	1 tbsp. of sugar
2 lbs. of sweet-sour apples	Salt
1 cup of dried currants	½ lb. of butter
	½ cup seedless raisins

Preparation: The dressed and well washed pig is rubbed

down with salt. The apples are peeled, cored and quartered, then mixed well with dried currants, raisins and sugar and stuffed into the pig which is then sewed up. Now bake just the same as No. 31.

Remarks: Sauerkraut and fried potatoes are good with it.

No. 33—SPANFERKEL A LA FRENCH STYLE.
Quantity for 8—10 Persons.

1 suckling pig
Liver, lungs and heart
½ lb. finely chopped pork
Salt, pepper
2 tbsps. of butter
1 egg

Preparation: The pig is washed well, dressed and rubbed with salt inside and outside. Liver, lungs and heart are chopped very fine and mixed well with butter, egg, salt, pepper and a few drops of lemon juice, then stuffed into the pig and this sewed up. The pig is brushed with fine salad oil and roasted slowly for 1½ to 2 hours. Water is added from time to time, garnish with lemon slices and serve with the gravy.

No 34—MEAT SALTING AND PICKLING.

60 lbs. of meat
2 tbsps. of ground white pepper
2 lbs. of salt

The Brine.

4¼ lbs. of salt
⅛ lb. of saltpetre
Scant ½ lb. sugar
9 qts. of water

Preparation: Rub the meat with the 2 lbs. of salt until it all disappears and rub the joints and cuts with pepper. Then pack it into a barrel, the big pieces at the bottom, the small ones to fill in the cavities. After 2 days, make the brine by heating it, but not boiling, pour it on the meat and leave it on for 20 to 30 days according to the size of the pieces.

No. 35—PICKLED HAM.

1 raw ham, 10 to 12 lbs.
2¼ lbs. of salt
2 tbsps. of sugar
1/20 lb. of saltpetre

Preparation: Salt is heated in a pan and mixed well with saltpetre, then the ham is rubbed with it for 45 minutes. After this, put the ham into a barrel, well weighted. Pour the salt water, which it produces, over it often and turn the ham over several times. It may remain in the brine 5 to 6 weeks.

CHAPTER 6.
POULTRY AND GAME BIRDS.

POULTRY.
Cooked and Roasted Poultry.
Complete directions for utilizing Poultry Remnants.

THE CHICKEN.

The young chicken has a slender body and a delicate color. All young poultry has long legs, soft skin, feathers with oily quill that can be pulled out easily, small red comb, long claws and an elastic breast bone.

Old hens have a small, pale comb. If you wish to keep poultry, hang it up for a few days with the plumage, then pick it and dress it, stuff it with white paper, hang it up or wrap it in a clean cloth and put it on ice.

Poultry must not be cooked directly after slaughtering, because it will not get tender. According to the season it will keep 1—3 days.

A young chicken is roasted or fried. It is best when 8 to 16 weeks old. Old hens are good for cooking.

No. 1—ROAST SPRING CHICKEN.
Quantity for 6 Persons.

2—3 young spring chickens	1 tbsp. of flour
Salt	½ cup of sweet cream
¼ lb. of butter	½ pt. of water
3 thin slices of bacon	

Preparation: The chicken is dressed, washed and dried well inside and outside and rubbed with salt.

Heart and liver may be put back into the chicken, gizzard and neck into the pan. The bacon slices are tied over the breast of the chicken, the pieces of butter put on top and then placed in the oven to roast one hour, basting it often until it is a golden yellow or light brown. Add water from time to time so that the butter will not get too brown. During the last 15 minutes put the cream, the flour and if necessary, water into the butter and let it simmer 15 minutes longer. Strain the gravy and serve with the chicken.

Remarks: You may leave off the bacon, but must baste the chicken every 5 minutes, because the breast gets dry very quickly.

No. 2—STUFFED ROAST CHICKENS.

Quantity for 6 Persons.

2 young chickens	Salt
2 slices of bacon to tie across the breast	½ tbsp. of flour
	½ cup of cream
¼ lb. butter for frying	½ pt. of water

The Stuffing.

The heart, liver and gizzard	1 tsp. of finely chopped parsley
1 roll	Salt
1 tbsp. of butter	1 pinch of pepper
2 eggs	1 pinch of nutmeg
½ tbsp. of lemon juice	

Preparation: The chickens are dressed, washed, dried and salted inside and outside. The stuffing made of finely chopped heart, liver, gizzard, from which the tough membrane has been removed, soaked roll, salt, pepper, parsley, nutmeg, butter, eggs and lemon juice, well mixed, is put into the chickens, the slices of bacon tied across the breast, the chickens sewed up and roasted exactly like No. 1.

Remarks: The stuffing may be made richer with ½ cup of chopped champignons and 3 truffles chopped fine.

No. 3—ANOTHER FORM OF STUFFED CHICKEN.

Quantity for 6 Persons.

2 young chickens	½ cup of sweet cream
¼ lb. of butter	½ pt. of water
2 slices of bacon	1 tbsp. of flour
Salt	

The Stuffing.

2 tbsps. of butter	1 pinch of pepper
1 tbsp. of finely sliced onion	1 pinch of nutmeg
Heart, liver, gizzard chopped fine	1 tsp. of finely chopped parsley
2 eggs	1 roll soaked and the water pressed out
Salt	

Preparation: The chickens are prepared as described in No. 1 and 2.

The stuffing is made by heating the butter and stewing the onion slices to a light yellow in it, then add the chopped heart, liver and gizzard and stew 5 minutes. Add the roll and all the other ingredients, stew another few minutes, stir in the eggs, stuff the chickens, sew them up, tie bacon across the breast and fry the same as in No. 1.

No. 4—STEWED CHICKEN WITH CHAMPIGNONS.

Quantity for 6 Persons.

2 young chickens	1 pinch of pepper
⅛ lb. of butter	1½ wineglassful of red wine
2 tbsps. of flour	½ pt. small champignons or
Bouillon or water	30 fresh, cleaned champignons
Salt	Juice of 1 lemon

Preparation: The chickens are dressed and washed and fried in ⅛ lb. of butter in the oven for 15 minutes, basting them several times. After this time, stir into the butter the 2 tablespoonfuls of flour, add bouillon or water, salt, pepper, wine and champignons, cover the pot or pan, stew the chickens for 1 hour. Lastly put in the lemon juice and serve the chickens and gravy on one platter.

No. 5—OLD OR YOUNG CHICKEN WITH RICE.

Quantity for 6 Persons.

1 old chicken or 2 young ones	¾ cup of rice
3 qts. of water	Water and chicken bouillon
Salt	½ tbsp. of fresh butter
	2 slices of onion

For the Gravy.

1 tbsp. of butter	½ wineglassful of white wine
2 tbsps. of flour	2 yolks of eggs
	Chicken bouillon

Preparation: The chickens are dressed, washed and boiled until tender in 3 qts. of water, the salt and onion slices. Boil a young chicken 45 minutes, old chicken 2—3 hours, according to its age. In the meantime, cook the rice in a double-boiler with a few cups of bouillon and a little salt. When the rice is done, stir in a piece of fresh butter. Do not cook it too mushy.

The Gravy: Stir 1 tablespoonful of butter and 2 of flour, add some of the chicken-broth, cook a few minutes till it thickens, add the white wine and stir in the 2 yolks of eggs.

The chickens are carved in nice pieces and placed in a heap in the middle of the platter, the rice around it and the gravy poured over the meat; or leave the chicken whole, place the rice around and serve the gravy separately.

Remarks: The gravy may be prepared without wine.

No. 6—CHICKEN PIE.

Quantity for 6 Persons.

2 young chickens or 1 old one	Salt
3 qts. of water	1 tbsp. of butter
	1½ tbsps. of flour

The Paste.

½ lb. of butter and lard, more butter than lard or butter only	½ lb. of flour, good measure
	1½ tumblerfuls of water

Preparation: The chickens are dressed, washed and put to boil in the water and salt. Young chicken will be tender in 45 minutes, old chicken in 2 to 3 hours.

The Paste: Butter and lard must be very cold. Cut it into the flour and add the very cold water, mix lightly and roll one-half of it out in ¼ inch thick layer. The paste must be dry; the butter must be visible after rolling. Put this layer into a baking-dish, cut up the chickens, put the pieces into the dish, pour in the bouillon so that meat and broth are even. Roll the other half of the paste, make a few cuts into it and cover the pie, trimming off the edge neatly. Bake in the oven 1 hour to a golden yellow color. Leave only enough broth for the gravy. Stir into the broth 1 tablespoonful of butter, 1½ of flour, cook, strain and serve with the pie.

Cabbage salad and fresh boiled potatoes go nicely with it.

No. 7—PUFF-PASTE PATTIES, FILLED WITH CHICKEN RAGOUT.

Quantity for 6 Persons.

1 small young chicken	Salt
	1½ qts. of water

For the Gravy.

2 tbsps. of butter	½ cup sweet cream
2 tbsps. of flour	Juice of ½ lemon
Chicken broth	Salt
½ wineglassful of white wine	1 pinch of white pepper
	½ pt. can champignons

The Paste.

½ lb. very cold fresh butter	1 tbsp. of strong brandy
½ lb. flour	½ of an egg
	¼ pt. very cold water

Preparation: The chicken is prepared well and cooked until tender in 1½ qts. of salt water, then cut up into very small pieces.

The Gravy: Melt the butter, stir in the flour, fill up with chickenbroth, add cream and wine, cook till it thickens, put in the chopped champignons and the meat, season with salt and pepper, fill hot into the ready baked patties. Then bake in moderately hot oven for about 10 minutes and serve immediately.

Bake the patties according to No. 29, Chapter 3, Veal Sweetbread Patties.

No. 8—CHICKEN RAGOUT IN SHELLS OR OTHER SMALL MOLDS.

Quantity for 6 Persons.

1¼ lbs. of cooked chicken	½ wineglassful of white wine
2 tbsps. of butter	Juice of ½ lemon
2 tbsps. of flour	Salt
Some bouillon	1 pinch of pepper
	½ cup of sweet cream

Preparation: The chicken meat is cut up into small pieces. Butter is melted and flour stirred in, broth, cream and white wine added, seasoned with salt, pepper and lemon juice, cooked and filled into the shells or other small molds. Sprinkle with bread crumbs, place pieces of butter on top and bake in oven to a nice brown color.

Remarks: This ragout may be improved with ½ pt. of finely chopped champignons and 4 truffles also chopped fine. This chicken ragout in shells makes an excellent side-dish.

No. 9—CHICKEN CROQUETTES.

The preparation and ingredients are the same as in No. 31, Veal Croquettes, or No. 30, Veal Sweetbread Croquettes. See Chapter 3.

No. 10—FINE CHICKEN FRICASSEE.

Quantity for 6—8 Persons.

2 young chickens	Salt
	¼ lb. of butter

For the Gravy:

2½—3 tbsps. of flour	½ cup champignon juice
½ pt. sweet or sour cream	1 wineglassful of Madeira or white wine
Bouillon or water	
½ pt. champignons	Salt
6 sliced truffles	1 pinch of white pepper
	Some lemon juice

Preparation: The chickens are dressed and washed, fried light brown in ¼ lb. of butter, and, when well done, carved.

For the gravy, stir into the drippings the flour, water or bouillon, cream, wine, champignons, juice and cook well. The gravy ought to be quite thick and light yellow, strain and season it with lemon juice, salt, if necessary, some pepper, and put in the whole champignons and the sliced truffles.

The chicken should be so carved that the meat will not fall from the bones and should be kept very hot. Put the meat on a platter and pour the gravy over it. Garnish the rim with puff-paste scallops and small meat dumplings.

The dumplings are made by chopping the chicken liver, heart and gizzard, mixing it well with ½ soaked roll, salt, pepper, 1 egg, ½ teaspoonful of lemon juice. Fry the mixture in 1 tablespoonful of butter; when cool, form small dumplings and fry them a light brown in very little butter. This is a very fine dish.

No. 11—VIENNA BAKED CHICKEN.
Quantity for 6 Persons.

3 young, fresh chickens
Salt
⅛ lb. of flour
1—2 eggs
2½ cups of bread crumbs
3 lbs. of lard for frying
1 lemon for garnishing

Preparation: The chickens are killed, dressed, washed, dried and prepared at once. Cut the chickens in half, salt them, dip them first into flour, then in beaten egg and then in bread crumbs. The lard is heated in an iron pot or kettle and the pieces of chicken placed into it carefully, one at a time, so as not to cool the fat too much and that the crumbs may not fall off. Bake them to a nice brown color. After the crust is hard, let them cook more slowly until well done. Then put on paper to drain, strew fine salt over the pieces and put on a platter after which they may be garnished with lemon slices.

No. 12—CHICKEN OR PIGEON CUTLET.
Quantity for 6 Persons.

3 young chickens or
6 young pigeons
Salt
1 pinch of pepper
2 eggs
Some flour
1½ cups of roll crumbs
Lemon
¼ lb. of butter

Preparation: The birds are dressed, washed and skinned. Each breast is quartered and pounded a little, on each piece fasten a scraped wingbone and season with salt and pepper.

Beat the egg well with 1½ tablespoonfuls of drawn butter, dip in the cutlets and then into roll crumbs, mixed with 2 tablespoonfuls of flour, then fry in butter 8 to 10 minutes, turning them often. With asparagus these poultry cutlets are very fine.

Remarks: The scraps of poultry may be utilized for soup, croquettes or fricassee

No. 13—CHICKEN PIE, ENGLISH STYLE.
Quantity for 6—8 Persons.

2 young chickens
¾ lb. of veal steak
½ lb. of boiled ham
2 tbsps. of chopped parsley
3 hard boiled eggs
2 tbsps. of flour
1 pt. of water or bouillon
Salt
1 pinch of pepper
1 tbsp. of butter

Preparation: The paste is made the same as the chicken pie in No. 6.

The chickens are prepared as in No. 6, the meat removed from the bones and cut into ¼ inch slices, the ham and veal too. The baking-dish is lined with the paste and filled with alternate layers of meat, salted and peppered, chopped parsley and champignons and the yolks of eggs put in whole.

The tablespoonful of butter and 2 of flour are browned a little, broth or water added, stewed, and this poured over the meat. Cover with the paste as described in No. 6, then bake in the the oven slowly for 1¾ hours. The pie may be eaten cold. Use no flour for the gravy, but clear broth.

No. 14—PIGEON PIE, ENGLISH STYLE.
Quantity for 6 Persons.

4 pigeons
¾ lb. of beefsteak
6 hard boiled eggs, the yolks only
¼ pt. finely chopped champignons
¼ lb. of butter
1½ tbsps. of flour
¾ pt. of bouillon
Salt
1 pinch of pepper
2 tbsps. of finely chopped parsley
¼ onion

Prepare the pie-crust as described in No. 6. See Chicken Pie.

Preparation: The pigeons are dressed, washed and fried in the butter for ½ hour, then cut in halves. Fry the steak, which has been cut into small pieces and the fat taken off, in the same butter for 10 minutes. Prepare a baking-dish with the crust as described in No. 6, put in the meat, salted and peppered, parsley and champignons and place the yolks of eggs here and there between the meat. Slice the ¼ onion and brown together with the flour in the drippings, add the bouillon, stew, strain and pour over the meat, then cover with crust according to No. 6 and bake in the oven 1¼ hours.

Remarks: For the crust, use butter only.

No. 15—FRIED PIGEON.
Quantity for 6 Persons.

6 young pigeons	1 cup of cream
¼ lb. of butter	½ cup of water
1 tbsp. of flour	

Preparation: The pigeons are dressed, washed, salted inside and outside. Heat the butter and fry the pigeons light brown on every side, basting with spoonfuls of water and cream. During the last ten minutes stir in the flour and add some more water if necessary, strain the gravy. On the stove it requires 1½ hours to fry the pigeons, to roast in the oven only one hour.

No. 16—STUFFED FRIED PIGEONS.
Quantity for 6 Persons.

6 young pigeons	½ cup of cream
¼ lb. of butter	1 cup of water
1 tbsp. of flour.	

For the Stuffing.

2 soaked rolls	¼ pt. finely chopped champignons
Chopped heart, liver, gizzard	4 truffles, chopped
1 tbsp. of butter	Salt, pepper
2 eggs	1 tsp. of chopped parsley.

Preparation: The pigeons are dressed, washed and salted inside and outside.

The stuffing is made by mixing well the chopped liver, heart and gizzard from which the inner membrane has been removed with all the other ingredients. Stuff the pigeons with it, sew them up and fry them as stated in No. 15; prepare the gravy likewise.

Remarks: You may make the stuffing more simply by omitting the champignons and truffles.

No. 17—FRIED PIGEONS WITH SWEET STUFFING.

4 pigeons	2 eggs
3 soaked rolls	3 tbsps. of sugar
½ cup of ground almonds	1 pinch of salt
½ cup of dried currants	⅛ lb. of butter

Preparation: The butter is melted, and the soaked rolls

stirred in and sautéed or dry fried. The almonds are scalded, skinned and ground and added with the rest of the ingredients. The pigeons are stuffed and prepared same as in No. 15.

No. 18—ROAST TURKEY.
Quantity for 10—15 Persons.

1 turkey weighing 8 to 10 pounds
½ lb. of butter
Salt
1 cup of cream
2 cups of water
2 tbsps. of flour
1 pinch of white pepper

Preparation: The turkey is dressed and soaked in cold water 30 minutes, then dried and seasoned with pepper and salt inside and outside. The butter is placed in bits on the turkey and if it is a young turkey, roast it in the oven 2 hours, basting frequently with cream and water.

For the gravy, brown the flour in the drippings, add water, cook, strain and serve with the turkey.

If the turkey is older it will require 3 hours to cook it well, and it is best to cover it so it will not get too brown. To prevent the butter from getting too dark, add water from time to time.

Remarks: The leavings may be utilized in many ways. Turkey ragout in shells, see No. 8 for Chicken ragout in shells; Turkey croquettes, see No. 31 or No. 30, Chapter 3, Veal and veal sweetbread croquettes; Turkey pie, see No. 7, Chicken pie. The bones make a good soup.

No. 19—ROASTED AND STUFFED TURKEY.
Quantity for 10—15 Persons.
The Stuffing.

3 soaked rolls
Chopped liver, heart and gizzard
Salt, pepper
2 tbsps. of butter
1 tbsp. of chopped parsley
1 tsp. of lemon juice

Preparation: Mix these ingredients well, stuff the turkey with the mixture and roast as directed in No. 18. Prepare the gravy the same as in No. 18.

The Goose.

The young goose or gosling has a soft gullet, a pale yellow bill and feet with pointed claws. The bill and feet of old geese are reddish yellow. The color of the skin must be white, not purple or blue.

The time for fat geese is from October to January.

No. 20—ROASTED YOUNG GOOSE.
Quantity for 6 Persons.

1 young goose	⅛ lb. of butter
Salt	½ onion, sliced
6 pepper-corns	2 tbsps. of flour
	1 pt. cold water

Preparation: The goose is cleaned and dressed. The wings, neck, head and feet chopped off. The fat is trimmed off, even from the bowels, and is soaked in water separately from the meat. The goose is washed and left to soak in cold water for 15 minutes, then dried and rubbed with salt inside and outside. Put it into the oven with 1 pt. of water, sliced onion and pepper-corns. When the water is boiled down pretty much, baste the goose frequently with browned butter. A young goose will be done in 1½ hours. It should be of a light brown color and very crisp. Sprinkle a tablespoonful of cold water over it to make it crisp.

Now prepare the gravy by stirring the flour into the drippings, cook it a few minutes and add water. Cook well, strain and serve with the goose.

No. 21—FAT GOOSE STUFFED WITH APPLES.
Quantity for 7—9 Persons.

1 goose, 7 to 8 lbs.	½ sliced onion
Salt	1½ pts. of water
	6 pepper-corns

The Gravy.

2 tbsps. of flour	Some water

The Stuffing.

1½ lbs. peeled, quartered apples ½ cup currants

Preparation: The goose is prepared as described in the previous number, washed and salted inside and outside.

The prepared apples are mixed well with the currants and stuffed into the goose, which is then sewed up. The goose is put into the oven in a covered roasting pan with the water, sliced onion and pepper-corns, and roasted for 1 hour. After that time, remove the cover, baste with the drippings every 10 to 15 minutes, and if the water boils down, add spoonfuls of it so the fat will not get too brown. It may require from 2 to 3 hours roasting before the goose is well done and crisp. Sprinkle a tablespoonful of cold water over the skin to make it more crisp. Then serve.

For the gravy, pour off nearly all of the grease and prepare as described in No. 20. If there is very much grease from the goose, skim some of it off while roasting.

No. 22—FAT GOOSE STUFFED WITH CHESTNUTS.
Quantity for 7—9 Persons.

The Stuffing.

2 lbs. of chestnuts, the liver
1 pinch of salt
1 pinch of pepper
3 tbsps. of butter
1 tsp. of sugar
Some water

Preparation: The preparation and ingredients for goose and gravy are the same as in No. 21. The chestnuts are put into the oven; when the shells burst take them out, peel them at once and chop them fine. Put them into a ketle over the fire with water, butter, 1 pinch of salt and 1 of pepper and sugar and cook until well done, then put in the chopped goose liver, stuff the goose with this mixture and sew it up. Prepare the roast and gravy as directed in No. 21.

No. 23—FRIED GOOSE LIVER.
Quantity for 7—9 Persons.

1 goose liver
½ pt. milk and water
1 egg
Some flour
Salt
1 pinch of pepper
1 piece of butter for frying
¼ cup of goose gravy or
¼ tablespoonful of flour mixed with broth

Preparation: Carefully remove the gall from the liver and put the liver into milk diluted with water for 2 hours, dry it well, salt and pepper, dip into beaten egg, then into flour. Heat the butter and fry the liver 5 minutes to a light brown, turning it several times. Serve on a hot platter. For the gravy, brown ¼ tablespoonful of flour in the butter, add broth or water, cook well and serve with the liver.

No. 24—GOOSE GIBLETS.
Quantity for 2—3 Persons.

From one goose the heart, gizzard, head, wings, feet and neck
1 qt. of water
Salt
4 pepper-corns
2 cloves
1 bay-leaf
½ onion, sliced

For the Gravy.

2 tbsps. of butter
3 tbsps. of flour
Bouillon
1 yolk of egg

Preparation: The feet are scalded and skinned, the gizzard emptied and also scalded and skinned, the gullet cut from the neck, the eyes taken out, wings, neck and head well cleaned and singed. Now put all this in a kettle over the fire with the water, onion, salt, peppers, cloves, bay-leaf and cook until tender.

For the gravy, melt the butter, stir in the flour, cook and add the goose broth. The gravy must be smooth; stir into it one yolk of egg and pour it on the giblets. Serve in a deep dish.

Fresh, peeled potatoes are good with it.

Remarks: You may also utilize these goose giblets for soup and put in small potatoes.

No. 25—GOOSE LIVER PIE.
Quantity for 6 Persons.

3 large goose livers
3/4 lb. veal
3/4 lb. fat pork
6 truffles
1 1/2 lemon
1/8 lb. of butter

2/3 pt. of bouillon
2 tbsps. of Madeira or red wine
Salt, pepper
3 yolks of eggs
1 tsp. of grated onion
Bacon slices to line the pan

4 tbsps. of flour

Preparation: Two of the goose livers are larded with oblong slices of peeled truffles. Drip the juice from 1 1/2 lemons on the livers and let stand for several hours.

The 1/8 lb. of butter is heated, mixed with the flour, salt and pepper and 3/4 pt. of broth and Madeira added. The finely chopped or ground veal and pork are stirred into the thick gravy. The one goose liver is chopped, fried 2 minutes in 2 tablespoonfuls of butter and the onion, salted and peppered and mixed into the filling. Fill all this into a deep baking pan or mold lined with bacon slices so that it makes 2 to 3 layers of stuffing, alternating with slices of goose liver. Cover with slices of bacon, set in steamer over a kettle of boiling water and boil for 1 1/2 hours or bake in oven for 1 hour.

A truffle or Madeira gravy may be served with it.

No. 26—GOOSE LIVER PUDDING.
Quantity for 6 Persons.

3 large goose livers
1/4 lb. of bacon
3 tbsps. of butter
3 rolls soaked in milk
1/4 onion

3 eggs
3 tbsps. grated Parmesan cheese
3 tbsps. of cream
Salt, pepper
Butter for the mold

Preparation: Liver and bacon are chopped fine. Fry the butter, grated onion, and the roll a few minutes, then put in the chopped liver and bacon, salt, pepper, cheese, cream, 3 yolks of eggs, the beaten whites and mix well. Put into a buttered mold, set in a steamer over a kettle of boiling water and boil for one hour, dump it on a plate and serve with a hot, brown gravy. This pudding may be made of duck liver as well; truffles may be added to make it richer. It makes a fine dish garnished with roasted blackbirds.

No. 27—ROASTED WILD GOOSE.
Quantity for 6 Persons.

1 wild, young goose	2 tbsps. of butter
8 large, sour apples	1 pinch of salt and pepper
	3 large onions

For Roasting.

⅛ lb. of butter	Some water
	Some slices of bacon

The Gravy.

1½ tbsps. of flour	1 cup of broth

Preparation: Wild geese are usually very tough, therefore take a young goose only. Clean and dress it well, let it soak in water for ½ hour, dry it and salt it inside and outside.

The filling or stuffing is made by heating the butter, chopping the scalded onion and put into the butter together with the peeled and sliced apples, cut into ⅛ths. Let these cook half done, then add 1 pinch of white pepper, salt and 2 pulverized cloves, fill the goose with this and sew it up.

Tie the slices of bacon across the breast of the goose and put into the oven with the water and ⅛ lb. of butter, basting it frequently. When the gravy gets too brown add more water. After it is well cooked, take off the string and bacon and serve it.

The Gravy: Stir some flour into the broth, add water or more broth, cook a few minutes, strain and serve.

No. 28—SMOKED GOOSE-BREAST.

The breast of one goose	1 tsp. of saltpetre
⅜ lb. of salt	1 tbsp. of sugar

Preparation: The breast is cut from an undressed goose. Cut off the legs and the meat off the breast down to the bone. Be careful not to injure the outer skin. The small fillets are separated from the breast and it is rubbed well with ½ the quantity of salt, which has been mixed with the saltpetre and sugar until it dissolves. Replace the small fillets after salting them also, fold and sew up the breast. Salt it well on the outside and place into a crock for 7 days, turning it twice a day and basting it well with the brine that collects. On the eighth day wrap in paper, place it between two boards, well weighted, and draw a string through the top end of fat and skin by which to hang it up. Hang it into a smoke house in medium smoke for 8 to 10 days. Then place again between two boards weighted down for a few days. By this process the fat becomes white and hard and the meat keeps better.

The Duck.

When the duck is 6 months old it makes the finest roast, but you may roast it up to a year old. The best time for duck is from August to the beginning of December.

No. 29—ROAST DUCK.
Quantity for 6—8 Persons.

2 ducks
Salt
1 pinch of pepper
Some butter for roasting
10—12 sweet-sour apples
1 cup currants
2 tbsps. of flour
1½ cups of water

Preparation: The duck is dressed, neck, wings and feet cut off and it is washed, dried and salted inside and outside. The apples are peeled, quartered, mixed well with the currants, filled into the duck and this sewed up. Put it into a pan with the water, 2 tbsps. butter, and roast for 1½ hours, basting frequently.

For the Gravy: If there is too much grease, pour some of it off, stir in the flour, brown it a little, add water, cook well, strain and serve with the duck.

No. 30—ANOTHER FORM OF STUFFED DUCK.
Quantity for 6—8 Persons.

2 ducks
Salt
1 pinch of pepper
2 tbsps. of butter for roast

The Stuffing.

Chopped heart, liver and gizzard
3 rolls, soaked
3 eggs
1 tbsp. of finely chopped parsley
1 tbsp. of lemon juice
Salt, pepper
⅛ onion chopped finely
1 tbsp. of butter

For the Gravy.

2 tbsps. of flour
1½ cups of water

Preparation: The ducks are dressed after cutting off

neck, wings and feet, then washed and salted and strewn with 1 pinch of pepper inside and outside.

The stuffing is made of chopped liver, heart, gizzard, mixed with all the other ingredients and put into the ducks, which are then sewed up and treated just the same as described in No. 29.

Prepare the gravy as given in No. 29.

No. 31—FRIED DUCK-LIVER.

This is prepared the same as described in No. 23.

No. 32—GOOSE AND DUCK SCHWARZ-SAUER.
Black Soup.
Quantity for 4 Persons.

Giblets of 1 goose or duck
Salt
¼ lb. prunes
¼ cup of sugar
1 small stick of cinnamon
½ lb. of peeled apples or pears
2 cloves
4 pepper-corns
Scant 1 pt. of goose or duck blood
1½ tbsps. of vinegar
1½ qts. of water
2 tbsps. of flour

Preparation: Neck, head, feet, wings, heart and gizzard are cleaned well and cooked until tender in 1 qt. of water with salt, pepper and 2 cloves. The prunes and quartered apples or pears are cooked until done in ½ qt. of water. The blood is stirred with the flour into ½ of the broth from the giblets and poured back on again. The chopped fruit added, then seasoned with vinegar and sugar and brought to boil, stirring constantly. It must not coagulate.

THE GAME BIRDS.

THE PHEASANT.

One can recognize the young bird by its less developed spurs and flexible bones. The pheasant may become 5 to 10 years old. Freshly shot pheasants are not good to eat because the meat is dry and hard. In winter the bird may be left hanging with its feathers for 2 to 3 weeks.

No. 33—FRIED PHEASANT.
Quantity for 6 Persons.

1 pheasant
Salt
⅛ lb. of butter
2 thin slices of bacon to tie across the breast
1½ tbsps. of flour
1 cup of water
½ pt. sweet or sour cream

Preparation: The young pheasant is dressed, carefully washed and dried, then salted inside and outside and the liver put back into the bird with a piece of butter. The slices of bacon are tied across the breast.

Put the pheasant into the oven with ⅛ lb. of butter, baste it frequently and roast to a golden yellow. After 30 minutes, baste frequently with the cream and water by spoonfuls. It will require 1 to 1½ hours to cook it well done. Before serving, remove the bacon slices.

Into the drippings stir the flour, brown it, if necessary add more water, cook and strain and serve the gravy with the bird.

No. 34—FRIED OLD PHEASANT.

The preparation is just the same as the one under No. 33, with the exception that it requires from 2½ to 3 hours to cook the bird well done, therefore take a little more cream and water for basting and cover the roasting pan during part of the time to keep the bird from getting too dark.

No. 35—PHEASANT PATTIES.
In Shells or Other Small Molds.
Quantity for 6—8 Persons.

½ lb. roasted pheasant meat
3 tbsps. of butter
3 tbsps. of flour
Pheasant broth from bones
½ wineglassful of white wine
3 chopped truffles
½ cup of chopped champignons
Salt
1 pinch of pepper
Some butter for the molds
2 eggs

Preparation: The skin is removed from the meat. The meat, truffles and champignons are chopped fine. The bones are put on the fire with 2 qts of water, salt, a small piece of onion and boiled down to ½ qt. of bouillon. Then the gravy is made by heating the 3 tablespoonfuls of butter and the same quantity of flour stirred in to brown, ½ qt. of bouillon added and cooked. Season with salt and pepper, add white wine, meat, truffles and champignons and stir in the 2 yolks of eggs. Beat the whites of eggs and stir lightly into the mixture.

When this is done, fill the shells or buttered molds with the filling and bake in the oven to a nice brown color.

Remarks: Truffles and champignons may be omitted.

No. 36—STEWED PHEASANT.
Quantity for 6 Persons.

1 pheasant	Salt
Broth cooked from neck, wings, gizzard, liver, heart	2—3 wineglassfuls of white wine or sherry
1 large onion, sliced	3 tbsps. of butter
6 pepper-corns	3 tbsps. of flour
1 small carrot, sliced	3 tomatoes, sliced
2 bay-leaves	

Preparation: The pheasant is cleaned, dressed, put into a stewpot with 3 tablespoonfuls of butter, fried a little on all sides, the flour stirred in and then enough broth added to cover the bird. Put in the rest of the ingredients named above and roast slowly in the oven for 2 to 2½ hours.

Strain the gravy through a fine sieve and serve with the pheasant.

No. 37—PHEASANT PIE.
Quantity for 8—10 Persons.

2 young pheasants	½ wineglassful of Madeira
⅛ lb. of butter	Juice of ½ lemon
Salt	½ pt. of champignons
1½ qts. broth from bones	1 small can of truffles

Pie Contents.

Liver, heart, gizzard, chopped fine	Salt
2½ soaked rolls	1 pinch of pepper
3 eggs	1 tbsp. of butter
	1 tsp. of chopped onion

Preparation: The pheasants are cleaned, dressed and fried in oven for 20 minutes with ⅛ lb. of butter. The meat is then removed from the bones and a good qt. of broth is made from the latter, seasoned with Madeira, salt, lemon juice. The champignons are quartered and the truffles sliced; liver, heart, gizzard chopped fine, the rolls, salt, pepper, and yolk of egg stirred in. The onions are cooked a little in the drippings and the whole mixture added and stewed a little while. The whites of eggs are beaten and stirred into the mixture after it has cooled. Now butter your dish and put in one-half of the giblet filling as the bottom layer, then one layer of meat, then champignons and truffles, and so on until all the meat, champignons and truffles have been used. The broth is poured over the whole, the other half of the giblet filling put on the top and it is now baked in the oven for 1¼ hours. Serve it in the dish or casserole.

No. 38—RED GROUSE AND GUINEA HEN.
Quantity for 6 Persons.

3 red grouse or 3 guinea hens
1/8 lb. of butter
Salt
1/2 pt. of cream
1 1/2 tbsps. of flour
1 cupful of water
Bacon slices to tie across the breast

Preparation: The preparation is the same as No. 33, Pheasant. It also requires 1 to 1 1/2 hours for cooking.

Remarks: Grouse gets very tender when kept in buttermilk over night.

No. 39—GROUSE PIE.
Quantity for 14 Persons.

3 red grouse
Buttermilk
1/8 lb. of butter
Salt

Pie Filling.

3/4 lb. beef with bones
3/4 lb. lean pork
1 small can of truffles
1 pt. can champignons
5 soaked rolls
4 eggs
3 tbsps. of butter
Juice of 1/2 lemon
1 tsp. of grated onions
1 glass Madeira
Salt
1 pinch of pepper

Preparation: The grouse must be well hung; dress, salt and bake in hot oven with 1/8 lb. of butter for one hour, basting frequently. If buttermilk is to be obtained, put the grouse in buttermilk for 24 hours before baking. After frying, cut off the breasts and divide them into 1/8ths. The other meat is cut from the bones and chopped fine, also the beef and pork. The soaked rolls are sautéed or dry fried in 3 tablespoonfuls of butter and 4 eggs stirred into them. Now add grouse meat, beef, pork, salt, pepper, juice of 1/2 lemon, 1 wineglassful of Madeira, 1 teaspoonful of grated onion and mix well. The bones of the birds and beef are put on the fire with the champignon and truffle juice and boiled down to 1/2 qt. of broth, half of which is stirred into the filling.

Butter your dish or casserole and after lining it with paste, put in a layer of filling, then one of meat, strewing on some chopped champignons and truffles. Pour in the other 1/2 of the broth, cover with paste and bake in oven 1 1/4 hours to a nice brown color. Serve with a Madeira gravy.

The paste is made by mixing lightly 1/4 lb. of flour with 1/4 lb. of cold butter, 1/2 glassful of cold water and 1 teaspoonful of brandy, then rolled out.

Remarks: These pies may be made of pheasants, heath cocks or hazel hens, snow hens, snipes, quails and partridges.

No. 40—FRIED PARTRIDGES.
Quantity for 6 Persons.

6 young partridges	¼ lb. of butter
Salt	½ pt. sour cream
Bacon slices	1 tbsp. flour
	Some water

Preparation: After the birds have been cleaned, singed, dressed, wiped out and salted, tie the bacon slices around them, put them into a pan, pour on the hot butter and fry them for ½ hour, basting frequently and adding the cream by spoonfuls. When well done, take off the bacon and serve with the following gravy. In the drippings, brown 1 tablespoonful of flour, add a little water if necessary, cook, strain and serve. A little white wine may be added to the gravy.

No. 41—PARTRIDGE WITH SAUERKRAUT.
Quantity for 6 Persons.

2 young partridges	1 wineglassful of white wine
1½ lbs. of sauerkraut	Water for the sauerkraut
2 tbsps. of butter	1 tbsp. of flour
2 thin slices of bacon	1 apple

Preparation: The partridges are cleaned, singed, dressed and wiped out, bacon slices tied on and fried in 2 tablespoonfuls of butter for 15 minutes. If the sauerkraut is too sour, soak it in water a while, drain, then put it on the stove with the partridges and a little water, white wine, sliced apple, cover and stew slowly for 2 hours. When the birds are tender, take off the bacon, stir a little flour into the sauerkraut; cook for a few minutes and serve with the birds.

No. 42—FINE RAGOUT OF PARTRIDGE.
Quantity for 6 Persons.

3 young partridges	½ lb. goose liver or
1 pint champignons	Calf sweetbreads
1 piece of bacon for larding	Salt

For the Gravy.

3 tbsps. of butter	1 tsp. of meat extract
3 tbsps. of flour	The champignon juice
Broth from the bones	3 pepper-corns
3 tbsps. of red wine	Salt
3 tbsps. of Madeira	1 pinch of sugar

For the Dumplings.

Heart, liver, gizzard, some meat from the bones	Salt, pepper Some butter to fry the dumplings
1 soaked roll	A few slices of toasted wheat bread
2 eggs	
1 tbsp. of butter	

Preparation: The partridges are well prepared. Cut off the breast and drum sticks and all other meat from the bones. The latter are cracked, put on the fire with 3 tablespoonfuls of butter and flour, fried quickly, then 1½ qts. of water, the champignon juice, some salt, 3 pepper-corns added and boiled slowly for 2 hours to make ½ to ¾ qt. of broth. Season this broth with red wine, Madeira, meat extract, sugar and strain it. Lard the breasts and fry them and the drum sticks or legs in butter. Cover and stew slowly for ½ hour until done. Drip the lemon juice on the goose liver, salt it and fry it in butter. If you have sweetbreads instead of goose liver, parboil in salt water for 10 minutes, remove the skin, drip on lemon juice and fry in butter.

To make the dumplings, chop the liver, heart, gizzard and meat from the bones very fine and mix well with the soaked roll, one egg, butter, salt, pepper, some chopped champignons and shape into dumplings. Fry these light brown in butter or cook 10 minutes in broth.

Toast the wheat bread slices, cut each partridge breast into 4 pieces, also the goose liver or sweetbreads. Place the toast on a hot platter, then on this the meat, breast, legs and the goose liver or sweetbreads. Put the champignons into the gravy and pour hot over the meat. Garnish the dish with the dumplings.

This ragout may be made of capon, quail, hazel hen, snow hen, pheasant or snipe.

No. 43—BLACKBIRDS.
Quantity for 6 Persons.

12 blackbirds
¼ lb. of butter
1 pinch of salt
1 pinch of pepper

½ tbsp. of flour
½ tbsp. of white wine
½ cup of water or broth
6 juniper berries

For Stuffing.

The intestines of the birds
2½ rolls

½ tsp. of lemon juice
Some salt and pepper

2 tbsps. of butter

Preparation: The blackbirds must be fresh. They are cleaned, the head skinned, the eyes taken out and bill and claws chopped off a bit. The legs are turned inward, the right foot stuck through the eye sockets and the claws joined. The intestines are taken out and the gizzard removed. Juniper berries and the cleaned intestines are chopped fine, seasoned with salt, pepper, ½ teaspoonful of lemon juice and 2 tablespoonfuls of butter. This stuffing is put into the birds and the openings closed, fastening with toothpicks. They are then closely packed into a pan and the browned hot butter poured on, seasoned with more salt, pepper and 5 pulverized juniper berries, then fried 15 minutes, turning them over several times. The rolls are sliced and toasted, placed on a platter and the birds arranged neatly on the toast after removing the toothpicks. For the gravy, brown ½ tablespoonful of flour in the drippings, add water, wine, cook, strain and serve with the birds.

You may drip some gravy on the toasted roll slices to make them more palatable.

No. 44—LEIPZIG LARKS.

These birds are prepared just like the blackbirds in No. 43. The intestines may also be used for the filling.

No. 45—FRIED SNIPES.
Quantity for 6 Persons.

3 snipes	½ tbsp. of flour
¼ lb. of butter	1½ toasted rolls
Salt, pepper	Some broth
Bacon slices to tie around them	

Preparation: The snipes are prepared the same as the blackbirds or larks in No. 43 and No. 44. The gizzard is removed, the bacon slices are tied around the birds, after salting and peppering inside and outside; then fry them in butter for 20 minutes and serve them on the toast which has been soaked with some of the gravy.

For the gravy, stir ½ tablespoonful of flour into the drippings, add broth, cook, strain and serve with the birds. These are garnished with snipe on toast made from the intestines.

No. 46—SNIPE ON TOAST.
Quantity for 6 Persons.

Intestines from the 3 birds with the gizzard removed	Salt, pepper
	A few drops of lemon juice
1½ tbsps. of butter	¼ cup of bread crumbs
1 yolk of egg	2½ rolls, sliced
1½ tbsps. of red wine	Some butter
1 tsp. of chopped capers	1 tbsp. Parmesan cheese

Preparation: The cleaned intestines are chopped and mixed well with butter, yolk of egg, red wine, parsley, capers, salt, pepper, bread crumbs and lemon juice. Cut the rolls in slices ½ inch thick, cut off the crust, toast them and put the above stuffing on thick, sprinkle some Parmesan cheese over and drip melted butter on, then bake them in the oven for 5 minutes and place around the fried snipes.

No. 47—FRIED WOODCOCK.
Quantity for 6 Persons.

1 woodcock
¼ lb. of butter
⅛ lb. of bacon for larding
Salt
¾ qt. of sour cream
½ pt. of bouillon or broth

Preparation: The woodcock may hang 5 days before being cooked. Skin, dress and pound it, wash and dry it well and salt it inside and outside, then lard with bacon. The woodcock is fried in the butter, the cream and broth are poured on gradually and the bird stewed for 2 hours, basting frequently. By this time the gravy will be boiled down and smooth, strain it and serve with the bird.

No. 48—ANOTHER FORM OF FRIED WOODCOCK.
Quantity for 6 Persons.

1 woodcock or hen
1 bottle of red wine
1 bottle wine vinegar
3 bay-leaves
10 pepper-corns
7 cloves
1 onion, sliced
1 carrot, sliced
A little thyme
Bacon slices
⅛ lb. of butter
Salt
1 pt. sour cream
1 pt. bouillon

Preparation: The woodcock is cleaned, dressed, tied, pressed into a jar and the bottle of red wine is emptied into this. The vinegar is boiled together with bay-leaves, pepper-corns, cloves, onion, carrot, thyme and when cooled, also poured on the bird; in this it remains 2 to 3 days.

After this time the bird is taken out, dried, rubbed with salt, bacon slices tied around it, fried in the butter, and stewed for 2 hours, basting frequently with cream and bouillon. The gravy is strained, the bacon slices are taken off the bird. It is served on a platter, some gravy poured over the bird and the rest served separately.

Remarks: You may serve a Madeira or pickle gravy with it.

No. 49—ROAST WILD DUCK.
Quantity for 6—8 Persons.

2 young, wild ducks
1 pt. water
⅛ lb. of butter
Bacon slices
2 cloves
1 bay-leaf
1 onion, sliced
2 tbsps. of flour
1 wineglassful of red wine
Salt
6 pepper-corns

Preparation: The ducks are picked, singed, dressed, washed and skinned, salted inside and outside and tied into bacon slices. The prepared ducks are put into a stewpot over the fire with 1 pt. of water, onion, cloves, pepper-corns, bay-leaves. Cover and stew. When the water is boiled down, pour the $\frac{1}{8}$ lb. of hot butter over them and add a little water or broth so that the butter may not get too brown, also add the red wine. 15 minutes before they are done, stir in the flour, add more broth or water if necessary and cook. The ducks should be of a nice golden brown color. Serve them with the strained gravy.

No. 50—ROAST CAPONS.

Quantity for 6 Persons.

1 capon	$\frac{1}{4}$ lb. of butter
Salt	Bacon for larding

For the Gravy.

1 tbsp. of flour	1 tbsp. of wine

Preparation: The capon is picked, dressed, the breast and drum sticks larded with bacon, and the bird salted inside and outside. Then the hot butter is poured over it and roasted $1\frac{1}{4}$ hours until done, basting frequently with cream.

For the gravy, brown the flour in the drippings, add the wine, and broth or water, cook, strain and serve with the bird.

No. 51—FRIED CAPON RAGOUT.

May be made from the capon. Prepare it just the same as described in No. 42, Fine Partridge Ragout.

No. 52—STEWED CAPON.

Quantity for 6 Persons.

1 capon	1 wineglassful of red wine
Salt	1 tsp. of lemon juice
6 pepper-corns	1 tsp. of sugar
2 onions, sliced	$\frac{1}{2}$ pt. champignons
$\frac{1}{8}$ of a celery	Some bouillon or water
$\frac{1}{2}$ carrot, sliced	$\frac{1}{8}$ lb. of butter
1 clove	2 tbsps. of flour
1 bay-leaf	

Preparation: The capon is prepared well and tied into bacon slices, then fried in $\frac{1}{8}$ lb. butter for $\frac{1}{2}$ hour.

For the gravy, stir in the flour, fill up with bouillon or water mixed with a teaspoonful of meat extract and the rest of the ingredients and in this gravy stew the capon 45 minutes to 1 hour, basting and turning it frequently. Serve the capon and strain the gravy. Quarter the champignons and put them into the gravy. Pour in the champignon juice while stewing.

Remarks: You can take oysters instead of champignons, allowing 3 or 4 to each person. Before serving the bird, remove bacon and strings.

No. 53—RED GROUSE CUTLETS.
Quantity for 6 Persons.

3 grouse	1—2 eggs
8 tbsps. thick, sweet cream	1½ cups of roll crumbs
Some salt	⅛ lb. of butter, good measure
	½ cup of flour

Preparation: The grouse or other poultry is cleaned well and the meat removed from the bones while raw. Chop the meat and remove skin and tendons. Mix with the cream and salt. Shape into cutlets 1½ inches thick, dip into flour, then into the well beaten egg and finally into the bread crumbs. Stick small bones into the cutlets and fry in butter to a nice color. These cutlets are very good served with vegetables.

Remarks: These cutlets may be made from all fine game birds, i e., partridge, pheasant, hazel hen, snow hen; also from chicken.

From the bones you can make soup, which will be better if the bones have been fried in butter and soupgreens a little while.

No. 54—ROAST POULARD.
Quantity for 6—8 Persons.

1 poulard	½ pt. sweet or sour cream
Salt	1 tsp. of lemon juice
¼ lb. of butter	2 tbsps. of flour
Bacon slices to tie over the breast	1 cup of water

Preparation: The Poulard or French pheasant is cleaned, dressed, washed, dried and salted inside and outside. Bacon slices are tied over the breast and drum sticks. Roast in hot butter, adding the water, for 1 to 1½ hours, a piece of butter being put inside the bird also. Baste frequently with water and cream. It should be roasted to a nice golden brown color.

Serve on a hot platter after taking off the bacon and strings.

Into the drippings stir some flour, water or cream if necessary, the lemon juice, cook, strain and serve with the bird. The gravy should be smooth and of a light brown color.

No. 55—POULARD FRICASSEE.
Quantity for 6—8 Persons.

Prepare like recipe No. 10, Chicken Fricassee. It will make a very fine side-dish.

No. 56—DUCK RAGOUT.
Quantity for 6 Persons.

1 duck	1 cup of water
1 tbsp. of butter	Salt

For the Gravy.

2 tbsps. of butter	6 pepper-corns
2 tbsps. of duck grease	3 sprays of parsley
2¼ tbsps. of flour	2 cloves
1½ pts. of bouillon or water	¼ pt. of port wine
Duck stock	Juice of ½ lemon
½ cup of champignon juice	3 truffles
Salt	½ pt. champignons

Preparation: The duck is cleaned, dressed, washed, salted and fried 1½ to 2 hours, in 1 tablespoonful of butter and 1 cup of water, basting frequently.

For the gravy, brown the flour in the 2 tablespoonfuls of butter, add the duck stock and cook a little while; then add the bouillon, red wine or port wine, champignon juice, lemon juice, salt, pepper-corns, cloves, parsley and truffle parings. Cook the gravy for 15-30 minutes, strain through a fine sieve. Cut the champignons in half and put them into the strained gravy. Carve the duck and put it into the gravy too and steep another 15 minutes. Heap the ragout in the middle of a hot platter. Put the peeled truffles which were fried in 1 teaspoonful of butter for 2 minutes, over the ragout. Garnish with puff paste scallops, (see preparation in No. 29, Chapter 3, Puff-paste Patties with Veal Ragout), and with dumplings. These are made by chopping very fine the heart, gizzard and liver, mixed well with one soaked roll, one egg, 1 tablespoonful of chopped champignons, 1 teaspoonful of chopped parsley, 1 pinch of salt, pepper, and nutmeg. Sauté or dry fry (which means cooking food in a small amount of fat) in ½ tablespoonful of butter and add ½ grated roll. Then form small dumplings from this mixture and fry them to a light brown in butter or duck grease.

Remarks: This duck ragout is a very fine side-dish.

CHAPTER 7.

GAME.

Game must not be soaked in water and it should be washed only when necessary and then quickly dried. The flavor of game depends greatly on its preparation, the latter makes it one of the finest dishes. Game ought to be fried and roasted; boiled game is never as savory.

Butter, bacon and cream are the best fats in which to fry game. Sweet-sour victuals are best to serve with game as: Red cabbage, apple sauce, currant jelly and Cumberland sauce.

No. 1—ROAST SADDLE OF VENISON.
Quantity for 6—10 Persons.

1 saddle of venison
Salt
1 pinch of pepper
Bacon for larding
1 pt of sour cream, good measure
1 tsp. of lemon juice
1½ tbsps. of flour
½ cupful water
½ lb. of butter

Preparation: The deer, fawn or doe must hang in its skin a few days before it is cooked. The neck is cut off. The ribs are chopped off if they are too long. The skin is taken off, the meat pounded and larded closely with bacon strips; place a thin slice of bacon under the fillets. Fry the venison on both sides with part of the ½ lb. of butter, put the rest of the butter into the pot or pan and roast the meat 45 minutes, basting frequently with the sour cream. The roast should be pink inside and very juicy. Put it on a hot platter and prepare the gravy.

Stir the flour into the frying butter, brown it a few minutes, add the water, cook 5 minutes and add the lemon juice, then strain.

Remarks: The remnants of this venison may be utilized in a soup. Fry them with some butter or lard and soupgreens and a tablespoonful of flour, add water and cook slowly for two hours. For directions refer to No. 63 and 64 under Soups, Chapter 1.

No. 2—LEG OF VENISON.
Quantity for 6 Persons.

1 leg of venison, 3½ to 4 lbs.
Salt
¼ lb. of butter
½ qt. sour cream
⅛ lb. of bacon cut in wide, thin slices, for lining the pan
1 tbsp. of flour
½ cup of water
⅛ lb. bacon strips

Preparation: The meat is pounded on both sides, washed, dried, skinned and larded with bacon. The joint of the leg is chopped. Scald the leg with a pint of boiling water and place it into the hot butter in the roasting pan, brown it on both sides, then place the bacon slices on the bottom of the pan and the leg of venison on top of them, roast in the oven for one hour, basting it often with spoonfuls of cream.

The Gravy: After the leg of venison is done, stir the flour into the drippings, brown it for 2 minutes, then add the water, cook for 5 minutes and strain.

Remarks: With a tablespoonful of red wine you can improve the gravy. If you wish to have the meat rare, allow ¾ hour for roasting. Add or subtract some of the time for frying according to the size of the piece of venison.

No. 3—VENISON CUTLETS.

2½ lbs. of venison from back or loin
Salt
Scant ⅛ lb. of butter

For the Gravy.

⅛ lb. of butter
3 tbsps. of flour
1 qt. of water
¼ pt. of Madeira
Some soupgreens
1 pinch of sugar
Salt
1 clove
1 tsp. of meat extract
½ tsp. of lemon juice
1 pinch of pepper

Preparation: The meat is skinned, cut into ½ inch slices, each having a rib bone, then they are pounded on both sides and salted. Chop the scraps and fry them with the soupgreens, light brown in hot butter, stir in the flour and brown it, add the water and season with salt, pepper, sugar, lemon juice, Madeira and clove and cook slowly for 1½ hours. Strain the gravy and put into it the meat extract and truffle slices and stew a little while. The cutlets are fried 4 minutes in the ⅛ lb. of butter; serve on a hot platter and pour the gravy, which should be smooth, over it.

Remarks: You may also pour tomato or champignon gravy over the meat. The platter with the cutlets would look well garnished with puff-paste scallops.

No. 4—DEER OR DOE LIVER.
Quantity for 2 Persons.

1 deer or doe liver	1 tbsp. of chopped onion
Salt	2 tbsps. of vinegar
1 pinch of pepper	2 tbsps. of water
⅛ lb. of butter	½ tsp. of meat extract
½ tbsp. of flour	

Preparation: The liver is washed and dried. Trim off the membrane, cut into even thin slices, salt and pepper and fry quickly in the hot butter. Onion and flour are stirred in and stewed with the liver. Then the water, vinegar and meat extract are added and cooked well; when done, serve at once because the liver will get hard and tough when standing.

No. 5—VENISON RAGOUT.
Quantity for 6 Persons.

3—4 lbs. of venison	6 pepper-corns
¼ lb. of butter	2 cloves
4 tbsps. of flour	1 bay-leaf
1½ qts. of water	Juice of ½ lemon
½ onion, sliced	1 tumblerful of red wine
Salt	

Preparation: The meat is cut into 3 inch squares. The ¼ lb. of butter is browned with the flour, then water is added and all the spices and cooked 5 minutes. The meat is put into this gravy, the pot well covered and ¼ hour before done, the red wine is added. If the gravy has boiled down too far, add some more water. When the ragout is done, take out the meat, strain the gravy and pour it over the meat, serve on a hot platter. The gravy should be smooth. This meat should be cooked in an iron pot.

Remarks: Potato dumplings are nice with venison ragout.

No. 6—TO CARVE A LEG OF VENISON.

Leg of deer, doe or reindeer may be carved like a leg of veal. From the leg, remove first the skin and membrane and you will recognize the parts called the fricandeaux. On top of the leg lies a flat piece, on the side of it a piece that has the shape of a small fillet. These pieces may be used for fricassee or they may be filled and roasted. You may leave these pieces on the leg and lard and roast it with them. The tail end is chopped off, chopped in small pieces, and with the last ribs which are attached to it, a soup is cooked.

Remarks: All uncooked game keeps in vinegar or milk.

No. 7—SADDLE OF VENISON.
Quantity for 14—16 Persons.

1 saddle of venison, 8 to 10 lbs.	2 tbsps. of white wine
Salt	6 pepper-corns
¾ lb. of butter	2 cloves
¼ lb. of bacon for larding	2 tbsps. of flour
1 pt. sour cream	1 cup of water
1 tsp. of lemon juice	1 tsp. of meat extract, if necessary

Preparation: The joints are chopped in several places so the meat lies flat in the pan, then it is skinned, washed, larded well, salted and fried on both sides in the hot butter; then put into the oven with all the spices and left to roast for 2 to 3 hours, basting frequently with the sour cream.

For the gravy, stir in the flour, brown it a little, then add the water and cook with the roast for 15 minutes. Strain the gravy and if the color is too light, add the meat extract.

No. 8—LEG OF VENISON.
Quantity for 14—18 Persons.

1 leg of venison, 10 lbs.	1 pt. of sour cream
Salt	2 tbsps. of flour
6 pepper-corns	1 cup of water
2 cloves	1 tsp. of lemon juice
¾ lb. of butter	2 tbsps. of white wine
	¼ lb. of bacon for larding

Preparation: The preparation is the same as described in No. 7, only the time for frying is longer, from 3 to 3½ hours.

Remarks: If the meat is from an old animal, it is best to keep it in milk, wine or vinegar for 2 to 3 days.

No. 9—ANOTHER FORM OF LEG OF VENISON.
Quantity for 14—18 Persons.

1 leg of venison, 10 lbs.	Some melted butter
Salt	Rolled out bread dough
	1 sheet of paper

For the Gravy.

¼ lb. of butter and	3 pepper-corns
¼ lb. of drippings	2 tbsps. of flour
Salt	Bouillon cooked from remnants
1 clove	1 tumblerful of port wine

Preparation: The meat is skinned, the bone trimmed out, washed and salted. A sheet of paper buttered or brushed with fine salad oil, is wrapped around the meat, then it is enveloped in a layer of white bread dough. Heat ¼ lb. of drippings and ¼ lb. of butter, place the leg of venison into it and roast for

5 to 5½ hours, basting it often. Remove paper and crust, when done, and brush the meat with gravy.

The gravy is prepared by browning the flour in the drippings, adding all the spices, the port wine, and the bouillon, then cooking it well. If the gravy is too greasy, skim it off and strain before serving.

Currant jelly or apple sauce is served with this meat.

No. 10—CHOPPED STEAK OF GAME.
Deer, Doe, Boar or Wild Rabbit Meat is Used.
Quantity for 6 Persons.

3 lbs. of meat
¼ lb. of bacon
⅛ lb. butter

Salt
1 pinch of pepper
Scant ½ lb. of butter for frying

For the Gravy.

1 tbsp. of flour
3 tbsps. of cream

1 tsp. of lemon juice
½ cup of water
1 tbsp. of capers

Preparation: The membrane and tendons are removed from the meat, then it is chopped or ground fine together with the bacon and mixed well with ⅛ lb. of butter, salt, pepper and shaped into steaks.

The other portion of butter is heated and in this the steak is fried 10 minutes on the stove, basting and turning often. Put it on a hot platter and prepare the gravy.

If there is too much drippings left, take some out, stir in the flour, brown a few minutes, then add all the ingredients and cook well, pour it over the steak, serve immediately.

No. 11—COLD GAME PIE.
Made From Deer, Doe, Boar or Rabbit Meat.

A good way to utilize the remnants of game roasts.
Quantity for 6 Persons.

2 lbs. fried or roasted game
¼ lb. of butter
Salt
1 pinch of pepper
1 tsp. of grated onion
¼ lb. finely grated Parmesan cheese

¼ lb. of truffles, sliced
4 eggs
¼ lb. finely chopped sardines
2 soaked rolls
Some butter for the dish

Preparation: The meat is chopped or ground very fine. The butter is melted—add to it the rolls, chopped sardines (from which the bones have been removed) and onions, one whole egg and 3 yolks of eggs. This mixture is stirred on the stove and left to stew until dry.

After cooling it off, add the chopped meat, salt and pepper. Press the whole through a sieve so there will be no chunks or pieces. Into this mass stir the truffle slices, the beaten whites of eggs, and the Parmesan cheese.

Fill a buttered dish or casserole with this mixture, cover it, set it in a steamer over a kettle of boiling water and boil 1½ hours. After cooling, turn it out on a platter, garnish the platter with prepared lettuce. This makes a fine dish for an evening dinner.

Remarks: This pie may also be served hot; then serve a game gravy or herb gravy with it.

No. 12—GAME RAGOUT MADE FROM REMNANTS.
Quantity for 6 Persons.

1½ lbs. cold game remnants, either deer, doe, rabbit or wild boar meat
⅛ lb. of bacon
1 tbsp. of butter
2½ tbsps. of flour
1½ tbsps. of lemon juice
1 small onion
Salt
1 pinch of pepper
1 pt. bouillon, boiled from the bones
½ cup sour or sweet cream
2 vinegar or dill pickles, sliced

Preparation: The meat is cut from the bones in nice, equal pieces. The bones are brought to boil in 2 qts. of cold water and boiled down to 1 pt. of broth or bouillon.

Cut the bacon into cubes and brown it in the butter, onion slices and flour and add the bouillon. If you have left-over game gravy, add that too, season with salt, pepper, lemon juice and cream and cook slowly for 20 minutes, then strain and cut the pickles into it. Put the meat pieces into this gravy and let it get hot, but do not cook or the meat will get tough. The gravy must be smooth. After heating, serve at once.

Remarks: If you wish to have the ragout very fine, omit the pickles and take truffles or champignons instead.

No. 13—LEG OR SADDLE OF WILD BOAR.
Quantity for 14—18 Persons.

10—14 lbs. of wild boar meat

For Pickling.

5 qts. of vinegar
10 pepper-corns
1 doz. juniper berries
1 large onion, sliced
3 cloves

For Frying.

1 bottle of red wine
Salt
1 qt. of bouillon

To Cover the Roast.

1 lb. grated rye bread	3 tbsps. of sugar
½ lb. of butter	4 pulverized cloves

For the Gravy.

3 tbsps. of flour mixed with some water
1 tsp. of meat extract

Preparation: The roast is pounded, the surface scored or cut in squares and the meat placed into a deep pot or jar. Vinegar, pepper, juniper berries, cloves and onion slices are put in and left with the meat for 3 days. After this time take the roast out and roast it in a deep roaster with all that was on it in the jar, except the vinegar. Instead of that, pour on the red wine and bouillon, season with salt and roast in the oven for 3½ hours. Then strew the roast with rye bread crumbs which have been mixed with ½ lb. of butter, pulverized cloves and 3 tablespoonfuls of sugar. Roast it 30 minutes longer so the crust will get hard and brown. In the meantime add the flour mixed with water to the gravy and cook it a while, then strain, add the meat extract, cook again, taste for salt and spices and skim off the fat.

Remarks: The remnants of roast are utilized in the same way as those of pork roast.

No. 14—HOW TO SKIN A RABBIT.

Hang the animal up by its hind legs on two nails, rip the rabbit from tail to throat, lengthwise. Take out the insides, cut the bile carefully from the liver, retain the latter and the heart and lungs, and throw away the rest of the intestines. Now separate the fur skin from the inner skin, make a cut through the fur around each ankle, pull the legs through, cut off the ears and pull the whole fur skin down from the hind legs over the head.

No. 15—RABBIT ROAST.
Quantity for 4 Persons.

1 rabbit	½ pt. sour or sweet cream
⅛ lb. bacon for larding	1 tsp. of lemon juice
Salt	1½ tbsps. of flour
1 pinch of pepper	1 cup of water
Scant ½ lb. of butter	

Preparation: The dressed rabbit is washed and dried, head, throat and the skin from the belly and its fore paws are cut off and the joints of its hind paws are chopped. The back and legs are larded with thin slices of bacon. The butter is heated and the larded hare is placed into it to roast for 45 minutes. Season with salt and pepper and baste frequently with cream. If it is an old hare, it will require 1¼ hours for roasting. Ten minutes before the hare is done, add the lemon juice and the flour and stew 5 minutes, then pour in the water, leave the hare in this gravy 5 minutes longer, then serve it with the strained gravy. ———

No. 16—STEWED RABBIT.
Quantity for 4 Persons.

1 rabbit
¼ lb. of butter
⅛ lb. of bacon

2 cloves
2 cups of rye bread crumbs
½ bottle of red wine

Salt, pepper

Preparation: The rabbit is prepared as described in No. 15, well larded, cut into pieces large enough for each person. The forelegs may be larded too. These pieces are fried in ¼ lb. of butter until they are light brown. Now pour the drippings into a deep roasting pot, add the bacon slices and make a layer of hare meat, season with salt, pepper, cloves and put on 1 cup of rye bread crumbs. Over this pour the red wine. After making another layer of meat and bread crumbs, cover the pot well and stew slowly 2 to 2½ hours. Serve the meat on a hot platter, strain the gravy, flavor and pour it over the meat. If the pot cannot be closed tightly, paste a strip of paper or cloth around the rim and cover.

Remarks: Potato dumplings are good with this meat.

No. 17—ANOTHER FORM OF STEWED RABBIT.
Quantity for 4 Persons.

The preparation is the same as given under No. 16 with the exception of taking ½ pt. of sour cream instead of wine and 2 tablespoonfuls of flour instead of rye bread crumbs.

The hare is prepared and cooked the same as given under No. 16. If the gravy is too thick, add more water.

No. 18—RABBIT CUTLETS.
Quantity for 4 Persons.

1 rabbit
Salt
1 pinch of pepper
2 eggs

1 small piece of bacon
Grated wheat bread for breading
1 egg
Some melted butter

For the Gravy.

½ pt. broth
1½ tbsps. of flour
⅛ lb. of butter
Juice of one lemon
½ tsp. of sugar
Salt
1 wineglassful of red wine

Preparation: All meat is cut from a well dressed rabbit, skin and membrane removed; the bacon and meat are chopped or ground fine, seasoned with salt and pepper and mixed well with 2 eggs and small cutlets formed. The butter is heated, the cutlets brushed with it, then dipped into the bread crumbs and finally into the beaten egg. Some ribs are cut off the skeleton and stuck into each cutlet. The butter for frying is put into a pan, heated and the cutlets fried to a nice brown color. The gravy has been prepared by browning the heart, liver and lungs in 1½ tablespoonfuls of flour, then adding 1 pt. of broth or water, putting into this all the bones and seasoning with salt, cloves, and 4 pepper-corns. Cook the gravy for ½ hour and add the red wine or port wine, lemon juice and sugar. Strain and serve with the cutlets. Garnish the platter with currant jelly.

No. 19—HASENPFEFFER (RABBIT PEPPER).
Quantity for 2—4 Persons.

The head, neck, breast, lungs, forelegs, heart, liver, 1 lb. of rabbit meat or lean pork
Some vinegar
1 small onion
⅛ lb. of bacon or butter
3 tbsps. of flour
Salt
4 pepper-corns
2 cloves
1 bay-leaf
2 pts. of water
1 tbsp. of sugar
½ cup of red wine (or not)

Preparation: The head, neck, breast, lungs, heart, liver and forelegs are cleaned well, cut in medium large pieces and left in vinegar for 1 day.

After the rabbit has been fried, cut 1 lb. of pork into medium large pieces. Cut the bacon into small cubes and fry it, or if you use butter, heat this and fry the finely sliced onion and pork in it and the rabbit meat which has been soaked in vinegar.

For the gravy, stir the flour into the drippings, stew a few minutes, then add water and all the spices and other ingredients. Then slowly cook the meat until tender in the gravy. When it is done, take the meat out and serve on a hot platter, strain the gravy and pour over the meat.

Remarks: You may omit the rabbit meat and pork and

use only the heart, lungs, liver, head, neck, breast and forelegs if these are sufficient. You may also stir a little vinegar into some rabbit blood and add to the gravy. The liver may be omitted and fried separately.

No. 20—RABBIT LIVER.
Quantity for 1 Person.

1 rabbit liver
1 pinch of salt and pepper
1 well beaten egg
Some flour
1 piece of butter for frying
1 slice of lemon

Preparation: The liver must be very fresh. As soon as the rabbit is shot, dress it, take the liver out and prepare it the same day. If you cannot do this the same day, it is better to leave the liver and prepare it with the rabbit.

The fresh liver is washed, sliced, seasoned with salt and pepper, dipped into egg and flour, then fried quickly in some hot butter and served at once on a hot platter. Place a lemon slice on it.

No. 21—RABBIT ROAST SALAD.
Quantity for 6 Persons.

¾ lb. of hare roast
3 medium sized, boiled potatoes
2 hard boiled yolks of eggs
2 raw yolks of eggs
¼ pt. fine salad oil
Wine vinegar according to taste
1 tsp. of mustard
Salt
1 pinch of pepper
1 tsp. of capers
1 tsp. of sugar
¼ cupful of cream

Preparation: The meat and potatoes are cut into small pieces. The 2 hard boiled yolks of eggs are mixed well and stirred with the 2 raw yolks, the oil dripped in, cream, vinegar and the other ingredients mixed in. Taste the gravy and stir lightly into it the meat and potatoes, then heap it in a glass dish, chop the 2 whites of eggs and strew over the salad.

No. 22—RABBIT PIE.

2 young rabbits
1 piece of bacon for larding
½ lb. chopped pork
1½ rolls
2 eggs
Salt
1 pinch of pepper
1 tbsp. of butter for the filling.

For Frying.

¼ lb. of butter
3 tbsps. of flour
1½ qts. of water or bouillon
1 small onion
¼ bottle of white wine
1 bay-leaf
6 pepper-corns
1 clove
Lemon peel
1 small can of truffles, sliced

Preparation: Shoulders and legs are cut off and the rest of the meat removed from the bones and chopped very fine, also the pork. Mix this well with the soaked rolls, eggs, butter, salt and pepper.

Line the bottom and sides of the dish with this mixture. The meat from the loins of the rabbits is cut into nice pieces, fried brown in ¼ lb. of butter and put into the pie with the sliced truffles.

Now prepare the gravy. Into the butter in which the pieces of meat have been fried, stir 3 tablespoonfuls of flour, brown and add 1½ qts. of water or bouillon. Season it with all the spices, onion, salt, bay-leaf, pepper, clove, lemon juice, white wine and the truffle peelings and cook slowly for 1 hour. Strain the gravy and pour ¾ of it into the pie, put on another layer of the filling, bake in medium hot oven for 1½ hours or cover the dish well and set it in a steamer over a kettle of boiling water and boil 1½ hours. The remainder of the gravy should be served hot with the pie.

Remarks: The bones are chopped up and broth cooked from them which is used for the gravy to make this rich and palatable.

Remarks: This pie may be served cold.

No. 23—DOMESTIC RABBIT ROAST.
Quantity for 4 Persons.

1 domestic rabbit	½ cup of sour or sweet cream
⅛ lb. of bacon	1½ tbsps. of flour
⅛ lb. of butter	½ cup of water
	Salt

Preparation: The domestic rabbit is prepared and cooked the same as described under No. 15, Rabbit Roast.

No. 24—STUFFED DOMESTIC RABBIT ROAST.
Quantity for 4—6 Persons.

1 domestic rabbit	½ cup of sour or sweet cream
⅛ lb. of bacon	1½ tbsps. of flour
⅛ lb. of butter	½ cup of water
	Salt

For Stuffing.

Heart, liver, kidneys of the rabbit	2 eggs
2 soaked rolls	1 tbsp. of butter
	1 tbsp. of lemon juice
	Salt, pepper, nutmeg

Preparation: The domestic rabbit is prepared like the rabbit under No. 14, but the legs, neck and breast are left on, because it is going to be stuffed. It is washed well inside and outside and salted. Heart, liver and kidneys are chopped fine and mixed well with the soaked rolls and the other ingredients. The rabbit is filled with this stuffing and sewed up, the back well larded and fried on all sides light brown in hot butter. Then it is roasted in the oven for 1½ hours, basting frequently with the cream and lemon juice.

Remarks: The domestic rabbit may be made into ragout. See No. 5, Doe or Deer Ragout.

Remarks: The stuffing may be improved by adding champignons or truffles or ¼ lb. of chopped pork.

No. 25—LAPINS.

Lapins, the European hare, are prepared like rabbit. See No. 23 and No. 24.

CHAPTER 8.

FISH.

THE VARIOUS PREPARATIONS OF FISH AND THE UTILIZING OF REMNANTS.

Every fish has a season when it is most savory. During the breeding or spawning season, no fish is good. When you buy a dead fish, observe carefully the following:
1. The meat of the fish must be firm and must not show any form of decay, neither in smell nor taste.
2. The skin must be tight on the fish.
3. Both eyes must be clear, not milky or sunken.
4. The gills must be red and slimy. Fish frozen very hard are not especially good.

The meat of middle sized fish is more savory than that of large ones.

When you buy live fish, take the lively ones, not those that swim on their side or back. The bought fish are best killed in the market. The quickest way of killing a fish is to stun it with a blow on the head or neck, then cutting its throat and its tail.

You scale the fish by taking hold of its tail and with a sharp knife or fish scaler scraping off the scales from there towards the head.

To retain the nourishing qualities of the fish, it is not soaked in water, only washed and boiled immediately. Whole fish are put on the fire with cold or hot water. Pieces of fish are put on with boiling water or prepared in hot butter or lard to retain the nutriment in the fish, since the hot water or fat contracts the cells at the cuts. The skin of a whole fish retains the nutriment, therefore it may be put on the fire in cold water.

Fish must not be covered up while cooking or frying so that the temperature will not get too high. Frozen fish must be thawed completely before using; if this is not done, the inside of the fish is mostly rare when serving it. No dish will be good when the fish or meat used is prepared in a frozen state.

Fish are dressed by making a slight cut along the whole under side and taking out all intestines. The inner darker membrane must be entirely removed and the fish washed well.

No. 1—TO BOIL.

Whitefish, shellfish, pike, codfish, pickerel, bass, black bass, white bass, flounders, plaice or sole, carp, salmon, trout, brook trout, cabeljou, river trout.

Quantity for 6 Persons.

3½—4 lbs. of fish	4 cloves
4 qts. of water	1 large onion
Salt	2 bay-leaves
10 pepper-corns	½ lemon, sliced

Preparation: The fish is dressed and washed. Into a fish kettle pour 4 qts. of water, all the spices and enough salt to make it quite salty. Place the fish on the tray of the kettle in a swimming position and bring slowly to boil 5 minutes in cold or hot water, then set back to draw ½ hour. When the meat near the gills is not bloody any more, the fish is done. Before serving, rinse it with hot water to remove the scum and place on the platter in a swimming position. It is then garnished with lemon slices, parsley, lettuce and potatoes.

With the fish is served a fish gravy, mustard gravy, Bearnaise gravy or fresh creamed butter, browned butter, mustard butter, parsley butter, etc.

No. 2—BAKED FISH.

Any of the varieties named in No. 1.

Quantity for 6 Persons.

3½—4 lbs. of fish	1½ cups of sour or sweet cream
¼ lb. of fresh butter	¼ tsp. of meat extract
Salt	Juice of ½ lemon
3 pepper-corns	1 tbsp. of capers
Some flour	1 tbsp. of Parmesan cheese

Preparation: The fish is dressed, washed and dried, salted inside and outside and rolled in flour. It is placed into a pan or if possible an earthen or porcelain dish in which the butter has been heated; then put into the oven and baked for 10 minutes to a light yellow color. Baste with the cream and lemon juice, sprinkle with the Parmesan cheese, and add the capers and pepper-corns. In this gravy stew it ½ hour, then prepare carefully on a hot platter and serve. Strain the gravy through a sieve to remove all lumps, i. e., make it smooth. If it is too thick, add some cream or milk and pour it on the fish or serve it extra.

Remarks: This preparation is very fine. A little meat extract makes the sauce look more delicate.

No. 3—FISH STEAMED OR STEWED IN RED WINE GRAVY.

Any one of the varieties named in No. 1.
Quantity for 6 Persons.

3½—4 lbs. of fish
Salt
⅛ lb. of butter
3 tbsps. of flour
1 pt. of water or bouillon
1 pt. of red wine
1 tsp. of meat extract
½ onion, sliced
3 slices of lemon
½ carrot, sliced
Small piece of celery root
1 small piece of parsley root
6 pepper-corns
2 cloves
2 bay-leaves
1 tbsp. of sugar

Preparation: The fish is dressed, washed, dried, salted inside and outside and left in a cold place for 1½ hours. The gravy is then prepared. Brown the butter and flour and mix in all the ingredients, also red wine; add water or bouillon and cook slowly 1½ hours and strain. It must be smooth and palatable.

Rub the salt off, put the fish into a porcelain or earthen dish in which the ounce of butter has been melted and roast in the oven for 10 minutes, basting frequently with the butter. After this, pour the gravy over it and stew the fish uncovered in the oven for ½ hour.

Remarks: The pan or dish should not be much larger than the fish, so that this is well covered with the gravy. Both fish and gravy are served on the same hot platter.

No. 4—BROILED OR ROASTED FISH.

Any one kind named in No. 1.
Quantity for 6 Persons.

3½—4 lbs. of fish
Salt, flour
½ cup of roll crumbs
¼ lb. of butter
1 beaten egg

Preparation: The fish is dressed, washed and dried, then ripped lengthwise into two halves and the bones removed. Then salt, dredge with flour, dip into beaten egg and roll in bread crumbs. Drip melted butter on the fish, place into a flat pan and roast or bake in the oven, basting with melted butter. Serve with brown butter gravy and garnish with lemon slices.

No. 5—BOILED SALMON.
Quantity for 6 Persons.

3 lbs. of salmon
3 qts. of water
½ cup of vinegar
1 cup of white wine
1 large onion, sliced

2 tbsps. of salt
1 tbsps. of pepper-corns
10 whole cloves
3 bay-leaves
½ lemon, sliced

Preparation: All ingredients are put into the water and then boiled. The fish is not scaled, but the insides taken out and washed. When the water boils, set it aside, put the fish in and let it draw ½—¾ hours. Cooking would make it tough. Serve a butter or madeira gravy with the fish.

Remarks: If the fish is a salmon, it requires 20 minutes to cook it.

No. 6—SALMON, BLUE.
Quantity for 15 Persons.

7 lbs. of salmon
7 qts. of water
¾ bottle of white wine
1 cup of wine vinegar
1 tbsp. of pepper-corns
6 cloves
3 bay-leaves

1 onion, sliced
1 lemon, sliced
1 piece of carrot
1 piece of celery root
1 piece of parsley root
⅛ lb. of butter
¼ cup of salt

Preparation: The salmon is dressed, washed and dried. The vinegar is heated and poured on the fish, then it is placed into a fish kettle in a swimming position and the water is poured on cold, so that it almost covers the fish. All the ingredients are added; bring it to boil and set aside to simmer 1 hour. The fish must be served carefully and garnished with parsley and lemon slices; potato balls are good with it. For gravy, serve creamed butter, drawn butter, egg gravy, remoulade gravy or mayonnaise dressing.

Remarks: Salmon is good served cold with a mayonnaise dressing.

No. 7—SALMON SALAD.
Quantity for 6 Persons.

2 lbs. of salmon
2 hard boiled eggs
1 raw yolk of egg
Fine salad oil
1 tsp. of mustard

Juice of 1 lemon
1 tbsp. of vinegar
1 tsp. of sugar
Salt
1 pinch of pepper

Preparation: The boiled fish is arranged on a glass dish in a mound after being cut into nice pieces and the bones removed. The gravy or dressing is made by stirring the raw yolk of egg into the boiled yolks, adding the oil a few drops at a time, also the lemon juice, vinegar and the other ingredients. It must be thick. The dressing is poured over the salad and slightly mixed with a wooden spoon. Garnish the salad with hard boiled eggs and green lettuce leaves.

No. 8—SLICED SALMON BROILED.
Quantity for 6 Persons.

2½ lbs. of salmon
Salt
¼ cup melted butter
2 tbsps. of lemon juice
1 tbsp. of finely sliced onion
1 bunch of parsley
⅛ lb. of butter for frying

Preparation: The salmon is cut into 2 to 3 slices, cleaned, washed and dried well. Brush the slices with the ¼ cup of melted butter, salt and put on the lemon juice, onion slices and parsley. Cover the dish and put on the stove for one hour but do not fry. After one hour, put into a broiler, broil for 10 to 15 minutes, basting with butter and turning frequently. You can also fry them in a buttered pan. Serve in a hot dish, garnish with lemon slices and parsley and serve with a tomato or olive gravy, or a cold, sour gravy.

No. 9—BOILED SALMON-TROUT.
Quantity for 6 Persons.

3½ lbs. of salmon-trout
Water enough to cover the fish
Salt
¾ pt. of vinegar
10 pepper-corns
2 cloves
1 bay-leaf
½ onion, sliced

Preparation: The fish is cleaned and washed. The water with all ingredients in it is brought to boil, the fish placed into it in a swimming position, cooked 10 minutes and served on a hot platter. A fish or egg gravy may be served with it.

No. 10—FRIED TROUT.
Quantity for 6 Persons.

3½ lbs. of trout
Salt, flour
1 beaten egg
¼ lb. of butter

Preparation: The fish is dressed, washed, dried, salted inside and outside, dipped into the beaten egg and then into flour. The butter is heated in a pan, the fish fried in it to a light brown color and a butter gravy served with it.

No. 11—EEL, BLUE.
Quantity for 6 Persons.

3½ lbs. of eel	4 cloves
1½ qts. of water	½ sliced onion
6 tbsps. of vinegar	½ sliced lemon
10 pepper-corns	Salt
2 bay-leaves	Water for cooking

Preparation: The eel is killed by wrapping the head into a cloth and giving it a few blows with a hatchet; then rub it with salt from head to tail until it looks blue. Skin the eel by making a cut in the skin around the head and pulling this down over the tail; if it does not strip off easily, cut it loose with a sharp knife. Cut the fish into equal pieces and clean each piece separately, pushing out the intestines and inner membrane and rubbing it with salt.

1½ qts. of water is brought to boil with 4 tablespoonfuls of vinegar and the eel scalded with it. Heat fresh water, 2 tablespoonfuls of vinegar, pepper-corns, bay-leaves, cloves, 1 onion, lemon slices and salt; in this water the eel is cooked slowly 15 minutes. The fish is then served on lettuce leaves and garnished with lemon slices. Caper, mustard or remoulade dressing is served with it. This fish is good eaten cold.

Remarks: The remnants of eel may be used to make aspic or head cheese. The eel broth and skin are utilized for it. See Head Cheese and Gelatines, No. 9 Eel in Jelly.

No. 12—BAKED EEL.
Quantity for 6 Persons.

3½ lbs. of eel	1 beaten egg
Salt	Flour for dredging
1 pinch of pepper	¼ lb. of butter or lard for frying

Preparation: The eel is prepared as described in No. 11. The bones are taken out of the pieces, (these may be 3 to 4 inches long) salt and pepper, roll in beaten egg and flour and bake in hot butter to a nice brown color.

A Dutch dressing may be served with it.

No. 13—EEL IN BEER.
Quantity for 6 Persons.

3½ lbs. of ell	¼ lemon, sliced
3 tbsps. of butter	Salt
2 tbsps. of flour	1 pinch of p-pper
1 qt. of white beer	1 clove
½ onion, sliced	½ bay-leaf

Preparation: The eel is prepared as in No. 11, the bones being removed from the pieces. The 3 tablespoonfuls of butter are stirred into the flour, the beer added and also all the spices and lemon and onion slices. Cook this gravy and put in the pieces of eel to boil 20 minutes. Serve the eel on a hot platter, strain the gravy and pour it over the eel. The gravy must be thick and very palatable.

Remarks: If the gravy is not thick enough, mix some more flour with water, stir it in and let it boil.

No. 14—EEL WITH RICE. (FRICASSEE).
Quantity for 6 Persons.

3½ lbs. of eel	1 pt. of cream
⅛ lb. of butter	Salt
2½ tbsps. of flour	Juice of 1 lemon

Preparation: The eel is prepared according to No. 11, cut into 4 inch pieces and cooked almost done in boiling water, salt, 2 tablespoonfuls of vinegar, ½ sliced onion, 8 peppercorns, 2 cloves, 1 bay-leaf. When almost done, take out the pieces and put them into the gravy, which is prepared in the following way: Heat the butter, stir in the flour, add the cream and stir well until smooth, add salt and lemon juice and let it simmer 10 minutes. Serve eel and dressing on a hot platter and place a rim of cooked rice around it. Then strew over the whole some fine minced parsley. If you wish you may sprinkle chopped parsley over the eel before serving, or you may cook the parsley in the dressing.

Remarks: The gravy must be smooth and savory.

No. 15—COLD EEL ROULADE.
Quantity for 6 Persons.

3 lbs. of eel	1 tbsp. of chopped capers
4 hard boiled, chopped eggs	Juice of one lemon
1 tbsp. of chopped parsley	Salt, pepper
½ tbsp. of chopped onion	

For Cooking.

2 qts. of water	1 small piece of carrot
10 pepper-corns	1 small piece of parsley root
3 cloves	1 small piece of celery root
1 bay-leaf	Salt
½ onion	

Preparation: The eel is prepared as described in No. 11, its head and tail cut off and ripped open lengthwise; intestines and bones carefully taken out; then cut it in two crosswise, to make 4 pieces. These pieces are washed, dried and rubbed with salt. The four hard boiled eggs are chopped and mixed well with the chopped parsley, onion, capers, lemon juice, salt and pepper. This stuffing is put inside of the four pieces of eel and these rolled up tightly and tied with string, then each tied up in a piece of white cloth. Into the 2 qts. of water put all the ingredients for cooking, and the head, tail and skin chopped up into small pieces and cook 15 minutes. This eel stock must be tasted as to seasoning, vinegar added and the prepared pieces of eel cooked in it slowly for 45 minutes. Leave them in the stock until pretty well cooled off, then take them out and place them between two platters. After a few hours, take off the strings and cloth and cut them into thin slices which are served on green lettuce leaves and garnished with hard boiled eggs. You may serve them also with pickles and mayonnaise or mustard dressing.

Remarks: These eel roulades may be made into eel jelly. See Chapter Nine, No. 9.

No. 16—LARDED PICKEREL.

Quantity for 6 Persons.

3½ lbs. of fish
⅛ lb. of bacon
Salt
1 pinch of pepper
¼ lb. of butter
1 tbsp. of flour
¾ pt. sweet or sour cream
½ tsp. of meat extract
1 tbsp. of Parmesan cheese
Juice of ½ lemon
1 tsp. of capers

Preparation: The fish is dressed, washed, dried and rubbed with salt inside and outside. The back is skinned by slitting the sides and pulling the skin off. The back is then larded with bacon strips. The butter is heated in a pan and the fish placed into it in a swimming position after dredging with flour and grated Parmesan cheese. The hot butter is dripped on, also the lemon juice, and the fish put into the oven to bake 15 minutes. During this time baste with the butter carefully so the flour and cheese make a crust on the fish. Gradually add the cream and capers, and bake the fish in this dressing for ½ hour, basting frequently. Serve on a hot platter. Color the gravy with the meat extract and if it is too thin, add 1 teaspoonful of flour, mixed with cream or milk, cook and strain. The gravy is served with the fish; garnish with potatoes and macaroni and serve with sauerkraut.

No. 17—LARDED AND STUFFED PICKEREL.
Quantity for 6 Persons.

3½ lbs. of fish	1 pt. sour or sweet cream
⅛ lb. of bacon	½ tsp. of meat extract
Salt, pepper	1 tbsp. of Parmesan cheese
¼ lb. of butter	Juice of ½ lemon
1 tbsp. of flour	1 tsp. of capers

The Stuffing.

1 pt. can of champignons	½ cup of sweet cream
2 tbsps. of butter	Salt, pepper
	1 tbsp. of flour

Preparation: The preparation is the same as given in No. 16. The filling or stuffing is made from chopped champignons stewed in the butter, flour, salt, pepper and cream. This is stuffed into the fish which is then sewed up. The fish is larded and cooked according to directions in No. 16. The gravy is also prepared as in No. 16. ———

No. 18—STUFFED AND LARDED PIKE.
Quantity for 6 Persons.

The preparation and ingredients are the same as given under No. 16 and No. 17.———

No. 19—FISH FRICASSEE FROM PICKEREL OR WHITEFISH.
Quantity for 6 Persons.

1 pickerel or whitefish, 3½ lbs.	¼ lb. of butter
⅛ lb. of bacon for larding	1 cup of cream

For the Fricassee.

18 crabs	⅛ lb. of butter
2½ qts. of salt water	20 champignons
1½ lbs. veal sweetbreads	10 peeled truffles
Juice of ½ lemon	2 tbsps. of butter
Salt, pepper	1 tbsp. of lemon juice

Preparation: The fish is dressed, washed, dried, the skin taken off the back and this larded with bacon. Then it is sprinkled with salt and put into a pan in a swimming position with ¼ lb. of butter and 1 cup of cream and fried slowly for 1 hour to a golden yellow color. During this time simmer the 18 crawfish or crabs in salt water for 45 minutes. They should not boil, but simmer. From eight crabs take out the meat and leave the other ten whole.

The veal sweetbreads are scalded, the membrane removed, salted and peppered, the lemon juice dripped on, then dredged with flour and fried in ⅛ lb. of butter to a nice brown color. The sweetbreads are cut into nice pieces. The champignons are heated in 1 tablespoonful of butter; lemon juice, salt, pepper, 2 tablespoonfuls of cream are added. The truffles are peeled and sliced and stewed with ½ tablespoonful of butter, 3 tablespoonfuls of bouillon, 1 pinch of salt. The crab meat from the 8 crabs is chopped fine and stirred with 1 tablespoonful of butter and 1½ tablespoonfuls of flour; add a little cream and boil. The lemon juice, salt, pepper and 1 yolk of egg are stirred in and set to cool. Small dumplings are formed from this mixture and fried in hot lard. The batter for the dumplings must be thick; try one first and if it does not hold together, add more flour. These small dishes must be prepared while the fish is cooking. That which is done must be kept hot in hot water. The fish, when done, is served on a hot platter in a swimming position, three crabs are placed on the fish's back, the other seven along its sides. The pieces of sweetbread are also arranged neatly around the fish and the champignons and truffles, as well as the fish dumplings. All must be very hot and kept so until the gravy is done.

The Gravy: Into the butter in which the sweetbreads were fried stir some flour and add bouillon or water, pour it into the pan in which the fish was fried and cook for 2 minutes, taste and strain. It must be smooth and be served with the fish.

Remarks: This is a fine dish for parties. Potato balls and green lettuce are served with it.

No. 20—PICKEREL WITH TOMATO SAUCE.
Quantity for 6 Persons.

3½ lbs. of pickerel, white fish or cod fish
Salt
1 sheet of paper
⅛ lb. of butter, good measure

Gravy.

⅛ lb. of butter
⅛ lb. of ham
6 tomatoes
3 tbsps. of flour
2 tbsps. of Parmesan cheese
Salt
Pinch of pepper
½ pt. bouillon
½ pt. of cream

Preparation: The fish is dressed, washed, dried, salted, placed into a pan and lightly covered with a buttered paper. Then the hot butter is poured over it and it is cooked in the oven until well done, basting frequently for about one hour. In the meantime the gravy is prepared thus: The ham is cut into small pieces and fried light yellow in the butter, with onion slices and flour, then add bouillon and cream, season with salt, pepper and add Parmesan cheese; also put in the sliced or chopped tomatoes and cook until pretty thick. Strain the gravy, taste it and heat it again. The fish, which must be a nice pink color, is brushed with the thick gravy and served in a swimming position. The rest of the gravy may be served separately.

No. 21—PICKEREL OR CODFISH SALAD.
Quantity for 6 Persons.

1¾ lbs. of pickerel or codfish	1 tsp. of mustard
2 tbsps. of butter	2 tbsps. of vinegar
1 scant tbsp. of flour	1 tbsp. of salad oil
1 small onion	Salt
1 pt. thick cream	1 pinch of white pepper
2 yolks of eggs	1 tbsp. of capers

Preparation: The boiled fish is cut up into nice pieces. The butter is melted, the peeled whole onion fried light yellow in it, then taken out. Stir in the flour, add the cream and cook 5 minutes. The 2 yolks are stirred in, but the gravy must not cook any more, cool it and season with salt, mustard, pepper, capers, vinegar and salad oil. Pour the gravy over the fish.

No. 22—BAKED RED SNAPPER.
Quantity for 6 Persons.

3½ lbs. of red snapper	Some flour
Salt	1 cup of rolled crackers
1 beaten egg	¼ lb. of butter

Preparation: The fish is dressed, washed, dried and rubbed with a little salt. It is then dredged with flour, dipped into the beaten egg and cracker crumbs. The butter is heated and put on the fish, then baked in the oven for ½ hour until a nice brown. Serve a parsley gravy with it.

No. 23—PICKEREL OR WHITEFISH WITH SAUERKRAUT.
Quantity for 6 Persons.

1 lb. boiled pickerel or whitefish	1 large piece of butter
1 lb. boiled sauerkraut	¾ pt. of cream
1 egg	Some salt

Preparation: A baking dish or casserole is buttered and filled with layers of sauerkraut and fish alternating. The bones must have been removed and the fish cut into nice pieces. There should be 3 layers of sauerkraut and 2 layers of fish. After the dish is filled, stir the cream with some salt and pour over the whole. Put a little butter on top and bake in oven for 45 minutes.

No. 24—BOILED TURBOT.
Quantity for 6 Persons.

3½ lbs. of fish
Salt
½ qt. of wine vinegar

Preparation: The turbot is drawn by making a cut across the dark side below the gills, then rub it with salt until all slime is gone. After washing it, pour ½ qt. of vinegar on and let it stand for ½ hour. Run the knife along the spine on the black side and slit the white side in several places to prevent the skin from bursting while cooking. Fins and tail are shortened. Put plenty of salt water into the fish kettle, put the fish in, white side up, and cook slowly for 5 minutes, then set aside to simmer for ½ hour. Do not cover up the kettle. When serving, the white side should be up and garnish the platter with any kind of lettuce or salad i. e., cucumber salad, head lettuce or endive. Place lemon slices on the fish or small boiled crabs. Serve with a butter gravy or creamed butter and potato balls.

No. 25—TURBOT FRICASSEE.
Quantity for 6 Persons.

1 lb. of fish remnants
A small calf's tongue
½ pt. of champignons
1 tbsp. of capers
3 tbsps. of butter
½ pt. of cream or milk
Juice of ½ lemon
Salt, pepper
½ pt. of bouillon
2 tbsps. of Parmesan cheese
2 tbsps. of flour

Preparation: The fish is cut into large pieces. A baking dish is buttered and the pieces of fish placed in. Add 3 tablespoonfuls of heated butter, stirred with 2 tablespoonfuls of flour, the cream, champignon juice and bouillon. The latter may be omitted. Cook the gravy until it is smooth and add the lemon juice, salt, pepper, chopped champignons and capers.

The tongue which has been boiled is skinned and sliced and put into the gravy, then boiled a few minutes and tasted as to seasoning. Pour this gravy over the fish, strew with Parmesan cheese and drip on some butter. Place the baking dish into a dish with water and bake in the oven to a nice color.

No. 26—BOILED RED SNAPPER.
Quantity for 6 Persons.

3½ lbs. of fish
Salt
10 pepper-corns
4 cloves
2 bay-leaves
½ onion, sliced
½ lemon, sliced
Water

Preparation: The fish is dressed, washed and put in a

swimming position, into water enough to cover it and brought to boil. All the ingredients are added and after boiling up once, set aside to simmer ½ hour. Garnish with lemon slices and parsley. Serve the fish with a butter gravy mixed with fine chopped parsley or with an egg dressing.

No. 27—RED SNAPPER WITH RED WINE DRESSING.
Quantity for 6 Persons.

The preparation and ingredients are the same as given under No. 3.

No. 28—FRIED SMELT OR SPARLING.
Quantity for 6 Persons.

3½ lbs. of sparling	2 tbsps. of milk
Salt	Flour
1 egg	½ lb. of butter for frying

Preparation: The fish is dressed, washed, rubbed with salt and left standing for 1½ hours. Then the salt is washed off a little. Beat the egg with the milk, brush the fish with it and dip it into the flour. Heat the butter and bake the fish in it in the oven to a nice brown color.

When served, pour the drippings over.

No. 29—FILLET OF SHELLFISH, WHITEFISH, CABELJOU, SOLE, WITH DRESSING.
Quantity for 6 Persons.

3½ lbs. of fish	Salt, pepper
¼ lb. of butter	Juice of 1 lemon

Fish Bouillon.

Bones, skin	2 slices of lemon
4 pepper-corns	½ onion
2 cloves	1½ qts. water
1 bay-leaf	Salt

Preparation: The fish is dressed, washed, the bones all removed and cut into equal fillets. These are salted a little and left with the salt ½ hour.

During this time prepare the fish bouillon. The bones and skin are brought to boil in 1½ qts. of water to which the pepper-corns, cloves, lemon and onion slices and salt have been added and then cooked until the water has boiled down to ¾ qt. Then put the fish fillets into a buttered pan, season with 1 pinch of pepper, lemon juice, the ¼ lb. of butter placed on in pieces and ½ cupful of the fish bouillon poured over them.

The pan must be covered and the fish stewed in the oven for 25 minutes, then served on a hot platter, the drippings poured over. A Dutch gravy is served with it and the bouillon used for that. See gravies or dressings, Dutch Dressing.

No. 30—FRIED MACKEREL.
Quantity for 6 Persons.

3½ lbs. of mackerel
Salt
1 egg
2 tbsps. of milk
Flour
½ lb. of butter for frying

Preparation: The mackerel is cleaned well, the head chopped off and the fish split open lengthwise. The bones are all taken out, the fillets rubbed with salt and let stand for 1 hour. Then it is washed a little, dried, dipped into the egg beaten with milk and into flour. The butter is heated and the fillets are fried in it to a nice color for about 10 to 15 minutes. Serve on a hot platter, pour the drippings over and garnish with lemon slices and parsley. If the drippings are not sufficient, make an extra gravy of drawn butter mixed with chopped parsley.

No. 31—ROLLED, STUFFED FISH FILLETS.
Made from whitefish, pickerel, cabeljou, shellfish, halibut.
Quantity for 6 Persons.

3 los. of fish
1½ rolls, soaked in milk
1 tbsp. of chopped parsley
½ tbsp. of chopped tion
1 pinch of salt
1 pinch of pepper
3 eggs
⅛ lb. of butter

For Stew.

½ pt. of white wi
1 oz. of butter
6 pepper-corns
¼ onion
2 lemon slices
3 tbsps. of lemon juice

The Gravy.

⅛ lb. of butter
2 tbsps. of flour
¾ pt. of fish gravy
3 yolks of eggs

Preparation: The fish is dressed, washed, skinned, split open lengthwise and the bones taken out, then it is cut into pieces 6 inches long and 3 inches wide. The trimmings which are left, must be fully ¼ lb. and are chopped fine. From 2 eggs make scrambled eggs. Cream the ⅛ lb. of butter and mix it well with the soaked roll, chopped fish trimming, 1 tablespoonful of parsley, scrambled egg, onion, salt, pepper. Press the whole mixture through a sieve and stir in another egg. This stuffing must taste very spicy or piquant and is spread evenly on the fish fillets. Then roll each one up and tie it with a white string, place them into a roasting pan, add ½ qt. of water, ½ pt. of white wine, 6 pepper-corns, ¼ onion, 2 slices of lemon, 3 tablespoonfuls of lemon juice and salt. The 1 ounce of butter is cut into pieces and put on the fish, then cover the pan with a buttered paper and bake in the oven ½ hour. Serve on a hot platter.

The gravy or dressing is prepared by mixing ⅛ lb. of butter with 2 tablespoonfuls of flour, add the strained broth from the fillets, cook and stir in 3 yolks of eggs, strain and serve with the fish fillets ———————

No. 32—BOILED CODFISH.

Quantity for 6 Persons.

3 lbs. of codfish	2 onions
⅛ lb. of soda	Salt
	4 qts. of water

Preparation: The fish is pounded well, and put into water for 36 hours, changing it every 12 hours and adding a teaspoonful of soda at every change. After that, skin the fish and cut it into pieces, place it into boiling water with the salt, and 2 sliced onions, and let it simmer for 45 minutes. Serve it with drawn butter or mustard gravy.

No. 33—CODFISH RAGOUT.

Quantity for 6 Persons.

1½ lbs. of boiled codfish	6 pepper-corns
⅛ lb. of butter	2 bay-leaves
2 tbsps. of flour	Salt
¾ pt. of bouillon	A small cup of herb vinegar
	½ onion

Preparation: The remnants of boiled codfish are cut in small pieces. The ⅛ lb. of butter is browned, 2 tablespoonfuls of flour stirred in, add the bouillon and season with vinegar, onion, pepper-corns and bay-leaves.

The gravy is cooked slowly ½ hour, seasoned and strained. Add the fish, reheat but do not boil and serve on a hot platter with potatoes. ———————

No. 34—FRIED SOLE.

Quantity for 6 Persons.

3½ lbs. of fish	1 cup grated rolls
Salt, white pepper	Juice of 1 lemon
1 egg	1 onion, sliced thin
2 tbsps. of milk	¼ lb. of butter for frying
	Some flour

Preparation: Skin the fish by running a sharp knife around the tail; loosen the skin from the meat and pull downward over the head. The white side is treated the same way, the tail and fins are shortened and the fish cut into convenient pieces. Every piece is cleaned well, salted and peppered, the lemon juice dripped on, the slices of onion placed on top, the pot covered up and the fish left in it to simmer 1½ to 2 hours. ½ hour before serving, each piece is dried, dredged with flour and dipped into the egg beaten with the milk and salt and then into roll crumbs.

The butter is heated and in it the pieces of fish are fried to a nice brown color. Serve it on a hot platter, garnish with lemon slices and parsley. The drippings may be used as gravy.

No. 35—BAKED SOLE.
Quantity for 6 Persons.

The ingredients and preparations are the same as in the preceding, No. 34. The pieces of fish are put into boiling hot lard deep enough so they float, and baked to a golden yellow color.

Serve with a mayonnaise or caviar gravy. See Gravies or Dressings.

Remarks: The pieces of fish may be rolled in finely chopped or ground hazel nuts instead of bread crumbs; this is very fine.

No. 36—BAKED GURNET.
Quantity for 6 Persons.

3½ lbs. of fish	2 tbsps. of milk
Salt	Juice of 1 lemon
1 egg	¼ lb. of butter

Preparation: The fish is cleaned well, dried, cut in halves, lengthwise, the bones taken out, salted, seasoned with lemon juice, dipped into egg beaten with milk and then into flour.

Heat the butter and fry the fish in the oven for ½ hour, basting frequently. Serve a butter dressing with it.

No. 37—SMALL FISH RAGOUTS IN SHELLS OR SMALL MOLDS; UTILIZING REMNANTS OF FISH.
Quantity for 6 Persons.

1 lb. of boiled fish	1 tbsp. of Parmesan cheese
1 oz. of butter	3 tbsps. of white wine
2 tbsps. of flour	Salt, white pepper
½ pt. of sweet or sour cream	2 tbsps. of roll crumbs
Juice of ½ lemon	1 small piece of butter

Preparation: The butter is heated, the flour stirred in, also the cream, wine and lemon juice and boiled. This gravy should be thick; if too thick, add more cream or milk, salt, pepper and Parmesan cheese, then boil one minute. Cut the fish into small pieces and put into the gravy. Butter the shells or molds and fill with this mixture, strew the bread crumbs on and bake in the oven about 10 minutes, to a light yellow color. Serve immediately after taking out of the oven.

Remarks: This dish may be served as a fine side-dish together with head lettuce.

No. 38—FISH CROQUETTES.
Quantity for 6 Persons.

1 lb. of boiled fish	Salt
1 oz. of butter	1 pinch of pepper
3 tbsps. of flour	2 whites of eggs, beaten with 1
¾ pt. of cream	tbsp. of milk
3 yolks of eggs	Flour
1 tbsp. of lemon juice	Lard enough for frying

Preparation: The fish is cut into small pieces. The butter is melted, the 3 tablespoonfuls of flour stirred in, then add cream and season with lemon juice, salt and pepper. This gravy is cooked a few minutes and must be thick, the 3 yolks of eggs are stirred in and the fish added. After this mixture has cooled off, small croquettes are formed which are dipped into the white of egg and flour or bread crumbs. Heat the lard to the boiling point, (it must be deep enough so the croquettes will float in it) and bake them to a golden yellow color.

Remarks: Fry one croquette first; if it should not hold together, add more flour.

No. 39—FISH CUTLETS.
Quantity for 6 Persons.

The preparation and ingredients are the same as under No. 38. Form small cutlets, bread them the same as the croquettes and fry them in butter to a nice color. You may improve them with champignons or crab tails.

No. 40—FISH AND POTATO PUDDING.
Quantity for 6 Persons.

1½ lbs. of boiled fish	2 tbsps. of Parmesan cheese
3 lbs. potatoes	Salt, pepper
1 pt. of cream or milk	1 tbsp. of capers
⅛ lb. of butter	1 tbsp. of roll crumbs
2 tbsps. of flour	

Preparation: The boiled fish is cut up fine, the bones all taken out; the raw potatoes peeled and sliced fine. The baking-dish or casserole is buttered and a layer of potatoes alternating with a layer of fish put in so that the last layer will be potatoes.

The gravy is made by heating the butter, stirring in the flour, adding the cream, salt, pepper, Parmesan cheese and capers. Cook one minute, then pour over the layers of fish and potatoes. Strew a few bread crumbs on top and place the pieces of butter on, then bake slowly 1½ hours. Serve in the dish with head lettuce.

No. 41—SALTED CODFISH CROQUETTES.
Quantity for 6 Persons.

The preparation and ingredients are the same as given under No. 38, Fish Croquettes. If the codfish is too salty, soak it in water a few hours or simmer in boiling water a few minutes.

No. 42—CODFISH HASH.
Quantity for 6 Persons.

1½ lbs. of codfish 1 tbsp. of flour
1 small piece of butter ½ pt. of cream

Preparation: The codfish is picked to pieces. If it is too salty, soak it a few hours. Heat the butter, stir in the flour, cream and fish and cook for 10 minutes. Toast slices of wheat bread and serve the fish hash on this.

No. 43—FRIED FRESH HERRING.
Quantity for 6 Persons.

12 fresh herring ½ lb. of butter or lard
Salt 1 cup of flour

For the Gravy.
Juice of 1 lemon ⅛ lb. butter
1 tbsp. parsley

Preparation: The head of the herring must have a yellow color, if it looks reddish, the herring is stale. The herring is dressed, washed, salted for 45 minutes, then it is dried and rolled in flour, that has been mixed with salt and pepper. Heat the butter or fat and fry the herring in it to a nice color, turning occasionally. For the gravy, brown the butter, add the juice of the lemon and finely chopped parsley.

Serve the herring on a hot platter and pour the gravy over it.

No. 44—TO MARINATE OR PICKLE FRIED HERRING.
Quantity for 6 Persons.

12 fresh herring	1 cup of flour
Salt	½ lb. of butter or lard

For Marinating.

¾ qt. vinegar	6 cloves
¾ qt. water	6 bay-leaves
1 large onion, sliced	Some Salt
20 pepper-corns	

Preparation: The herring are dressed, washed, salted for 45 minutes; after that they are dried, then rolled in flour mixed with salt and pepper and fried in butter or lard to a nice color.

For marinating, boil vinegar, water, pepper, cloves, bay-leaves, sliced onion and salt and cool it. The fried herring are cooled and put into a stone jar and the fluid poured over. To be prepared one day before serving.

No. 45—MARINATED SALT HERRING.
Quantity for 6 Persons.

6 salt herring	12 pepper-corns
1 pt. sour or sweet cream or milk	4 cloves
2 sour apples	2 bay-leaves
	Vinegar to taste
1 small onion	

Preparation: The salt herring are soaked for one day, then dressed and skinned. If you wish, you may cut them into pieces or leave them whole and put them into a dish. The gravy is then prepared.

The milt and roe, taken out of the herring, are well cleaned, chopped and beaten with vinegar, cream, grated apples and onions, pepper, cloves and bay-leaves. Pour this dressing over the herring and let stand for ½ to 1 day. Serve the herring in the gravy and potatoes in their jackets.

Remarks: Sour cream is best to use for marinating salt herring. This preparation is very good.

No. 46—MARINATED SALT HERRING.
A Simple Way.
Quantity for 6 Persons.

6 salt herring	12 pepper-corns
1 pt. wine vinegar	6 cloves
1 large onion, sliced	2 bay-leaves

Preparation: The herring are dressed, skinned and soaked in water for ½ day, then cut into desirable pieces or left whole.

Cook the vinegar with ½ pt. of water and cool. Put all the spices on the herring and pour the cold vinegar over. The milt may be put in also.

No. 47—HERRING SALAD.
Quantity for 6 Persons.

3 salt herring	1 onion
15 boiled, peeled potatoes	1 tsp. mustard
3 apples	4 tbsp. of oil
¼ lb. cold roast	1 pinch of salt
⅛ lb. tongue sausage	Pepper
¼ lb. pickled beets	1 pinch of sugar
2 salt pickles	Vinegar to taste
2 pepper pickles	½ pt. bouillon
3 hard boiled eggs	

Preparation: The herring are soaked in water for ½ day, then dressed, skinned, the bones taken out, and cut into equal parts. Potatoes, apples, roast, sausage, eggs, onion, pickles, beets are all cut up, mixed well and seasoned with oil, salt, pepper, mustard, sugar and vinegar, then bouillon added. The salad is served in a glass dish and garnished with minced white of egg, yolk of egg, pickles and beets. You may also garnish with sardines cut in halves and rolled.

No. 48—BOILED LOBSTER.
Quantity for 6 Persons.

3 lobsters, 2½ lbs.	Salt
Boiling water	12 pepper-corns

Preparation: The lobster is cleaned in water with a brush, by taking hold of its back with the left hand and using the brush with the right. In this way it is harmless. The water is brought to boil in the meantime with salt and the 12 pepper-corns, then the lobsters are put in head first, which kills them instantly. Boil 5 minutes, then set aside to simmer 45 minutes. After this time take out the lobsters, dry them and put them on a board, break off the claws and tail and split the body into halves from head to tail. Arrange these halves upright on a platter, put a bunch of parsley in the top, place lettuce leaves around and garnish neatly with the tails, cracked claws and legs.

Creamed butter or butter balls are served with it, also a mayonnaise dressing.

Remarks: Claws and legs are placed into a cloth and carefully cracked so the meat is not crushed. Large lobsters may boil 1 hour.

No. 49—COLD LOBSTER.
Quantity for 6 Persons.

Preparation and ingredients are the same as in the preceding, No. 48. When the lobster is done, pour a cupful of cold water into the hot water and let the lobster cool in it. Then take it out, dry it and press it under a heavy board for one hour. When serving, brush it with oil and prepare it like the warm lobster. A mayonnaise dressing is nice with it.

No. 50—LOBSTER CROQUETTES OR CUTLETS.
Quantity for 6 Persons.

Utilizing remnants of lobsters.

The preparation and ingredients are the same as those given under No. 38 and 39, Fish Croquettes or Cutlets.

No. 51—LOBSTER RAGOUT IN SHELLS OR ON TOAST.
Quantity for 6 Persons.

2 lobsters, 3 lbs.
1/8 lb. of butter
2 tbsps. of flour
1/2 pt. bouillon
1 tsp. of meat extract
1 pinch of salt
1 pinch of pepper
1 pinch of sugar
1 tbsp. of lemon juice

4 pepper-corns
1 clove
1/4 bay-leaf
1/8 of an onion
2 tbsps. of Madeira
1/8 pt. of white wine
1/4 pt. of champignons
3 truffles
1 cup tomatoes

Preparation: The lobster is prepared as given under No. 48. After the lobster is cooked, all meat is picked out, reserving the coral, which is pulverized. The 1/8 lb. of butter is browned with the flour, bouillon or water added and the coral put in. Meat extract, salt, pepper, sugar, lemon juice, cloves, bay-leaf, onion, Madeira, white wine and tomatoes added and and smooth. It is strained and must be about 3/4 of a pint. this is all cooked 1/2 hour. This gravy must be very savory The champignons are cut into small pieces, the truffles peeled and chopped, then add the champignons, truffles and lobster to the strained gravy. This mixture is filled into buttered shells or small molds and baked in the oven for 5 to 10 minutes. Serve on slices of toast.

Remarks: This is a fine side-dish.

No. 52—BAKED LOBSTER.
Quantity for 6 Persons.

The preparation and ingredients are the same as given under No. 48. When the lobster is cooked and split, hot butter is dripped on and the lobster baked in it for 10 to 15 minutes.

A mayonnaise dressing and chopped pickles are nice with it.

Remarks: It is best to bake the lobster in a gas oven.

No. 53—BOILED CRAWFISH OR CRABS.

Quantity for 6 Persons.

24 crabs	2 tbsps. of caraway
Sufficient water	Salt
	1 large onion, sliced

The Gravy.

⅛ lb. of butter	2 tbsps. of chopped parsley

Preparation: The crabs are cleaned like the lobster. See No. 48. The water with caraway seeds, salt and sliced onion is boiled and the crabs put in one by one. The water must boil constantly, so that the crabs are killed instantly. Boil 3 minutes, then set aside to simmer ¾ to 1 hour. Serve the hot crabs on a napkin. For gravy or dressing, take hot butter mixed with minced parsley.

No. 54—CRAB CUTLETS WITH VEGETABLES.

Quantity for 6 Persons.

36 crabs	Salt, pepper
1 oz. of butter	1 tsp. of lemon juice
2 yolks of eggs	1 cupful of roll crumbs
1 egg	½ lb. of butter for frying

Preparation: The crabs are prepared and cooked as given under No. 53. The meat picked out, 18 claws or legs laid aside. The meat is coarsely minced, then mixed well with creamed butter, 2 yolks of eggs, lemon juice, salt and pepper and small croquettes made from this mixture. Dip in beaten egg and roll crumbs. Heat the butter and fry these croquettes in it on both sides to a nice color. Into each put a claw or leg. Arrange the croquettes around asparagus or peas.

Remarks: A good crab dressing may be prepared from the meat of crabs.

No. 55—CRAB RAGOUT.
Quantity for 6 Persons.

50 crabs
¼ lb. of butter
3 tbsps. of flour
1 pt. bouillon
Some champignon water
¼ wineglassful of white wine
1 tbsp. of lemon juice
1 pinch of salt and pepper
2 yolks of eggs
½ pt. champignons

Preparation: The crabs or crawfish are cooked the same way as given under No. 53, the meat all picked out, also out of the tails and cut into small pieces. The coral is pulverized and cooked in ¼ lb. of butter together with flour browned in it. The bouillon, the champignon juice, white wine, lemon juice, salt and pepper are added and cooked for 15 minutes in a covered pan. This gravy is then strained through a fine sieve and the crab meat and champignons put in. This mixture is filled into shells or patties and baked in oven 5 minutes. (See Chapter 3, No. 29, Veal Sweetbread Patties). You can also serve this ragout on toast.

No. 56—OYSTERS.
Quantity for 6 Persons.

6 doz. oysters
1½ lemon

Preparation: The oysters are opened with an oyster knife and cleaned with a small knife, then placed neatly on a platter covered with a napkin, garnishing with slices of lemon.

No. 57—OYSTER PATTIES.
Quantity for 6 Persons.

2½ doz. oysters
1 tbsp. of butter
1 tbsp. of flour
1 tsp. of lemon juice
Salt, pepper
Pie crust
2 tbsps. of cream

Preparation: The butter is melted, flour, cream, lemon juice, salt, pepper and oysters put in, then boiled up once. Small patties are made as given under Chapter 3, No. 29, Veal Sweet Bread Patties. Fill the patties with the oyster ragout, bake in oven a few minutes, then serve at once. This is a fine dish.

No. 58—FRIED OYSTERS OR CLAMS.
Quantity for 6 Persons.

3 doz. oysters
Salt, pepper
1 cupful of fine roll crumbs
⅛ lb. of butter
Some lemon juice

Preparation: The prepared oysters are put into a dish,

the lemon juice dripped on and breaded with crumbs, which are mixed with salt and pepper. In the meantime brown the butter and fry the oysters crisp, turning frequently. Serve them with spinage, sauerkraut and fish.

No. 59—OYSTER OR CLAM SALAD.

Quantity for 6 Persons.

50 oysters or clams
Juice of 2 lemons
Salt, white pepper
2 tbsps. of chopped parsley
4 tbsps. of oil

Preparation: The oysters or clams are mixed with the other ingredients, put into a glass dish and garnished with green lettuce leaves.

No. 60—OYSTER OR CLAM PUDDING WITH RICE.

Quantity for 6 Persons.

50 clams
1 pt. white wine
1 tsp. of salt

For the Rice.

¼ lb. of rice
1 pt. bouillon

For the Gravy.

¼ lb. of butter
3 tbsps. of flour
¾ pt. cream or milk
1 tbsp. of lemon juice
3 yolks of egg
½ tbsp. of Parmesan cheese
2 tbsps. chopped champignons

Preparation: The clams are cleaned in cold water with a brush. Change the water several times until it remains clear.

The white wine and salt are put into a dish and the clams put in and shaken over the fire until they open. The inside is then taken out, the shells thrown away. The clam liquor is used for dressing or gravy. Heat ¼ lb. of butter, stir in the flour and add cream, the liquor from the clams, chopped champignons and let it boil a few minutes, stirring constantly; then stir in the 3 yolks of eggs and set aside.

While the clams and dressing are being prepared, the rice is cooked with the bouillon to a thick mush.

A baking dish or casserole is buttered and filled with layers of rice alternating with layers of clams, rice for the top layer. The prepared gravy or dressing is then poured on, cheese strewn over, 1 tablespoonful of hot butter dripped on and then baked in the oven for 20 minutes. This dish may also be made of fresh oysters.

CHAPTER 9.

Head-Cheese and Gelatines.

The various preparations of Gelatines, Aspic, Head-Cheese, Poultry and Fish Jellies.

No. 1—HOW TO PREPARE GELATINE.

4 lbs. of pork sward or skin	7 whites of eggs and the shells
4 lbs. of pigs' feet	1 qt. of white wine
6 qts. of water	Juice of 3 lemons

Preparation: The pork sward and pigs' feet are cleaned well in cold water, then put in cold water and brought to boil. As soon as they begin to boil, pour this water off and cut the sward up into small pieces, chop the feet into several pieces and put on the stove with 6 qts. of cold water to boil for 7 hours. The feet may be taken out before this time if you wish to use them for a meal. The broth must boil down to 2½ qts.; this is strained through a fine sieve, set aside to cool, and all fat removed from the top.

Whites of eggs, wine and lemon juice are thoroughly beaten together; the egg shells are crushed and all this put into the broth. Then put the broth over the fire once more and stir constantly until it boils. Remove at once, cover up the pot and place it in a moderate oven until the liquid is perfectly clarified. Put a clean white cloth over a pot and strain the broth through it. This must be as clear as water. Put into glass jars, seal and set them in a boiler with water at the bottom, the jars resting on a tray. Cover the kettle and boil for 1 hour. This gelatine will keep and may be used for sweet or sour gelatines.

Remarks: The pigs' feet may be served with a brown sweet-sour gravy. They may be eaten cold if put in vinegar, onion slices, salt and pepper-corns for 2 days.

No. 2—MEAT GELATINE FOR PATIENTS.
Quantity 1½ qts.

1 lb. of beef	Salt
2½ lbs. veal cartilage	¾ qt. of water
1 small carrot	

Preparation: The beef and the veal cartilage are washed and cut into small pieces, the carrot is scraped, but left whole.

Then this meat, the carrot and 1 pinch of salt are put into a glass jar with ¾ qt. of water, sealed and slowly cooked in a boiler with water at the bottom, the jar resting on a tray, for 4 hours. After that, strain the broth, let it get cold and remove the fat, then serve it to the patient in spoonfuls.

Remarks: Instead of beef, you may use poultry.

No. 3—GELATINE OR HEAD-CHEESE FROM POULTRY BOUILLON.

Quantity for 4—6 Persons.

1 young, fried or boiled chicken	½ tsp. of meat extract
¾ qt. good beef bouillon	5 layers of ½ box of white gelatine
2 tbsps. of Madeira or white wine	2 sour pickles.

Preparation: The fried chicken is cut into small pieces, the pickles are peeled and sliced. The strong beef broth is heated and the gelatine dissolved in it with wine, meat extract and salt added, then strained and tasted as to seasoning. Put ¼ pt. of the warm fluid into a porcelain dish, skim off all fat, let it get cold and put on the sliced pickles and a few tablespoonfuls of broth, let it cool, arrange the chicken meat on it in the form of scales, pour the rest of the broth on and let it get cold and stiff. Then turn it out on a platter and garnish with parsley. Asparagus cut into small pieces may also be used in this gelatine.

Remarks: Instead of chicken you may use veal roast, tongue or goose liver from which all hard fried meat and cartilage is removed.

No. 4—HEAD-CHEESE FROM PIGS' FEET AND CALF'S TONGUE.

Quantity for 6 Persons.

4 pigs' feet	1 small onion
2 calves' tongues	½ bay-leaf
Juice of ½ lemon	¼ tsp. of meat extract
⅛ pt. of white wine	1 sour pickle, cut into small pieces
3 tbsps. of vinegar	
Some salt	2 qts. of water
4 pepper-corns	

Preparation: Pigs' feet and calves' tongues are cleaned well, put on to boil with the water, salt, pepper, onion, bay-leaf. Cover the pot and boil until well done, then take the skin off the tongue and cut it with the rest of the meat into small pieces.

Strain the bouillon and add vinegar, lemon juice, wine and meat extract. Put the meat into a dish, pour the bouillon on and set to cool. Then turn it out on a platter and serve with head lettuce or potato salad, vinegar and oil, mayonnaise dressing or with fried potatoes.

No. 5—HEAD-CHEESE FROM OX-TONGUE.
Quantity for 6 Persons.

1 pickled ox-tongue
½ qt. strong beef bouillon
4 pieces of white gelatine
1 tbsp. of capers
4 sliced pickles

½ pt. sliced champignons
⅛ pt. white wine
Some champignon water
½ tsp. of meat extract
Some vinegar

Preparation: The tongue is cleaned and put on to boil in cold water until tender. It is then skinned and sliced, ½ pt. of vinegar poured on and left for a few hours. The bouillon is seasoned with salt, wine, champignon juice, lemon juice, some vinegar and the 4 pieces of gelatine are dissolved in the bouillon. The tongue, champignon and pickle slices and capers are put into a porcelain dish, the bouillon poured on and cooled; then turned out on a platter and served.

No. 6—HEAD-CHEESE FROM GOOSE OR DUCK.
Quantity for 6 Persons.

1 goose, 8 to 10 lbs.
6 calves' feet

For Cooking.

6 qts. of water
Salt
6 pepper-corns
2 cloves
1 bay-leaf

1 large sliced onion
Some soupgreens
1 tsp. of meat extract
½ cup of good vinegar
4 whites of eggs and shells

Preparation: The goose and calves' feet are cleaned and well jointed, then put to boil in cold water with all the other ingredients. When the goose is tender, take it out of the broth, remove all spices that may adhere to it, place it into a porcelain or stone jar. Let the calves' feet cook until boiled down to 3 qts., remove all fat and season with vinegar, meat extract and salt if necessary. Put in the crushed egg shells, beat the white of egg with water and add it to the bouillon, let it come to boil and then set aside to simmer until the white of egg curdles. After one hour, strain the bouillon and pour it through a white cloth over the goose meat.

Remarks: If you wish to prepare the head-cheese quickly, omit the calves' feet and use 35 pieces of gelatine dissolved

—155—

in 3 qts. of bouillon, which is also clarified with white of egg and egg shells.

Remarks: The meat of the calves' feet may be breaded in roll crumbs, fried in butter and served with a raisin gravy. If you wish to make this head-cheese from duck, take 2 ducks.

No. 7—HEAD-CHEESE FROM PARTRIDGE.
Quantity for 6 Persons.

3 partridges	2 tbsps. of lemon juice
2 qts. of water	4 tbsps. of Madeira or good
Salt	white wine
4 pepper-corns	2 whites of eggs and egg shells
½ onion	15 pieces of gelatine or
2 cloves	1/20 of a lb.
1 bay-leaf	¼ tsp. of meat extract

Preparation: The partridges are cleaned and dressed and put to boil in cold water with the spices. When it is done, carve it and put it into a porcelain dish. Let the bouillon boil down to 1¼ qts., season with white wine or Madeira, lemon juice and meat extract and remove all fat, then dissolve the gelatine in it. Stir the whites of eggs with some bouillon and add it with the egg shells, then boil for a few minutes and set aside to simmer until the bouillon is clear. Strain it through a sieve and a cloth and pour it on to the meat to cool. Turn it out on a platter and garnish with lettuce and lemon slices.

No. 8—FISH IN JELLY.
Quantity for 6 Persons.

2½ lbs. of fish	2 lemon slices
2½ qts. of water	2 tbsps. of vinegar
Salt	4 tbsps. of lemon juice
4 pepper-corns	¼ pt. of white wine
2 cloves	10 pieces of white gelatine
1 bay-leaf	

Preparation: Put the water on with all the other ingredients and boil, then put in the fish after being dressed and cleaned and let it simmer gently for ½ hour. Take out the fish, remove the bones and cut it up into large pieces. The fish stock is boiled down to 1¼ qts. and the gelatine dissolved in it, then boiled for one hour, strained and poured on the fish to cool. Serve it on a glass platter garnished with head lettuce.

No. 9—EEL IN JELLY.
Quantity for 6 Persons.

3 lbs. of eel	1 sliced onion
1½ qts. of water	Some soupgreens
¼ qt. of wine vinegar	¼ lemon, sliced
10 pepper-corns	12 layers of white gelatine
3 cloves	¼ tsp. of meat extract
Salt	2 hard boiled eggs
2 bay-leaves	White of 1 egg

Preparation: The eel is skinned, cut in pieces and the intestines taken out. The 1½ qts. of water are brought to boil with vinegar, pepper-corns, salt, bay-leaf, onions, lemon slices and soupgreens; add the eel and simmer gently for 15 minutes. Take out the pieces of eel and boil the broth down to 1 qt.. Into this put the crushed egg shells, the white of egg mixed with some broth, ¼ teaspoonful of meat extract and the gelatine and cook for a minute, then set aside. When the bouillon is clear, strain it through a fine cloth. Slice the two hard boiled eggs and cover the bottom of a porcelain dish with them, then pour on some jelly and fish bouillon and let it get cold. After that put the eel pieces on and the rest of the sliced egg, then pour the rest of the stock over and let it get cold. When it is stiff, turn it out on a plate and garnish with head lettuce. It is best to prepare this dish the day before using it.

No. 10—SALMON IN JELLY.
Quantity for 6 Persons.

2½ lbs. of salmon	12 pepper-corns
1½ qts. of water	5 cloves
½ cup of wine vinegar	2 bay-leaves
1 cup of white wine	10 pieces of gelatine
½ sliced onion	2 whites of eggs and shells
¼ sliced lemon	10 crab tails if you like
Salt	

Preparation: Into the water put the wine vinegar, the wine, salt, pepper-corns, bay-leaves, cloves, onion slices, lemon slices and let it come to boil. Clean the fish well and put it into this water to simmer gently for ½ to ¾ hour. After this take the fish out, remove the bones, cut in pieces and boil down the stock to 1 qt. Beat the whites of 2 eggs with some of the broth and add it, also the crushed shells and 10 pieces or layers of gelatine. Let this mass cook a second and set aside to clarify, then strain through a fine cloth.

Place the pieces of fish and crab tails into a porcelain dish, pour the fish stock on and put it on ice to cool quickly. Then turn it out on a glass platter and garnish with head lettuce and lemon slices. Serve with a mayonnaise dressing.

No. 11—OYSTERS AND CAVIAR IN JELLY.
Quantity for 6 Persons.

1 qt. strong beef bouillon	12 layers of gelatine
3 tbsps. of white wine	4 doz. oysters
1 tsp. of lemon juice	¼ lb. of caviar, ice
2 whites of eggs and shells	

Preparation: The beef bouillon must be clear and free from fat; season it with white wine and lemon juice, and dissolve the gelatine in it. Stir the white of egg with some bouillon and add it, put in the crushed egg shells to cook for a second, then set aside to clarify. Strain it through a fine cloth. Fresh oysters are opened, cleaned and cut out of the shells. A dish is set on chopped ice, some oysters are placed in a circle into the dish and sufficient cold bouillon put on to cover; then let them get stiff. Repeat this until all oysters have been used. Put the rest of the bouillon on top and let it get stiff.

The caviar is poured into a sieve, let very cold water run over it until it becomes granular. In the center of the oyster jelly cut out a round hole, large enough to hold the quantity of caviar at hand. Heat the oyster jelly that has been cut out and pour it over the caviar. When it is perfectly stiff, turn it out on a platter and garnish with lemon slices and lettuce leaves. Serve with a cold mustard dressing.

No. 12—GOOSE-LIVER IN JELLY.
Quantity for 6 Persons.

1½ lbs. of fat goose liver	½ tsp. of meat extract
¼ lb. of truffles	3 tbsps. of Madeira
¼ lb. of champignons	10 pieces of white gelatine
¾ qt. very strong beef or chicken broth	1 white of egg and shell for clearing

Preparation: Remove all fat from the broth. Dissolve the gelatine in it, color with the meat extract and season with Madeira. Add to it the white of egg beaten into some of the broth, and the crushed shell, cook a second and set aside to clarify, then strain through a fine cloth.

Skin the goose liver and cut it into 1½ inch slices, also the truffles and lard the liver slices with the truffles, then stew slowly in a little butter. When done, place them on blotting paper to drain off the fat. The champignons are cooked in bouillon for 10 minutes.

Into a dish set in crushed ice put part of the bouillon, let it get stiff and put in half of the goose liver, also half of the champignons. Some more bouillon is poured over this and cooled; then repeat this same process until all goose liver, champignons and broth have been used. Let it get stiff, turn it out on a platter and serve with a cold mustard dressing and potato salad.

CHAPTER 10.
DRESSINGS or GRAVIES.

DRESSINGS FOR MEAT, POULTRY, GAME AND FISH. SAUCES FOR PASTRY AND SWEET DISHES.

Flour Gravies.

Good butter and good flour are the essentials for a gravy and constitute the main part of it. For the preparation of white gravies, earthen, pewter or enameled dishes are the best. Gravies must always be smooth and it is best to strain them through a fine sieve. If you have them ready before the meal, put them into a double boiler. They must neither be too thick nor too thin.

No. 1—WHITE GRAVY.
Quantity for 6 Persons.

1 oz. butter
¼ small onion
2 tbsps. of flour
¾ pt. of bouillon
1 pinch of salt and pepper
2 yolks of eggs

Preparation: Melt the butter, add the peeled onion and steep a little while, then stir in the flour and bouillon and cook 10 minutes, season with salt and pepper. Beat the 2 yolks of eggs with a little water and slowly stir it into the gravy. Do not boil any more.

No. 2—DUTCH GRAVY.
For Fish, Chicken or Veal With Rice.
Quantity for 6 Persons.

1 oz. of butter
2 tbsps. of flour
½ pt. of fish stock, chicken or veal broth
1½ tsps. of lemon juice, for fish
2 tbsps. white wine, for chicken
Salt
2 yolks of eggs
¼ cup of cream

Preparation: Melt the butter, stir in the flour, stew a few minutes, fill up with fish stock, stirring constantly, then season with salt and lemon juice and add the 2 yolks of eggs as given under No. 1.

Remarks: If the gravy is for chicken or veal with rice, season it with white wine.

No. 3—FINE DUTCH GRAVY FOR FISH OR VEAL.
Quantity for 6 Persons.

1 oz. of butter
2 tbsps. of flour
½ pt. fish stock or bouillon
½ cup sour cream
1 tbsp. of lemon juice

1 tbsp. of capers
3 sardines
Salt
1 pinch of white pepper
2 yolks of eggs

Preparation: Melt the butter, stir in the flour, simmer gently, fill up with fish stock, or bouillon if it is intended for veal. Cook, stirring constantly, add sour cream, lemon juice, salt and pepper.

The sardines are cleaned, chopped and put into the gravy with the capers. Cook slowly for ten minutes, stirring frequently, then strain through a fine sieve, heat it again and add the 2 yolks of eggs.

No. 4—WHIPPED DUTCH GRAVY.
For Fish, Asparagus, Cauliflower, Oyster Plants and Scorzonera.
Quantity for 6 Persons.

½ pt. of fish stock for fish, or
½ pt. of vegetable broth for vegetables
1½ tbsps. of flour

1 oz. of butter
3—4 yolks of eggs
Salt, pepper

Preparation: The flour is mixed well with fish stock or vegetable broth and whipped while over the fire, until it thickens; then add the fresh butter and the yolks of eggs, which have been beaten with water. Let it boil, stirring constantly. Serve at once.

Remarks: The gravy may be seasoned with 1 teaspoonful of lemon juice.

No. 5—GOOD FISH GRAVY.
Quantity for 6 Persons.

1 oz. of butter
2 tbsps. of flour
1/3 pt. of fish stock

Juice of ½ lemon
Salt
2—3 yolks of eggs
½ cup of cream

Preparation: Melt the butter, stir in the flour, add the fish stock and cream and cook a little while, stirring constantly, then season with lemon juice and salt if necessary. Finally stir in the yolks of eggs.

No. 6—CAULIFLOWER GRAVY.

Quantity for 6 Persons.

1 oz. of butter
2 tbsps. of flour
½ pt. of cauliflower broth
Salt to taste
2 yolks of eggs
Nutmeg to taste

Preparation: Melt the butter, stir in the flour, gradually pour in the cauliflower broth and boil, stirring constantly. Then season with salt and nutmeg and stir in the 2 yolks of eggs.

No. 7—ASPARAGUS GRAVY.

Quantity for 6 Persons.

⅛ lb. of butter
1 tbsp. of flour
4—6 yolks of eggs
½ cup of cream
1/3 pt. of asparagus broth
Salt to taste

Preparation: Cream the butter, add the yolks of eggs, flour and cream; then add the boiling asparagus broth, while stirring. Let it boil, stirring constantly. Serve at once or keep warm in water. It is very fine.

No. 8—FINE MUSTARD GRAVY.

For Beef and Fish.

Quantity for 6 Persons.

⅛ lb. of butter
3 yolks of eggs
2 tbsps. of mustard
1 tbsp. of flour
1 tbsp. of lemon juice
1 slice of lemon
1 pinch of sugar
1 pinch of salt
½ pt. bouillon

Preparation: Cream the butter, add the yolks of eggs, mustard, flour, and gradually pour in the bouillon, stirring constantly, then cook. Season it with lemon juice, sugar and salt if necessary. Put in the lemon slice which should be taken out when served.

No. 9—PLAIN MUSTARD DRESSING.

For Fish and Beef.

Quantity for 6 Persons.

1/10 lb. of butter
1½ tbsps. of flour
2 tbsps. of mustard
1 tbsp. of vinegar
1 pinch of salt
Sugar, pepper
½ pt. of bouillon

Preparation: Brown the butter and flour, add the bouillon, cook and season with pepper, salt, sugar and vinegar.

No. 10—FINE BEARNAISE SAUCE.
For Fillets, Saddle of Mutton, Mutton Cutlets.
Quantity for 6 Persons.

1 leek	¼ cup of bouillon
3 tbsp. of vinegar	½ tsp. of meat extract
¼ lb. of butter	1½ tsps. of chopped parsley
4 yolks of eggs	Salt, pepper

Preparation: The leek is cut into small pieces, vinegar added, then boiled down to one-half of the portion and strained through a fine sieve. Cream the butter, stir in the yolks of eggs, the leek vinegar, meat extract and bouillon. Place into a double boiler and let it thicken, stirring constantly; season with salt, pepper and finely chopped parsley. It must be smooth. Serve at once.

No. 11—TOMATO GRAVY.
For Fillet, Saddle of Mutton and Mutton Cutlets.
Quantity for 6 Persons.

1 leek	¼ cup of bouillon
3 tbsps. of vinegar	¼ cup of tomato pulp
⅛ lb. of butter	1 tsp. of sugar
3 yolks of eggs	Salt, pepper
	½ tsp. of flour

Preparation: The leek is cut into small pieces and boiled down in vinegar to half of the portion. Cream the butter, add yolks of eggs, tomatoes, flour, bouillon and the strained leek vinegar. Put into a double boiler and let it thicken, stirring constantly. Season with sugar, salt and pepper and serve at once.

No. 12—FINE TOMATO DRESSING.
Quantity for 6 Persons.

1 oz. of butter	1 pt. bouillon
1½ tbsps. of flour	Salt to taste
1 lb. or ¼ qt. can of tomatoes	1 pinch of sugar and pepper
¼ lb. raw ham	½ tbsp. of lemon juice
½ onion	2 yolks of eggs

Preparation: Ham and onion are cut into fine pieces and fried brown in butter. The chopped tomatoes are added and cooked a little while; then stir in the flour and add the bouillon. Season it with salt, pepper, lemon juice and sugar. Cook the gravy slowly for 1 hour, strain through a fine sieve and stir in the 2 yolks of eggs.

No. 13—FINE GRAVY.
For Poultry, Meat and Fish.
Quantity for 6 Persons.

⅛ lb. of butter
⅛ lb. of raw ham
1 small onion
1½ tbsps. of flour
1/3 pt. bouillon

1/3 pt. cream or milk
¼ cup of ground poultry, fish or meat
Salt, pepper
1 tsp. of lemon juice

Preparation: The lean ham is cut into small cubes and fried in the butter. Add the sliced onion, stir in the flour and stew a little while, add the bouillon and cream. Now the gravy is cooked for 15 minutes and the ¼ cupful of ground fish added. When served with meats, add meat instead of fish. Season with salt, pepper and lemon juice. Let it boil a while and strain through a fine sieve.

No. 14—HORSE RADISH GRAVY.
Quantity for 6 Persons.

½ cup of horse radish
1½ tsps. of flour
1 tbsp. of butter

¾ cup of cream or bouillon
1 pinch of salt
1 tsp. of sugar

Preparation: The horse radish must be scraped and grated very quickly, flour and butter stirred in and the cream added. Let it boil 15 to 20 minutes, stirring constantly, and season with salt and sugar.

No. 15—HORSE RADISH DRESSING, RAW.
Quantity for 6 Persons.

½ cup of horse radish
3 tbsps. of vinegar

1 pinch of salt
1 tsp. of sugar

Preparation: The prepared horse radish is mixed with vinegar, salt and sugar and served that way.

No. 16—SARDINE GRAVY.
For Fish and Meat.
Quantity for 6 Persons.

⅛ lb. of butter
2 tbsps. of flour
½ pt. of strong bouillon or fish stock
¼ pt. of white wine

Juice of ½ lemon
4—6 sardines
Salt
1 pinch of pepper
2 yolks of eggs

Preparation: The sardines are soaked in water for ½ hour, then chopped fine and rubbed through a sieve. Melt the butter, stir in the flour and stew a while, then add the bouillon, or fish stock if used for fish. Add wine and lemon juice and the sardines, cook it slowly for 15 minutes and season with salt and pepper; then stir in the yolks of eggs, but do not boil it any longer.

No. 17—CAPER SAUCE.
Quantity for 6 Persons.

1/10 lb. of butter	2 tbsps. of capers
1/4 of an onion	1 tbsp. of lemon juice
1½ tbsps. of flour	Salt
¾ pt. of bouillon (or fish stock, for fish)	1 pinch of pepper
	2 yolks of eggs

Preparation: Melt the butter, add the sliced onion and stew a while, then stir in the flour and add the bouillon, season with salt, pepper, lemon juice, and boil 15 minutes, stirring constantly. Strain through a fine sieve. Put in the capers and let it simmer gently. Stir in the yolks of eggs and a pinch of sugar.

No. 18—OYSTER DRESSING.
Quantity for 6 Persons.

18 oysters	1 sardine or
1/10 lb. of butter	1 tbsp. sardine butter
1½ tbsps. of flour	1 pinch of salt
1 pt. strong bouillon	Pepper
	½ cup of cream

Preparation: Melt the butter, stir in the flour, add the bouillon, and oyster liquor. If the oysters are fresh, you may use some of the beards. Cook the gravy slowly for ½ hour, then strain through a fine sieve and season with salt and pepper. Put in the sardine butter or finely chopped sardines. The oysters are put into boiling water for ¼ minute, then placed into a colander to drain. Put into the hot gravy and serve at once.

No. 19—CRAB OR LOBSTER GRAVY.
For Fish, Chicken and Fricassee.
Quantity for 6 Persons.

18 crabs	Salt
2 qts. salt water	1 pinch of pepper
1/10 lb. of butter	Sugar
2 tbsps. of flour	2 tbsps. of cream
	½ pt. of rich bouillon

Preparation: The crabs are brushed well in cold water, then cooked very red in 2 qts. of boiling salt water. The claws and tails are broken off and the meat picked out and cut up. Remove the gravy substance from the bodies and crush the coral in a mortar.

Heat the butter and put in the crushed coral, stir while stewing, add the 2 tablespoonfuls of flour, stew a while and add the bouillon, cook it slowly until it is smooth, then strain through a sieve and season with salt and pepper. Stir in the 2 tablespoonfuls of cream, let the gravy get very hot and put in the meat from the tails and claws. It must not boil any more.

Lobster gravy is prepared the same way. Instead of crabs or crab butter, take lobsters or lobster butter.

Remarks: A left-over body of a lobster may be utilized for a gravy.

No. 20—REMOULADE SAUCE.
Quantity for 6 Persons.

3 tbsps. of fine oil
1½ tbsps. of flour
½ pt. of bouillon
2 hard boiled yolks of eggs
1 raw yolk of egg
1½ tbsps. of lemon juice
1 tsp. of mustard
Salt
1 pinch of pepper
½ tsp. of sugar

Preparation: Stew the oil and flour a little while, add the bouillon, cook, strain and stir until cold. Stir the hard boiled yolks of eggs together with the raw yolk, lemon juice, mustard and gradually stir in the oil mixture. Season with salt, pepper and sugar. It is served with beef, eggs and headcheese.

No. 21—WHITE FRICASSEE SAUCE.
For Chicken Fricassee or Veal Fricassee.
Quantity for 6 Persons.

1 small piece of butter
2 tbsps. of flour
1 pt. bouillon
1 tbsp. of lemon juice
Salt
1 pinch of pepper
½ wineglass of white wine

Preparation: Melt the butter and stir in the flour, add the bouillon, stir and boil 5 minutes, add white wine, lemon juice, salt, pepper and set to simmer gently.

No. 22—ONION GRAVY.
For Boiled Beef.
Quantity for 6 Persons.

1 small piece of butter
1 medium sized onion
1 tbsp. of flour
Salt
1 pinch of pepper
1 tbsp. of vinegar
½ pt. bouillon

Preparation: Brown the butter with the sliced onion, stir in the flour, add the bouillon and season with salt, vinegar and pepper. Cook the gravy 10 minutes and strain through a fine sieve.

No. 23—PEARL ONION GRAVY.

Quantity for 6 Persons.

1 small piece of butter
½ tbsp. of sliced onion
1½ tbsp. of flour
½ pt. of bouillon

1½ tbsps. of vinegar
Salt
1 pinch of pepper
2 yolks of eggs

2 tbsps. of small pearl onions

Preparation: Prepare the gravy just like onion gravy, No. 22. After the gravy has been strained, put in the pearl onions, cook for 1 minute and stir in the yolks of eggs, but do not cook any longer.

No. 24—PICKLE GRAVY.

Quantity for 6 Persons.

1 piece of butter
2 tbsps. of sliced onion
1½ tbsps. of flour
¾ pt. of bouillon

¼ tsp. of meat extract
Salt, pepper
½ tbsp. of vinegar
1 tsp. of sugar

2 small chopped pickles

Preparation: Brown the butter, stir in the onion and flour, cook a minute, and add the bouillon. Add the meat extract and cook 15 minutes, then strain and season with salt, pepper, vinegar, sugar. Put in the finely chopped pickles and set to simmer. You can improve this gravy with pieces of cauliflower and small pearl onions. Serve with mutton roast or lamb.

No. 25—BURGUNDY OR MADEIRA SAUCE.

For Ham, Fish or Tongue.

Quantity for 6 Persons.

1/10 lb. of butter
2 tbsps. of flour
¾ pt. of bouillon
1 cup of Burgundy, red wine or Madeira
Salt

1 clove
1 bay-leaf
1 lemon slice
1 tbsp. lemon juice
1 tsp. sugar
½ tsp. meat extract

6 pepper-corns

Preparation: Brown the butter and flour, add the bouillon and all the other ingredients.

Cook this gravy for 1 hour slowly, stirring frequently, then strain through a fine sieve, add a few tablespoonfuls of wine, season and serve hot. It must be a nice brown color and smooth.

No. 26—BACON GRAVY.
Quantity for 6 Persons.

⅛ lb. of bacon
2 tbsps. of flour
¾ pt. bouillon
¼ onion
Salt
6 pepper-corns
1 clove
1 bay-leaf
2 tbsps. of vinegar
Sugar

Preparation: Cut the bacon into small cubes and fry to a nice yellow color, add the finely sliced onion and fry a little while, add the flour and bouillon and season with salt, pepper, cloves, bay-leaf, vinegar and sugar. Cook for 15 minutes and serve with potatoes in their jackets.

No. 27—HERB GRAVY.
Quantity for 6 Persons.

3 tbsps. of minced herbs
1 tbsp. of minced parsley
1 tsp. of minced onions
1 spray of thyme
6 pepper-corns
2 tbsps. of flour
1¼ pts. of bouillon
½ tsp. meat extract
1 tsp. lemon juice
Salt to taste
2 tbsps. of butter

Preparation: Parsley, onion, thyme, pepper-corns are fried in butter, the flour stirred in and browned; add the bouillon and meat extract and boil down to ½ the quantity, strain through a fine sieve, heat again and put in the herbs. Season with lemon juice and salt and stir in a small piece of butter.

No. 28—BROWN CHAMPIGNON SAUCE.
Quantity for 6 Persons.

1/12 lb. of butter
2 tbsps. of flour
1 tsp. of sliced onion
1 pt. of bouillon
1 tsp. of meat extract
½ cup champignon liquor
¼ cup of red wine or
4 tbsps. of Madeira
1 tbsp. lemon juice
Salt to taste
1 pinch of sugar
½ pt. of champignons

Preparation: Brown the butter, stir in flour and onion and cook 1 minute, add the bouillon and champignon liquor, season with meat extract, red wine or Madeira, lemon juice and cook for ½ hour. Strain the gravy, add the champignons, which may be quartered if they are too large, set aside to simmer gently. Now flavor with salt, sugar and lemon juice.

No. 29—TRUFFLE SAUCE.
Quantity for 6 Persons.

1/12 lb. of butter	2 cloves
3 tbsps. of flour	1 bay-leaf
1 tsp. of chopped onion	1 pinch of sugar
1 pt. bouillon or beef gravy	Salt to taste
1 cup red wine	1 small can of truffles
½ cup Madeira	½ tsp. meat extract
6 pepper-corns	

Preparation: Butter and onion are browned, flour stirred in and bouillon added, together with red wine, Madeira, pepper, meat extract, cloves, bay-leaf and put in the peelings of truffles, cook slowly for 1 hour, strain through a fine sieve. Chop the peeled truffles and add them, season with salt and a little sugar.

No. 30—MOREL SAUCE.
Quantity for 6 Persons.

1 lb. of fresh morels or	1 pinch of pepper
½ can of morels	½ pt. morel liquor
1 pt. of bouillon	½ tsp. meat extract
2 tbsps. of butter	⅛ lb. raw, lean ham
2½ tbsps. of flour	1 tsp. minced parsley
1 tsp. onion	1 tsp. of butter
Salt	

Preparation: The fresh morels are cleaned, washed in lukewarm water and put on the fire with lukewarm water, stirring carefully while heating the water. Then they are poured into a colander. This process is repeated until there is no more sand on the morels. The last water is put aside. After a while pour it off carefully from the settlings and boil down to ½ pt. The ham and onion are cut into small dice, fried brown in 2 tablespoonfuls of butter, the flour stirred in and browned 1 minute, then add the bouillon and morel liquor and cook slowly for 45 minutes. Add the meat extract, pepper, salt and strain it. Cut up the morels, put them into the gravy, let it come to boil again, add parsley and serve very hot.

No. 31—PARSLEY GRAVY.
Quantity for 6 Persons.

1/12 lb. of butter	1 tbsp. of lemon juice
1 tbsp. chopped onion	1 pinch of pepper
2½ tbsps. of flour	Salt
1 pt. bouillon	4 tbsps. of finely chopped parsley

Preparation: The finely chopped onions and flour are browned in butter, bouillon added and cooked 10 minutes, stirring constantly. Season with salt, pepper and lemon juice, add the chopped parsley, but do not cook any longer.

Remarks: ¼ cup of sweet cream will improve the gravy.

No. 32—DILL, CHIVE OR TARRAGON GRAVY.

These gravies are prepared like the parsley gravy, the ingredients are the same also, but instead of parsley take dill for dill gravy, chives for chive gravy, and tarragon for tarragon gravy. These gravies are good with fish, chicken, beef and asparagus.

No. 33—SORREL GRAVY.
Quantity for 6 Persons.

1/12 lb. of butter	2 yolks of eggs
2½ tbsps. of flour	½ tsp. of sugar
1 pt. bouillon	1 pinch of pepper
½ cupful of sweet cream	Salt to taste
	½ cup of sorrel puree

Preparation: Melt the butter, stir in the flour, gradually add the bouillon and cream, stirring constantly, cook a few minutes and add the sorrel. Strain and season with salt, pepper and sugar. Stir in the yolks of eggs and serve very hot.

Remarks: The sorrel is cleaned and treated like spinage and boiled the same way, then rubbed through a sieve.

Cold Dressings.
No. 34—OIL DRESSING A LA TARTARE.

For Hard Boiled Eggs, Cold Beef and Head-Cheese.
Quantity for 6 Persons.

¼ cup of fine salad oil	1½ tbsps. of minced herbs or minced mixed pickles
1 tbsp. finely sliced onion	1 pinch of pepper
2 tbsps. of flour	Salt to taste
½ pt. of bouillon	
	Juice of ½ lemon

Preparation: Oil, onion and flour are fried light brown, bouillon and lemon juice added, cook a little while. then strain and stir until cold. Add the herbs or pickles and season with salt, pepper and more lemon juice, if necessary. If the gravy is too thick, when cold, add more bouillon.

No. 35—COLD MUSTARD DRESSING.

For Cold Lamb or Veal Roast.

Quantity for 6 Persons.

2 hard boiled yolks of eggs
1 raw yolk of egg
½ cup of fine salad oil
Juice of ½ lemon
1 pinch of pepper
Sugar
1 tbsp. of cream
1 tbsp. of mustard
Salt to taste

Preparation: Hard boiled and raw yolks of eggs are well stirred together, the oil added in drops, season with mustard, lemon juice, salt, pepper and sugar. If the dressing is too thick, thin it with 1 tablespoonful of cream. This dressing is very good with cold roast.

No. 36—TARTARE DRESSING.

Quantity for 6 Persons.

3 tbsps. of oil
2 tbsps. of flour
1 tbsp. of finely chopped onions
¾ pt. strong bouillon
1 tsp. mustard
Salt to taste
1 pinch of pepper
2 yolks of eggs
2 tbsps. of chopped mixed pickles
1 tbsp. of chopped capers
3 tbsps. lemon juice or vinegar

Preparation: Oil, onion, flour are fried light brown, bouillon added, seasoned with mustard, lemon juice, salt and pepper and cooked slowly for 15 minutes, then strained through a fine sieve. Stir until cold, then stir in the 2 yolks of eggs and the pickles and capers. Taste it again. It should be quite thick.

No. 37—COLD HERB DRESSING.

Quantity for 6 Persons.

2 hard boiled eggs
1 raw yolk of egg
½ cup of fine salad oil
1½ tbsps. of minced herbs
1 mustardspoonful of mustard
1 tsp. of lemon juice or vinegar
Salt to taste
1 pinch of pepper

Preparation: The 2 hard boiled and 1 raw yolk of eggs are thoroughly beaten together, the oil added a few drops at a time, the herbs and mustard put in and then seasoned with salt and pepper and the finely chopped white of egg put in also.

No. 38—COLD REMOULADE DRESSING.
Very fine.
Quantity for 6 Persons.

3 hard boiled yolks of egg
2 raw yolks
¾ cup of fine salad oil
¼ cup thick sour cream
3 tbsps. lemon juice or vinegar
1 tbsp. chopped capers
¼ tbsp. chopped sardines
¼ tbsp. mustard
1 pinch of salt
Pepper

Preparation: The two kinds of yolks of eggs are mixed well, the oil added a few drops at a time, cream and lemon juice slowly stirred in, then capers, sardines and mustard are added. Season with salt and pepper and keep cold.

No. 39—COLD CHIVE DRESSING.
For Beef.
Quantity for 6 Persons.

½ cup of cream or milk
1/6 cup of vinegar
1 pinch of pepper and sugar
¼ cup of finely chopped chives
Salt to taste

Preparation: Cream, vinegar and chives are stirred together, then seasoned with salt, pepper and sugar.

No. 40—COLD CAVIAR DRESSING.
Quantity for 6 Persons.

⅛ lb. of caviar
3 yolks of eggs
½ cup of cream
2 tbsps. of vinegar
1 pinch of pepper and sugar
Salt to taste

Preparation: Put the 3 yolks of eggs and cream into a double boiler and cook until it thickens, stirring constantly, add the vinegar and stir until cold, then season with pepper, sugar and salt.

Put the caviar into a sieve, and let cold water run over it until it becomes granular, then stir into the dressing. This dressing is good with blue fish.

No. 41—MAYONNAISE DRESSING No. 1. (COLD).
Quantity for 6 Persons.

6 yolks of eggs
½ pt. olive oil
Juice of ¼ lemon
1/10 tsp. of mustard
¼ tsp. of sugar
Salt to taste
1 pinch of white pepper

Preparation: The 6 yolks of eggs are stirred with the oil, then seasoned with lemon juice, pepper, mustard, sugar and salt.

Remarks: Mayonnaise dressing is good with salmon.

No. 42—MAYONNAISE DRESSING No. 2.
Quantity for 6 Persons.

- 4 yolks of eggs
- 1/3 pt. fine salad oil
- 3 tbsps. of bouillon
- 2 tbsps. of vinegar
- ¼ tsp. of mustard
- ¼ tsp. of grated onion
- 1 pinch of pepper
- Salt to taste

Preparation: The yolks of eggs are stirred adding the oil and vinegar a few drops at a time, season with onion, pepper and salt and add sufficient bouillon to give it the required thickness.

No. 43—COOKED MAYONNAISE DRESSING.
Very Good With Lobster or Chicken Salad.
Quantity for 6 Persons.

- 4 yolks of eggs
- ¾ cup of sour cream
- 2 tbsps. of vinegar
- ¼ tsp. ground mustard
- 1 pinch of white pepper
- 1 pinch of salt
- 1 pinch of sugar
- ½ pt. of thick, sour whipped cream

Preparation: Yolks of eggs, cream, vinegar, mustard, pepper, salt and sguar are mixed well and cooked in a double boiler, stirring constantly until it thickens. When the gravy is cold, add sour whipped cream.

Remarks: You may peel a dill pickle, chop it very fine and add to the dressing

No. 44—MAYONNAISE DRESSING No. 3.
Very Good With Poultry Salad.
Quantity for 6 Persons.

- 4 yolks of eggs
- 1 tsp. of flour
- 1 cup of sweet cream
- ¼ cup of good poultry broth
- 1 pinch of white pepper
- Salt
- ¼ tsp. of grated onion
- 2 tbsps. of fine oil
- 2 tbsps. of vinegar

Preparation: Yolks of eggs, cream, broth and vinegar are mixed well and boiled in double boiler as before mentioned in No. 43, then seasoned with salt, pepper and onion. Stir the dressing until cold, then add 2 tablespoonfuls of oil a few drops at a time.

Sweet Sauces or Dressings.
Sauces for Puddings and Pastries.

No. 45—WHITE WINE SAUCE.
Quantity for 6 Persons.

- 2 eggs
- 1 tsp. of flour
- 2 slices of lemon
- 2 tbsps. of sugar
- 1 tumblerful of white wine

Preparation: The 2 whole eggs, flour, wine, sugar are

mixed well on the stove and stirred until it becomes foamy and begins to thicken, but must not cook. Then add the lemon slices.

Remarks: This sauce may be served cold or warm.

No. 46—ARRACK SAUCE.
Quantity for 6 Persons.

¼ cup of arrack or brandy 2 tbsps. of lemon juice
1 pt. of water 1 slice of lemon
3 yolks of eggs 1½ tbsps. of flour
⅛ lb. of sugar

Preparation: All ingredients except the arrack or brandy are mixed well and treated the same as mentioned under No. 45. The arrack or brandy is stirred in last. This sauce may be served cold or warm.

No. 47—VANILLA SAUCE.
Quantity for 6 Persons.

1 pt. of milk 4 yolks of eggs
½ vanilla bean or 1 tsp. of flour
1 tbsp. vanilla extract ¼ cup of sugar

Preparation: The vanilla bean is left to soak in milk for 1 hour, then the sugar is added. The milk is brought to boil, the yolks of eggs and flour are mixed with a little cold milk, slowly stirred into the boiling milk and cooked for one minute. If you wish to use this sauce cold, it must be stirred several times while getting cold so it will not form a skin.

Remarks: The sauce must be stirred well while boiling.

When it is used cold you may add ½ cup of whipped cream or the white of egg beaten to a froth.

No. 48—COCOA SAUCE.
Quantity for 6 Persons.

1 pt. milk 3 tbsps. of cocoa
½ tsp. of vanilla extract ¼ cup of sugar
4 yolks of eggs

Preparation: Stir the cocoa with the yolks of eggs and a little cold milk and prepare the sauce like vanilla sauce given under No. 47.

No. 49—CHOCOLATE SAUCE.
Quantity for 6 Persons.

The preparation is the same as given under No. 47 and No. 48, but instead of cocoa, ¼ lb. of chocolate is grated and stirred into the yolks of eggs and milk and less sugar is needed.

No. 50—LEMON SAUCE.
Quantity for 6 Persons.

1 pt. of milk
1/3 lemon peel
1 tsp. of flour
¼ cup of sugar
4 yolks of eggs

The preparation is the same as given under No. 47, but instead of vanilla use lemon peel.

No. 51—MARASCHINO SAUCE.
Quantity for 6 Persons.

4 tbsps. of maraschino
1 pt. of milk
1 tsp. of flour
¼ cup of sugar
4 yolks of eggs

The preparation is the same as given under No. 47, but instead of vanilla, use 4 tablespoonfuls maraschino.

No. 52—CHERRY SAUCE.
Quantity for 6 Persons.

1 lb. sour cherries
¾ qt. of water
Sugar to taste
1 small piece of cinnamon
1½ tbsps. of corn starch

Preparation: The cherries are stoned and boiled in the water for 1 hour, then rubbed through a fine sieve. The corn starch is dissolved in a little water, then stirred into the boiling cherry sauce mixed with sugar and cooked 5 minutes, stirring constantly. The sauce is served cold.

No. 53—PRUNE SAUCE.

Preparation and ingredients are the same as given under No. 52. Instead of cherries use 1 lb. of fresh or dried prunes.

No. 54—APRICOT SAUCE.

Preparation and ingredients are the same as given under No. 52. Instead of cherries use 1 lb. of fresh or dried apricots.

No. 55—STRAWBERRY SAUCE.
Quantity for 6 Persons.

1 pt. strawberry juice
⅛ lb. of sugar
1 stick of cinnamon
1½ tbsps. of corn starch
1 tsp. of vanilla or lemon extract

Preparation: The corn starch is mixed with some juice. The remaining juice is mixed with sugar and spices and put over the fire until it boils, then the dissolved corn starch added and boiled 5 minutes, stirring constantly. The sauce is served cold or warm.

Remarks: When the juice from preserved fruit is used, less sugar is needed.

No. 56—RASPBERRY SAUCE.

Preparation and ingredients are the same as given under No. 55; instead of 1 pt. of strawberry juice, use 1 pt. of raspberry juice.

No. 57—CHERRY, CURRANT, BLUEBERRY SAUCE.

Preparation and ingredients are the same as given under No. 55 but instead of strawberry juice, use either cherry, currant or blueberry juice.

No. 58—FRUIT PUREE SAUCE.
Quantity for 6 Persons.

Sauce made from prunes or fresh plums, cherries, strawberries, raspberries, gooseberries, currants, grapes, apples or apricots.

½ lb. of fruit puree ¾ qt. of water
Sugar to taste 1½ tbsps. of corn starch
1 small piece of cinnamon ½ cup of white wine
¾ lemon

Preparation: The fruit puree is made very savory with sugar and spices. The corn starch is mixed with a little water and stirred into it, also the rest of the water, then the whole is cooked and rubbed through a fine sieve. If the sauce should be too thin, use more corn starch. The wine may be omitted.

CHAPTER 11.

POTATOES.

The various recipes for the preparation of potatoes.

The potato is a very useful food and may be prepared in many ways. Salt is necessary to make the potato savory. It must be boiled well done and quickly. It may be peeled long before using, but should be kept covered with water after it is peeled, otherwise it will turn brown. Potatoes lose their good flavor if they are kept in a moist cellar where they will grow poisonous sprouts. They sprout also in the spring; the sprouts should be immediately removed.

No. 1—POTATOES IN THEIR SKINS OR JACKETS.
Quantity for 6 Persons.
2 lbs. of medium sized potatoes   Water sufficient to cover them
3 tbsps. of salt

Preparation: The potatoes must be of equal size. They are cleaned in cold water and put to boil in cold water in a covered kettle. When done, drain off the water, shake them a little and set them aside to dry and their jackets will burst.

No. 2—NEW POTATOES IN THEIR JACKETS.
Quantity for 6 Persons.
2 lbs. of potatoes   3 tbsps. of salt
Water sufficient to cover them   1 tsp. of caraway seeds if desired

Preparation: The potatoes are cleaned in cold water and with a kitchen knife, a small piece of peeling is cut off. Put on the fire with cold water and caraway. When done, pour off the water, leave the dish covered, shake it and set it aside to dry, and their jackets will burst.

Remarks: The potatoes must be kept constantly boiling.

No. 3—BAKED POTATOES.
Quantity for 6 Persons.
2 lbs. of potatoes

Preparation: The potatoes should be of even size. They are cleaned in cold water, the point of each is cut off and they are baked in the oven for 1 good hour. The oven must be very hot. Serve in their jackets.

No. 4—PEELED POTATOES.
Quantity for 6 Persons.

2½ lbs. of raw potatoes   Water sufficient to cover them
1½ tbsps. of salt

Preparation: The potatoes are cleaned in cold water and peeled. The very large ones are quartered, the medium-sized ones are cut into halves and the small ones rounded, with the eyes well pierced out. Put into clear water at once after peeling. Then put them over the fire with cold water and salt, boil quickly, drain well and set them aside to dry a little.

No. 5—SMALL POTATO BALLS.
To Be Served With Fish.
Quantity for 6 Persons.

5—6 lbs. of large potatoes   Water sufficient to cover them
1 tbsp. of salt

Preparation: The potatoes are cleaned in cold water, peeled, and with a vegetable scoop cut out round balls. They are then put over the fire in a kettle with water and salt and boiled until done which requires about 15 to 20 minutes. Drain the water off at once and set aside to dry.

Remarks: You may steam these potatoes, which requires ½ hour. They are very nice when steamed.

No. 6—UTILIZING THE REMNANTS OF POTATO BALLS, MASHED POTATOES.

The remnants from potato balls   1½ tbsps. of salt
Water sufficient to cover them   2 tbsps. of butter

Preparation: The potato remnants are boiled until tender in salt water, which is then drained off and the potatoes pressed through a potato masher. The butter is added, the pot with these potatoes placed into hot water and beaten until well mashed, seasoned with salt, then served in a hot dish.

Remarks: The remnants may also be used for potato soup or dumplings.

The whites of 5 eggs, well beaten, may be stirred into the above and then baked in a buttered pan in the oven.

No. 7—PARSLEY POTATOES.
Quantity for 6 Persons.

5—6 lbs. of large potatoes   1 tbsp. of finely chopped parsley
1 tbsp. of salt   2 tbsps. of fresh butter
Water sufficient to cover them

Preparation: The potatoes are peeled, scooped out and cooked as given under No. 5. When they are done, stir in the butter mixed with parsley and cover a few minutes.

No. 8—FRENCH FRIED POTATOES, POMME SOUFFLE.

Quantity for 6 Persons.
1½ lbs. of raw potatoes   1 tsp. fine salt
1½ lbs. clear lard

Preparation: The potatoes are peeled and cut into thin oblong or round slices as thick as the back of a knife or cut out in small balls. The lard is heated until it smokes, but must not boil.

The potatoes are dried with a clean cloth and fried to a golden yellow color in the lard, then they are placed into a colander to drain, sprinkled with salt, shaken a little and served very hot.

No. 9—POTATO CHIPS.

Quantity for 6 Persons.

The ingredients are the same as given under No. 8, French Fried Potatoes.

Preparation: The potatoes are cleaned, peeled and sliced so thin that you can see the knife through them. The lard is heated until it smokes, a handful of potato slices at a time are dried and fried golden yellow in the hot lard, then taken out with a skimmer and placed on paper to drain. Salt and serve very hot. They must never be covered, neither while cooking nor afterwards.

No. 10—STUFFED POTATOES.

Quantity for 6 Persons.

12 large potatoes	¼ tsp. of grated onion
1/10 lb. of butter	1 pinch of pepper
2 yolks of eggs	Salt to taste
½ tbsp. of Parmesan cheese	Some butter for frying
1 tsp. of finely chopped parsley	

Preparation: The potatoes are washed well and cooked in their jackets, removed from the fire when barely done, strained, peeled, then carefully cut into halves and scooped out. The pieces which have been removed, are pressed through a potato masher and mixed with butter, Parmesan cheese, onion, parsley and yolk of egg. Season with salt and pepper and put back into the scooped out potato halves, smooth off on top, sprinkle with salt and fry in butter to a golden yellow color.

Remarks: They are very fine to serve with cold meats or to garnish hot meat platters.

No. 11—POTATO CROQUETTES.
Quantity for 6 Persons.

1 lb. of potatoes	Salt to taste
⅛ lb. of butter	⅛ lb. finely grated bread
3 yolks of eggs	Butter or lard for frying
1 pinch of pepper	

Preparation: The potatoes are washed, cooked, peeled, grated and pressed through a potato masher. The butter is creamed with the yolks of eggs and grated potatoes stirred in and seasoned with salt and pepper. Small croquettes are formed, rolled in bread crumbs and fried in butter or lard to a nice color. Serve hot.

No. 12—POTATO BALLS, FRIED.
Quantity for 6 Persons.

1 lb. of potatoes	1 pinch of pepper
⅛ lb. of butter	Salt to taste
4 yolks of eggs	½ cup of flour
1 tbsp. of Parmesan cheese	1 cup of roll crumbs
1 pinch of nutmeg	Lard for frying

Preparation: The potatoes are boiled, peeled, grated or mashed. Cream the butter, stir in the yolks of eggs, Parmesan cheese, nutmeg, pepper and salt, the mashed potatoes and flour. Balls, walnut size, are formed from this mass, rolled in roll crumbs and fried in hot lard to a nice golden yellow color. The lard should be deep enough for the balls to float. Drain in a colander or on paper.

Remarks: These potato balls are nice to garnish meat platters.

No. 13—SOUR POTATOES.
Quantity for 6 Persons.

1 lb. of potatoes	1 pt. good beef bouillon
¼ lb. of butter or good drippings	1 pinch of pepper
	2 tbsps. of vinegar or to taste
1 tsp. of chopped onions	Salt to taste
3 tbsps. of flour	

Preparation: The potatoes are cooked, peeled and sliced. While they are boiling, the dressing is prepared. Brown the butter or lard with the onions, stir in the flour, stew a little while, add the bouillon and season to taste with vinegar, salt and pepper and cook a few minutes. Put in the boiled sliced potatoes, cook a few minutes and serve.

No. 14—CREAMED POTATOES.
Quantity for 6 Persons.

1 lb. of potatoes
⅛ lb. of butter
2 tbsps. of flour
¾ pt. of milk or
½ pt. of milk and
¼ pt. of sweet cream
1 pinch of pepper
Salt

Preparation: The potatoes are cooked in the jackets, then peeled and sliced or cut into small dice. Or bake the potatoes in the oven, peel them and cut into dice. Melt the butter, stir in the flour, cook 1 minute, add the milk and cream, cook a little while, season with salt and pepper, put in the potatoes, cook and serve. The dressing must neither be too thin nor too thick.

Remarks: Creamed potatoes are nice with soup meat, mutton chops or fried sausage.

No. 15—BAKED POTATO PUDDING.
Quantity for 6 Persons.

1½ lbs. of potatoes
Fully ⅛ lb. of butter
4—6 eggs
½ tbsp. of Parmesan cheese
1 pinch salt
Pepper
½ cupful of flour
Butter for the mold

Preparation: The potatoes are boiled, peeled and mashed. The butter is creamed with yolks of eggs, cheese, pepper and salt. Stir in the mashed potatoes, the flour and lastly the beaten white of egg. Butter the mold, put the mixture in and bake in medium hot oven for 45 minutes.

No. 16—STEAMED POTATO PUDDING.
Quantity for 6 Persons.

Preparation and ingredients are the same as given under No. 15. The prepared mixture is put into a mold that has been buttered and sprinkled with bread crumbs. Set in a steamer over a kettle of boiling water and boil for 1 hour. Then turn it out on a platter and serve.

Remarks: Caper sauce is good with potato pudding.

No. 17—POTATO PANCAKES.
Quantity for 6 Persons.

3 lbs. of raw potatoes
3—4 eggs
1¼ cupfuls of flour
1 pinch of pepper
½ tbsp. of salt
1 large sour apple, peeled and grated
½ tsp. of grated onion
Enough lard for baking

Preparation: The raw potatoes are peeled, washed and put into cold water. Take out of the water and grate quickly.

Drain off the water that collects on the grated potatoes, mix them with the yolks of eggs, flour, pepper, salt, apple, onion and lastly with the beaten whites of eggs. Heat the lard and bake 3 to 4 thin pancakes in the pan at once. They must be baked brown and crisp. The dish or plate on which they are served, should not be covered.

Remarks: Apple sauce is good with them.

No. 18—BOUILLON POTATOES.
Quantity for 6 Persons.

2½ lbs. of raw potatoes
1½ qts. of beef bouillon
1 medium sized onion
1 pinch of pepper
Salt to taste
1 piece of butter, half the size of an egg
3 tbsps. of finely chopped parsley

Preparation: The potatoes are peeled and cut into quarters or sixths, according to their size, then partly boiled in water. Drain off the water and pour on the boiling bouillon, season with salt, pepper and onion, do not cover them and cook slowly until the bouillon has been absorbed by the potatoes. Add the butter, cook a little longer, then add the parsley.

Remarks: With new potatoes you need only 1 qt. of bouillon, because they are not so mealy.

No. 19—SARDINE OR HERRING POTATOES.
Quantity for 6 Persons.

3 lbs. of boiled potatoes
Scant ½ lb. of sardines or
2 herrings

For the Gravy.

⅛ lb. of raw ham
⅛ lb. of butter
2 sliced onions
⅛ lb. of flour
¾ qt. of beef bouillon
1 pinch of pepper
Very little salt
1 tbsp. Parmesan cheese
¾ qt. of sweet cream or milk

Preparation: The boiled potatoes are peeled and sliced, sardines or herring are soaked in water and cut in small pieces. The ham, which may be remnants, is also cut and fried in ⅛ lb. of butter and the sliced onion. The butter must not get brown; stir in the flour and after cooking a little, add the bouillon and cream, season with salt and pepper if necessary. Cook this dressing slowly for ½ hour, then rub through a sieve. Fill a buttered baking-dish or casserole with layers of sliced potatoes and herring or sardines alternately, pour the dressing over, strew with cheese and drip on a little butter, then bake in oven 20 minutes, being careful that the dressing does not boil, as that will make it thin. It is best to put the dish into another dish with water before baking. Bake until a golden yellow.

Remarks: This may also be prepared without sardines or herring.

No. 20—POTATOES WITH CRACKERS.
Quantity for 6 Persons.

2 lbs. of raw potatoes	1 pinch of pepper
¼ lb. of salt crackers	Salt
1 qt. of sweet cream or milk	¼ lb. of butter

Preparation: The raw potatoes are peeled, sliced thin, and the crackers rolled. Butter a baking-dish or casserole, fill with layers of potatoes and crackers alternately, with small pieces of butter, salt and pepper between each, repeating until all has been used. Then pour the cream or milk over, put a few pieces of butter on top and bake 1½ hours.

Remarks: This dish is good with cold meats.

No. 21—FRIED RAW POTATOES.
Quantity for 6 Persons.

2½ lbs. raw potatoes	1 small, chopped onion
⅛ lb. of butter or good drippings	¼ pt. of water
	Salt to taste

Preparation: The raw potatoes are peeled, sliced very thin and washed well. Butter or drippings are put into a pan, add the sliced potatoes, onion, salt and pepper. Cover and fry slowly, gradually adding the water. In ½ hour the potatoes are done and of a golden yellow color.

No. 22—SWEET POTATOES.
Quantity for 6 Persons.

3 lbs. of sweet potatoes

Preparation: The potatoes are washed well and baked in their skins in the oven for ¾ to 1 hour. Fresh butter is served with them.

No. 23—POTATO DUMPLINGS FROM BOILED POTATOES.
Quantity for 6 Persons.

3½ lbs. of boiled potatoes	½ tsp. of onion
1½ cups of roll crumbs	1 pinch of pepper
½ roll cut into cubes	1 heaping tbsp. of salt
⅛ lb. of butter	½ cup of flour
3—4 eggs	Salt water

Preparation: The potatoes are boiled, peeled and grated when they are cooled off or mashed while still hot. When cold, the mashed potatoes are mixed well with roll crumbs, eggs, onion, pepper, salt, the 1/8 lb. of melted butter and the flour. The roll cubes are fried in butter crisp and yellow. These pieces are put in the middle of dumplings formed of the mashed potatoes, rolled in flour and cooked in salt water 15 to 20 minutes in an open kettle. The water must be boiling when the dumplings are put in.

Remarks: Try a dumpling; if it does not hold together, add more flour. The dumplings must be taken out of the water as soon as done. Serve hot.

No. 24—ANOTHER KIND OF POTATO DUMPLINGS.
Quantity for 6 Persons.

3½ lbs. of boiled potatoes	1 tbsp. of salt
1/12 lb. of butter	2 cups of flour
4—5 eggs	1 roll cut into cubes
1 pinch of nutmeg	Salt water for cooking

Preparation: The potatoes are boiled, peeled and grated. When they are cold, butter, eggs, nutmeg, salt and flour are stirred in. The roll cubes are fried in butter until crisp, then medium sized dumplings are formed from this mixture with the roll cubes in the center. Dip your hands into flour and make the dumplings round and firm, then roll them in flour and boil them in an open kettle 15 or 20 minutes. The salt water must boil briskly before the dumplings are put in.

Remarks: Try a dumpling first and if it does not hold together add more flour. Sour roast goes nicely with potato dumplings.

No. 25—RAW POTATO DUMPLINGS.
Quantity for 6 Persons.

5 lbs. of large potatoes	1 tbsp. of salt
1½ pts. of milk	1 roll cut into cubes
1/8 lb. of fine farina	Salt water for cooking
3 eggs	

Preparation: The raw potatoes are peeled, grated and pressed dry in a cloth. Bring the milk to boil, pour in the farina slowly and boil it 3 to 4 minutes, stirring constantly. Mix the grated potato with the boiling farina, yolks of eggs, salt and beaten whites of eggs. Fry the roll cubes in butter very crisp. Rinse your hands in cold water, make dumplings from the mixture with the roll cubes in the center. While the dumplings are being made the salt water is brought to boil and the dumplings are put in for 15 to 20 minutes. Do not cover the pot. The raw potato dumplings must be prepared quickly or they will turn black.

Remarks: They may be served with any kind of meat.

No. 26—UTILIZING REMNANTS OF POTATO DUMPLINGS.

The dumplings left over are sliced and fried in butter to a golden yellow color.

CHAPTER 12.

VEGETABLES.

The various preparations of vegetables.
Vegetables are known to be the best and most wholesome food.

Mushrooms, all kinds of cabbage, legumes are good for anemics. The legumes and cabbages must be washed well and scalded.

The Preservation of Vegetables During the Winter.

Cauliflower is cut off above the roots, the outer leaves removed, a string tied to the stem and hung up on the ceiling of the cellar. White and red cabbage and savoy cabbage are preserved in the same manner.

Kohlrabi, carrots, turnips, parsley roots, celery roots and shallots are kept in dry sand over winter.

Fresh parsley is kept in glass jars by putting in alternate layers of salt and parsley. Close the glass well each time after taking some out. Rinse the parsley before using.

No. 1—ASPARAGUS WITH BROWN BUTTER.
Quantity for 6 Persons.

3 lbs. of asparagus   1½ tbsps. of salt
3 qts. of water   ¼ lb. of fresh butter

Preparation: The asparagus stalks are washed and peeled thin at the top and thicker toward the end. If the ends are woody cut them off. Then tie the asparagus into small bundles and put them into salt water to boil until tender, about ½ hour. Place them on a platter with the heads all lying one way, lightly brown the butter and pour it over. Serve hot.

No. 2—ASPARAGUS WITH CREAMED BUTTER.
Quantity for 6 Persons.

3 lbs. of asparagus   1½ tbsps. of salt
3 qts. of water   ½ lb. fresh butter

Preparation: Preparation and cooking of this asparagus are the same as given under No. 1. Serve the asparagus on a platter covered with a napkin, then cream the butter and serve in a separate dish.

No. 3—ASPARAGUS WITH CREAM DRESSING.
Quantity for 6 Persons.

3 lbs. of asparagus   1½ tbsps. of salt
3 qts. of water

For the Dressing.

⅛ lb. of butter   4 tbsps. of sweet cream
1 even tbsp. of flour   ½ pt. asparagus liquor
4 yolks of eggs

Preparation: The asparagus are prepared and cooked as given under No. 1. When they are tender pile them on a platter keeping the heads all one way and prepare the dressing.

Melt the butter, stir in the flour, the yolks of eggs and the cream and gradually pour in the boiling asparagus liquor. Let it come to a boil, stirring constantly, pour over the asparagus and serve hot.

No. 4—CANNED ASPARAGUS.
Quantity for 6 Persons.

This asparagus is carefully heated and served with any kind of dressing prepared for it as given either under No. 1, No. 2 or No. 3.

No. 5—FRENCH ASPARAGUS WITH CREAM DRESSING.
Quantity for 6 Persons.

2 lbs. of fresh or   2 qts. of water
2 lb. can of asparagus   1 tbsp. of salt

For the Dressing.

⅛ lb. of butter   ¾ pt. of asparagus liquor
2 tbsps. of flour   2 yolks of eggs
½ cup of sweet or sour cream   3 tbsps. of lemon juice

Preparation: Thin stalks of asparagus may be used for this; they are peeled and cut into 2 inch lengths, then cooked in boiling salt water for 20 minutes. The water is poured off, the asparagus put into a dish and the gravy or dressing poured over. For the dressing melt the butter, stir in the flour and pour in gradually the boiling asparagus liquor, add sour or sweet cream, 3 teaspoonfuls of lemon juice, stirring constantly, boil 1 minute, then add the 2 yolks of eggs, but do not boil any more.

No. 6—PRESERVED ASPARAGUS WITH CREAM.
Quantity for 6 Persons.

Preparation and ingredients are the same as given under No. 5, French Asparagus with Cream Dressing.

No. 7—GREEN ASPARAGUS.
Quantity for 6 Persons.

4 lbs. of asparagus
3½ qts. of water
2 tbsps. of salt
¼ lb. of butter
3 slices of toasted wheat bread

Preparation: The green asparagus is washed, but not peeled, and cooked 20 minutes in boiling salt water. The slices of toast are placed on a platter and the asparagus, from which the water is drained in a colander, put on each slice of toast, heads all one way. The butter which has been heated to a golden color is poured on. Serve very hot.

No. 8—ASPARAGUS.
Quantity for 6 Persons.

2 lbs. of fresh or
2 lbs. of canned asparagus
2 qts. of water
1 tbsp. of salt
⅛ lb. of butter
½ pt. sweet or sour cream
½ pt. asparagus liquor
½ tbsp. of Parmesan cheese
2 tbsps. of grated rolls
1 tbsp. of butter
3 scant tbsps. of flour

Preparation: The fresh asparagus is peeled and cooked as given under No. 5.

For the dressing melt the butter, stir in the flour, add the cheese, the sweet or sour cream, and cook, stirring constantly. The dressing must be thick.

Drain the water off the asparagus, butter a baking dish, put in the asparagus and dressing, strew the roll crumbs over and drip the tablespoonful of butter on. Bake this by setting the baking-dish in a dish with hot water in the oven about 10 to 15 minutes.

Boiled ham or tongue is nice with this dish.

Remarks: It makes a fine side-dish.

No. 9—CAULIFLOWER.
Quantity for 6 Persons.

1 head of cauliflower, 2 lbs.
4 qts. of water
2 tbsps. of salt

For the Dressing.

⅛ lb. of fresh butter
2 tbsps. of flour
¾ pt. of cauliflower liquor
¼ pt. of sweet cream
2—3 yolks of eggs
A little nutmeg

Preparation: Pick off the outer leaves and put the head of cauliflower, the top downward, in cold water for 15 minutes to remove the insects that might be on it. The salt water is brought to boil and the cauliflower boiled in it a half hour.

For the dressing stew the butter and flour, add the cauliflower liquor and cream, and boil, stirring constantly. Add the yolks of eggs and do not boil any more.

The cauliflower is carefully placed on a platter or into a vegetable dish so it does not fall apart and the dressing is poured over, then the nutmeg is strewn over it.

No. 10—CAULIFLOWER WITH BUTTER SAUCE.

Quantity for 6 Persons.

1 head of cauliflower, 2 lbs.　　2 tbsps. of salt
4 qts. of water　　　　　　　　¼ lb. of butter

Preparation: The cauliflower is prepared and cooked the same as given under No. 9. It is carefully placed in a dish, and the hot browned butter poured over.

No. 11—CAULIFLOWER WITH CRAB OR LOBSTER DRESSING.

Quantity for 6 Persons.

1 head of cauliflower, 2 lbs.　　2 tbsps. of salt
4 qts. of water　　　　　　　　Crab dressing

Preparation: The preparation of cauliflower is the same as given under No. 9. Make a dressing as described under No. 19, in Gravies or Dressings and pour it over the head of cauliflower.

No. 12—SCALLOPED CAULIFLOWER AU GRATIN.

Quantity for 6 Persons.

1 head of cauliflower, 2 lbs.　　2 tbsps. of salt
4 qts. of water

For the Dressing.

⅛ lb. of butter　　　　　　　1 tbsp. of Parmesan cheese
2½ tbsps. of flour　　　　　　1 tbsp. of lemon juice
1 pt. sweet or sour cream　　2 tbsps. of fine roll crumbs
1 pinch of salt　　　　　　　1 tbsp. of butter

Preparation: The cauliflower is cleaned and put in water ¼ hour, then boiled in salt water ½ hour until almost tender, placed into a buttered dish until the dressing is made.

The butter is melted, flour stirred in, and cooled 1 minute. Add the sweet cream, boil, season with cheese, lemon juice and salt to taste. This dressing is poured over the cauliflower, roll crumbs strewn on and a little butter dripped over it; then baked in oven 20 to 30 minutes until it is a nice yellow color.

No. 13—ARTICHOKES WITH BUTTER.
Quantity for 6 Persons.

3 large or 6 small artichokes
4 qts. of water
3 tbsps. of salt
1 tbsp. of vinegar
¼ lb. of fresh butter

Preparation: With a sharp knife cut off the points of the artichokes about 1½ inches, then boil them tender in salt water and vinegar. Serve them on a dish, cream the butter and serve with the artichokes or brown it and pour it over.

No. 14—STEWED ARTICHOKES.
Quantity for 6 Persons.

3 large artichokes or 6 small ones
4 qts. of water
3 tbsps. of salt
2 tbsps. of vinegar
¼ lb. of butter
½ tbsps. of flour
½ pt. strong bouillon
1 tsp. of meat extract
½ wineglass Madeira or red wine
2 tbsps. of grated Parmesan cheese
4 tbsps. of champignons
Salt to taste
1 pinch of pepper

Preparation: The artichokes are cleaned and prepared as given under No. 13 and cooked partly done in salt water and vinegar. Then each one is cut into half and the inside white fibers removed carefully. These pieces are put into a pot, 3 tablespoonfuls of butter, chopped champignons, cheese and ½ pt. of bouillon added, the pot covered and the artichokes stewed 2 hours, turning them over several times. The stewed artichokes are put into a vegetable dish and the dressing prepared. Heat the rest of the butter with the flour, add the artichoke liquor, the rest of the bouillon, Madeira or red wine and the meat extract. Cook this well and season with pepper and salt, then pour over the artichokes.

No. 15—CANNED ARTICHOKES.
Quantity for 6 Persons.

2 lb. can artichokes
⅛ lb. butter
2½ tbsps. of flour
¼ pt. of bouillon
¼ pt. sweet cream
Juice of 1/ lemon
1 pinch of pepper
Salt to taste

Preparation: The canned artichokes are heated and the dressing is prepared. The butter is heated, the flour stirred in, cooked 2 minutes, the bouillon and cream added and cooked well. Season the dressing with salt, pepper and lemon juice.

Take the artichokes out of the liquor and put them into this dressing to simmer 10 minutes. If you like add 3 tablespoonfuls of white wine and chopped champignons or truffles.

No. 16—SCALLOPED ARTICHOKES WITH CHEESE
Quantity for 6 Persons.

3 large or 6 small artichokes	3 tbsps. of salt.
4 qts. of water	2 tbsps. of vinegar

For the Dish

¼ lb. of butter, good measure	¼ pt. of rich bouillon
¼ lb. of grated Parmesan cheese	1 pinch of pepper and salt

Preparation: The artichokes are prepared as given under No. 13. Cooked partly done with vinegar in the boiling salt water. From the pieces of cooked artichokes remove the white fibers. Place them into a buttered baking-dish or casserole, strewn with cheese and put on the ¼ lb. of butter in small pieces, season with pepper and salt, add the bouillon, cover the dish and bake them slowly in the oven 2 to 3 hours

No. 17—OYSTER PLANTS. SALISFY.
Quantity for 6 Persons.

2 lbs. of oyster plants	1½ tbsps. of salt
2 qts. of water	2 tbsps. of vinegar.

For the Dressing.

⅛ lb. of butter	1 pt. sweet cream
2 tbsps. of flour	¼ tsp. meat extract
½ pt. of bouillon, or	1 pinch of pepper and salt to taste.
¼ pt. of bouillon and	

Preparation: The oyster plants are scraped and at once placed into water mixed with flour or milk so that they keep their white color, then cut into 2 inch lengths and cooked until tender in boiling salt water with vinegar. While they are cooking, prepare the dressing. Melt the butter, stir in the flour, cook and add bouillon or half bouillon and half cream, add meat extract, cook and season with pepper and salt. Then drain the water from the oyster plants, put them into the dressing and set aside to simmer gently for 10 minutes.

No. 18—SCORZONERA.
Quantity for 6 Persons.

2 lbs. of scorzonera	1 tbsp. of salt
2 qts. of water	2 tbsps. of vinegar

For the Dressing.

⅛ lb. of butter	¼ pt. sweet cream or milk
2 tbsps. of flour	Juice of ½ lemon
¼ pt. of bouillon	2 yolks of eggs, if desired

Preparation: The vegetable is scraped, cut into 2 inch lengths and immediately put into water, mixed with flour or milk, then cooked until tender in salt water and vinegar. This will require ½ hour, during which time you prepare the dressing.

Melt the butter, stir in the flour, stew a few minutes, add the bouillon and cream or milk, boil again and season with lemon juice, pepper and salt. Drain the water from the vegetables, put them into the dressing and cook 10 minutes or set aside to simmer gently. When serving stir in the yolks of eggs.

Remarks: For scorzonera salad make a dressing of oil and vinegar mixed with mayonnaise.

No. 19—FRESH GREEN PEAS.
Quantity for 6 Persons.

1½ lbs. of fresh green peas	½ tsp. of meat extract
qts. of water	1 pinch of pepper
sp. of salt	Salt to taste
lb. of fresh butter	½ tbsp. of chopped parsley
tbsp. of flour	½ tsp. of sugar
¼ pt. of sweet cream	

Preparation: The fresh, green peas are taken out of the pods and boiled until tender in boiling salt water. This will require ½ hour; then drain the water off, add butter and flour, shake the pan, but do not stir it; add cream, meat extract, 1 pinch of pepper, sugar and salt to taste. Let it cook slowly and when you serve it put in the chopped parsley.

No. 20—ANOTHER WAY OF PREPARING PEAS.
Quantity for 6 Persons.

1½ lbs. of fresh, green peas, or 2 lb. can	1 pinch of pepper
2 qts. of water	Salt to taste
1 tbsp. of salt	½ tsp. of sugar
	1 tbsp. minced parsley
⅛ lb. fresh butter	

Preparation: The fresh green peas are prepared and cooked as directed under No. 19. When they are done drain them, put the drawn butter on, season with pepper, salt, sugar, shaking the pan, and sprinkle with minced parsley before serving. Canned peas are prepared the same way, but not cooked in salt water.

No. 21—FRESH GREEN PEAS WITH CRAB MEAT.
Quantity for 6 Persons.
1½ lbs. fresh green peas   25 crabs or crawfish

Preparation: The preparation and ingredients are the same as given under No. 20. When they are done shake them with the hot butter, add the crab meat, mix, drip the crab butter on.

Remarks: This is a very fine dish.

No. 22—PEA-OMELET.
Look for the preparation in chapter 15, Omelets.

No. 23—ASPARAGUS AND CAULIFLOWER OMELET.
Look for the preparation in chapter 15, Omelets.

No. 24—MARROW PEAS.
Quantity for 6 Persons.
2 lbs. of marrow peas   Salt to taste
1½ pts. of bouillon   ½ tsp. of sugar
1/10 lb. of butter   ½ tbsp. of flour
1 pinch of pepper   1 tbsp. of chopped parsley

Preparation: The marrow peas are strung like beans, washed and cooked until tender in bouillon and butter, then add the flour, stir and season with salt, pepper and sugar. Lastly add the parsley.

No. 25—YOUNG CARROTS.
Quantity for 6 Persons.
2½ lbs. of carrots   1 pinch of pepper
1 pt. bouillon   1 tsp. of sugar
1/10 lb. of butter   1 tbsp. of flour
Salt to taste   1 tbsp. of finely chopped parsley

Preparation: The carrots are scraped, cut into small pieces or sliced, then washed and cooked until tende in bouillon and butter. This will require from ½ to 1 hour. Season them with salt, pepper, sugar to taste, stir in the flour and let them cook a little while longer, lastly add the parsley. The carrots may be scooped out and the openings filled with boiled green peas, then stewed until soft.

No. 26—FRESH GREEN PEAS AND CARROTS.
Quantity for 6 Persons.
The peas are prepared as directed under No. 19, but take only 1 lb. of peas and ½ of all other ingredients. Take ½ of

the quantity of carrots also, and prepare according to directions in No. 25. When serving, place the carrots in the center of the dish and the peas around them.

No. 27—SPINAGE.
Quantity for 6 Persons.

1 peck of spinage
5 qts. of water
3 tbsps. of salt
⅛ lb. of butter
¼ pt. sweet cream
¼ pt. bouillon
1 pinch of pepper
Salt to taste
2 tbsps. of flour

Preparation: The spinage is picked over, the stems cut off and washed well. Cook it in boiling salt water for 15 minutes, drain the water off and chop the spinage or rub it through a colander.

Melt the butter, stir in the flour, cook and stir in the spinage, add sweet cream and bouillon, season with salt and pepper and cook a little longer, stirring constantly.

Remarks: The dish may be garnished with hard boiled eggs.

No. 28—SORREL.

Sorrel is prepared just like spinage, see No. 27, Spinage.

No. 29—LETTUCE.

Lettuce as a vegetable dish is prepared like spinage. See No. 27, Spinage.

No. 30—SPINAGE IN INDIVIDUAL MOLDS.
Quantity for 6 Persons.

1 peck of spinage
5 qts. of water
3 tbsps. salt
⅛ lb. of butter
1 pinch of pepper
Salt to taste
3 yolks of eggs
¼ pt. sweet cream
2 tbsps. of flour

Preparation: The spinage is picked over, the stems cut off, washed well, cooked in boiling salt water for 15 minutes, the water then drained off and the spinage rubbed through a sieve.

Melt the butter, stir in the flour, cook, add the spinage, season with salt, pepper, stir in the cream and yolks of eggs. Put in small buttered molds and set in a steamer over a kettle of boiling water and boil until the mixture stiffens, then turn them out on a platter and serve.

No. 31—SAVOY CABBAGE.
Quantity for 6 Persons.

2 heads of Savoy cabbage, 4-5 lbs.
6 qts. of water
4 tbsps. of salt
⅛ lb. of butter or half butter and half lard
½ tbsp. of flour
½ tbsp. finely chopped onion
¾ pt. bouillon
1 pinch of pepper
Salt to taste

Preparation: The head of cabbage is cut into half, remove the outer leaves and cut out the heart or core, then cut up the rest into several pieces, wash it and cook it 20 minutes in boiling salt water.

Butter and onions are stewed a little while, add the flour and stew a few minutes. Drain the water from the cabbage, chop it or rub it through a colander, then add it to the butter, onion and flour; add the bouillon, season with salt and pepper and cook slowly for 15 minutes.

No. 32—BRUSSELS SPROUTS.
Quantity for 6 Persons.

3 lbs. of Brussels sprouts
4 qts. of water
2 tbsps. of salt
⅛ lb. of butter
½ pt. of bouillon
¼ tsp. of meat extract to taste
1 pinch of pepper
Salt to taste
½ tbsp. of flour

Preparation: The sprouts are cleaned, the yellow leaves removed, then slowly boiled in salt water. Drain off the water. Melt the butter, stir in the flour, cook a little while, add the bouillon and meat extract and put in the Brussels sprouts. Season with salt and pepper and cook 20 minutes longer. The little sprouts must not fall apart.

Remarks: When served it may be garnished with a wreath of fried chestnuts.

No. 33—ANOTHER WAY OF PREPARING BRUSSELS SPROUTS.
Quantity for 6 Persons.

3 lbs. of Brussels sprouts
4 qts. of water
2 tbsps. of salt
½ cup of fine roll crumbs
¼ cup of strong bouillon
1 pinch of pepper
¼ lb. of butter

Preparation: The sprouts are prepared as before, (See No. 32.) After the water has been drained off, melt ⅛ lb. of butter, add the sprouts, pour in some bouillon, season with salt and pepper and serve. Fry the roll crumbs in the other ⅛ lb. of butter and put over the sprouts before serving.

No. 34—KALE OR BORECOLE.
Quantity for 6 Persons.

3—3½ lbs. of kale
6 qts. of water
3 tbsps. of salt
¼ lb. of butter or good drippings
1 tbsp. of flour
½ to 1 pt. strong bouillon
1 pinch of pepper
Salt to taste

Preparation: The ribs of the leaves are cut out, then the kale is washed carefully 4 to 5 times, to remove all sand. Cook in boiling salt water for ½ hour or until tender, then pour it into a colander to drain. Now chop it fine or rub it through the colander.

The butter or drippings are melted, the flour stirred in, stewed, the prepared kale added, and then the bouillon. Season with salt and pepper. Cook slowly 1 to 1½ hours and add ½ cup of sweet cream if you like.

No. 35—STEWED RED CABBAGE.
Quantity for 6 Persons.

1 head of red cabbage, 4 lbs.
⅛ lb. of butter or good drippings
½ glass red wine to taste
2 tbsps. of vinegar
1 tbsp. of sugar
2 peeled and sliced apples
2 cloves
1 pinch of pepper
Salt to taste
1 pt. water

Preparation: The bad leaves are cut off, the cabbage cut into half, the heart cut out and the cabbage sliced. Pour a pint of boiling water on, add butter or drippings, cook one hour, add all the other ingredients. Cook 1 to 2 hours longer, stirring occasionally. Ten minutes before serving it, add 1 tablespoonful flour and stew 10 minutes longer.

Remarks: Taste the cabbage so that it is neither too sweet nor too sour. You may use vinegar instead of wine.

No. 36—WHITE CABBAGE.
Quantity for 6 Persons.

White cabbage, 4 lbs.
5 qts. of water
⅛ lb. of good drippings
1 pt. bouillon
1 tbsp. of flour
¼ tbsp. caraway seeds
1 pinch of pepper
Salt to taste

Preparation: The bad leaves are removed, the head of cabbage cut in half, the heart cut out and the cabbage cut into 16 parts. It is cooked in boiling salt water for 15 minutes, drained, drippings and bouillon added and stewed for 1 hour. Add caraway seeds, flour, salt and pepper and stew a while longer.

No. 37—STEWED WHITE CABBAGE.

Quantity for 6 Persons.

4 lbs. of white cabbage	1 tbsp. of flour
5 qts. of water	1 pinch of pepper
1/8 lb. of drippings	Salt to taste
1 tbsp. of sugar	1 pt. of bouillon or water

3—5 tbsp. of vinegar

Preparation: The cabbage is prepared as directed under No. 36. The sliced cabbage is stewed for 15 minutes, the water drained off, bouillon or water and drippings added and stewed for one hour. Sugar, vinegar, flour, pepper, salt are added and the cabbage stewed another hour, stirring frequently.

No. 38—WHITE CABBAGE PREPARED LIKE CAULIFLOWER.

Quantity for 6 Persons.

4 lbs. of white cabbage	4 tbsp. of salt

6 qts. of water

For the Dressing.

1/8 lb of butter	1 pinch of pepper
2 1/2 tbsps. of flour	Salt to taste
1 pt. of milk	2 yolks of eggs

Preparation: The outer leaves are removed and the head of cabbage cooked until tender in 6 qts. of boiling salt water. The butter is melted, flour stirred in, milk added, cooked and seasoned with salt, pepper and if you like, stir in the yolks of eggs. Put the head of cabbage on a platter and pour the thick dressing over it, then serve at once.

No. 39—WHITE CABBAGE SAUSAGES.

Quantity for 6 Persons.

1 head of cabbage, 4 lbs.	1 tbsp. of butter
5 qts. of water	Salt to taste
3 tbsps. of salt	1/4 lb. of bacon, cut fine
1/4 lb. chopped pork	1 onion, cut fine
1/2 lb. of chopped beef	1/2 pt. gravy

1 pinch of pepper

Preparation: The bad leaves are removed and after cleaning the cabbage well, it is cooked partly done in boiling salt water. The outer leaves are then carefully cut off. The leavings of the cabbage are chopped fine, also the pork and beef and all this is mixed well, seasoned with butter, salt and pepper. Some of this mixture is put on each cabbage leaf and the leaf is rolled round it and tied with a clean string. The bacon is put into a pan and the cabbage sausages fried brown in it. The gravy is poured in and all is cooked a few minutes, then served on a platter.

No. 40—WHITE CABBAGE WITH LAMB.
Quantity for 6 Persons.

1 head of white cabbage, 5 lbs.
5 qts. water
2—3 lbs. of lamb
1 pinch of pepper
Salt to taste
1 qt. of water

Preparation: The bad leaves are trimmed off, the heart cut out, the cabbage cut up into 8 parts and cooked 15 minutes in boiling water, then the water is drained off. 1 to 2 qts. of water are poured on the cabbage, the meat is put in, season with salt and pepper and boil until tender. By the time the meat is done, the water ought to be boiled down so the vegetables are not too juicy.

No. 41—KOHLRABI.
Quantity for 6 Persons.

6—8 medium sized kohlrabis
3 qts. of water
1 tbsp. of salt
1/10 lb. of butter
1½ tbsps. of flour
½ pt. of bouillon
½ tsp. of meat extract
½ cup of sweet cream
1 pinch of salt
1 pinch of pepper

Preparation: The kohlrabis are peeled, sliced and cooked until tender in boiling salt water. Drain off the water. Melt the butter, add the flour and bouillon and cook. Put in the kohlrabis, season with salt and pepper, add the cream and stew slowly for 15 minutes.

No. 42—TURNIPS.
Quantity for 6 Persons.

6—8 medium sized turnips
4 qts. of water
2 tbsps. of salt
1/10 lb. of butter
½ tbsp. of flour
¼ pt. of bouillon
1 pinch of pepper
Salt to taste

Preparation: The turnips are peeled, sliced, cooked until tender in boiling salt water, which is drained off when done. Put the butter on the turnips, add the flour and bouillon, season with salt and pepper and stew 15 minutes more.

No. 43—TELTOW TURNIPS.
Quantity for 6 Persons.

2 lbs. of Teltow turnips
3 qts. of water
2 tbsps. of salt
⅛ lb. of butter
1 tbsp. of flour
1 pt. of bouillon
½ tsp. of meat extract
1½ tsps. of sugar
1 pinch of pepper
Salt to taste

Preparation: The vegetable is scraped, washed well in warm water, put into boiling salt water and boiled partly done, then drained. The turnips are stewed in butter to which the flour, sugar and bouillon are added, then the dish is covered and left to stew until tender. Season with salt and pepper. The vegetable must not be too juicy.

No. 44—STEWED GREEN STRING BEANS.
Quantity for 6 Persons.

2½ lbs. fresh, green beans
⅛ lb. of butter or good drippings
1½ pt. of bouillon
1 tbsp. of flour
1 tsp. of sugar
1 small piece of summer savory
1 tbsp. of chopped parsley
Salt and pepper
1—2 tbsps. of vinegar

Preparation: String the beans, slice them or break into 4 parts each, wash them, put over the fire with the butter or drippings, some bouillon and cook until tender, gradually adding more bouillon. ½ hour before well done, flour, vinegar, sugar are added, also salt and pepper. When they are cooked, add the parsley. If you like, you can put in a little summer savory.

No. 45—GREEN STRING BEANS, PREPARED ANOTHER WAY.
Quantity for 6 Persons.

2½ lbs. of fresh, green beans
3 qts. of water
⅛ lb. of butter
2 tbsps. of salt
2 tbsps. of flour
1 pt. of milk
¼ pt. sweet cream
Salt to taste
1 pinch of pepper
1 tbsp. of minced parsley

Preparation: The beans are prepared as given under No. 44, and boiled until tender in salt water, which is then drained off. The butter is melted, flour stirred in and the milk added. This dressing is cooked a few minutes, stirring constantly, and the beans put into it. Season with salt and pepper, stew 5 minutes and add the minced parsley.

Remarks: The dressing for the beans must not be too thick.

No. 46—SALTED GREEN BEANS.
Quantity for 6 Persons.

2½ lbs. of salted beans
3 qts. of water
⅛ lb. of butter
2 tbsps. of flour
1 pt. of milk
¼ pt. of cream
1 pinch of pepper
1 tbsp. of parsley

Preparation: Soak the beans in water for a few hours, drain and put over the fire in boiling water. Then boil until tender, drain and prepare the beans as given under No. 44 or No. 45.

Remarks: The salted beans need more time to cook than fresh beans and when seasoning, be careful not to add too much salt.

No. 47—CANNED GREEN BEANS.
Quantity for 6 Persons.

1 qt. can of green beans
1/10 lb. of butter
1½ tbsps. of flour
½ pt. of bouillon
1 pinch of pepper and one of salt
1 tsp. of finely chopped parsley

Preparation: The water is poured off the beans, butter is melted and the beans put into it and cooked slowly for 15 minutes. Flour is lightly stirred in, the bouillon poured in and the beans stewed in it a little while, then seasoned with salt, pepper and the parsley.

No. 48—CANNED WAX BEANS.
Quantity for 6 Persons.

1 qt. can of beans
1/10 lb. of butter
1½ tbsps. of flour
½ pt. of bouillon
½ tbsp. of sugar
Salt to taste
1 pinch of pepper
1 tsp. of chopped parsley
1 tbsp. of vinegar

Preparation: Pour off the water, melt the butter and put the beans in to steep a little while. Then stir in the flour, add the bouillon, season with vinegar, sugar, salt and pepper and stew 15 minutes, then add the parsley.

No. 49—FRESH WAX BEANS.
Quantity for 6 Persons.

2 qts. of fresh beans
3 qts. of water
2 tbsps. of salt
⅛ lb. of butter
2½ tbsps. of flour
¾ pt. of water
3 tbsps. of vinegar
Salt to taste
1 pinch of pepper
2 yolks of eggs

Preparation: The beans are strung and broken into 2 to 3 pieces, washed and cooked until tender in boiling salt water. The butter is melted, the flour and water added. Boil a few minutes, stirring constantly, and season with salt, pepper and vinegar. Put the beans into this gravy, stew them a little, then stir in the yolks of eggs, but do not boil any more.

No. 50—CANNED SWEET-SOUR BEANS.
Quantity for 6 Persons.

2 qts. fresh, yellow beans
3 qts. of water
2 tbsps. of salt
1 cup of water
½ cup of vinegar
½ cup of sugar
2 cloves
1 stick of cinnamon

Preparation: The beans are strung, broken into pieces

and cooked until tender in boiling salt water. One cup of water mixed with vinegar, sugar, cloves, cinnamon, boiled and poured over the beans, from which the salt water has been well drained. Serve cold.

No. 51—BEETS.
Quantity for 6 Persons.

3 lbs. of beets
4 qts. of water
1/10 lb. of butter
1 pt. of milk
Salt to taste
1 pinch of pepper
2 tbsps. of flour

Preparation: The beets are put over the fire in cold water and cooked until tender, then the water is drained off and the beets peeled and sliced. The butter is heated, the flour and the milk stirred in, then boiled, seasoned with salt and pepper, the beets put in and cooked a little while longer.

No. 52—YOUNG ONIONS.
Quantity for 6 Persons.

3 lbs. of onions
3 qts. of water
2 tbsps. of salt
1/8 lb. of butter
2 tbsps. of flour
1 pt. of milk
Salt to taste
1 pinch of pepper

Preparation: The onions are peeled and cooked until tender in boiling salt water, which is drained off when done. The butter is heated, the flour stirred in, stewed a little, milk added and cooked, stirring constantly. Lastly add the onions, season with salt and pepper, and simmer a few minutes.

No. 53—STUFFED ONIONS.
Quantity for 6 Persons.

6 large onions
2 qts. of water
2 tbsps. of salt
1/2 lb. of fine meat filling
2 tbsps. of chopped champignons
1 tsp. of chopped truffles
1 tbsp. of flour
3/4 pt. bouillon
1/2 tsp. of meat extract
Salt to taste
1 pinch of pepper
4 tbsps. of red wine
2 tbsps. of butter

Preparation: The onions are peeled, scooped out, put into boiling salt water for a few minutes and then taken out and dried. The meat stuffing is mixed well with champignons and truffles, then carefully put into the onions. The inside of the onions is stewed in butter, the flour stirred in and then the bouillon. Season with wine and meat extract and stew the stuffed onions in this gravy for 1 hour until they are brown.

Strain the gravy and add salt and pepper.

No. 54—TOMATOES.
Quantity for 6 Persons.

1 qt. of fresh or canned tomatoes   1/10 lb. of butter
2 cups of fine rolled crackers   1 pinch of salt and one of pepper

Preparation: The tomatoes are sliced and put into a buttered baking-dish in layers alternating with crackers, seasoned with butter, salt and pepper and baked in the oven 1/2 hour, then served in the dish.

No. 55—STUFFED TOMATOES.
Quantity for 6 Persons.

6 nice, red tomatoes   1 pinch of pepper
1 cup of grated rye bread   Salt to taste
1/10 lb. of butter   1/4 tsp. of grated onion
1 tbsp. of chopped parsley   2 yolks of eggs

Preparation: The tomatoes are wiped clean, a slice is cut off at the top, the pulp carefully taken out with a small spoon and rubbed through a fine sieve. Put the butter, grated bread and onions in a pan to cook, then add the tomato pulp, salt, pepper and parsley, stew it a little while, stir in the yolks of eggs and fill the tomatoes with this mass. Sprinkle with roll crumbs and butter, place these stuffed tomatoes in a buttered baking pan and bake them in the oven 1/2 hour.

No. 56—TOMATOES FILLED WITH MEAT.
Quantity for 6 Persons.

6 nice, red tomatoes   Salt to taste
1/2 lb. fine chopped veal or sweetbreads   1 pinch of pepper
   3 tbsps. of minced champignons
1 yolk of egg   3 tbsps. of butter
3 tbsps. of cream

Preparation: Prepare the tomatoes as given under No. 55. The butter is melted, the veal stewed in it, yolks of eggs, cream, champignons stirred in and seasoned with salt and pepper, 2 tablespoonfuls of tomato pulp added and the whole mixture cooked a few minutes. Now fill the tomatoes with this, sprinkle with roll crumbs and butter, then place in a buttered baking pan and bake in the oven 1/2 hour.

Remarks: You may omit the champignons. These tomatoes look very nice on the table and are served at parties.

No. 57—STUFFED CUCUMBERS.
Quantity for 6 Persons.

6 medium sized cucumbers   1 pinch of nutmeg
1 lb. finely chopped veal   1 1/2 tsps. finely chopped parsley
1/2 roll   1/10 lb. of butter
Salt to taste   2 eggs
1 pinch pepper

For Stewing.

⅛ lb. of butter   1 pt. bouillon or gravy

Preparation: The cucumbers are peeled and carefully scooped out. Mix the chopped veal with the soaked roll, stew it in the butter, add salt, pepper, nutmeg, eggs and parsley, cook 2 minutes and fill the cucumbers with this mixture. Melt the ⅛ lb. butter in a shallow pan, place the cucumbers in and gradually add the bouillon, and stew ½ hour. Place the cucumbers carefully on a platter and serve very hot.

No. 58—STEWED CUCUMBERS.
Quantity for 6 Persons.

4 large cucumbers	Salt to taste
1 tbsp. of salt	4 tbsp. of vinegar
6 tbsps. of sugar	¼ cup of sugar
4 tbsps. of wine vinegar	⅛ lb. of butter
1 pinch of pepper	1 small onion
1 qt. of bouillon	2 tbsps. of flour

1 tsp. of meat extract

Preparation: The cucumbers are peeled and cut in halves. The seeds are taken out and the cucumbers cut into equal parts, which are marinated for 1½ hours in 4 tablespoonfuls of vinegar, 1 tablespoonful of salt, 6 tablespoonfuls of sugar and a pinch of pepper.

The bouillon is cooked with meat extract, vinegar, sugar, salt and pepper and the cucumbers put in to cook until tender. Then the butter is melted, the sliced onion and flour browned in it, and the cucumber liquor added. The cucumbers are put in and slowly stewed ¼ hour until they are a shining brown color. Season the gravy to taste.

Remarks: Preserved cucumbers are at once placed in the gravy and stewed ¼ hour.

No. 59—STUFFED ROOT CELERY OR CELERIAC.
AU JUS.
Quantity for 6 Persons.

3 medium sized roots of celery	1 pt. of gravy
4 qts. of water	½ pt. of Madeira of red wine
3 tbsps. of salt	1 yolk of egg

½ lb. of savory veal stuffing

Preparation: The celery is cleaned well and peeled, then carefully scooped out and cooked in salt water for 20 minutes. Line with yolk of egg and stuff with meat stuffing. See preparation of Stuffed Veal, Chapter 3. The slice which had been cut from the top of the celery before this was scooped out, is tied on to the stuffed celery and this is put into a pot with the gravy, mixed with Madeira or red wine and stewed slowly 1½ hours until tender, turning several times. Cut each celery in half, pour dressing over and serve.

No. 60—"GARDI AND FINOCCI" AS VEGETABLES.

This is a southern species of thistle and is prepared like Stuffed Root Celery, No. 59. You can prepare this vegetable without stuffing, by cooking it tender in salt water, and stewing a few minutes in a savory wine dressing.

No. 61—MIXED OR LEIPZIG VEGETABLES.
Quantity for 6 Persons.

1 lb. of asparagus	4 qts. of water
1 small head of cauliflower	3 tbsps. of salt
30 small, young carrots	¼ lb. of butter
½ lb. of morels or fresh champignons	2 tbsps. of flour
	Salt to taste
12 crabs	1 pinch of pepper

Preparation: The asparagus is peeled and cut into 1½ inch pieces, cauliflower is cleaned and broken into small roses, morels or fresh champignons brushed well. If you use morels, put them over the fire in lukewarm water and let them get hot, stirring gently, then strain. Repeat this process until all sand is removed. Asparagus and cauliflower are cooked until tender in salt water. The carrots are scraped and stewed until tender in butter and ¼ pt. of bouillon. The crabs are washed, brushed and cooked in boiling salt water, then the meat is picked out, the coral broken fine and stewed in 2 tablespoonfuls of butter and 1 pt. of vegetable liquor from cauliflower and asparagus. The flour is mixed with a little water and stirred in and all this is cooked ½ hour, then seasoned with salt and pepper and strained. The crab sauce is added to the carrots, the asparagus, cauliflower, morels and crab meat added, heat it over the fire, put into a dish with a little butter over top and serve very hot.

Remarks: This is a very fine dish and it may be prepared from canned vegetables.

No. 62—CHAMPIGNONS.
Quantity for 6 Persons.

2 lbs. of fresh champignons	½ pt. of cream
⅛ lb. of good butter	¼ pt. champignon liquor
Salt to taste	2 tbsps. lemon juice
1 tbsp. flour	1 pinch of pepper

Preparation: The fresh champignons must be hard and white. Remove the brown skin, trim off the roots and wash them. The butter is heated and the champignons put in, season with salt and pepper and gradually pour on ¼ cup of water, stew until tender. Stir the flour with the cream, add to the mushrooms and stew a few minutes.

Remarks: If you take canned champignons, take ¼ pt. of cream and ¼ pt. of champignon liquor.

No. 63—CHAMPIGNON PUREE.

The preparation is the same as given under No. 62. The champignons are chopped fine and while preparing them, add ½ teaspoonful of meat extract.

Remarks: May be served on toasted bread.

No. 64—TRUFFLES IN BROWN DRESSING.
Quantity for 6 Persons.

½ lb. of fresh truffles
⅛ lb. of butter
1½ tbsps. of flour
1 pt. of strong bouillon
1 tsp. of meat extract
1 wineglassful of Madeira or red wine
Salt to taste
1 pinch of pepper
½ tsp. lemon juice

Preparation: The truffles are put into cold water so the dirt will dissolve, then brushed in lukewarm water. Put them on the fire with butter, gradually add the bouillon, cover the pot and cook slowly until tender. When done, take them out, peel them carefully and cut them up into 6 to 8 parts. The rest of the butter is browned, flour and the truffle peelings added, and the bouillon in which the truffles were boiled. Season with meat extract, Madeira, salt, pepper, sugar and lemon juice. Cook a nice, brown dressing of this, strain, put the truffles in and stew a few minutes. Serve on toast.

Remarks: This may be used for stuffing.

No. 65—TRUFFLE PUREE.
Quantity for 6 Persons.

1/3 lb. of truffles
½ pt. of good bouillon
⅛ lb. of butter
1½ tbsps. of flour
5 tbsps. of Madeira or red wine
Salt to taste
1 pinch of pepper
¼ tsp. of sugar
¼ tsp. of lemon juice
½ tsp. of meat extract

Preparation: The truffles are cleaned and the dressing is prepared from the peelings of the truffles, according to No. 64. The truffles are chopped very fine, put into the strained dressing and seasoned. Then put into shells or small porcelain dishes or serve on cutlets or scrambled eggs.

No. 66—MORELS.
Quantity for 6 Persons.

2 lbs. of morels
1 piece of butter as large as an egg
½ tbsp. flour
½ tsp. of meat extract
½ pt. morel liquor
½ cup of cream
Salt to taste
1 pinch of pepper
1 tsp. of finely chopped parsley.

Preparation: The morels are cleaned well and put on the fire with lukewarm water and let them get hot, stirring gently, then strain. Repeat this until all sand is removed. The last water is boiled down to ½ pt. The butter is browned with the flour, the morel liquor is added and the meat extract, and then cooked slowly for 15 minutes. Put in the cream and season with salt and pepper. Now put the morels into the dressing, cook, put in a piece of butter and the parsley.

This dish is fine with smoked salmon or scrambled eggs.

Remarks: Canned or dried morels are prepared the same way. If you use canned morels, then utilize the liquor in the can. Dried morels are soaked in water for 2 to 3 hours.

No. 67—MUSHROOMS.
Edible Boletus.
Quantity for 6 Persons.

2 lbs. of mushrooms
¼ lb. of butter
½ tbsp. of flour
1 medium sized onion
½ pt. of sour cream
Salt to taste
1 pinch of pepper
1 tbsp. of parsley

Preparation: Mushrooms must be firm, they are brushed and very dark ones only are peeled. The lighter colored ones do not need to be peeled. They are cut up into equal pieces. The butter is heated, the mushroom pieces put in with the whole peeled onion and stewed for 15 to 20 minutes. The dish must be covered. Strew the flour on, stirring lightly, add the sour cream, ¼ teaspoonful of meat extract, salt and pepper, and lastly the parsley, stew 2 minutes and serve.

No. 68—CHANTERELLES.
Another Species of Mushrooms.
Quantity for 6 Persons.

2½ lbs. of chanterelles
2 qts. of water
2 tbsps. of salt
¼ lb. of butter
½ tbsp. of flour
Salt to taste
1½ tbsps. of finely chopped parsley
2 tbsps. of cream
1 pinch of pepper

Preparation: The chanterelles are cleaned, washed, but not left in water; cook them 1 minute in 2 qts. of boiling salt water, drain in a colander. Heat the butter, put in the chanterelles with flour, salt and pepper and stew 2 minutes, then add the cream and parsley and serve at once.

No. 69—OLIVES AS VEGETABLES.
Quantity for 6 Persons.

60 olives
¼ lb. of butter, scant
1 tbsp. of flour
1 pt. of bouillon
¼ tsp. of meat extract
Salt to taste
1 pinch of pepper
½ tsp. parsley
¼ pt. of cream

Preparation: The stones are taken out and the olives cooked tender in the bouillon; to this add 1 tablespoonful of butter. The rest of the butter is melted, flour stirred in, then the olives, bouillon, cream and meat extract. Season with salt and pepper, stew for 15 minutes and add the chopped parsley.

No. 70—STUFFED OLIVES.
Quantity for 6 Persons.

36 olives
½ lb. of finely ground chicken
1 egg
Salt and pepper to taste
4 tbsps. of cream
¼ tsp. of lemon juice
1 tbsp. of butter
½ pt. of Madeira sauce

Preparation: The preserved olives are scooped out and stuffed with cooked chicken, which has been ground fine and mixed with egg, butter, salt, pepper and lemon juice. One-half pint of Madeira sauce is prepared. See under Gravies and Dressing, No. 25. The stuffed olives are put in and cooked until tender.

No. 71—FILLED OR STUFFED OLIVES WITH CHAMPIGNONS.
Quantity for 6 Persons.

The preparation is the same as given under No. 70. One-half pound of champignons, which have been cooked until tender in butter, are stirred into the dressing.

Remarks: This is a fine dish to serve at parties.

No. 72—ROASTED CHESTNUTS.
Quantity for 6 Persons.

1 lb. of sweet chestnuts
¼ lb. of fresh butter
1 lb. of salt

Preparation: The skins are rubbed off and the chestnuts slit with a sharp knife. Into an iron frying pan or spider put 1/3 of the salt, place the chestnuts on the salt in one layer and cover them with the rest of the salt. Put the pan into a medium hot oven and bake them scarcely ½ hour, then take them out and place them on a napkin to eat with fresh butter.

No. 73—CHESTNUT PUREE.
Quantity for 6 Persons.

1½ lbs. of chestnuts	4 tbsps. of red wine
⅛ lb. of butter	Salt to taste
1 tbsp. of flour	1 pinch of pepper
½ pt. of bouillon	1 tbsp. of sugar
¼ pt. of cream	1 tsp. of chopped parsley

Preparation: The chestnuts are taken out of the outer shell, then hot water poured on and the inner skin pulled off. Cook them in bouillon until tender and strain. Heat the butter, stir in the flour, stew a few minutes, add the chestnuts and stir in cream, red wine, salt, pepper, sugar and parsley. Let it get hot, stirring briskly, arrange mound-shaped and serve.

No. 74—FRIED CHESTNUTS.
Quantity for 6 Persons.

1 lb. of chestnuts	1 pinch of salt
¼ lb. of butter	1 tbsp. fine sugar

Preparation: Shell the chestnuts, scald them and pull off the inner skin. Brown the butter and after the chestnuts are cooked slightly in water, put them into the hot butter, add salt and sugar and fry them light brown, shaking frequently. Serve them with roast goose stuffing or as a garnish with cabbage.

CHAPTER 13.
SALADS.

The various preparations of green salads, potato salads, vegetable salads and meat salads.

Green salads such as head lettuce, endive, romaine and escariol salads are pleasing and refreshing with meats and fish.

Salads must be prepared carefully. They may be served with every meal.

Good oil and good vinegar or lemon juice are essentials for preparing salads.

No. 1—GREEN LETTUCE.
Head Lettuce, Endive Lettuce.
Quantity for 6 Persons.

2 heads of lettuce
¼ cup of fine oil
⅛ cup of vinegar
¼ tsp. of salt
1 pinch of pepper
1 tsp. of minced parsley

Preparation: The head lettuce is picked over, the ribs cut through, also the largest leaves, then washed well and dried. The oil, vinegar or lemon juice, salt and pepper are mixed well and poured over the lettuce. Mix thoroughly with two spoons.

No. 2—GREEN LETTUCE WITH EGG DRESSING.
Head Lettuce, Endive, Romaine, Escariol Lettuce.
Quantity for 6 Persons.

2 heads of lettuce
2 yolks of eggs
¼ cup of cream
¼ tsp. salt
1 pinch of pepper
¼ tsp. of sugar
Juice of ½ lemon

Preparation: The lettuce is picked over, washed and drained. The yolks of eggs are thoroughly beaten with cream, then vinegar stirred in slowly and salt, pepper and sugar added. Pour over the lettuce, mix well with two spoons, and serve at once.

No. 3—GREEN LETTUCE WITH MAYONNAISE DRESSING.
Head, Endive, Escariol Lettuce.
Quantity for 6 Persons.

2 heads of lettuce
2 yolks of eggs
4 tbsps. of sour cream
2 tbsps. of vinegar
¼ tsp. of mustard
¼ tsp. of salt
1 pinch of white pepper
1 pinch of sugar

Preparation: The lettuce is prepared as before mentioned.

Yolks of eggs, cream, vinegar, mustard, salt, pepper and sugar are mixed well and cooked in a double boiler until thick, stirring constantly, cooled and mixed with the lettuce.

No. 4—GREEN LETTUCE WITH BACON.
Head, Endive Lettuce.
Quantity for 6 Persons.

2 heads of lettuce	1 pinch of pepper
⅛ lb. of bacon	1 pinch of sugar
5 tbsps. of vinegar	½ tsp. of mustard
	½ tsp. of salt

Preparation: Prepare the lettuce as before. The bacon is cut into small cubes and fried to a nice yellow color; add vinegar, salt, pepper, sugar and mustard, cool and add the lettuce, stirring lightly.

No. 5—GREEN LETTUCE PREPARED SWEET.
Head Lettuce.
Quantity for 6 Persons.

2 heads of lettuce	⅛ cup of vinegar
1 egg	¼ tsp. of salt
3 tbsps. of sugar	1 pinch of pepper
	¼ cup of cream

Preparation: Prepare the lettuce as before. The whole egg is beaten with sugar, cream, vinegar, salt and pepper and mixed well with the lettuce.

Remarks: Three tablespoonfuls of oil may be used.

No. 6—POTATO SALAD.
Quantity for 6 Persons.

4 lbs. of potatoes	Salt to taste
½ cup of good oil	¼ tsp. of pepper
½ cup of vinegar	1 tsp. finely sliced onions
	½ cup of warm bouillon or water

Preparation: The potatoes should be medium sized and not mealy. They are boiled in the jackets, peeled and sliced. The vinegar and bouillon are poured over while potatoes are still warm, add the oil, salt, pepper and onions and mix well, being careful not to break the potatoes. This salad must be prepared one hour before serving. Taste before serving and add more seasoning if necessary.

No. 7—POTATO SALAD WITH SPICED DRESSING.
Quantity for 6 Persons.

2 lbs. of potatoes	1 tsp. of salt
4 yolks of eggs	¼ tsp. of red pepper
1 large cup of milk	1½ tsps. of sugar
½ large cup of vinegar	1 tsp. of flour
2 mustardspoonfuls of mustard	Piece of butter, the size of an egg

Preparation: The potatoes are prepared as given under

No. 6. Yolks of eggs, milk, vinegar, mustard, salt, pepper, sugar, flour and butter are mixed well and cooked in double boiler until thick, stirring constantly. Mix the sliced potatoes with this dressing.

No. 8—POTATO SALAD WITH SOUR CREAM.
Quantity for 6 Persons.

2 lbs. of potatoes
1 pt. thick, sour cream
¼ cup of vinegar
1 tbsp. of sugar
½ tbsp. of salt
1 pinch of pepper

Preparation: Prepare the potatoes as in No. 6. The cream, vinegar, sugar, salt and pepper are put on the sliced potatoes and mixed well. **Remarks:** Nos. 7 and 8 are fine salads.

No. 9—POTATO SALAD WITH BACON.
Quantity for 6 Persons.

2 lbs. of potatoes
¼ lb. of bacon
½ cup of vinegar
½ tbsps. of salt
1 tbsp. of finely sliced onions
1 pinch of pepper
½ cup of bouillon or water

Preparation: Prepare the potatoes as in No. 6. Cut the bacon into small dice, fry to a light yellow color, add the onions and fry a few minutes, then add bouillon, vinegar, salt, pepper and let come to a boil. Pour over the sliced potatoes.

No. 10—CUCUMBER SALAD.
Quantity for 6 Persons.

2 large cucumbers
½ tbsp. of salt
3 tbsps. of oil
4 tbsps. of vinegar
1 pinch of pepper
1 tsp. of finely chopped parsley

Preparation: The cucumbers are peeled and sliced very thin, salted and left standing for a while. Drain well, add oil, vinegar, pepper, parsley and mix well.

No. 11—SWEET CUCUMBER SALAD.
Quantity for 6 Persons.

2 large cucumbers
1 egg
¼ cup of cream
1 pinch of pepper
½ tbsp. of salt, for salting
1 tsp. of finely chopped parsley
3 tbsps. of sugar

Preparation: The cucumbers are prepared as given under No. 10. Egg, cream, vinegar, sugar, pepper, parsley, are beaten well and mixed with the cucumbers.

No. 12—CUCUMBER SALAD WITH SOUR CREAM.

2 large cucumbers
½ tbsp. of salt, for salting
½ pt. thick sour cream
2 tbsps. of vinegar
1 pinch of pepper

Preparation: The cucumbers are prepared as given under No. 10 and mixed well with cream, vinegar and pepper. They are very good.

No. 13—CUCUMBERS AND HEAD LETTUCE MIXED.

Quantity for 6 Persons.

1 large cucumber	2 tbsps. of lemon juice
1 head of green lettuce	1 pinch of salt
½ pt. of thick, sour cream	1 pinch of pepper

Preparation: The lettuce and cucumber are prepared as before given under No. 1 and No. 10. The cucumber slices are mixed well with cream, vinegar, pepper, salt and mixed lightly with the green lettuce.

No. 14—TOMATO SALAD.

Quantity for 6 Persons.

2 lbs. of tomatoes	½ tsp. of onion, sliced fine
¼ cup of fine oil	1 tsp. of finely chopped parsley
1 tsp. of salt	¼ cup of vinegar
	1 pinch of pepper

Preparation: The tomatoes are scalded, skinned, sliced and mixed well with oil, vinegar, salt, pepper, onion and parsley.

No. 15—TOMATO SALAD WITH MAYONNAISE DRESSING.

Quantity for 6 Persons.

6 nice medium sized tomatoes	½ tsp. of mustard
1 head lettuce	½ tsp. of salt
3 yolks of eggs	1 pinch of pepper
½ cup of very fine oil	Juice of 1 lemon
	¼ cup of thick, sweet cream

Preparation: The tomatoes are scalded, skinned and placed on ice. The yolks of eggs are mixed with oil, which is put in a few drops at a time; add cream, lemon juice, pepper, salt and mustard. The mayonnaise dressing must be thick. The head lettuce is treated as under No. 1, placed on salad plates and the cold tomatoes put on them, the mayonnaise dressing poured over the tomatoes.

Remarks: This is a fine salad.

No. 16—TOMATO SALAD WITH COOKED MAYONNAISE.

Quantity for 6 Persons.

6 medium sized tomatoes	½ tsp. of mustard
3 yolks of eggs	1 pinch of salt
6 tbsps. of sour cream	1 pinch of white pepper
2—3 tbsps. of vinegar	1 pinch of sugar

Preparation: Preparation is the same as given under No. 15. Yolks of eggs, cream, vinegar, mustard, salt, pepper and sugar are mixed well and cooked in the double boiler until thick, stirring constantly. Let it get cold and pour over the whole tomatoes. The tomatoes may be garnished with green lettuce as under No. 15.

No. 17—ASPARAGUS SALAD.
Quantity for 6 Persons.

2 lbs. of asparagus	2 tbsps. of good vinegar
2 qts. of water	1 pinch of salt
1 tbsp. of salt	1 pinch of pepper
	4 tbsps. of fine oil

Preparation: The asparagus are peeled, cut into equal pieces or left whole and boiled until tender in boiling water. When cold, mix them with the oil, vinegar, pepper and salt.

No. 18—ASPARAGUS SALAD WITH MAYONNAISE.

Preparation and ingredients are the same as given under No. 17. The asparagus is covered with mayonnaise dressing. See No. 16, Cooked Mayonnaise Dressing for Tomato Salad.

No. 19—CAULIFLOWER SALAD.
Quantity for 6 Persons.

1 large cauliflower	4 tbsps. of vinegar
2 qts. of water	1 pinch of pepper
1 tbsp. of salt	1 pinch of salt
	4 tbsps. of oil

Preparation: The cauliflower is broken up into roses, boiled until tender but not too soft, in boiling salt water, drained and mixed with oil, vinegar, pepper and salt.

No. 20—CAULIFLOWER WITH COOKED MAYONNAISE.

Preparation and ingredients are the same as given under No. 19. Instead of the other dressing use cooked mayonnaise dressing. See No. 16.

No. 21—CARROT SALAD.
Quantity for 6 Persons.

2 lbs. of small, young carrots	¼ cup of vinegar
2 qts. of water	1 pinch of salt
½ tbsp. of salt	1 pinch of pepper
	¼ cup of fine oil

Preparation: The carrots are scraped, cut up into equally large pieces and cooked until tender in salt water, drained and mixed well with oil, vinegar, salt and pepper.

No. 22—BEAN SALAD.
Quantity for 6 Persons.

2 lbs. of yellow string beans	1 tsp. of grated onion
3 qts. of water	1 pinch of salt
1 tbsp. of salt	Pepper
¼ cup of oil	1 tbsp. of chopped parsley or
¼ cup of vinegar	chives

Preparation: The beans are strung, broken into pieces, boiled until tender in salt water, drained, and while still warm, mixed with oil, vinegar, salt, pepper, onion and parsley. It must not be too dry.

No. 23—ROOT CELERY OR CELERIAC SALAD.
Quantity for 6 Persons.

2 large celery-roots	6 tbsps. of vinegar
3 qts. of water	1 pinch of salt
1 tbsp. of salt	Pepper
5 tbsps. of oil	¼ pt. of cold bouillon

Preparation: The celery is washed well, cooked until tender in 3 qts. of water, peeled, sliced and while still lukewarm, mixed with vinegar, oil, salt, pepper, bouillon, then covered and left standing for 1 hour before serving. ½ cup of sugar may be mixed with it.

No. 24—ROOT CELERY SALAD MIXED WITH POTATO SALAD WITH MAYONNAISE DRESSING.
Quantity for 6 Persons.

1½ lbs. of potatoes	½ tsp. of mustard
1 celery-root	¼ tsp. of pepper
4 yolks of eggs	Salt to taste
1 cup of cream	1 tsp. of sugar
	½ cup of vinegar

Preparation: The potatoes and celery are cleaned, cooked until tender, peeled and sliced thin. Yolks of eggs, cream, vinegar, mustard, pepper, salt and sugar are mixed well and cooked in double boiler until thick, stirring constantly. This dressing is mixed with warm potatoes and celery.

No. 25—CELERY SALAD WITH MAYONNAISE DRESSING.
Quantity for 6 Persons.

2 large celery-roots	½ portion of mayonnaise dressing

Preparation: The celery is prepared according to No. 23. One-half of the portion of mayonnaise dressing is made according to No. 24 and mixed with the celery.

No. 26—BEAN SALAD.
Quantity for 6 Persons.

2 lbs. of green or yellow beans
3 qts. of water
2 tbsps. of salt
¼ cup of fine oil
¼ cup of vinegar
½ cup of bouillon
1 tbsp. of finely chopped parsley
¼ tsp. of finely chopped onion
Salt to taste
Pepper

Preparation: The beans are strung, broken into 3 pieces, cooked until tender in boiling water, drained and mixed with oil, vinegar, bouillon, parsley, onion, salt and pepper. This salad must be prepared a few hours before serving and should be kept covered until served.

No. 27—MIXED SALAD.
Quantity for 6 Persons.

½ lb. of asparagus
1 small head of cauliflower
½ small celery-root
¼ lb. of green beans
¼ lb. of yellow beans
5 potatoes
6 young carrots
Salt water
¼ cup of fine oil
¼ cup of vinegar
Salt to taste
Pepper
½ tsp. grated onion
1 tbsp. of finely chopped summer savory
1 head lettuce

Preparation: The vegetables are cleaned, cut up and each separately cooked until tender in salt water and drained. The potatoes are boiled until tender, peeled and cut. When the vegetables and potatoes are cold, mix with oil, vinegar, salt, pepper, onion, summer savory and parsley, being careful not to break the pieces.

No. 28—FINE MIXED VEGETABLE SALAD.
Quantity for 6 Persons.

1 portion of mayonnaise dressing
½ cup of minced truffles and olives
¼ lb. smoked salmon
6 sardines
½ lb. asparagus
½ small celery-root
6 young carrots
4 boiled potatoes
1 small head of cauliflower broken into small roses
¼ lb. green beans
¼ lb. yellow beans
1 head of green lettuce

For Mayonnaise Dressing.

4 yolks of eggs
1 cup of cream
Juice of 1 lemon
1 pinch of white pepper
Salt to taste
4 tbsps. of fine oil
¼ tsp. mustard

Preparation: All the vegetables are cut into small pieces and boiled separately in salt water until tender, but not too soft. The water is drained off and the vegetables mixed with the potatoes, truffles, salmon, sardines and olives, which have also been cut into pieces.

The mayonnaise dressing is made by stirring the 4 yolks of eggs into cream; add lemon juice, mustard, pepper and salt and cook in double boiler until thick, stirring constantly. After it has cooled off, stir in the oil.

The salad is mixed carefully with one half of this dressing. The head lettuce leaves are picked off and placed into the salad dish, the salad piled up in the center of it and the rest of the dressing poured over. You may garnish it with olives. This is a very fine salad.

No. 29—MIXED SALAD WITH MEAT.
Quantity for 6 Persons.

1 head lettuce
1 cup of prepared endive lettuce
½ cup of wax beans, cut in pieces
½ cup of green cut beans
½ cup of sliced radishes
¼ cup of very small pearl onions
½ small cauliflower, cut into roses
1 apple, cut into pieces
2 sour pickles, cut into pieces
½ lb. boiled potatoes, cut into pieces
2 cups of meat, cut into pieces
Salt to taste
1 pinch of pepper
¼ cup of fine oil
½ cup of vinegar
¼ tsp. of mustard

Preparation: The vegetables are all prepared according to No. 28. The meat may be beef, veal or poultry, which has been cooked or fried and is cut up like the vegetables, then mixed with these and vinegar, oil, pepper, salt and arranged on the leaves of the head lettuce.

Remarks: This salad may be served with mayonnaise dressing as No. 28.

No. 30—CHAMPIGNON SALAD.
Quantity for 6 Persons.

2 lb. can of champignons or
2 lbs. of fresh ones
5 potatoes
1 lb. of boiled sweetbreads
1 cup sour cream
Juice of 1 lemon
½ tsp. of chopped parsley
Salt to taste
1 pinch of pepper
10 olives
¼ cup of fine oil

Preparation: The larger champignons are cut into pieces, the smaller ones left whole. The potatoes are boiled until tender, peeled and cut into small dice. The sweetbreads are boiled in salt water, skinned and minced. All this is mixed with the sour cream, oil, lemon juice, salt and pepper and arranged on the head lettuce leaves, strewn with parsley and garnished with olives.

No. 31—TRUFFLE SALAD.
Quantity for 6 Persons.

¼ lb. of truffles
1 lb. of salad potatoes
3 hard boiled eggs
¼ cup of fine oil
½ cup of bouillon
Salt to taste
1 pinch of pepper
3 tbsps. of fine white wine
¼ cup of vinegar

Preparation: Preserved truffles are scraped and sliced fine, fresh ones are brushed well in much water, then put into a small pot with the bouillon and 2 tablespoonfuls of oil and cooked until tender, taken out of the bouillon, peeled and sliced. Into the water or bouillon in which the truffles had been cooked, put the rest of the oil, vinegar, salt and pepper to cook and pour it on the sliced potatoes. Add the sliced truffles and the chopped hard boiled eggs and the white wine. Mix it all carefully, cover the dish and set aside for 3 hours before serving.

Remarks: If you take canned truffles cook the bouillon with the truffle liquor and peelings for 15 minutes, strain it and mix it with the other ingredients.

No. 32—COLD SLAW.
Quantity for 6 Persons.

1 small head of red or white cabbage
2 qts. boiling water
¼ cup of vinegar
2 yolks of eggs
Salt to taste
1 pinch of pepper
3 tbsps. of oil
1 cup of sour or sweet cream

Preparation: Pick off the bad leaves and slice or cut the cabbage very thin, scald it 5 minutes and drain the water off through a colander. Mix it well with vinegar, cream, yolks of eggs, pepper, salt and oil.

No. 33—BEEF SALAD.
Quantity for 6 Persons.

For preparation and ingredients for this salad look to No. 24, Chapter 2, Beef salad.

Remarks: Lamb and veal salad are prepared the same way.

No. 34—RABBIT ROAST SALAD.
Quantity for 6 Persons.

For preparation and ingredients for this salad look to No. 21, Seventh Chapter, Game.

No. 35—CHICKEN SALAD.
Quantity for 6 Persons.

1 chicken
3 qts. of water
Salt to taste
1 cup of cream
¼ cup of vinegar
½ cup of chicken broth
4 yolks of eggs
¼ tsp. of mustard
Salt to taste
1 pinch of pepper
½ cup of sliced champignons
½ pt. sour whipped cream
2 tbsps. of sliced truffles
1 bunch of stalk-celery

Preparation: The chicken is well cleaned and cooked until tender in 2 qts. of water and salt. The skin is removed and the meat cut fine. The bouillon is boiled down and ½ cup of it poured on the meat. The cup of cream, yolks of eggs, vinegar, mustard, pepper and salt are mixed well and cooked until thick, stirring constantly. This dressing is poured over the meat, the chopped champignons and truffles added and mixed with the rest or they may be omitted. Cover the salad and set it aside for one hour before serving. This salad may be made from any kind of poultry. You may add celery cut in small pieces. Lastly add the whipped cream.

No. 36—HERRING SALAD.
Quantity for 6 Persons.

For preparation and ingredients see Chapter 8, No. 47.

No. 37—SALMON SALAD.
Quantity for 6 Persons.

For preparation and ingredients see Chapter 8, No. 7.

No. 38—PIKE SALAD.
Quantity for 6 Persons.

2 lbs. of pike
2 qts. of boiling water
1 tbsp. of salt
1 piece of butter the size of an egg
1 medium sized onion
1¼ tbsps. of flour
¾ qt. thick cream
3 yolks of eggs
2 tsps. of mustard
4 tbsps. of vinegar
2 tbsps. of fine oil
Salt to taste
1 tbsp. of capers

Preparation: The fish is scaled, dressed, washed, cooked until tender in salt water and set to simmer gently 15 minutes. Remove the skin and bones, cut the meat into small pieces. Heat the butter and onion, but do not brown, stir in the flour, add the cream, stirring constantly, cook, add the yolks of eggs, but do not boil any longer. When the dressing is cold, add the vinegar, oil, mustard, capers and salt. Stir the dressing for 15 minutes more, pour over the fish and mix lightly. Take out the onion before adding the cream.

No. 39—OYSTER OR CLAM SALAD.
Quantity for 6 Persons.
For preparation and ingredients see Fish, Chapter 8, No. 59.

No. 40—LOBSTER SALAD.
Quantity for 6 Persons.

3 lbs. of lobster	3 yolks of eggs
3 tbsps. of vinegar	Juice of ½ lemon
2 tbsps. of oil	1 tsp. of capers
Salt to taste	½ tsp. of mustard
1 pinch of pepper	¼ tsp. of sugar

1 cup of cream

Preparation: The lobster is cooked, cooled, the meat picked out and cut into small oblique pieces. Mix it with vinegar, oil, salt and pepper.

The cream, yolks of eggs, lemon juice, mustard and sugar are mixed well and cooked until thick, stirring briskly; then put in the capers. The head lettuce is prepared and the large leaves cut into smaller pieces. Now arrange on a platter one layer of lettuce and one of lobster salad, pour over some mayonnaise dressing and repeat 2 or 3 times until all is used up. Garnish the dish or plate with radishes. It makes a fine salad. This salad may be mixed with mayonnaise dressing as in Chapter 10, No. 42.

No. 41—FRUIT SALAD AS DESSERT.
Quantity for 6 Persons.

3 oranges	¼ pt. cognac-cherries
3 bananas	Sugar to taste
½ pineapple	1 pt. whipped cream

½ pt. strawberries

Preparation: Oranges, pineapple, bananas are peeled and sliced. Strawberries are cleaned, the cherries are stoned, all this fruit mixed and whipped cream poured on in a glass dish. The whipped cream may be omitted. If you like you may mix ½ cup of Sherry wine in with it.

No. 42—LETTUCE COMBINATION SALAD.

Head lettuce	4 green onions
4 medium sized tomatoes	6 radishes
1 small cucumber	½ cup mayonnaise dressing
2 tbsps. vinegar	Roquefort cheese

¼ tsp. Worcestershire Sauce

Preparation: Line salad bowl with the crisped lettuce; peel and quarter the tomatoes; slice and crisp the cucumbers; slice the onions and radishes in very thin slices. Arrange the vegetables on the lettuce; mix the vinegar with the mayonnaise dressing and pour over the salad. A little Roquefort cheese crumbled and mixed with the dressing is fine. Excellent, served with steak ———

No. 43—FRUIT SALAD DRESSING.

Preparation: Take 1 cup boiled mayonnaise, a little powdered sugar, juice of an orange or a lemon, ½ pint of whipped cream.

No. 44—FRUIT SALAD No. 1.

2 apples
1 small bunch celery
1 cup chopped walnuts
1 cup pineapple

Preparation: Mix all the cut fruit with fruit salad dressing.

No. 45—FRUIT SALAD No. 2.

4 oranges
1 cup pineapple
½ cup chopped nuts
2 cups cherries
½ cup shredded cocoanut

Preparation: Mix all the cut fruit with the fruit salad dressing.

No. 46—FRUIT SALAD No. 3.

6 large peaches
1 pt. strawberries
3 bananas
½ cup nuts

Preparation: Mix all the cut fruit with the fruit salad dressing.

No. 47—FRUIT SALAD No. 4.

1 lb. dates
1 cup chopped apples
1 cup chopped celery
3 sliced oranges

Preparation: Mix all the cut fruit with the fruit salad dressing.

CHAPTER 14.

EGGS.

The preparation of eggs. Eggs are a valuable food and indispensable in the kitchen. Some dishes cannot be prepared without eggs.

Eggs can be tested as to their freshness in a basin with ½ pt. of water mixed with a tablespoonful of salt. Fresh eggs sink to the bottom, others float on top.

To preserve eggs for the winter, put them into salt, so that they do not touch and are covered well. Use a stone jar for this purpose and cover it.

No. 1—SOFT BOILED EGGS.
Quantity for 6 Persons.
12 eggs   3 qts. of water

Preparation: The eggs are washed well, then carefully put into boiling water with a spoon and cooked 3 minutes. Take from the stove and let stand 1 more minute.

No. 2—HARD BOILED EGGS.
Quantity for 6 Persons.
12 eggs   3 qts. of water

Preparation: The eggs are washed well and carefully put into boiling water to boil 20 minutes. These hard boiled eggs are easily digested.

No. 3—HARD BOILED EGGS FOR GARNISHING.
Quantity for 6 Persons.
4—5 eggs   2 qts. of water

Preparation: The eggs are boiled 20 minutes in 2 qts. of boiling water, then shelled and either sliced or quartered and used for garnishing spinage and ragout.

No. 4—FRIED EGGS.
Quantity for 6 Persons.
12 eggs   Salt and pepper
1 tbsp. of butter

Preparation: The butter is heated in a clean spider and each egg carefully put in and fried until the white around the yolk has become opaque or firm. Sprinkle with salt and pepper and take out with a cake turner, place on platter and garnish with parsley.

No. 5—POACHED EGGS.
Quantity for 6 Persons.

12 eggs
1½ qts. of water
1 tsp. of vinegar
6 slices of toast
Salt to taste

Preparation: Add salt and vinegar to the water, boil it and put each egg in on a ladle, hold it there until the white has become firm, then put it on a skimmer to let the water drip off, place it on the warm buttered toast and put into oven until all eggs are poached.

No. 6—FRIED EGGS IN TOMATO SAUCE.
Quantity for 6 Persons.

10—12 eggs
1 cup of fine oil

Tomato Sauce or Dressing.

6 very ripe tomatoes
¼ lb. of raw ham
Salt to taste
1 pinch of pepper
1 tsp. of sugar
1 tbsp. of butter
1 tbsp. of flour
¼ medium sized onion

Preparation: The tomatoes are sliced and the ham cut into small pieces. Melt the butter, stew the sliced onion and ham in it for 10 minutes, then stir in the flour, 1 pt. of water, tomatoes, salt, pepper and sugar and cook ½ hour, then strain through a fine sieve. Sprinkle each egg with salt and pepper and fry in the salad oil, which should be very hot. Tip the pan or dish a little so the oil covers the egg. When the white of egg is firm, take it out and put it into the hot tomato dressing which is set where it will remain hot.

No. 7—BOILED EGGS IN BRINE.
Quantity for 6 Persons.

6 eggs ½ lb. of salt 2 qts. of water

Preparation: The eggs are boiled five minutes in boiling water. If you wish them hard, cook them 15 minutes, then crush the points of the egg shells and put the eggs into 2 qts. of salt water.

No. 8—BRINE EGGS IN CREAM SAUCE.
Quantity for 6 Persons.

6 eggs
¼ lb. of salt
2 qts. of water
2 tbsps. of butter
1½ tbsps. of flour
1 pt. cream
Juice of ½ lemon, or
2 tbsps. of vinegar
Salt to taste
1 pinch of pepper

Preparation: The eggs are boiled 15 minutes, the shells crushed and the eggs placed into strong salt water for 4 hours. The butter is heated, flour stirred in, cream, lemon juice, salt and pepper added and this cooked, stirring continually.

Shell the eggs, quarter them, heat them in the gravy and serve very hot.

No. 9—SCRAMBLED EGGS.
Quantity for 6 Persons.

10 eggs
¼ cup of milk
½ tsp. of salt
1 tbsp. of butter

Preparation: Beat the eggs well into milk and salt for 5 minutes. Heat the butter in a pan, pour in the mixture of egg and milk and slowly stirring them, let them get firm, then serve on a hot platter.

No. 10—SCRAMBLED EGG PANCAKE.
Quantity for 6 Persons.

10 eggs   ¼ tsp. of salt.   1 tbsp. of butter

Preparation: Beat the eggs in a dish 5 minutes, adding salt. Heat the butter in a broad pan or spider, pour in the eggs and let them get firm over a slow fire. Lift with a knife once or twice and carefully slip on a hot platter to serve.

No. 11—SCRAMBLED EGGS, ENGLISH STYLE.
Quantity for 6 Persons.

10 eggs
3 tbsps. of finely chopped champignons
Salt
1 pinch of white pepper
1 tbsp. of butter
¼ cup of cream

Preparation: The eggs are beaten 5 minutes with cream, salt, pepper, then champignons added. The butter is heated in a pan, the eggs poured in and stirring gently, let them get firm, then serve on a hot platter.

No. 12—SCRAMBLED EGGS WITH RED HERRING.
Quantity for 6 Persons.

3 red herrings
6 eggs
1 pinch of pepper
2 tbsps. of butter
1 pinch of salt

Preparation: The herrings are skinned and the bones removed from them, then stewed in the hot butter. Eggs, salt and pepper are well beaten and poured over the fish. Let the eggs get firm and serve on a hot platter.

No. 13—SCRAMBLED EGGS WITH CHIVES.
Quantity for 6 Persons.

10 eggs
2 tbsps. of chives
¼ tsp. salt
1 pinch of white pepper
¼ cup of milk

Preparation: The preparation is the same as No. 9. The chives are strewn on or mixed in while baking.

No. 14—STUFFED EGGS, (DEVILED EGGS).

Quantity for 6 Persons.

6 eggs
1 tbsp. of butter
½ tsp. finely chopped parsley
1 tsp. chopped capers
1 tsp. of mustard
1 pinch of pepper
1 pinch of sugar
1 tsp. of lemon juice
¼ tsp. of salt

Preparation: The eggs are cooked 15 minutes, cooled, peeled, cut into halves, the yolk taken out and mixed well with butter, parsley, capers, salt, pepper, sugar, lemon juice and mustard and put back into the whites of the eggs. Place lettuce leaves on a platter, garnish with sardines and put the stuffed eggs on.

No. 15—ANOTHER FORM OF STUFFED EGGS.

Quantity for 6 Persons.

8 eggs
⅛ lb. of caviar
12 crab tails
2 tbsps. of oil
¼ tsp. of salt
1 pinch of pepper
2 tbsps. of cream or bouillon
1½ layers of white gelatine
1 tbsp. of lemon juice

Preparation: The eggs are cooked 15 minutes, cooled, the top carefully cut off and the inside carefully scooped out with a small spoon, so the shell is not destroyed or broken. The white of egg is chopped fine, the yolk stirred with oil, which is put in by drops, mixed with lemon juice, salt, pepper, sugar, cream. The gelatine is dissolved in a tablespoonful of warm water, strained and also stirred in with the yolk mixture. The crab tails are cut into small pieces. The caviar is poured into a sieve and cold water poured on plentifully, then drained off. Now fill each egg with a little dressing, then crab meat, then chopped white of egg, dressing and caviar; repeat this until the egg is filled. Re-place the tip of the egg and put the eggs on ice or prepare them the day before serving, then no ice is needed. Garnish with lettuce.

CHAPTER 15.

Omelets, Pancakes, Waffles, Noodles and Pie.

The Various Preparations of Omelets, Pancakes, Waffles, Noodles, as Sweet Pastry and Small Side-dishes.
PIES.

No. 1—OMELET FOR BREAKFAST.
Quantity for 6 Persons.

10 eggs
4 tbsps. of cream or milk
1 tbsp. butter
1½ tsps. of flour
¼ tsp. salt

Preparation: The yolks of 10 eggs are beaten 3 minutes with cream, flour, salt. The beaten whites are stirred in lightly. A large round spider is heated, the butter melted in it, the egg batter poured in and baked 1 minute on the stove, then put into the oven for 5 minutes. The omelet must be a nice yellow color; do not turn it over. Serve on a hot platter.

No. 2—SWEET OMELET AS DESSERT.
Quantity for 6 Persons.

8 eggs
3 tbsps. of milk or cream
¼ tsp. of salt
1 tbsp. of butter
½ glass jelly or preserves
Sugar to sprinkle
1 tsp. of flour

Preparation: The preparation is the same as under No. 1, also the baking. When the omelet is done, put jelly or preserves on one-half of it and fold the other half over to cover it. Sprinkle sugar over and serve at once.

No. 3—ASPARAGUS OMELET.
Quantity for 6 Persons.

8 eggs
3 tbsps. of cream or milk
¼ tsp. of salt
1 lb. canned asparagus or cooked fresh ones
1 tbsp. of butter
1 tsp. of flour

The preparation is the same as No. 1. The asparagus pieces are mixed into the batter and baked the same as No. 1. Serve at once.

No. 4—PEA OMELET.
Quantity for 6 Persons.

8 eggs
3 tbsps. of cream or milk
¼ tsp. of salt
1 tsp. of flour
½ pt. can of fine peas
1 tbsp. of butter

Preparation: The water is drained from the peas. Beat the yolks, cream, flour and salt 3 minutes and stir in the peas and the beaten whites of eggs. Bake as given under No. 1 and serve at once.

No. 5—OMELET WITH PARMESAN CHEESE OR OYSTERS.
Quantity for 6 Persons.

10 eggs
4 tbsps. of cream or milk
¼ tsp. of salt
2 tbsps. of Parmesan cheese
⅛ lb. of butter
1 cup of roast gravy
1 pinch of pepper

Preparation: Eggs, cream, salt, pepper are beaten 5 minutes and the melted butter stirred in. A broad spider is heated with a little butter, the omelet batter poured in, the pan shaken to and fro until the batter is baked. Then slip the omelet carefully on a hot platter, sprinkle with cheese, roll it up, pour a little gravy over and serve at once. Stewed oysters may be rolled in the omelets.

No. 6—OMELETS WITH MEAT OR CHAMPIGNONS.
Quantity for 6 Persons.

8 eggs
¼ cup of cream
1 tsp. of salt
1 pinch of pepper
⅛ lb. of fresh butter
1 portion of champignon puree or
1 portion of veal hash
1 tbsp. of Parmesan cheese.

Preparation: Preparation and baking are the same as given under No. 5, Omelet With Cheese. When the omelet is done, cover it well with champignon puree, (see Chapter 11, No. 62,) roll up the omelet, sprinkle it with cheese and serve at once. **Remarks:** Pour a cup of gravy over the omelet.

No. 7—WHIPPED CREAM OMELET.
Quantity for 6 Persons.

6 fresh eggs
1 pt. of whipped cream
¼ tsp. of salt
Scant ¼ cup of fresh butter
½ cup of flour

Preparation: Yolks of eggs, flour and salt are mixed well with the beaten whites of eggs and the cream. Melt the butter in a broad spider, pour in the omelet batter and bake in medium hot oven 10 minutes until golden yellow.

Remarks: The omelet may be sprinkled with Parmesan cheese.

No. 8—WHIPPED CREAM OMELET AS DESSERT.

Prepare the omelet No. 7, fill it with jelly or preserves and serve a fruit sauce with it.

No. 9—WHIPPED CREAM OMELET WITH FROSTING.
Quantity for 6 Persons.

6 fresh eggs	¼ lb. of sugar
1 pt. whipped cream	¼ cup of butter
½ cup of flour	1 cup of strawberry or plum marmalade
¼ tsp. of salt	

Frosting.

6 whites of eggs — Fruit for garnishing
½ lb. of sugar

Preparation: Yolks of eggs, flour, salt and sugar are mixed well. Add the beaten whites of eggs and the whipped cream. The butter is heated in a broad spider, the omelet batter poured in and baked in medium hot oven 10 to 12 minutes until golden yellow. When done, spread it with plum, prune, strawberry or apricot marmalade.

Beat the 6 whites of eggs to a stiff froth, stir into it the ½ pound of sugar, then put into a cornucopia from which the point has been cut off. Now press the frosting through the opening and make figures on the omelet, put it into the oven for 15 minutes until the frosting is of a light yellow color. When done, serve on a warm platter and garnish with sugared fruit. Serve at once.

Remarks: The frosting must be ready when the omelet is taken out of the oven the first time. Cover it with fruit marmalade and the figures or designs of frosting and finish baking it in the oven.

No. 10—PANCAKES.
Quantity for 6 Persons.

4 eggs	1¼ tsps. baking powder
½ pt. of milk	¼ tsp. of salt
1 cup of flour	Butter or lard for baking

Preparation: Yolks of eggs, milk, flour and salt are mixed well with beaten whites of eggs and lastly the baking powder. Heat the butter or lard in a small pan or spider, put in 2 tablespoonfuls of batter and bake it to a nice color. When baked on one side, turn the pancakes and bake on the other side. **Remarks:** If you use a large spider, put in 2 to 3 pancakes and bake them at once.

Potato Pancakes.

For preparation see No. 17, Chapter 11, Potato Pancakes.

No. 11—FILLED PANCAKES.
Quantity for 6 Persons.

6 eggs
½ pt. of milk
½ cup of flour
¼ tsp. of salt
1 tbsp. of sugar
Butter for baking
Jelly or fruit marmalade for stuffing
Sugar and cinnamon to sprinkle

Preparation: The eggs are beaten 5 minutes with milk, flour, sugar and salt. Heat a large spider and put in the butter, then 4 to 5 tablespoonfuls of pancake batter and bake until golden yellow on both sides. Spread with the jelly or marmalade, roll up the pancake, place it on a platter and sprinkle with sugar and cinnamon. This recipe will make 6 pancakes. They must be baked very thin.

No. 12—WAFFLES.
Quantity for 6 Persons.

½ qt. of flour
3 eggs
1¼ cups of milk
4 tbsps. of melted butter
¼ tsp. of baking powder

Preparation: Flour, yolks of eggs, milk, butter and salt are stirred well with beaten whites of eggs and baking powder.

Grease a waffle iron, put in 2 to 3 tablespoonfuls of batter and bake the waffles to a nice brown color, turning it to bake on both sides. Serve at once.

No. 13—ANOTHER FORM OF WAFFLES.
Quantity for 6 Persons.

4 eggs
2 cups of sour milk
2 tbsps. of sour cream
2½ cups of flour
½ tsp. of soda
Lard for baking

Preparation: The 4 yolks of eggs, milk, cream, flour, are mixed well and the soda dissolved in 1 tablespoonful of milk stirred in; add the beaten whites of eggs and bake according to No. 12.

No. 14—SAND-CAKE WAFFLES.
Quantity for 6 Persons.

½ lb. of butter
4 eggs
½ lb. of sugar
¼ lb. of fine flour
¼ lb. of corn starch
¼ tbsp. of grated lemon peel
Lard for baking
Vanilla sugar to sprinkle over

Preparation: The butter is washed so it does not contain any salt, then creamed. Add the eggs, sugar, flour and lemon and bake the batter in a waffle iron. Put ½ teaspoonful of lard on each half of the iron, then put in three tablespoonfuls of batter, close the iron and bake 8 minutes, turning it to bake on both sides. Sprinkle with vanilla sugar.

No. 15—YEAST WAFFLES.
Quantity for 6 Persons.

½ lb. of butter	¾ pt. of milk or cream
4 eggs	1—2 cents worth of yeast
¼ cup of sugar	½ lb. of flour
½ grated lemon peel	Lard for baking

1 pinch of nutmeg

Preparation: Cream the butter, stir in eggs, sugar, lemon peel, nutmeg. The yeast is dissolved in the cream which has been warmed, stirred into the mixture, then flour added to make a stiff batter. Set to rise in a warm place. Grease the waffle iron, put in 3 tablespoonfuls of batter, close the iron and bake the waffles light brown, turning the iron to bake on both sides. Waffles must be baked and served quickly, because they are apt to lose their crispness and become tough. When serving, sprinkle with sugar and cinnamon.

No. 16—LEMON PIE.
Quantity for 6 Persons.

¼ lb. of fresh, very cold butter   ½ glass of very cold water
1½ cups of flour

For the Filling.

1 large cup of sugar	1 large cup of boiling water
2 tbsps. of flour	2 tbsps. of boiling water
Juice of one large lemon	2 yolks of eggs
1 small lemon peel	1 egg

For Frosting.

2 whites of eggs   6 tbsps. of sugar

Preparation: The 1½ cups of flour are put into a dish, the hard butter cut into it and rubbed, not kneaded; gradually add ½ glass of cold water, work lightly, roll it out and line a pie tin with the paste, making a high rim. Then bake it in oven and prepare the filling. Mix the sugar with 2 tablespoonfuls of flour, lemon juice, grated lemon rind and hot water and boil 1 minute, stirring constantly, then cool and mix in the 2 yolks and one whole egg. Put this filling into the baked crust and set aside for a few minutes to thicken. The frosting is made by beating the 2 whites of eggs to a stiff froth, stir in the 6 tablespoonfuls of sugar, cover the pie filling with it and put back into the oven and bake to a light brown color.

No. 17—APPLE PIE.
Quantity for 6 Persons.

¼ lb. of butter   ½ glass of water
1½ cups of flour

For the Filling.

4 medium sized sour apples — ½ cup of sugar

For Frosting.

2 eggs — 2 tbsps. of sugar
½ cup of cream — ¼ tsp. of cinnamon

Preparation: The paste is prepared as given under No. 16. The apples are peeled, cored, sliced, placed into a pie tin lined with paste, sugar strewn over and baked in oven.

The frosting is then made by beating the 2 yolks of eggs with cream, sugar, cinnamon and the beaten whites. When the apples in the pie are done, pour on the frosting and put back into the oven until the frosting turns a light brown color. Apple pie must be served warm.

No. 18—ANOTHER KIND OF APPLE PIE.
Quantity for 6 Persons.

1/3 lb. of cold butter — ¾ glass of cold water
3 cups of flour

For the Filling.

4 medium sized apples — ¼ tsp. of cinnamon
½ cup of sugar — ¼ glass white wine

Preparation: The paste is prepared like No. 16. Half of it is rolled out and the pie tin lined with it. The apples are peeled, cored, sliced, put into the crust which is not yet baked, sugar and cinnamon strewn on, the white wine sprinkled over, the rest of the paste rolled out, 4 slits cut in the center and placed over the apples, fastening the edge well by pressing it down and cutting off the superfluous crust. Bake to a nice brown color.

No. 19—STRAWBERRY OR HUCKLEBERRY PIE.
Quantity for 6 Persons.

1/3 lb. of cold butter — ¾ cup of cold water
2¼ cups of flour

For the Filling.

1—2 qts. of berries — 1 cup of sugar

Prepare the crust as before, (See No. 16, Lemon Pie), roll out half of the crust, line a pie tin with it, fill with berries and sugar, cover as before, (see No. 18), and bake in oven to a nice brown color.

No. 20—STRAWBERRY PIE WITH WHIPPED CREAM.
Quantity for 6 Persons.

¼ lb. of butter — ½ cup of water
1½ cups of flour

For the Filling.

1—2 qts. of berries — 1 cup of sugar

For the Frosting.

1 pt. whipped cream — 2 tbsps. of sugar — 1 tsp. of vanilla

Preparation: The pie crust is prepared and baked as given under No. 16. Then the berries and sugar are put in and put back into oven 15 minutes until berries are cooked, cool off, mix the whipped cream with sugar and vanilla and garnish the pie with it or spread evenly over the top and garnish with raw strawberries.

No. 21—PEACH PIE.
Quantity for 6 Persons.

1/3 lb. of cold butter
2¼ cups of flour
2 lbs. of peaches
¾ cup of sugar
¾ cup of cold water

Preparation: Prepare the pie crust as in No. 16, but do not bake. Peel the peaches and remove the stones, then slice them, put into the pie and sprinkle the sugar over. Cover with the rest of the crust and bake to a nice brown color.

No. 22—SQUASH PIE.
Quantity for 6 Persons.

¼ lb. of butter
½ glass of water
1½ cups of flour

For the Filling.

1 pt. of squash
3 eggs
1 tsp. of vanilla
1 pinch of nutmeg
½ cup of cream or milk
½ tbsp. of corn starch

Preparation: Prepare the crust as in No. 16, but do not bake it. Cook the squash, rub through a sieve or colander, add eggs, vanilla, nutmeg, cream, corn starch and put into the crust, bake 45 minutes.

No. 23—PUMPKIN PIE.
Quantity for 6 Persons.

¼ lb. of cold butter
½ glass of cold water
1½ cups of flour

For Filling.

¼ medium sized pumpkin
½ cup of molasses
¾ pt. of boiling milk
1 tsp. of salt
½ cup of sugar
2 tsps. of cinnamon
1 pinch of nutmeg
2 eggs

Preparation: The pie crust is prepared as in No. 16. The pumpkin is cut into pieces and cooked until tender. Rub through a colander or sieve, take 2½ cups of pumpkin puree, mix it with molasses, milk, salt, sugar, cinnamon, nutmeg and cook 15 minutes, stirring constantly. Lastly stir in 2 eggs, put into the crust and bake 45 minutes.

No. 24—MINCE PIE.
Quantity for 6 Persons.

¼ lb. of cold butter
½ glass of cold water
1½ cups of flour

Mince Filling.

1 lb. of lean beef
1 lb. of sour apples
½ cup of molasses
¼ cup of sugar
½ tsp. of ground cloves
½ tsp. of ground cinnamon
¼ tsp. of grated nutmeg
¼ cup of brandy
¼ tsp. of salt
½ pt. of cider
¼ lb. of raisins
¼ lb. of dried currants
1 tbsp. of chopped, sugared, citron
2 tbsps. of butter
¼ lb. of suet

Preparation: The pie crust is prepared as in No. 16. The mince filling is prepared by cooking the lean beef in a little water, then removing fat and membranes, and chopping it fine. Apples are peeled, cored, chopped. Mix apples, meat, molasses, sugar, cloves, cinnamon, nutmeg, suet, chopped fine, cider, raisins, currants, citron, butter, salt and brandy, put into the crust and bake 45 minutes.

Remarks: This filling may be sufficient for 2 pies. The mince meat not used is kept in a sealed glass can.

No. 25—ANOTHER KIND OF MINCE MEAT.
Quantity for 4 Pies.

2 lbs. of lean beef
1 lb. of beef suet
5 lbs. sour apples
1 lb. of raisins
2 lbs. of currants
¾ lb. of minced citron
1 tsp. of salt
½ lb. of brown sugar
1 cup of molasses
1 orange
1 lemon
½ pt. of brandy
2 tsps. of all kinds of spices

Preparation: The meat is prepared as in No. 24. Apples, suet and citron are treated as given in No. 24 and the whole mixed with the spices, i. e., 1 teaspoonful of pulverized cinnamon, ¾ teaspoonful of cloves, ¼ teaspoonful of nutmeg, salt, sugar, molasses, raisins, currants, juice of orange and lemon and brandy. Stir it for 10 minutes, put it into a glass can and seal.

No. 26—PIEPLANT PIE, RHUBARB.

1/3 lb. of cold butter
¾ glass cold water
2¼ cups of flour

For the Filling.

1 tbsp. of flour   1½ qts. pie plants, cut up   1½ cups of sugar

Preparation: Prepare the pie crust as in No. 16. The pie plants are skinned and cut into 1 inch pieces, then put into pie crust, strew sugar and 1 tablespoonful of flour over, cover with a crust, making slits in the center, and bake 45 minutes.

No. 27—GRAPE PIE.
Quantity for 6 Persons.

¼ lb. of cold butter ½ glass water
1½ cups of flour

For the Filling.

2 cups of crushed and strained grapes   2½ cups of sugar

Preparation: The dough is prepared as in No. 16. The grapes crushed in a sieve or colander, to remove the seeds and shells, then mixed with the sugar, put into the crust. Cover with strips of pie crust and bake 45 minutes.

No. 28—SOUR CREAM PIE.
Quantity for 6 Persons.

¼ lb. of cold butter ½ glass of water
1½ cups of flour

For the Filling.

1 cup of light brown sugar 2 eggs
1 cup of sour cream 1 tsp. of grated lemon peel

Preparation: Prepare the crust as in No. 16 and bake it. Sour cream, sugar, yolks of eggs, lemon peel, beaten whites of eggs are mixed well and put into the baked crust and baked 15 minutes in medium hot oven.

No. 29—VANILLA CREAM PIE.
Quantity for 6 Persons.

¼ lb. of cold butter ½ glass of water
1½ cups of flour

For the Filling.

2 cups of cream 3 eggs
½ cup of sugar 9 tbsps. of sugar
2 tbsps. of flour 1 tbsp. of vanilla

Preparation: Prepare the crust as in No. 16 and bake it. For the filling, mix the cream, ½ cup of sugar, flour, vanilla and cook in double boiler until thick, then stir in the 3 yolks of eggs, put into the crust and bake in oven 10 minutes. Now make the frosting with 3 beaten whites of eggs and the 9 tablespoonfuls of sugar stirred in, cover the pie and bake in oven until light brown.

No. 30—CHICKEN PIE.
Quantity for 6 Persons.

Ingredients and preparation are given under No. 6, Chapter 6, Poultry, see Chicken Pie.

No. 31—PATTY-PASTE.
Quantity for 6 Persons.

½ lb. of good cold butter
½ lb. of fine flour
¼ pt. of cold water
1 white of egg
1 tbsp. of rum
¼ tsp. of baking powder

Preparation: Flour, water, egg, rum and baking powder are mixed into a paste. The cold butter is cut on the paste, folded around it and rolled out. This repeated 3 times and the paste rolled out, cut into 6 small tarts or 1 large one.

No. 32—SWEET PUFF PASTE.
Quantity for 6 Persons.

Preparation: The ingredients and preparation are the same as given under No. 31. The rolled out paste is cut into all kinds of shapes, sprinkled with sugar and covered with fruit marmalade, then folded over, baked to a nice brown color, brushed with white of egg and sprinkled with sugar and cinnamon.

No. 33—PUFF PASTE SCALLOPS.
Quantity for 6 Persons.

Preparation: Ingredients and preparation are the same as under No. 31. The paste is rolled out to ¼ inch thickness, cut out with a medium large tumbler, cut into halves and baked.

Remarks: These scallops are used for garnishing ragout.

No. 34—PUFF PASTE TARTS.
Quantity for 6 Persons.

Preparation: Prepare the paste as given under No. 31, roll it out to ¼ inch thickness and cut out 12 disks, then with a smaller cutter cut out the centers of these, so as to form 12 rings. 6 of the small disks cut out of the centers are used to cover the tarts and the other 6 are folded together and rolled out to 1/6 inch thickness and 6 disks cut out a little larger than the rings. These are for the under crust. Set the rings upon the larger disks and fasten them on with beaten egg, brush the ring with beaten egg and put on a second ring. Then bake them in the oven, also the small disks as covers. Fill each tart with anything you like and put the cover on, put back into oven for a few minutes and serve.

No. 35—SWEETBREAD PATTIES.
Quantity for 6 Persons.

Ingredients and preparation are the same as given in Chapter 3, Veal, No. 28, Sweetbread Patties.

No. 36—CHICKEN PATTIES.
Quantity for 6 Persons.

Ingredients and preparation are the same as given under Chapter 6, No. 7, Puff Paste Patties.

No. 37—PIGEON PIE, ENGLISH STYLE.
Quantity for 6 Persons.

Ingredients and preparation are given in No. 14, Chapter 6.

No. 38—GOOSE LIVER PIE.
Quantity for 6 Persons.

Ingredients and preparation are given in No. 25, Chapter 6, Goose Liver Pie.

No. 39—PHEASANT PIE.
Quantity for 6 Persons.

Ingredients and preparation are given under No. 37, Chapter 6, Pheasant Pie.

No. 40—PIE MADE FROM GROUSE, HAZELHEN, SNOWHEN, SNIPE, QUAIL, PARTRIDGE.
Quantity for 6 Persons.

Ingredients and preparation are given under No. 39, Chapter 6.

No. 41—COLD GAME PIE.
Venison, Doe, Boar, Rabbit.
Quantity for 6 Persons.

Ingredients and preparation are given under No. 11, Chapter 7, Cold Game Pie.

No. 42—RABBIT PIE.
Quantity for 6 Persons.

Ingredients and preparation are given under No. 22, Chapter 7, Rabbit Pie.

No. 43—OYSTER PATTIES.
Quantity for 6 Persons.

Ingredients and preparation are given under No. 57, Chapter 8, Fish.

No. 44—NOODLES.
Quantity for 6 Persons.

4 eggs   Piece of butter size of walnut   2 cups of flour

Preparation: Beat the eggs and butter well, mix in the flour gradually, knead the dough 20 minutes, roll it out very thin, so it is almost transparent, then roll it up and cut in $\frac{1}{4}$ inch slices for cooking and baking and still finer for soup, then dry them thoroughly.

No. 45—COOKED NOODLES.
Quantity for 6 Persons.

Ingredients and preparation are given under No. 44. These dried noodles are cooked in 5 qts. of boiling salt water 10 minutes, then the water is drained off.

No. 46—SOUP NOODLES.
Quantity for 6 Persons.

Ingredients and preparation are given under No. 44. The fine soup noodles are cooked in bouillon 15 minutes.

No. 47—HAM NOODLES.
Quantity for 6 Persons.

Ingredients and preparation are given under No. 12, Chapter 5, Pork, Boiled Ham and Noodles.

No. 48—NOODLE PUDDING WITH APPLES AS DESSERT.
Quantity for 6 Persons.

2 eggs
Piece of butter, size of ½ walnut
1 cup of sugar
¼ cup of currants
1 cup of flour
Salt water
1 lb. of apples
½ cup of peeled, chopped almonds
1 cup of water
½ tsp. of cinnamon

Preparation: The noodles are prepared like No. 44, cooked in salt water 10 minutes and the water drained off. The apples are peeled, cored and sliced. Butter a baking-dish or casserole and put in a layer of noodles, then apples, currants, sugar, cinnamon and almonds, repeat 2 or 3 times until all is used. The last layer should be noodles. Pour the cup of water over, place little pieces of butter on top and bake in oven 1 hour.

No. 49—APPLE STRUDEL.
Quantity for 6 Persons.

2 eggs
Piece of butter, size of ½ egg
1 cup of flour

For the Filling.

4 medium sized apples
½ cup of almonds
2 tbsps. of citron
¼ cup of currants
½ cup of sugar
¼ tsp. of cinnamon
1 tbsp. of butter
⅛ lb. of butter for baking

Preparation: The eggs and butter are mixed with the cup of flour and a noodle dough made which is rolled out to be almost transparent. The apples are peeled, cored and chopped into quite small pieces, the almonds peeled and almonds and citron chopped quite fine. All these are placed on the dough, then sugar, cinnamon, currants and lastly the tablespoonful of butter cut into small pieces added, these rolled up in the dough and placed into a long pan. The ⅛ lb. of butter is cut in pieces and put on the strudel and this is baked in the oven to a nice color. Cream may be served with this as dressing.

No. 50—ROLLED UP APPLES.
Quantity for 6 Persons.

2 eggs	6 medium sized apples
Butter, the size of ½ egg	12 strawberries
¼ cup of milk	Sugar
2 cups of flour	Cinnamon
½ tsp. of baking powder	Lard for baking

Preparation: Butter and eggs are mixed well, then milk and flour added and lastly the baking powder, a smooth paste made and rolled out thin. The apples are peeled, cored and left whole, then each apple filled with fresh or preserved strawberries. Each apple is wrapped into a piece of paste, which is pressed around it, so it cannot come off and fry in deep fat. When done, strew with sugar and cinnamon and serve hot.

No. 51—APPLE FRITTERS.
Quantity for 6 Persons.
For the Pancake Batter.

3 eggs	½ cup of sugar
1 cup of flour	¼ tsp. of cinnamon
½ cup of milk	Butter for baking
¼ tsp. of salt	Sugar and cinnamon for sprinkling.
3 medium sized apples	
½ glass white wine	

Preparation: Eggs, flour, milk and salt are stirred to a pancake batter. The apples are peeled and cut into thick slices, the core carefully removed, the white wine with sugar and cinnamon poured over the slices, covered and left standing for 1 hour.

Heat the butter in a pan, dip the apple slices into the batter and put them into the hot butter, then put on another tablespoonful of batter and bake on both sides to a nice brown color. Strew sugar and cinnamon over. Serve hot.

No. 52—MACARONI WITH PARMESAN CHEESE.
Quantity for 6 Persons.

½ lb. of macaroni	2 cloves
3 qts. of water	⅛ lb. of butter
1 tbsp. of salt	1 pinch of pepper
1 medium sized onion	⅛ lb. of grated Parmesan cheese

Preparation: The macaroni is broken into pieces and

cooked well in boiling salt water, which will require ½ hour. Drain the water off, strew pepper and grated cheese on, put the butter on and cook a while longer. Serve hot with a tomato or lobster dressing.

No. 53—BAKED MACARONI.
Quantity for 6 Persons.

Ingredients and preparation are the same as given under No. 52, but these are put into a buttered baking-dish, ¾ pt. of cream poured on, roll crumbs and butter on top and baked in the oven to a nice color.

No. 54—MACARONI WITH HAM.
Quantity for 6 Persons.

Ingredients and preparation are given in Chapter 5, No. 13, Boiled Ham With Macaroni.

No. 55—FISH MACARONI.
Quantity for 6 Persons.

½ lb. of macaroni
3 qts. of water
1 tbsp. of salt
2 lbs. of boiled fish
¼ lb. of grated Parmesan cheese
½ pt. white wine
1 tbsp. of flour
1 pt. of cream or milk
2 tbsps. of lemon juice
Salt to taste
1 pinch of pepper
½ cup sliced champignons
¼ lb. of butter

Preparation: The macaroni is broken into inch pieces and boiled in 3 qts. of salt water. The fish is cleaned, dressed and boiled in salt water, then the skin and bones are taken out and the fish cut into small pieces. Butter a baking-dish, put in a layer of macaroni, then fish and Parmesan cheese and champignons, sprinkled with white wine. Repeat this 3 times, the last layer being macaroni. A dressing is made of ⅛ lb. of melted butter into which the flour, cream or milk, lemon juice, salt and pepper are stirred, this poured over the macaroni, the ⅛ lb. of butter cut in small pieces, sprinkled over the top and baked in the oven to a nice color.

No. 56—MACARONI PUDDING.
Quantity for 6 Persons.

½ lb. of macaroni
3 qts. of water, for cooking
1 tbsp. of salt
Scant ¼ lb. of butter
⅛ lb. of grated Parmesan cheese
4 eggs
½ pt. of cream
1 pinch of pepper and one of salt

Preparation: The macaroni is broken into 1 inch pieces,

cooked in 3 qts. of salt water, and drained. Cream the butter, stir in the yolks of eggs, cheese, salt, pepper and macaroni. Beat the whites of eggs and add, stirring lightly. Put into a buttered baking-dish or casserole, which has been strewn with bread crumbs, cover well, set in a steamer over a kettle of boiling water and cook 1 hour. Serve with a truffle or brown butter dressing and turn pudding out on a platter.

No. 57—MUFFIINS.

Quantity for 6 Persons.

½ pt. of flour
½ pt. of corn meal
1/3 cup of sugar
2 eggs
½ pt. of milk
2 tbsps. of melted butter
2 tsps. of baking powder

Preparation: Flour, corn meal, sugar, eggs, milk and melted butter are mixed to a smooth batter, the baking powder added, then small muffin tins buttered and filled with dough. Bake 20 minutes.

No. 58—CHOCOLATE PIE WITH WHIPPED CREAM.

Quantity for 6 Persons.

¼ lb. of butter
1½ cups of flour
½ glass water

For the Filling.

¼ lb. of sugar
¼ lb. grated sweet chocolate
3 eggs
¼ cup of water
1 tsp. vanilla

For the Frosting.

Whipped cream

Preparation: The pie crust is made as given under No. 16. For the filling, cook the chocolate 5 minutes with the water, sugar and vanilla, stirring constantly, remove from the stove and stir in the yolks of eggs and the beaten whites.

This mixture is poured into the baked pie crust and put back into the oven to thicken. When cold, cover with whipped cream mixed with sugar and vanilla.

CHAPTER 16.

SAUCES.

FRUIT.

Stewed fruit used as a sauce is a wholesome and valuable food. It is served with poultry and game. It is refreshing for patients. The fruit must be cooked in a pot or kettle free from any kind of grease. The spices must be removed from sauces and jams before serving. Fruit jams and sauces look best when served in glass dishes.

No. 1—APPLE SAUCE.
Quantity for 6 Persons.

2 lbs. of apples
3 cups of water
Sugar to taste
½ cup of white wine, if you like it
1 slice of lemon
1 tsp. of lemon juice

Preparation: The apples are pared, cored, cut up into eighths, boiled until tender with water, wine, lemon slice, lemon juice and sugar. They should be cooked on a moderate fire to prevent scorching, rubbed through a colander, served cold in a glass dish.

No. 2—CHERRY SAUCE.
Quantity for 6 Persons.

2 lbs. of cherries
Sugar to taste
1 cup of water

Preparation: The cherries are cleaned, the stems picked off, cooked until tender in sugar and water and served cold. Sour cherries require much sugar.

No. 3—STRAWBERRY SAUCE.
Quantity for 6 Persons.

2 qts. of strawberries
1 cup of sugar
½ cup of water

Preparation: The berries are cleaned and washed. Water and sugar are boiled down to a syrup; cool it and put in the strawberries and shake them until they are well mixed with the syrup. Then put them in a cool place.

No. 4—RASPBERRY SAUCE.
Quantity for 6 Persons.

1 qt. of raspberries   ¾ cup of sugar
½ cup of water

Preparation: Clean the berries, boil the water and sugar 5 minutes, then put in the berries and cook a little while. Carefully remove the scum and serve the fruit cold.

No. 5—CURRANT SAUCE.
Quantity for 6 Persons.

2 qts. of currants   1 cup of water
1½ cups of sugar

Preparation: Clean the currants and pick them off the stems. Boil the sugar and water, put in the berries and cook them a few minutes, take them out and put them into a dish. Boil the syrup until thick, then pour over the berries and serve cold.

No. 6—WHORTLEBERRY OR HUCKLEBERRY SAUCE.
Quantity for 6 Persons.

1½ qts. of whortleberries   1 tbsp. of lemon juice
½ cup of sugar   1 lemon slice

Preparation: The berries are picked over, washed, put on the fire with water and sugar to cook. When boiling, add lemon slice and juice, let it boil up a few times, remove the lemon slice and serve cold.

No. 7—BLACK MULBERRY SAUCE.
Quantity for 6 Persons.

2 qts. of mulberries   ½ cup of white wine or water
½ cup of sugar   1½ tbsps. of lemon juice

Preparation: The berries are picked over, washed and the water drained off. White wine and sugar or water and sugar are brought to boil. Add lemon juice and mulberries, cook 1 minute, take them out with a skimmer. Boil down the juice and pour over the berries. Serve cold.

No. 8—FRESH PLUM SAUCE.
Quantity for 6 Persons.

2 lbs. of fresh plums   ½ cup of water   ½ cup of sugar

Preparation: The plums are cut into halves and the stones are taken out. The water and sugar boiled a few minutes, the plums put in, covered and cooked slowly without stirring until tender. Carefully place them into a dish so they will not be crushed. Boil down the juice and pour it over the fruit. Serve cold.

No. 9—GOOSEBERRY SAUCE.

Quantity for 6 Persons.

1½ qts. of gooseberries 2 cups of sugar
¼ cup of water 1 piece of lemon peel

Preparation: The unripe berries are cleaned, i. e., stems and calix removed, scalded and left in the water a few minutes and drained.

Water and sugar are boiled, the berries put in and covered. Let them simmer ½ hour, strew with sugar and serve cold.

Remarks: If there should be much syrup, boil some of it down with sugar until it becomes pink and forms bubbles, then pour on to a moistened plate. This jelly may be used for garnishing.

No. 10—BILBERRY OR BLUEBERRY SAUCE.

Quantity for 6 Persons.

1 qt. berries 2 cups of water
1 cup of sugar

Preparation: The berries are washed, cooked until tender in water and sugar, rubbed through a sieve or colander and served cold.

No. 11—PEACH SAUCE.

Quantity for 6 Persons.

2½ lbs. of peaches ½ cup of water
¾ cup of sugar 10 peach stones

Preparation: The peaches are pared, cut into halves and the stones removed. Sugar and water are boiled a few minutes, the peaches put in and 10 of the stones, set to simmer a few minutes; then take them out with a skimmer, boil down the syrup and pour over the fruit when cold.

No. 12—APRICOT SAUCE.

Quantity for 6 Persons.

The ingredients and preparation are the same as given under No. 11, Peach Sauce.

No. 13—PLUM SAUCE.

Mirabelle Plum.

Quantity for 6 Persons.

1½ lbs. mirabelle plums ¾ cup of white wine or water
1 cup of sugar

Preparation: Sugar and wine are boiled for ½ minute, prick each plum, put them into the boiling sugar and stew them slowly until tender. Serve cold.

No. 14—GREENGAGE SAUCE.
Quantity for 6 Persons.

The preparation of this fruit is the same as given under No. 13, Mirabelle Plum.

No. 15—PINEAPPLE SAUCE.
Quantity for 6 Persons.

1 pineapple
1 cup of sugar
2 tbsps. of lemon juice
1 cup of water

Preparation: The pineapple is peeled, cut up into neat pieces and cooked well done in sugar and water mixed with lemon juice. If there is too much syrup, take out the fruit, boil down the syrup and pour over the fruit. Serve cold.

No. 16—MELON SAUCE.
Quantity for 6 Persons.

2 melons
Juice of 1 lemon
1 cup of sugar
½ cup of water

Preparation: The melons are peeled, the seeds taken out, the fruit cut into neat pieces and boiled until tender in sugar, water and lemon juice. Then take out the melon with a skimmer, boil down the juice to a syrup and pour it over the fruit. Serve cold.

No. 17—ORANGE AND APPLE SAUCE.
Quantity for 6 Persons.

6 sweet-sour apples
6 oranges
½ cup of white wine
½ cup of water
1 cup of sugar

Preparation: The apples and oranges are peeled, the core and seeds removed and each sliced or cut into 8 to 10 equal pieces. The sliced apples are boiled in white wine, water and ½ cup of sugar. Cook slowly, taking care that the pieces do not break. Let them cool. The white skin is removed from the oranges. The yellow skin or peeling is cut up and thickly sugared, set on the stove so the sugar will adhere to the pieces, then set to cool. The orange slices are also sugared well. Now in a glass dish, alternate layers of boiled apples and sliced oranges are placed, repeating twice, and the apple and orange juice poured over. The sugared orange peel is used for garnishing the dish; but the rind of one orange should be sufficient for that.

No. 18—STEWED SLICED APPLES FOR SAUCE.
Quantity for 6 Persons.

12 sweet-sour apples   ¾ cup of sugar
2 cups of water   ½ cup of white wine
¼ cup of currants

Preparation: The apples are peeled, cored and cut into 8 or 10 equal parts. The currants are washed and put to boil with apples, water, wine and sugar. Boil until tender, but not broken. Serve them cold.

No. 19—DRIED APPLES FOR SAUCE.
Quantity for 6 Persons.

½ lb. of dried apples   1 slice of lemon
¾ qt. of water   Juice of ½ lemon
¼ lb. of sugar   1 cup of white wine, if you wish

Preparation: The apples are washed, drained and put to boil in ¾ qt. of water. Set them on the back of the stove where they will heat very slowly and soak while heating. Add the sugar, lemon slice, lemon juice and white wine, let them boil until tender and serve cold.

Remarks: These dried apples may be made into a smooth sauce by rubbing them through a colander or sieve when done.

No. 20—PRUNES FOR SAUCE.
Quantity for 6 Persons.

1 lb. of prunes   1 pt. of water
¾ cup of sugar   1 slice of lemon
Juice of ½ lemon

Preparation: The prunes are washed and set to boil with 1 pt. of water, sugar, lemon slice and lemon juice. If there is too much juice, take the prunes out, boil down to a thicker syrup and pour over the prunes. Serve cold.

No. 21—RHUBARB SAUCE.
Quantity for 6 Persons.

2 bunches of pie plants   1 cup of water
Sugar to taste

Preparation: Skin the rhubarb and cut it up in 2 inch pieces, cook until tender in water and much sugar. Serve cold. Rhubarb requires much sugar, as it is very sour.

Remarks: If you like, you can thicken this sauce with a little corn starch dissolved in water.

No. 22—PEAR SAUCE.
Quantity for 6 Persons.

2 lbs. of juicy pears
1½ qts. of water
¼ lb. of sugar
1 clove
1 stick of cinnamon
1 slice of lemon
1 tbsp. of corn starch

Preparation: The pears are peeled, large pears cut into 4 parts, small ones into halves. The core is cut out and the pears cooked until tender in water, sugar, cloves, cinnamon and lemon slice. It is best to cook them very slowly in a granite or porcelain dish. When the pears are soft, take them out, add the corn starch to the syrup, boil it down and pour over the fruit. Serve cold or warm.

No. 23—TOMATO SAUCE.
Quantity for 6 Persons.

12 medium sized tomatoes
2 cups of sugar
1½ cups of water
3 cloves
½ sliced lemon

Preparation: The tomatoes are scalded and skinned. Water, sugar, cloves and lemon slices brought to boil and the tomatoes put in 2 or 3 at a time. When they are done, take them out and put in others until all are boiled. Boil down the syrup if there is too much of it and pour over the tomatoes after straining.

CHAPTER 17.

DESSERTS.

Directions for preparing all kinds of desserts, cold and warm; puddings, puff pastes, souffles, sherbets, creams, ices and ice creams.

Steamed Puddings.

No. 1—RICE PUDDING.
Quantity for 6 Persons.

½ lb. of rice
1 qt. of milk
¼ lb. of fresh butter
¼ lb. of sugar, scant
¼ lb. of raisins
¼ lb. of ground almonds
7 eggs
1 pinch of salt

Preparation: The rice is washed and brought to boil in 1 cup of water. When the water is boiled down, add the milk gradually and 1 pinch of salt and boil to a thick mush. When done, cool it off. Cream the butter, add sugar, 7 yolks of eggs, raisins, almonds and the beaten whites of eggs. Butter a pudding-mold, strew in some bread crumbs, put in the rice pudding, close the mold well and set in a steamer over a kettle of boiling water and boil for 1½ hours. When serving, turn the pudding out on a platter and serve cold with a vanilla or wine sauce or sweet cream.

No. 2—APPLE RICE PUDDING.
Quantity for 6 Persons.

½ lb. of rice
¾ qt. of milk
⅛ lb. of butter
¼ lb. of raisins
7 eggs
1 pinch of salt
6 sweet-sour apples
1 cup of sugar
¼ lb. of blanched, ground almonds

Preparation: The rice is cooked slowly with one cup of water; when the water is boiled down, add the milk gradually and cook it to a thick mush. Cream the butter, add the sugar, then the yolks of eggs, raisins and almonds. Let rice cool, then mix all together. The apples are peeled, cored, cut into 16 parts and stewed until tender in a little water and sugar. Butter a pudding-mold and strew with bread crumbs. Stir the well-beaten whites of the 7 eggs into the rice, put a layer of rice into the mold, then a layer of apples and repeat this twice; the last layer to be rice. Close the mold, set in a steamer over a kettle of boiling water and boil 1½ hours, then turn over on platter and serve with sweet cream.

No. 3—CHERRY RICE PUDDING.
Quantity for 6 Persons.

½ lb. of rice
¾ qts. of milk
⅛ lb. butter
7 eggs
¼ lb. of peeled and ground almonds
¼ lb. of raisins
1 lb. stoned sour cherries
1 cup of sugar

Preparation: The preparation is again the same as No. 2, instead of apples put in layers of sour cherries, boiled until tender in 1 cup of sugar and 1 cup of water. Boil down the cherry juice with sugar to taste and serve it with the pudding.

No. 4—PEACH RICE PUDDING.
Quantity for 6 Persons.

½ lb. of rice
¾ qt. of milk
7 eggs
⅛ lb. of butter
¼ lb. of peeled and ground almonds
¼ lb. of raisins
1½ lbs. of peaches
½ lb. of sugar

Preparation: The preparation is again the same as No. 2, instead of apples put in layers of peaches, boiled until tender in 1 cup of water and one of sugar. Boil down the peach juice, putting in a few stones which should be removed before serving, and serve the syrup with the pudding.

No. 5—APRICOT RICE PUDDING.
Quantity for 6 Persons.

½ lb. of rice
¾ qt. of milk
⅛ lb. of butter
7 eggs
1½ lbs. of stoned apricots
¼ lb. of sugar
¼ lb. of peeled and ground almonds
¼ lb. of raisins

Preparation: The preparation is the same as given under No. 2, see Apple Rice Pudding. Instead of apples put in layers of apricots boiled until tender in 1 cup of water and ½ cup of sugar. Boil down the juice with some sugar and serve with the pudding.

No. 6—PLAIN RICE PUDDING.
Quantity for 6 Persons.

½ lb. of rice
1 qt. of milk
¼ lb. of butter
7 eggs
¼ lb. of sugar

Preparation: The preparation is the same as given under No. 1, Rice Pudding.

No. 7—FROTH OR FOAM PUDDING.
Quantity for 6 Persons.

½ pt. of milk
¼ lb. of butter
¼ lb. of sugar
¼ lb. of fine flour
1 lemon peel
8 eggs

Preparation:. The milk is brought to boil, the butter added, sugar and flour are mixed and stirred into the boiling milk until the mixture comes off the sides of the skillet. Then cool it, grate the lemon peel and stir it in with the yolks of eggs and the beaten whites. Butter a pudding-mold and strew in bread crumbs, then put in the pudding, set in a steamer over a kettle of boiling water, cover the mold tightly and boil for 2 hours. Turn it, and serve with a fruit sauce.

No. 8—CABINET PUDDING.
Quantity for 6 Persons.

8 zwieback
12 lady fingers
¼ lb. of raisins
¼ lb. of currants
1 pt. of milk
1 pt. of cream
6 eggs
¼ lb. of sugar

Preparation: The zwieback is broken into 3 parts, the lady fingers into halves. Butter a mold and make a layer of zwieback, raisins, currants, then one of lady fingers, repeat this 2 to 3 times, the last layer being zwieback. Then mix well the milk, cream, sugar and eggs and pour on the pudding, set in a steamer over a kettle of boiling water and boil 1½ hours. When done, turn it out on a platter and serve with a wine sauce.

No. 9—WHEAT BREAD PUDDIING.
Quantity for 6 Persons.

¼ lb. of fresh butter
6 eggs
¼ lb. of sugar
½ cup of raisins
¼ cup of currants
½ cup of fine cut citron
½ cup blanched, grated almonds
4 milk rolls

Preparation: Cream the butter with yolks of eggs, sugar, raisins, currants, citron and almonds, mix and stir well. The crust of the rolls is grated off, then they are soaked in milk.

the surplus milk pressed out and the rolls stirred with the rest of the ingredients, also the beaten whites of eggs. Butter a mold, strew with bread crumbs, put in the pudding and steam 1 hour. Serve with a fruit sauce.

No. 10—PLUM PUDDING.
Quantity for 6—8 Persons.

1 pinch of salt	6 eggs
1 lb. raisins	1 lemon peel
1 lb. currants	2 cups of milk
1 lb. of flour	2 small cups of grated bread
1 lb. of sugar	½ cup of brandy
1 lb. beef kidney suet	Rum

Preparation: Raisins and currants are washed well and dried. The suet is chopped very fine and mixed well with 6 eggs, sugar, raisins, currants, grated lemon peel, milk, bread crumbs, brandy and lastly the flour. Butter a mold, strew with bread crumbs, put in the pudding and steam for 5 hours. Turn the pudding out on a platter, pour the rum over and light it. The flaming pudding is brought to the table and served with a wine sauce.

No. 11—CHOCOLATE PUDDING.
Quantity for 6 Persons.

1 pt. of milk	Scant ¼ lb. of sugar
Scant ¼ lb. of butter	⅛ lb. blanched, ground almonds
¼ lb. grated sweet chocolate	6 eggs ¼ lb. fine flour

Preparation: The milk is brought to boil, butter, sugar, flour, chocolate well stirred in until the mixture comes off the sides of the skillet, then take from the stove. Cool it and stir in the almonds, yolks of eggs and the beaten whites.

Butter a mold, strew with bread crumbs, fill with the pudding, cover tightly and steam 1½ hours, then turn out on a platter and serve with a vanilla sauce.

Remarks: The dish must be only ¾ full because the pudding raises very much.

No. 12—FLOUR PUDDING.
Quantity for 6 Persons.

¼ lb. of fine flour	½ grated lemon peel
8 eggs	¼ lb. of sugar 4 tbsps. of lemon juice

Preparation: Beat the yolks of eggs with sugar 20 minutes, add lemon juice and grated rind and lastly stir in the flour, which must be sifted 4 times. The whites of eggs are beaten to a stiff froth and mixed in. Butter a mold, put in the pudding, close it well and steam 1¼ hours. Turn the pudding on a platter and serve with a wine sauce.

No. 13—LAYER PUDDING.

Quantity for 6 Persons.

½ pt. of cream	5 beaten whites of eggs
¼ lb. of flour	¼ lb. of sugar
⅛ lb. of butter	½ lemon peel — 5 yolks of eggs

For the Filling.

½ lb. peach marmalade, or   1 qt. of cherry or strawberry preserves

For Between Layers, 4 Small Pancakes.

¼ lb. of flour   1 pinch of salt
3 tbsps. of butter   ¼ lemon peel
4 eggs   Butter, for baking   ¼ pt. of milk

Preparation: Cream, flour, butter, yolks of eggs are mixed well and brought to boil. When the batter rolls from the sides of the pot, take it off the fire to cool. Then add sugar, grated lemon peel, and 5 whites of eggs beaten to a stiff froth.

Now bake the pancakes. Mix well the milk, flour, 3 tablespoonfuls of melted butter, 4 eggs and a little salt. Heat a pan with butter and bake the pancakes the size of the pudding dish. Now butter the mold, strew bread crumbs in, make 1 layer of pudding batter, one layer of fruit marmalade or preserved fruit as peaches, cherries, strawberries or raspberries; on this fruit layer, place a pancake, then another layer of pudding batter, again a layer of fruit, another pancake and so on according to the number of pancakes you have. The top layer must be the pudding batter. Close the dish well and steam for 1½ hours. When done, turn the pudding out and serve with a fruit sauce.

No. 14—FARINA PUDDING No. 1

Quantity for 6 Persons.

1 pt. of milk	¼ lb. of blanched, ground almonds
1 cup of fine farina	
⅛ lb. of butter	The rind of ¼ lemon
Scant ¼ lb. of sugar	6 eggs

Preparation: Milk and butter are brought to boil, the farina stirred in, the sugar and lemon rind added and all stirred and cooked until the batter rolls from the sides of the skillet, then cool it off and add almonds, yolks of eggs and beaten whites. Butter a mold, strew with roll crumbs, put in the pudding, close the mold well and steam 1½ hours. Turn the pudding out on a platter and serve with cherry or raspberry sauce.

No. 15—MACARONI PUDDING.
Quantity for 6 Persons.

Ingredients and preparation are the same as given under No. 56, in Chapter 15, Macaroni Pudding.

No. 16—POTATO PUDDING.
Quantity for 6 Persons.

Ingredients and preparation are given in Chapter 10, No. 16, Potato Pudding.

No. 17—MEAT PUDDING WITH RICE LAYERS.
Quantity for 6 Persons.

Ingredients and preparation are the same as given as in Chapter 2, Beef, No. 2, Meat Pudding, from Roast Beef, Stew or Soup Meat.

No. 18—ANOTHER FORM OF MEAT PUDDING.
Quantity for 6 Persons.

Ingredients and preparation are the same as given in Chapter 2, Beef, No. 26, Meat Pudding.

No. 19—MUTTON KIDNEY PUDDING.
Quantity for 6 Persons.

Ingredients and preparations are given in Chapter 4, Lamb, No. 20, Lamb Kidney Pudding.

No. 20—VEAL ROAST PUDDING.
Quantity for 6 Persons.

Ingredients and preparation are the same as given in Chapter 3, Veal, No. 6, Veal Roast Pudding.

No. 21—GOOSE LIVER PUDDING.
Quantity for 6 Persons.

Ingredients and preparation are given in Chapter 6, Poultry, No. 26, Goose Liver Pudding.

No. 22—CHERRY PUDDING.
Quantity for 6—8 Persons.

8 milk rolls
¾ qt. of milk
¼ lb. of butter
8 eggs
Rind of 1 lemon
¼ tsp. of cinnamon
2 lbs. stoned cherries
¾ cup of sugar

Preparation: The milk rolls are grated and soaked in milk. When well soaked, press out the milk and rub them through a strainer or colander. Melt the butter in a spider, put in the mashed rolls and sauté or dry fry them on the stove. Now mix this well with yolks of eggs, grated lemon rind, cinnamon, sugar, stoned cherries and cherry syrup. Beat the whites of eggs to a stiff froth and add to the mixture. Butter a pudding mold, strew in bread crumbs, then fill with the pudding and steam for 2 hours. Turn out and serve.

No. 23—FARINA PUDDING No. 2.
Quantity for 6 Persons.

1 qt. of milk
¼ lb. of butter
¾ cup of sugar
1 grated lemon peel
¾ cup of fine farina
8 bitter almonds
¼ lb. sweet almonds
8 eggs

Preparation: The milk and butter are brought to boil, then the sugar, lemon peel and farina poured in and cooked 5 minutes to a thick paste, stirring constantly. Now take from the fire, cool off and add blanched and ground sweet and bitter almonds, the 8 yolks of eggs and the beaten whites. Butter a pudding mold, strew with bread crumbs, put in the pudding and steam 1½ hours. Turn the pudding out and serve with a fruit or wine sauce.

No. 24—SOUR CREAM PUDDING.
Quantity for 6 Persons.

½ pt. thick, sour cream
Juice and peel of ½ lemon
10 eggs
¾ lb. of roll crumbs
¼ tsp. of salt
1 cup of currants
½ cup of sugar

Preparation: The thick sour cream is mixed well and stirred 10 minutes with juice and grated peel of lemon, yolks of eggs, roll crumbs, salt, currants and beaten whites of eggs. A mold is buttered and strewn with roll crumbs, the pudding filled in and steamed 1½ hours. Then it is turned out on a platter and served with a wine or fruit sauce.

No. 25—BLACK PUDDING.
Quantity for 6 Persons.

⅛ lb. of ground almonds
¼ lb. sweet chocolate
¼ lb. of sugar
⅛ lb. of small raisins
¼ cup chopped citron
¼ tsp. cinnamon
⅛ tsp. ground cloves
¾ cup of roll crumbs
¼ cup of white wine
6 eggs

Preparation: The unblanched almonds are ground, the chocolate grated. Sugar and yolks of eggs are stirred 20 minutes, then mixed well with almonds, chocolate, raisins, citron, cinnamon, cloves, roll crumbs, white wine and beaten whites of eggs. Butter a mold, strew it with crumbs, put in the pudding, close it well and steam 1½ hours. Turn it out and serve with a chocolate sauce.

No. 26—PUDDING A LA BRANDENBURG.
Quantity for 6—8 Persons.

1 pt. of milk	1 tbsp. chopped bitter almonds
⅛ lb. of butter	2 tbsps. chopped citron
¼ lb. flour, good measure	1 tbsp. chopped orange rind
¼ lb. of sugar	½ grated lemon peel
⅛ lb. of blanched, chopped sweet almonds	7 eggs
	¼ cup of rum

Preparation: Milk and butter are brought to boil, add the flour and boil, stirring constantly till it comes from the sides of the skillet. Cool and stir in the sugar, sweet and bitter almonds, citron, orange and lemon peel, yolks of eggs and the beaten whites. Butter a pudding mold, strew it with roll crumbs, put in the pudding, close well and steam for 2 hours. Turn the pudding out on a platter, pour on ¼ cup of rum, light it and bring it to the table. Serve with a wine sauce.

Warm Puddings, Baked Puddings.
No. 27—BAKED CREAM PUDDING.
Quantity for 6 Persons.

¾ qt. of sour cream	2 tbsps. of lemon juice
¾ cup of sugar	3 tbsps. of flour
½ lemon peel	7 eggs

Preparation: The sour cream is mixed well with sugar, grated lemon peel, lemon juice, flour, 7 yolks of eggs and beaten whites. Then bake in the oven in a buttered pudding dish for 25 to 30 minutes.

No. 28—BAKED RICE PUDDING.
Quantity for 6 Persons.

1 cup of rice	⅛ lb. of butter	
¾ qt. of milk	4 eggs	½ cup of sugar

Preparation: The rice is boiled to a thick mush with milk. Cream the butter with sugar and yolks of eggs, add the rice and the beaten whites of eggs, fill into a buttered pudding dish and bake in oven ½ hour.

Remarks: The pudding may be made richer with ¼ lb. blanched, ground almonds, ½ cup of raisins, 6 to 8 eggs instead of 4.

No. 29—BAKED RICE PUDDING WITH FRUIT LAYERS.
Quantity for 6 Persons.

1 cup of rice	1 qt. boiled fruit, (cherries, apricots or peaches)	
¾ qt. of milk		
⅛ lb. of butter	6 eggs	½ cup of sugar

Preparation: The preparation of the rice is the same as given under No. 28, Baked Rice Pudding.

The buttered pudding dish is filled with alternating layers of rice and fruit, from which the juice has been drained. Put in 3 layers of each and the top layer should be rice. Bake in oven for 1 hour and serve with the sauce from the fruit used in the pudding.

No. 30—BAKED FARINA PUDDING WITH FRUIT.
Quantity for 6 Persons.

1 qt. of milk
1 cup of farina
¼ lb. of butter
1 grated lemon rind
3 tbsps. of lemon juice
¼ lb. sugar
5 eggs
1 qt. cherries

Preparation: The milk is brought to boil, the farina put in and stirred 10 minutes. Let it get cold. Cream the butter, add grated lemon rind, lemon juice, sugar, 5 yolks of eggs and the farina and stir in the beaten whites of eggs. Butter a pudding dish and fill it with alternating layers of farina and cherries, 2 layers of each; the top layer should be farina. Put a few pieces of butter over the top and bake in oven 1 hour.

No. 31—BAKED CHERRY PUDDING.
Quantity for 6 Persons.

¼ lb. of butter
¼ lb. of sugar
6 eggs
¼ lb. blanched, ground almonds
3 rolls
3 lbs. sweet cherries

Preparation: Soak the rolls in milk, cream the butter with sugar, add the yolks of eggs, almonds and rolls, after pressing out the milk; mix well, add the stoned cherries and beaten whites of eggs. Butter a baking-dish, put in the pudding and bake in oven 1 hour.

No. 32—BAKED LEMON PUDDING.
Quantity for 6 Persons.

8 eggs
¼ lb. of sugar   1 tbsp. corn starch
½ lemon peel
Juice of 1½ lemons

Preparation: The 8 yolks of eggs are beaten ¼ hour with sugar, lemon juice and grated lemon peel, the corn starch and beaten whites of eggs added last. Butter a baking-dish, fill in the pudding and bake 15 minutes.

No. 33—BAKED POTATO PUDDING.
Quantity for 6 Persons.

½ lb. boiled, grated potatoes   ½ pt. of cream
6 eggs   ¼ lb. of sugar   1 grated lemon rind

Preparation: Cream the yolks of eggs and sugar, add the grated lemon peel, grated potatoes, cream, beaten whites of eggs, and mix well. Put the batter into a buttered baking-dish and bake in oven 45 minutes. Serve with a fruit sauce.

No. 34—BAKED POTATO PUDDING.
To be Served with Meat.
Quantity for 6 Persons.

8 medium sized potatoes — ½ tbsp. Parmesan cheese
1/10 lb. of butter — 1 pinch of pepper
2—3 eggs — Salt to taste

Preparation: The potatoes are boiled, peeled and grated. Cream the butter with the yolks of eggs, add the potatoes, cheese, salt, pepper and beaten whites of eggs. Butter a casserole or pudding-dish, put the pudding in, sprinkle bread crumbs and pieces of butter over the top and bake in oven 45 minutes.

No. 35—BAKED CHARLOTTE PUDDING.
Quantity for 6 Persons.

6 rolls — ½ cup of blanched, ground almonds
½ pt. of milk
¼ pt. of white wine — ½ cup of raisins
¼ lb. of sugar — ½ grated lemon peel
4 eggs

Preparation: The rolls are soaked in milk and wine, add ground almonds, sugar, raisins, lemon peel, yolks of 4 eggs and lastly the beaten whites of eggs. A baking dish is buttered, the pudding filled in and baked in oven 45 minutes. A fruit or wine sauce is served with the pudding.

No. 36—BAKED ALMOND PUDDING.
Quantity for 6 Persons.

8 eggs — ¾ cup of sugar
¼ lb. blanched, ground almonds — ¼ lb. fine flour

Preparation: The yolks of eggs, almonds and sugar are stirred 20 minutes, then the flour and whites of eggs added. A pudding-dish is buttered, the pudding filled in and baked 45 minutes.

No. 37—BAKED YORKSHIRE PUDDING.
Quantity for 6 Persons.

1 egg — 1 pinch of salt
1 white of egg — 6 tbsps. of butter
½ pt. of milk — 6 tbsps. of mutton suet — 1 cup of flour

Preparation: Egg, white of egg, milk and flour are mixed well. Butter is heated in a pudding-dish, the batter put in, the suet heated and poured over and the pudding baked in a hot oven 20 minutes.

No. 38—BAKED CHOCOLATE PUDDING.
Quantity for 6 Persons.

1¼ pts. of milk — ¼ lb. of sugar
¼ lb. of sweet chocolate — ¾ cup of butter
4 tbsps. of flour — 7 eggs — 1 tsp. of vanilla

Preparation: The chocolate is grated and mixed with

flour and sugar. The milk is brought to boil and the chocolate with the flour and sugar added, stirred over the fire until the mixture is thick, then cooled. Cream the butter with the yolks of eggs and vanilla, mix with the chocolate batter and the beaten whites of eggs. Butter a pudding-dish, fill in the pudding and bake in oven for 1 hour.

No. 39—BAKED APPLE AND FARINA PUDDING.
Quantity for 6 Persons.

1 pt. of milk
½ cup of fine farina
4 eggs
¼ lb. of butter
6 large sweet-sour apples
¼ lb. of raisins or currants
⅛ lb. blanched, ground sweet almonds
6 blanched, ground bitter almonds
One lemon peel

Preparation: The milk is brought to boil, the farina added and cooked 10 minutes, stirring constantly, then cooled. Cream the butter, mix with yolks of eggs, sugar, grated lemon peel, the boiled farina, and the beaten whites of eggs.

The apples are peeled, sliced into ¼ inch slices, mixed with ½ cup of sugar. Butter a pudding-dish and put in layers of farina, apples, currants and almonds alternating, repeat 3 times; then bake in oven for 1 hour.

No. 40—BAKED APPLE STEW PUDDING.
Quantity for 6 Persons.

⅛ lb. of good butter
8 medium sized sweet-sour apples
½ cup of sugar
1½ heaping tbsps. of flour
1 pt. thick sweet cream
4 eggs
1 lemon peel

Preparation: The apples are peeled, cut into 4 inch slices and stewed in ⅛ lb. of butter, then cooled. Beat 4 yolks of eggs for 30 minutes with sugar, add flour, grated lemon peel, cream and the stewed apples. Lastly add the beaten whites of eggs. Butter a pudding-dish, put in the pudding and bake 45 minutes.

No. 41—FINE BAKED APPLE PUDDING:
Quantity for 6 Persons.

6 medium sized, sweet-sour apples
½ cup of currants
¼ cup of blanched, ground almonds
2 tbsps. of sugar
¼ tsp. of cinnamon
½ grated lemon peel
¾ qt. thick, sweet cream
5 eggs
½ cup of sugar
2 tbsps. of flour

Preparation: The apples are peeled, cored and filled with a mixture of currants, almonds and 2 tablespoonfuls of sugar. Butter a pudding-dish, put in the filled apples, make a batter of cream, cinnamon, lemon peel, yolks of eggs, sugar, flour and beaten whites of eggs, then pour over the apples and bake slowly.

No. 42—BAKED OMELET PUDDING.
Quantity for 6 Persons.

6 eggs   ½ grated lemon peel   6 tbsps. of sugar

Preparation: The yolks of eggs are beaten 25 minutes with the sugar, the beaten whites of eggs lightly mixed in, then put into a buttered pudding dish, and bake in oven 20 minutes.

No. 43—BAKED CREAM PUDDING.
Quantity for 6—8 Persons.

1 pt. of milk   1 tbsp. of butter
7 eggs   ½ grated lemon peel
⅛ lb. of corn starch   ⅛ lb. of sugar

Preparation: Milk, butter and sugar are brought to boil. Four yolks of eggs are stirred smooth with the corn starch and added to the boiling milk to cook 3 minutes, stirring constantly; then cooled and three yolks of eggs, grated lemon peel, beaten whites of 7 eggs added.

Butter a dish, put in the pudding and bake in oven ½ hour. Serve with a fruit sauce.

No. 44—BAKED FLOUR PUDDING.
Quantity for 6 Persons.

¾ qt. of milk   ¼ lb. blanched, ground
½ cup of flour   almonds
¼ lb. of sugar   5 eggs

Preparation: Flour and ½ cup of milk are stirred smooth, the rest of the milk brought to boil and the flour stirred in to boil 1 minute. The almonds, sugar and eggs are stirred in and beaten 10 minutes. Butter a pudding dish, put in the batter and bake in oven for 1 hour. Serve with a raspberry sauce.

No. 45—BAKED SPONGE PUDDING.
Quantity for 6 Persons.

6 eggs   ¾ cup of sugar
4 tbsps. of thick, sour cream   2 tsps. of vanilla

Preparation: Yolks of eggs, cream, sugar and vanilla are stirred 20 minutes. The beaten whites of eggs are mixed in and put into a buttered pudding dish. Bake in medium hot oven for ½ hour. A fruit sauce is served with it.

No. 46—BAKED VEAL ROAST PUDDING.
Quantity for 6—8 Persons.

Ingredients and preparation are given in Chapter 3, Veal, No. 6, Veal Roast Pudding.

No. 47—BAKED SWEET PUDDING WITH WINE FROSTING.

Quantity for 6 Persons.

6 rolls	⅛ lb. chopped citron or almonds
1 pt. of milk	1¼ grated lemon peel
¼ lb. of good butter	¼ tsp. of cinnamon
¼ lb. of sugar	6 eggs

For Wine Frosting.

6 eggs	¼ tsp. of cinnamon
⅛ lb. of sugar	2 glasses of French white wine
Peel and juice of 1 lemon	1 glass of arrack

Preparation: The crust is grated off the rolls, these are cut up, soaked in milk for 1 hour, then the milk is pressed out and the soaked rolls stirred with the melted butter to a creamy mass. Add sugar, citron, cinnamon, 6 yolks of eggs, and the beaten whites. Butter a pudding dish, put in the batter and bake 1 hou

Prepare the frosting by mixing 6 yolks of eggs, sugar, grated lemon peel and lemon juice, cinnamon, French white wine and arrack and heating it on the fire while beating constantly. Then add the 6 beaten whites of eggs to the hot sauce. Pour the wine sauce over the hot baked pudding and serve at once.

No. 48—BAKED RYE BREAD PUDDING WITH APPLES.

Quantity for 6 Persons.

2½ cups of soaked rye bread	6—8 medium sized, sweet-sour apples	
3 eggs		
1 cup of sugar	⅛ lb. of butter	¾ cup of currants

Preparation: The apples are peeled, cored, cut into slices ¼ inch thick. Cream the butter, add sugar, yolks of eggs, rye bread, currants and beaten whites of eggs. Butter a pudding dish and fill it with alternating layers of rye bread mixture and apples with sugar sprinkled over, repeat 2 or 3 times. The top layer should be rye bread. Put on small pieces of butter and bake in oven 1 hour. Serve sweet cream with the pudding.

No. 49—BAKED NOODLE PUDDING.

Quantity for 6 Persons.

Noodles made from 2 eggs	¾ cup of sugar
Salt water	½ cup of currants
6—8 medium sized, sweet-sour apples	1 cup of water

Preparation: The noodles are cooked in salt water for 10 minutes, then the water is drained off. The apples are peeled, cored and sliced. Butter a pudding dish and fill with alternating layers of noodles and apples with sugar and currants. The top layer should be noodles. Pour on a cup of water, put on small pieces of butter and bake in oven 1 hour.

No. 50—BAKED QUINCE PUDDING.
Quantity for 6 Persons.

6—8 quinces
¼ lb. of sugar
Juice and peel of 1 lemon
6 eggs

Preparation: The quinces are boiled until soft in water, then skin and grate them. The grated quince should weigh about ¾ lb. Stir until white. Add sugar, grated lemon peel and juice, yolks and beaten whites of eggs. Put into a buttered dish and bake in oven ½ hour.

No. 51—BAKED MACAROON PUDDING.
Quantity for 6 Persons.

2 tbsps. of butter
½ pt. of milk
Scant ⅛ lb. of flour
2 tbsps. of cream
3 cups of sweet macaroons
¼ cup of bitter macaroons
5 eggs
⅛ lb. of sugar
⅛ lb. blanched, ground almonds
1 tbsp. of vanilla

Preparation: Butter, milk, flour, crushed macaroons are stirred over the fire until they form a thick batter; remove from the fire and stir until it has cooled off. Add the yolks of eggs, sugar, almonds, vanilla, beaten whites of eggs. Put into a buttered dish and bake in oven for 1 hour. Serve with a fruit sauce.

Remarks: This pudding may be steamed for 1½ hours.

Sweetmeats Baked or Fried in Pans On the Stove.

No. 52—FRENCH TOAST.
Quantity for 6 Persons.

6 milk rolls
1 pt. of cream or milk
¼ cup of sugar
2 eggs
½ tsp. of cinnamon
Butter or lard for baking

Preparation: The rolls are sliced, cream, sugar, eggs, cinnamon are mixed and poured over the slices to soak. Butter is heated in a pan, the roll slices baked a golden yellow in it and sprinkled thickly with sugar and cinnamon. Serve dried or fresh fruit sauce with it.

No. 53—CARTHUSIAN DUMPLINGS WITH WINE SAUCE.
Quantity for 6 Persons.

6 fresh rolls
1½ pts. of milk
2 eggs
¼ cup of sugar
½ tsp. of cinnamon
Butter for baking

Preparation: The crust of the rolls is grated off, then

quarter them and soak in a pint of milk. After soaking, press out the milk, mix the milk well with eggs, sugar, cinnamon and pour it back on the roll slices to soak for a while longer. Now roll each piece in the crumbs from the crusts and bake in butter to a nice color. Serve on a hot platter with wine sauce.

No. 54—APPLE FRITTERS OR BANANA FRITTERS.
Quantity for 6 Persons.

4 sweet-sour apples or bananas   ½ glass of white wine
½ cup of sugar

For the Batter.
3 eggs   ¼ tsp. of salt
1 cup of flour   1½ cups of milk   Butter for frying

Preparation: The apples are peeled, the core removed, sliced in ½ inch thick, round slices, white wine and sugar poured over. Eggs, milk, flour and salt are mixed to a batter. Butter is heated in a pan, each apple slice dipped into the batter, put into the hot butter and fried a nice color. Serve on a hot platter, sprinkled with sugar and cinnamon.

No. 55—APPLE STRUDEL.
Quantity for 6 Persons.

Noodle dough from 3 eggs   Flour   ⅛ lb. of butter

For the Filling.
6 medium sized, sweet-sour apples   ½ tsp. of cinnamon
½ cup of sugar   ¼ lb. blanched, chopped almonds
½ cup of currants   ¼ cup of chopped citron
   Butter for baking

Preparation: The noodle dough is rolled out very thin. Melt the butter and brush it on the dough. Peel and core the apples and slice them thin. Then put the apple slices, sugar, cinnamon, almonds and citron on the dough, roll it up, brush it with butter and bake in a buttered pan 30 to 45 minutes. Sprinkle with sugar and cinnamon and serve.

No. 56—CHOCOLATE STRUDEL.
Quantity for 6 Persons.

Noodle dough from 3 eggs   ⅛ lb. of butter   Flour

For the Filling.
5 eggs   10 blanched, chopped bitter almonds
Scant ½ cup of sugar
⅛ lb. blanched, chopped sweet almonds   1/3 lb. grated sweet chocolate
   Butter for baking

Preparation: The noodle dough is kneaded with ⅛ lb. of butter, then rolled out very thin. The 5 yolks of eggs are stirred with sugar for 15 minutes, almonds and chocolate are added, and lastly the beaten whites of eggs. This mixture is spread on the dough which is then rolled up. A baking pan is buttered and the strudel baked ½ to ¾ hour.

No. 57—CHOCOLATE STRUDEL WITH DRESSING.
Quantity for 6 Persons.

The ingredients and preparation are the same as given under No. 56, Chocolate Strudel. When ready to be baked, place it into the pan in the form of a snail, pour on ¾ pt. of hot cream mixed with ⅛ lb. of fine grated chocolate and 1 tablespoonful of vanilla, then bake ½ hour.

No. 58—STEAM NOODLES.
Quantity for 6 Persons.

⅛ lb. of flour
½ pt. of milk
1 cent's worth of yeast
¼ lb. of butter

3 eggs
1½ cups of flour
1 qt. of cream
⅛ lb. of butter

½ cup of sugar

Preparation: Mix flour, milk and yeast to a batter and set to rise. When risen, mix in butter, sugar, eggs and flour. Put on a well-floured baking board and form dumplings from the dough, leaving them on the board to rise. Stew them 15 minutes in the hot cream and ⅛ lb. of butter until light brown, then sprinkle with sugar and pour drawn butter over.

No. 59—FRIED APPLE POCKETS.
Quantity for 6 Persons.

6 small apples   ½ cup of sugar   Raspberry jelly

Pancake Batter.

3 eggs
¾ cup of milk

Salt
2 cups of flour

Lard for baking

Preparation: The apples are pared, cored, filled with jelly and strewn with sugar.

Eggs, milk, salt and flour are stirred into a dough that is rolled out to ¼ inch thickness. With a tumbler cut out 12 round disks. Put each apple between two disks and press the edges together, so as to completely cover the apple. Then fry in much hot lard, place into a colander to drain off the fat and sprinkle with sugar and cinnamon. They may be served warm or cold.

No. 60—BISCUIT TORTONI. MACAROON MOUSSE.
Quantity for 6 Persons.

6 eggs
1 cup of powdered sugar
1 cup of grated macaroons
1 tsp. vanilla
1 pt. whipped cream

Preparation: Whip the yolks of eggs, vanilla and sugar well, mix in the macaroons, beaten whites of eggs and whipped cream. Oil a mold, put in the mixture and let it stand in ice 6 hours before serving.

No. 61—RUM CREAM WITH CHERRY SAUCE.
Quantity for 6—10 Persons.

6 eggs
¾ cup of rum
¼ lb. of sugar
1½ tsps. of vanilla
5 layers of gelatine or ½ package
½ pt. of milk
1 pt. whipped cream

Preparation: Yolks of eggs, rum and sugar are whipped to a froth. Milk and vanilla are brought to boil, the gelatine dissolved in a little milk and mixed with the boiling milk to which also the mixture of yolks of eggs, rum and sugar is added. This mixture must be stirred until it is cold, then the beaten whites of eggs and finally the whipped cream is stirred in. Rinse a mold with cold water, put in the pudding and place on ice or in a cold place. Turn the pudding out on a platter and serve with cherry sauce.

No. 62—WHIPPED CREAM PUDDING.
Quantity for 6 Persons.

1 pt. of whipped cream
½ cup of sugar
2 tsps. of vanilla
2 qts. of fresh strawberries
1 cup of sugar
1 cup of grated pumpernickel
¼ lb. of grated chocolate
¼ cup of sugar

Preparation: The cream is mixed with sugar and vanilla. The strawberries are cleaned and mixed with 1 cup of sugar. Pumpernickel, chocolate and ¼ cup of sugar are mixed. Now arrange in a glass dish layers of strawberries, pumpernickel and whipped cream. The latter garnished with strawberries make the top layer.

No. 63—WINE PUDDING.
Quantity for 6 Persons.

¾ pt. good white wine
Juice of 2 lemons
1 grated lemon rind
½ lb. of sugar
8 eggs
4 layers or 1/3 package of white gelatine
Fruit for garnishing

Preparation: White wine, lemon juice, and lemon rind, sugar, 8 yolks of eggs are stirred well on the stove and brought to boil ¼ minute. The gelatine is dissolved in 4 tablespoonfuls of wine and mixed in with the rest, also the beaten whites of eggs. Oil a mold, put in the mixture and put on ice or in a cold place. When stiff, turn it out on a platter and garnish with fruit.

No. 64—WINE CREAM.
Quantity for 6 Persons.

¾ pt. good white wine
¼ cup of French brandy or cognac
½ cup of cherry juice
Juice of 1 lemon
¼ lb. of sugar
6 eggs
6 layers or ½ package of red gelatine
Juice of 1 orange
1 pinch of salt

Preparation: White wine, brandy, cherry juice, lemon juice, orange juice, sugar, yolks of eggs and the gelatine dissolved in wine are mixed well and stirred over a slow fire until it thickens, but do not let it boil. While still warm, add the whites of eggs beaten to a froth and salt. Oil a mold, put in the cream and place on ice or prepare it a day before using. When serving, turn it out and garnish with cherries.

No. 65—WINE JELLY WITH RICE LAYERS.
Quantity for 6 Persons.

Wine Jelly.

½ bottle of white wine
9 layers of gelatine or ¾ package
1½ cups of water
Juice of 2 lemons and 1 orange

Rice Layer.

¼ lb. of sugar
¾ cup of good rice
3 qts. of water
Juice and grated rind of ½ lemon
1 pinch of salt
½ pt. of white wine
3 layers or ¼ package of white gelatine
3 oranges

Preparation: White wine, lemon and orange juice, sugar and gelatine dissolved in 1½ cups of water are well mixed over a slow fire. The rice is washed and cooked 25 minutes in 3 qts. of water, then poured into a colander or sieve. Now add the wine, sugar, lemon juice and rind, salt and dissolved gelatine, cover and cook very slowly. When the juice has been absorbed by the rice, take it from the stove and cool. A dish is placed into ice or very cold water and a layer of wine jelly poured in to stiffen. When that is stiff, cut out oblong dumplings of cold rice and place them on the jelly layer in circles, pour on another layer of wine jelly and so on until the rice and jelly are used up. When stiff, turn it out and garnish the jelly and platter with orange slices.

No. 66—WHITE WINE JELLY WITH FRUIT LAYERS.
Quantity for 6 Persons.

½ bottle of white wine
9 layers or ¾ package of white gelatine
¾ pt. of water
¾ cup of sugar
Juice of 2 lemons and one orange

Fruit for Layers.
Bananas
Strawberries or pineapples

Preparation: White wine, dissolved gelatine, sugar, lemon and orange juice are well mixed and stirred over the fire until it starts to boil, then strain through a cloth. Place a dish on ice or into very cold water, pour in a cup of jelly to stiffen, on this place a layer of fruit, strawberries, sliced bananas or pineapples and repeat several times

If you have no fresh fruit, use preserves from which the syrup has been drained. The jelly layer must be on top. Turn it out before serving. The platter may be garnished with various kinds of fruit.

No. 67—LEMON JELLY.
Quantity for 6 Persons.

¾ qt. of water
Juice of 4 to 5 lemons
10 layers or 1 package of white gelatine
½ lb. of sugar

Preparation: The gelatine is dissolved in ¾ qt. of warm water, sugar and lemon juice added and the whole warmed a little, then strained through a cloth. Put into a mold and when stiff, turn it out on a platter.

Remarks: You may put layers of fruit into the jelly according to No. 66, Wine Jelly With Fruit Layers.

No. 68—ORANGE JELLY.
Quantity for 6 Persons.

1¼ pts. of orange juice, (about 10 oranges)
5 tbsps. of lemon juice
¼ lb. of sugar
9 layers or ¾ package of red gelatine
1 cup of champagne or good white wine

Preparation: The oranges are cleaned, cut into halves, and the juice carefully pressed out with a lemon squeezer. The gelatine and sugar are dissolved in this juice, then warmed and lemon juice and wine added. Strain through a cloth. The orange rinds are carefully cleaned out without breaking them and filled with the above gelatine, then placed on ice. When stiff, place the oranges on a platter and garnish with fresh leaves.

No. 69—PINEAPPLE JELLY.
Quantity for 6 Persons.

1 large pineapple
1 pt. of water or white wine
1½ cups of sugar
8 layers or ¾ package of white gelatine

Preparation: The pineapple is peeled and grated on a fine grater. The gelatine is dissolved in 1 pt. of warm water, then mixed well with sugar and the grated pineapple. This mixture is strained through a fine sieve, poured into a mold, placed on ice to harden. When cold, turn it out.

No. 70—CHERRY JELLY.
Quantity for 6 Persons.

2 qts. of sour cherries
1 pt. of water
½ lb. of sugar
2 cloves
1 stick of cinnamon
10 layers or 1 package of gelatine
½ cup of red wine

Preparation: The cherries are cleaned and stoned. Two dozen of the stones are crushed and boiled with the crushed cherries, cloves and cinnamon for 20 minutes in 1 pt. of water, the dish being covered. Strain, add gelatine and sugar, then strain again and add the red wine. Put the jelly into a mold, place on ice and when cold, turn out on a platter.

No. 71—STRAWBERRY JELLY.
Quantity for 6 Persons.

2 qts. of nice, ripe strawberries
¾ lb. of sugar
Juice of 2 lemons
1 pt. of water
8 layers or ¾ package of red gelatine
2 tsps. of vanilla

Preparation: The strawberries are crushed, water, sugar, lemon juice mixed in and cooked over a slow fire for 10 minutes, then strained through a fine sieve. The gelatine is dissolved in this juice and the whole strained again. Fill into a mold, place on ice to stiffen, then turn out and garnish with strawberries and whipped cream.

No. 72—ORANGE GELATINE.
Quantity for 6 Persons.

1 pt. of cream
Grated rind of 1 orange
Juice of 3 oranges
6 layers or ½ package of white gelatine
½ lb. of sugar

Preparation: Cream, grated orange rind and juice, sugar and gelatine are mixed well and cooked ¼ hour, stirring constantly, then strained through a fine sieve. Oil a mold, put in the jelly and place on ice or prepare the day before serving. Turn out on a platter or glass dish.

No. 73—ARRACK CREAM WITH WHIPPED CREAM.
Quantity for 6 Persons.

6 yolks of eggs
½ lb. of sugar
5 layers or ½ package of red gelatine
½ cup of warm water
6 tbsps. of arrack
1 pt. of whipped cream

Preparation: Yolks of eggs and sugar are whipped ½ hour. The gelatine is dissolved in warm water and strained, then mixed with the yolks of eggs and sugar, arrack and lastly the whipped cream. This is filled into a glass dish and set to stiffen.

No. 74—STRAWBERRY CREAM.
Quantity for 6 Persons.

1 qt. of preserved strawberries, or 2 qts. of fresh ones
¼ lb. of sugar
1 tsp. of vanilla
5 layers or ½ package of white gelatine
½ cup of warm juice
1 pt. of whipped cream
12 lady fingers

Preparation: The juice is drained from the strawberries and strained to remove the seeds. The gelatine is dissolved in ½ cup of the juice and mixed with strawberries, vanilla, sugar and whipped cream. Oil a mold, strew with sugar, put in a layer of lady fingers, then the cream on top of the lady fingers, place on ice to harden, turn it out and serve with strawberry juice.

Remarks: If you take fresh strawberries, use more sugar.

No. 75—RASPBERRY CREAM.
Quantity for 6 Persons.

Ingredients and preparation are the same as given under No. 74, Strawberry Cream. If you use fresh raspberries, you need 2 pts.

No. 76—PINEAPPLE CREAM.
Quantity for 6 Persons.

1 pt. of preserved pineapple
½ cup of sugar
1 tsp. of vanilla
6 layers or ½ package of white gelatine
1 pt. whipped cream

Preparation: The juice from the pineapple is drained off and warmed, the gelatine dissolved in some of it and strained through a fine sieve. Sugar and vanilla are stirred in and the pineapple cut up into small pieces. Lastly add the whipped cream which has been drained on a sieve. Oil a mold, strew in a little sugar, fill in the cream and place on ice or prepare the day before serving. Turn out on a platter.

No. 77—VANILLA CREAM.
Quantity for 6 Persons.

½ pt. of milk
3 eggs
1 vanilla bean or 2 tbsps. of vanilla
5 layers or ½ package of gelatine
1 pt. of whipped cream
¼ lb. of sugar

Preparation: The vanilla bean is put into the milk to soak, or the vanilla extract put into the milk; also the yolks of eggs, sugar and gelatine. Let this mixture come to a boil, stirring constantly, boil ¼ minute, mix in the beaten whites of eggs and stir until cold. Now add the whipped cream. Oil a mold, fill in the cream, and place on ice; turn it out when stiff.

No. 78—COLD APPLE CREAM.
Quantity for 6 Persons.

6 apples
½ pt. white wine
½ lb. of sugar
1 qt. of cream   5 eggs
1 tbsp. of flour
½ lemon peel
1 qt. of strawberries or raspberries

Preparation: The apples are peeled, cored and cut into 8 parts, then boiled until soft in ½ pt. of white wine and ¼ lb. of sugar. When done, cool them.

The cream, yolks of eggs, flour, grated lemon peel and ¼ lb. of sugar are mixed well, then boiled to a cream, stirring constantly. Now oil a mold and put in a layer of boiled apples, then strawberries or raspberries, then a layer of cream, then frosting made of the whites of eggs beaten to a froth with 6 tablespoonfuls of sugar. This is baked 10 minutes in a medium hot oven. Let it get cold and serve in the dish.

Remarks. This cream may be served hot, but it is better cold. If you have no fresh fruit, use preserved, but drain off the juice.

No. 79—COLD APPLE PUDDING.
Quantity for 6 Persons.

12 sweet-sour apples
Water
2 cups of white wine
8 layers or ¾ package of white gelatine
1 cup of sugar

Preparation: The apples are cut up and put into a pot with enough water to cover them, then boiled until soft, very slowly, so they do not get slushy. Pour them into a sieve or cloth and drain off the juice. This is boiled down to 1 qt., add to it the sugar and gelatine and strain; boil up again, then mix in the white wine. Fill the whole into a glass dish to stiffen and serve with a vanilla sauce.

Remarks: The apples may be used for apple sauce.

No. 80—NECTAR.
Quantity for 6 Persons.

1 qt. of sour cream
½ lb. of sugar
1½ tsps. of vanilla

9 layers or ¾ package of red gelatine
4 tbsps. of rum
¼ cup of milk

Preparation: Sour cream, sugar, vanilla and rum are mixed well. The gelatine is dissolved in warm milk, strained and mixed with the other ingredients. Pour into a mold and set on ice to stiffen. Turn it out before serving.

No. 81—CORN STARCH PUDDING.
Quantity for 6—8 Persons.

1 qt. of milk
Scant ¼ lb. of corn starch
¼ lb. of sugar

⅛ lb. peeled, ground almonds
1 tbsp. of vanilla
8 eggs

Preparation: ¾ qt. of milk, sugar, almonds and vanilla are mixed well and brought to boil. Then the corn starch is stirred into ¼ qt. of milk, poured into the boiling mixture and boiled 5 minutes, stirring constantly. Yolks of eggs are stirred in as soon as the pudding is taken from the fire, also the beaten whites of eggs. Put into a dish to stiffen, turn it out and serve with a vanilla or wine sauce.

No. 82—COLD LEMON CREAM.
Quantity for 6 Persons.

6 eggs
½ lb. of sugar
Juice and rind of 1 lemon
3 tbsps. of arrack

½ glass white wine
5 layers or ½ package of white gelatine

Preparation: The yolks of eggs and sugar are stirred hour, then add the grated rind and juice of 1 lemon and the arrack. Dissolve the gelatine in warm white wine, stir until cold and strain before mixing with the other ingredients. Add the whites of eggs beaten to a froth, place on ice or prepare a day before serving. Turn it out on a platter.

No. 83—RUSSIAN CREAM.
Quantity for 6 Persons.

6 eggs
¾ cup of sugar
2 tbsps. of rum

Preparation: Yolks of eggs and sugar are beaten for 15 minutes, add the rum, then the beaten whites of eggs. Serve in glass dishes.

No. 84—ORANGE CREAM PREPARED COLD.
Quantity for 6 Persons.

5 eggs
½ lb. of sugar
Grated rind of ½ orange

2 tbsps. lemon juice
4 layers or 1/3 package of white gelatine
8 tbsps. of orange juice

Preparation: The yolks of eggs and sugar are beaten ½

hour, add the gelatine dissolved in the orange juice, and strained. Then add the lemon juice, grated orange rind and the beaten whites of eggs. Put into glass dishes and set to stiffen.

No. 85—COLD LEMON CREAM.
Quantity for 6 Persons.

The preparation is the same as given under No. 84, Orange Cream Prepared Cold. Instead of 8 tablespoonfuls of orange juice and rind, take the same quantity of lemon juice and rind.

No. 86—COFFEE CREAM PREPARED COLD.
Quantity for 6 Persons.

The preparation is the same as given under No. 84, Orange Cream Prepared Cold. Instead of the juice of oranges, the juice of lemons and the rind, take ¼ pt. of coffee extract in which you dissolve 1 tablespoonful of cocoa.

No. 87—CHOCOLATE CREAM PREPARED COLD.
Quantity for 6 Persons.

The preparation is the same as given under No. 84, Orange Cream Prepared Cold. Instead of the juice of oranges, the juice of lemons and the rind, take 1/10 lb. of bitter chocolate or cocoa dissolved in ¼ cup of water and 1 teaspoonful of vanilla.

No. 88—CHOCOLATE CREAM.
Quantity for 6 Persons.

¼ lb. of chocolate 6 layers or scant ½ package of
⅛ lb. of sugar white gelatine
1 pt. of water 4 eggs 1 tsp. of vanilla

Preparation: The chocolate is dissolved in ½ pt. of water and the gelatine in the other ½ pt., mix the two. Add sugar and vanilla and boil this mixture ½ minute. Take from the fire and add the yolks of eggs, a little later the whites of eggs beaten to a froth. Rinse a mold with cold water, put in the mixture to stiffen, turn it out and serve with a vanilla sauce.

No. 89—CHOCOLATE MOUSSE.
Quantity for 6 Persons.

½ cup of cocoa 4 layers or 1/3 package of
¾ cup of sugar gelatine
1 tbsp. vanilla ½ cup of water 1 pt. of whipped cream

Preparation: Dissolve the cocoa and gelatine in ½ cup of water on a small fire, with sugar and vanilla well mixed in. Stir until cold, add the whipped cream. Rinse a mold with cold water; put in the mixture, close the dish well, pack in ice and salt and let stand several hours. When serving, dry the dish and turn the cream out on a platter.

No. 90—VANILLA MOUSSE.
Quantity for 6 Persons.

1 qt. of whipped cream	5 tbsps. of warm water
4 layers or 1/3 package of white gelatine	2 tsps. of good vanilla ½ lb. of sugar

Preparation: The gelatine is dissolved in the warm water and strained. The sugar and vanilla are added and the whipped cream in spoonfuls. Rinse a mold with cold water, fill in the mixture, close well and pack in ice and salt for several hours. Then dry and turn out on a platter.

No. 91—COFFEE MOUSSE.
Quantity for 6 Persons.

The preparation is the same as given under No. 90, Vanilla Mousse. Instead of vanilla, take 6 to 8 tablespoonfuls of coffee extract.

No. 92—HAZELNUT MOUSSE.
Quantity for 6 Persons.

The preparation is the same as given under No. 90, Vanilla Mousse. Mix in ¼ lb. roasted, coarsely chopped hazelnuts.

No. 93—PINEAPPLE MOUSSE.
Quantity for 6 Persons.

The preparation is the same as given under No. 90. Instead of vanilla, take ½ lb. of pineapple, cut into small pieces, or pineapple puree.

No. 94—RUM OR COGNAC MOUSSE.
Quantity for 6 Persons.

The preparation is the same as given under No. 90, Vanilla Mousse. Instead of vanilla, take 8 tablespoonfuls of rum or cognac.

No. 95—COUNT PUECKLER OR LAYER MOUSSE.
Quantity for 6 Persons.

1½ pts. whipped cream	⅛ lb. of macaroons
½ lb. chocolate	1½ tsps. of vanilla
½ lb. of sugar	12 layers or 1 package of wh'te gelatine
½ cup of raspberry jelly	
2 whites of eggs	½ cup of warm water

PART I.

Preparation: ½ lb. of chocolate is grated and mixed well with ¼ cup of warm water and ⅛ lb. of sugar. Dissolve the gelatine in the other ¼ cup of warm water, strain and divide into 3 parts; mix ⅓ of it with the chocolate, ½ teaspoonful of vanilla and ½ pt. of thick whipped cream.

PART II.

Dissolve the raspberry jelly over the fire, mix in ⅛ lb. of sugar, 2 beaten whites of eggs, and 1/3 of the dissolved gelatine, also ½ teaspoonful of vanilla and ½ pt. of thick whipped cream.

PART III.

The macaroons are crushed, mixed with ½ pt. of whipped cream, ⅛ lb. of sugar, ½ teaspoonful of vanilla and 1/3 part of the dissolved gelatine.

A form is rinsed with cold water and layers of the chocolate, raspberry and macaroon mixtures are put in. Then the mold is closed well and packed in salt and ice for some hours. When serving, dry the mold and turn it out on a platter.

No. 96—COLD RICE STARCH PUDDING.
Quantity for 6 Persons.

¼ lb. rice starch
¼ lb. of sugar
1 pt. of milk
1 grated lemon peel
5 eggs
1 pinch of salt

Preparation: The milk and grated lemon peel are brought to boil; sugar, rice starch and yolks of eggs are mixed well with a little cold milk, stirred into the boiling milk and boiled again 5 minutes, stirring constantly; then take from the stove. When the mass has cooled, mix in the beaten whites of eggs. Rinse a mold with cold water, fill in the pudding and set to stiffen. Turn it out on a platter and serve with a fruit sauce.

No. 97—COLD CHOCOLATE PUDDING WITH FARINA.
Quantity for 6 Persons.

½ lb. of fine chocolate
⅛ lb. of fine farina
½ cup of sugar
1 qt. of milk
1 tsp. of vanilla

Preparation: The chocolate is grated and mixed with farina, vanilla and sugar. The milk is brought to boil, the farina mixture put in and boiled 15 minutes, stirring constantly. Rinse a mold with cold water, fill in the pudding and set to stiffen. Vanilla sauce is served with it.

No. 98—COLD RICE PUDDING WITH PEACHES.
Quantity for 6—10 Persons.

1 cup of good rice
¾ qt. of milk
1 pinch of salt
1 cup of sugar
1 tsp. of vanilla
½ cup of raisins
1 cup of blanched, ground almonds
5 finely chopped macaroons
5 layers or ½ package of white gelatine
1 pt. of whipped cream
1 qt. preserved or fresh stewed peaches

Preparation: Wash and boil the rice for 5 minutes in 1 cup of water with a pinch of salt, then add the milk gradually and cook until the rice is done and thick, but not mushy. Mix with sugar, vanilla, raisins, almonds and macaroons. Dissolve the gelatine in ¼ cup of warm water and mix with the rice, then cool and stir in the whipped cream. Rinse a mold with milk and sprinkle with sugar, then make alternating layers of rice and peaches from which the syrup has been drained. The top layer must be rice. Close the mold well and place on ice or into a very cold place. When serving, use the fruit juice for a sauce.

No. 99—PLAIN COLD RICE PUDDING.
Quantity for 6 Persons.

1 cup of rice
¾ qt. of milk
1 cup of sugar
1 tsp. of vanilla
5 layers or ½ package of white gelatine
1 pt. of whipped cream
1 pinch of salt

Preparation: Wash and boil the rice 5 minutes in 1 cup of water and a pinch of salt, then gradually add the milk until the rice is thick, but not mushy. Now stir in the sugar and vanilla. Dissolve the gelatine in ¼ cup of warm water and stir into the rice, then cool and mix in the whipped cream. Rinse a mold or dish with milk and sprinkle with sugar. Put in the pudding, close it well and place on ice or into very cold water. Turn it out on a platter and serve with cherry sauce.

No. 100—CHAMPAGNE CREAM.
Quantity for 6 Persons.

8 eggs
Scant ½ lb. of sugar
1 pt. champagne
5 layers or ½ package of white gelatine
1 pint of thick whipped cream

Preparation: 5 yolks of eggs, 3 whole eggs, sugar and champagne are mixed and boiled to cream, stirring constantly. The gelatine is dissolved in ¼ cup of water and mixed into the cream, also the beaten whites of 5 eggs. Put it into a mold or into glasses and put on ice. Serve with macaroons.

Remarks: Omit the gelatine when using the whipped cream.

No. 101—CURRANT AND RASPBERRY PUDDING.
Quantity for 6 Persons.

2 qts. of currants and
1 qt. raspberries
1 pt. of water
¾ lb. of sugar
1 cup of fine farina or sago
¾ cup of corn starch

Preparation: Currants and raspberries are picked over and cooked in 1 pt. of water ½ hour, then strained through a cloth and the juice brought to boil. Add the sugar and farina and cook for 20 minutes, stirring constantly; fill the mass into a mold rinsed with cold water to stiffen. Turn it out and serve with cream or milk.

Remarks: If you use corn starch instead of farina, mix it with 1 cup of cold juice before putting it into the boiling juice. Then boil it 5 to 8 minutes and fill it into the mold. If the farina is not sweet enough, add more sugar while boiling.

No. 102—GOOSEBERRY PUDDING.
Quantity for 6 Persons.

2 qts. of gooseberries	1 lb. of sugar
1 qt. of water	¾ cup of fine farina

Preparation: Gooseberries are best when still unripe. Cook them in water for ½ hour, then press through a fine sieve and put in the sugar and cook again with the farina for 10 minutes. Fill it into a dish rinsed with cold water and set aside to stiffen, turn it out and serve with cream or milk.

No. 103—CHERRY PUDDING.
Quantity for 6 Persons.

2 lbs. of sour cherries   ¼ lb. of sugar
1 pt. of water   1 tbsp. of lemon juice   ¼ lb. of corn starch

Preparation: Clean and stone the cherries, then crush about 20 stones and cook them with the cherries in the water slowly for ½ hour, after that strain them and add lemon juice and sugar. Then let it come to boil again. Mix the corn starch with 1 cup of cold juice and stir it into the boiling juice to cook 5 to 8 minutes more, stirring constantly. Put into a dish rinsed with cold water and after stiffening, turn it out and serve with cream or milk.

Remarks: If the pudding is too thin, add more corn starch.

No. 104—HILL CREAM.
Quantity for 6 Persons.

¾ qt. sweet cream   ¼ lb. of sugar
5 yolks of eggs   3 whites of eggs
½ lemon peel   1 glass of raspberry jelly   1 tbsp. of flour

Preparation: Cream, yolks of eggs, grated lemon peel, flour and sugar are mixed well and boiled to a cream. The 3 beaten whites of eggs and the jelly are stirred 1 hour, then fill the cream into a glass dish and set to cool. After cooling, fill the jelly on top of it. Serve cold.

Desserts That Are Frozen.
No. 105—VANILLA ICE CREAM.
Quantity for 10 Persons.

1 qt. of cream
1 pt. of milk
¾ tbsp. of flour
2 tbsps. of vanilla
Sugar to taste
3 eggs

Preparation: ½ pt. of milk 3 yolks of eggs and flour are boiled to a cream, stirring constantly; mix the beaten whites of eggs with sugar and add to the cream. To this add the rest of the milk, cream and vanilla. Freeze the mass and pour a hot chocolate sauce over it when serving. It is very fine.

No. 106—STRAWBERRY ICE CREAM.
Quantity for 6 Persons.

3 qts. of fresh or 1 qt. preserved strawberries
1 tsp. of vanilla
1 qt. of cream
Sugar to taste

Preparation: The strawberries, fresh or preserved, are rubbed through a sieve, cream and vanilla, sugar to taste added, then frozen.

No. 107—RASPBERRY ICE CREAM.
Quantity for 6 Persons.

2 pts. of fresh or 1 pt. preserved raspberries
1 tsp. of vanilla
Sugar to taste
1 pt. of cream

The preparation is the same as given under No. 106, Strawberry Ice Cream.

No. 108—PEACH ICE CREAM.
Quantity for 8—10 Persons.

2½ qts. of fresh or 1 qt. preserved peaches
1 qt. of cream
1 tsp. vanilla
Sugar to taste

Preparation: Fresh peaches are peeled, stoned and rubbed through a sieve, mixed with cream, vanilla and sugar and frozen.

No. 109—APRICOT ICE CREAM.
Quantity for 8—10 Persons.

2½ qts. of fresh or 1 qt. of preserved apricots
1 tsp. of vanilla
Sugar to taste
1 qt. of cream

The preparation is the same as given under No. 108, Peach Ice Cream.

No. 110—LEMON ICE CREAM.
Quantity for 6 Persons.

1 pt. of milk
½ pt. of cream
2 cups of sugar
Juice of 2½ lemons

Preparation: Milk, cream and sugar are mixed and put into the ice cream freezer to freeze a little, then the juice of 2½ lemons are added and frozen.

No. 111—PINEAPPLE ICE CREAM.
Quantity for 6—8 Persons.

1 qt. of cream
1 large pineapple
Sugar
Juice of ½ lemon

Preparation: The pineapple is peeled and grated, then rubbed through a sieve, mixed with cream, sugar and lemon juice and frozen.

No. 112—CHOCOLATE ICE CREAM.
Quantity for 6 Persons.

1 pt. of cream
1 pt. of milk
4 yolks of eggs
½ lb. of chocolate
1½ tsps. of vanilla
About ½ lb. of sugar

Preparation: Dissolve the chocolate in milk, add sugar, cream, vanilla, yolks of eggs and heat to the boiling point, stirring constantly. Remove from the fire immediately, stir until cold and freeze.

No. 113—COFFEE ICE CREAM.
Quantity for 6 Persons.

1 pt. of cream
¼ lb. of finely ground strong coffee
1 pt. of milk
½ lb. of sugar
4 yolks of eggs

Preparation: The coffee must steep in the milk for 1 hour, then strain through a fine cloth. Cream, yolks of eggs and sugar are mixed well and cooked to a cream, stirring constantly. Then take it off the stove and stir until cold, mix with coffee and milk and freeze.

No. 114—NUT ICE CREAM.
Quantity for 6 Persons.

1 pt. of cream
1 pt. of milk
About ¼ lb. of sugar
½ lb. ground hazelnuts
3 yolks of eggs

Preparation: Milk, cream, sugar and yolks of eggs are mixed well and boiled, stirring constantly; then cooled, the nuts mixed in and the mass frozen.

Remarks: One teaspoonful of vanilla may be added.

No. 115—TEA ICE CREAM.
Quantity for 6 Persons.

1 pt. of cream
1 pt. of milk
⅛ lb. of sugar
2 tbsps. of fine tea
4 yolks of eggs

The preparation is the same as given under No. 113, Coffee Ice Cream. Instead of steeping the coffee in the milk, put in tea.

No. 116—VANILLA ICE CREAM WITH FRUIT.
Quantity for 6 Persons.

1 qt. of cream
1½ tbsps. of vanilla
¼ lb. of sugar
4 eggs
¼ cup of chopped citron
¼ lb. of crushed macaroons
25 preserved cherries
1 cup of large raisins
3 tbsps. of maraschino

Preparation: Cream, vanilla, sugar and yolks of eggs are mixed well and brought to boil, stirring constantly, then cool it. The raisins are scalded, put into a colander, cut into small pieces, mixed with the cut citron, crushed macaroons and quartered cherries, also 3 tablespoonfuls of maraschino and mixed into the cold cream. Add also the beaten whites of eggs and freeze.

No. 117—STRAWBERRY ICE.
Quantity for 6 Persons.

4 qts. of fresh or 1 qt. preserved strawberries
1 tsp. of vanilla
Sugar to taste

Preparation: The strawberries are rubbed through a sieve, sugar and vanilla added, then frozen. Serve with whipped cream.

No. 118—RASPBERRY ICE
Quantity for 6 Persons.

3 pts. of fresh or 1 qt. of preserved raspberries
1 tsp. of vanilla
Sugar to taste

The preparation is the same as given under No. 117, Strawberry Ice.

No. 119—PEACH ICE.
Quantity for 6 Persons.

3—4 qts. of fresh or 1½ qts. of preserved peaches
Sugar to taste

Preparation: The fresh peaches are peeled, stoned, pressed through a sieve, mixed with sugar and frozen.

No. 120—APRICOT ICE.
Quantity for 6 Persons.

Preparation and ingredients are the same as given under No. 119, Peach Ice.

No. 121—PINEAPPLE ICE.
Quantity for 6 Persons.

1 large pineapple
½ pt. of water
½ lb. of sugar, (good measure)
2 whites of eggs
Juice of ½ lemon

Preparation: The pineapple is peeled, grated, mixed with sugar, whites of eggs, lemon juice and water, then frozen.

No. 122—TUTTI FRUTTI ICE.
Quantity for 6 Persons.

1 large pineapple
½ pt. of water
3 whites of eggs
Juice of ½ lemon
2 oranges
1 cupful of preserved cherries
½ lb. of sugar, (good measure)

Preparation: This tutti-frutti ice is prepared like No. 121, Pineapple Ice. Oranges are peeled and cut into small pieces and sugared, the cherries are quartered and sugared. When the pineapple ice is nearly frozen, mix with orange and cherry and freeze a little more, but do not turn the freezer.

No. 123—CHAMPAGNE SHERBET.
Quantity for 6 Persons.

1 pt. of water
1 qt. of champagne
2 cups or 1 pt. of sugar
1 pt. of orange juice

Preparation: Dissolve the sugar in a little water then add champagne and orange juice. Fill the mixture into a freezer and pack with finely chopped ice and salt. Do not turn freezer, stir contents occasionally with spoon.

No. 124—CHAMPAGNE FRAPPE.
Quantity for 8 Persons.

1 pt. of water
Whites of 2 eggs
Juice of 1½ lemons or to taste
2 cups of sugar   1 bottle of champagne

Preparation: Dissolve the sugar in water and add the juice of lemon, beat the whites of eggs well and add, then let it freeze. Before serving the lemon ice, it should be put into a larger dish when taken out of the freezer. Pour the champagne over the mass and beat quickly, serve at once in glasses.

No. 125—MAPLE SYRUP ICE.
Quantity for 8 Persons.

Yolks of 8 eggs
2 tbsps. of water
1 cup of maple syrup
1 qt. of whipped cream

Preparation: The yolks of eggs and water are beaten 15 minutes, add the syrup, let it come to a boil in a double boiler, stirring constantly. Let it cool, add the whipped cream, pour into a mold, close the mold and pack in ice with salt.

No. 126—ROLL DUMPLINGS.
Quantity for 6 Persons.

6 rolls	½ cup of sugar	2—3 eggs	1 pinch of salt
1 piece of butter, (egg size)		4 qts. of water mixed with 1 tbsp. of salt	
1 cup of flour			

Preparation: The rolls must be soaked in water or milk and the liquid pressed out. Cream the butter with the eggs and sugar, then mix all this with the soaked rolls, flour and salt. Now boil 4 qts. of water with one tablespoonful of salt, cut off dumplings from the batter with a tablespoon, drop into the boiling salt water and boil them 10 minutes. Always try one dumpling first, if too loose, mix a little more flour into the batter.

No. 127—BETTER KIND OF ROLL DUMPLINGS.
Quantity for 6 Persons.

6 rolls
3 eggs
¼ lb. of butter
½ cup of sugar
½ cup of currants
¼ lb. of blanched, ground almonds
Rind of ½ lemon
A pinch of salt
¾ cup of flour
4 qts. of salt water

Preparation: The rolls must be soaked in milk and the milk pressed out. Cream the butter with the yolks of eggs and sugar, add the almonds, currants, grated lemon rind, rolls, flour and salt. Beat the whites of eggs to a stiff froth and stir into the mixture. Let the 4 qts. of salt water boil, cut off dumplings from the batter with a tablespoon, drop into the boiling salt water and boil them 10 minutes.

Remarks: Always try one dumpling first, if too loose, mix a little more flour into the batter.

No. 128—LEMON ICE GARNISHED WITH FRUIT
Quantity for 6 Persons.

1 pt. of milk
Juice of 1 lemon
1½ cupfuls of sugar
6 slices of canned pineapple
6 boiled prunes
6 tsps. of whipped cream
6 tsps. of brandied cherries
½ cupful of fruit juice
6 preserved apricots cut in half

Preparation: Mix the milk, lemon juice and sugar, but do not freeze. On each dessert plate put a slice of pineapple, on this the half of an apricot, a prune on the apricot, then a teaspoonful of whipped cream, finishing with the brandied cherries, adding a small piece of lemon ice to the fruit. Mix some of the pineapple and apricot juice, boil with sugar and 2 tablespoonfuls of sherry until it thickens. Add 3 tablespoonfuls of this sauce to each plate of dessert.

CHAPTER 18.

BEVERAGES.

Cold and Hot Beverages.

No. 1—COLD PUNCH.

2 bottles of white wine   Juice of 3 lemons
½ bottle of arrack   1 lb. of sugar   1 thin lemon rind

Preparation: The ingredients are mixed well, put into a punch bowl and covered to stand several hours.

No. 2—HOT PUNCH.

1 bottle of fine rum   Juice of 2 lemons
1 bottle of white wine   Rind of 1 lemon
1½ lbs. sugar   2½ qts. of boiling water

Preparation: The punch bowl is put into hot water. Pour into it 1 pt. of boiling water, sugar and lemon rind and let stand for a while, then add white wine, rum, lemon juice and 2 qts. of hot water, stir with a wooden ladle and serve hot.

No. 3—HOT KING'S PUNCH.

1 bottle of white wine   ½ lemon peel
1 pt. fine rum   ¾ lb. of sugar
Juice of 1 lemon   1 qt. of water

Preparation: Mix the ingredients, boil and serve hot.

No. 4—PRESIDENT'S PUNCH.
Cold or Warm.

1 bottle of fine white wine   ½ lb. of sugar
1 wineglassful of fine rum   ⅛ lb. of preserved pineapple
3 pts. of water   1 cup of pineapple juice

Preparation: Sugar and water are boiled 15 minutes, then wine, rum, pineapple juice and preserved pineapple added. This punch is served hot or put on ice and served cold.

No. 5—EGG PUNCH.

1 bottle of white wine   ½ lemon rind
¾ pt. of arrack   Juice of 1½ lemon
1¼ cups of sugar   7 eggs

Preparation: Mix white wine, sugar, lemon juice and rind, add the well beaten eggs and bring to a boil, beating constantly, then take from the stove and mix in the arrack. Serve at once.

No. 6—WARM BURGUNDY PUNCH.

½ bottle of Burgundy wine
½ bottle of good white wine
½ bottle of arrack
½ pt. pineapple juice
2 oranges
½ bottle German champagne
¼ lb. of sugar
¼ pt. of water

Preparation: Sugar, water, Burgundy wine, white wine, arrack and pineapple juice are mixed well and heated but not boiled. The orange is sliced with the peel and put into the bowl, then the hot fluid is poured in and the champagne added at the table.

No. 7—HOT WINE.

1 bottle of red wine
¼ lb. of sugar
10 cloves
1 stick of cinnamon
½ lemon rind

Preparation: The ingredients are mixed well and brought to the boiling point, but not boiled, strained and served hot.

No. 8—GROG.

½ pt. of rum   Liberal ½ lb. of sugar   ¾ qt. of boiling water

Preparation: Mix the ingredients and serve at once.

No. 9—BISHOP.

1 tbsp. of Bishop essence, or the thin peel of a small orange
1 bottle of red wine   ¼ lb. of sugar   ½ cup of water

Preparation: The sugar is dissolved in the red wine and the Bishop essence mixed in or the orange peel is soaked in water for ½ hour and mixed with the wine.

No. 10—CARDINAL, (COLD).

2 bottles of good white wine
Juice of 2 oranges
½ lb. of fresh pineapple
1 bottle of champagne
1 lb. of sugar
⅛ orange peel

Preparation: The pineapple is cut into small pieces, put into a bowl, the piece of orange peel and juice, with the sugar added and left to stand 15 minutes, then the white wine is poured on. Put the beverage on ice and when serving, add the champagne.

No. 11—CREAM PUNCH.

5 eggs
½ lb. of sugar
1½ qts. of whipped cream
¾ pt. of arrack.

Preparation: Yolks of eggs and sugar are beaten to a froth, the arrack mixed in, the beaten whites of eggs added and lastly whipped cream. Serve this punch in glasses or tumblers.

No. 12—PINEAPPLE PUNCH.

1 large, fresh pineapple   2 bottles of white wine
½ lb. of sugar   ¾ bottle of champagne

Preparation: The pineapple is peeled and sliced very thin. The sugar is added, ½ bottle of the wine poured over and let stand several hours, then add the rest of the wine and when serving, pour in the champagne.

Remarks: Instead of the champagne you may put in a small bottle of Seltzer-water.

No. 13—STRAWBERRY PUNCH.

2 qts. of fresh strawberries   2 bottles of white wine
Scant ½ lb. of sugar

The preparation is the same as No. 12, Pineapple Punch. If you like you may add ½ bottle of champagne.

No. 14—RASPBERRY WINE.

Raspberries and sugar   Light white wine

Preparation: The berries are crushed and strained through a cloth. With 1 qt. of raspberry juice, use 2 lbs. of sugar and 2 qts. of white wine and let it come to a boil. Cool it and fill into bottles that are well corked and kept in a cool place.

No. 15—PEACH PUNCH.

3 lbs. of peaches   2 bottles of white wine
½ lb. of sugar   1 bottle of red wine

Preparation: The peaches are peeled and sliced, put into a bowl with sugar, ¼ bottle of white wine and let stand 3 to 4 hours. Then pour on the rest of the white wine and red wine and serve very cold.

No. 16—MAY BOWL OR WOODRUFF PUNCH.

2 bottles of white wine   About 1/20 lb. of woodruff
¼ lb. of sugar

Preparation: One-half bottle of white wine is poured on the woodruff. Cover the bowl and let stand several hours. Then add the rest of the wine and sugar. Place the bowl on ice.

Remarks: This May bowl may be improved by mixing a bottle of champagne and 1 cupful of strawberries with it when serving.

No. 17—CURRANT WINE.

10 qts. of currant juice
20 qts. of water
15 lbs. of sugar
1 qt. corn brandy

Preparation: Red and white currants are mashed and strained through a cloth. To 10 qts. of juice, add 15 lbs. of sugar and 20 qts. of water. Put it into a clean cask, and leave it to ferment for 3 weeks. After that time empty the cask, clean it well, then pour back the wine and leave it two weeks longer, then add the brandy. Now close up the cask tightly and place it so that it need not be moved when the wine is drawn off. Bottle the wine after six months, without moving the cask.

No. 18—WARMBEER.

1 qt. beer
Sugar to taste
A piece of butter the size of an egg
½ pt. of milk
3 yolks of eggs
1 piece of cinnamon

Preparation: Beer, sugar and butter are brought to boil; then milk and yolks of eggs are mixed well and added; season with cinnamon, let all come to a boil and serve hot.

No. 19—COLD LEMONADE.

1 qt. of cold water
Juice of 1 lemon
¾ cup of sugar

Preparation: Dissolve the sugar in the water, add the lemon juice, mix well and serve very cold.

No. 20—FINE LEMONADE.

1 qt. of cold water
Sugar
Juice of 1 orange
2 bananas
Juice of ½ lemon

Preparation: Dissolve the sugar in the water, mix in the lemon and orange juice and pour the whole over the sliced bananas.

No. 21—ALMOND MILK.

½ lb. sweet almonds
1¼ qts. of water
Scant ½ lb. of sugar
4 tbsps. of rose water

Preparation: The almonds are blanched and ground, then put into a porcelain dish. Add the water and sugar and let stand 20 minutes, then strain through a cloth and add the rose water.

No. 22—CHOCOLATE.
Quantity for 6 Persons.

½ lb. of chocolate Sugar to taste
½ cup of water 1½ qts. of milk

Preparation: The chocolate is broken into pieces and dissolved in the water on the stove, the milk is added and brought to boil. Mix in sugar to suit your taste.

Remarks: You may stir in 2 yolks of eggs. Plain chocolate is made by using more water and mixing 1 tablespoonful of flour with water and adding this to the chocolate while cooking.

No. 23—ICE CHOCOLATE.

Ingredients and preparation are the same as given under No. 22, Chocolate. When cooled off, strain through a sieve, add 1 teaspoonful of vanilla, place into ice and salt for 3 hours and serve in tumblers or sherbet cups with whipped cream on top.

No. 24—COCOA.
Quantity for 6 Persons.

4 tbsps. of cocoa ½ tsp. of vanilla
1½ qts. of milk Sugar to taste 2 yolks of eggs

Preparation: The cocoa is stirred smooth with milk, add the sugar, let it get hot, stirring constantly. Add the rest of the milk, cook 1 minute and add the vanilla. Mix the yolks of eggs well with one tablespoonful of milk and stir into the cocoa.

Remarks: You may omit the yolks of eggs and instead stir a tablespoonful of flour, mixed with water, into the boiling cocoa.

No. 25—TEA.
Enough for 12 cups.

8 even tsps. of tea 2 qts. of water

Preparation: The tea is put into a well covered pot. Pour on 1 pt. of boiling water, cover and let it steep 3 minutes, then pour on the rest of the water and set to draw again 5 minutes before serving.

No. 26—TEA WITH VANILLA.

Ingredients and preparation are the same as given under No. 25, Tea. But add to this ½ teaspoonful of vanilla.

Remarks: You may add a small piece of lemon peel when pouring on the water.

Dried tea leaves may be used for sweeping carpets. Moisten the leaves and sprinkle them on the carpet. This will clean the carpet and absorb the dust when sweeping.

No. 27—ICED TEA.

The ingredients and preparation are the same as given under No. 25, Tea. After the tea has steeped long enough, pour it off, cool it and put in pieces of clean ice, sugar and into each glass 1 to 2 slices of lemon.

No. 28—COFFEE.
Enough for 12 cups.

6 tbsps. of ground coffee   14 cups of boiling water

Preparation: It is best to grind the coffee fresh and fine every time you wish to make some. The water must boil when you pour it on. Close the pot well.

Remarks: There are various ways of making coffee. **A.** An egg may be stirred into the ground coffee before pouring on the hot water. **B.** It may be made in a machine in which the water boils and little water gets onto the coffee at a time. This is the best way. **C.** Pour the hot water on the coffee, simmer 5 minutes and strain. This is the quickest way of making coffee.

No. 29—GOOSEBERRY OR CURRANT WINE.

For a 6 gallon cask use 18 lbs. of sugar   3—4 gallons of juice   Water to fill the cask

Clean and pick over the berries, wash them and press out the juice well. The cask must be very clean and odorless. Scald it several times and then dry it in the fresh air, put in the sugar and enough water to dissolve it while shaking the cask. When the sugar is dissolved, add the strained juice. Place the cask into a place like the garret where it is warm. It will soon ferment, then remove the foam from the bunghole every morning, stir the wine with a clean wooden stick and fill in fresh water so the cask remains full. After about 6 weeks the fermenting will cease, then close the bunghole with a cork, leave it in the cask another 3 to 4 months and then put the wine into bottles. Cork and seal them well and set them upright in the cellar, where it is dark and cold.

CHAPTER 19.

BREAD AND CAKES.

No. 1—WHEAT BREAD No. 1.
Enough for 2 Loaves.

8 cups of wheat flour		1½ cents' worth of yeast
1 pt. of milk	1 pt. of water	2 tbsps. of salt

Preparation: The 4 cups of flour are put into a mixing bowl, lukewarm milk and water added and mixed into a smooth batter. The yeast is dissolved and stirred in ¼ cup of milk and mixed into the batter; sprinkle a little flour over it and put the sponge in a warm place to rise. If the pan is ¼ full, it must rise to half fill the pan. Put in the salt and the rest of the flour, knead the dough for 15 minutes and put into two greased bread pans to rise again. If the pans are half full, the bread must rise to the brim of the pan. Brush the top of the bread with cold water and bake it in medium hot oven for 45 minutes.

No. 2—WHEAT BREAD No. 2.
Enough for 2 Loaves.

8 cups of flour		1½ cents' worth of yeast
1 qt. of milk	2 tbsps. of salt	1 tbsp. of lard

The preparation is the same as given under No. 1. When the second part of the flour is kneaded into the dough, work in 1 tablespoonful of lard.

Remarks: You may take butter instead of lard. One cup of boiled and grated potatoes may be mixed with the flour.

No. 3—RYE BREAD WITH LEAVEN.
Enough for 2 Loaves.

11 cups of rye flour	2 tbsps. of salt
1 qt. of water	1 tsp. of caraway seed if you like
	3 cents' worth of leaven

Preparation: Mix 4 cups of flour with lukewarm water, then add the leaven or yeast, strew a little flour over and set to rise to double its bulk. Then knead in the salt and caraway seed and the rest of the flour and continue kneading for 20 minutes. Make two loaves and put them into greased pans and set to rise again to twice its size, brush it with cold water and bake 1 hour.

No. 4—RYE BREAD WITH YEAST.
Enough for 2 Loaves.

11 cups of rye flour 2 cents' worth of yeast.
1 qt. of water 1 tsp. of caraway seed if desired 2 tbsps. of salt

The preparation is the same as given under No. 3, using yeast instead of leaven. Dissolve the yeast in ¼ cup of lukewarm water and mix it with the flour.

No. 5—HEALTH BREAD OR GROATS BREAD.
Enough for 2 Loaves.

8—9 cups of coarse meal or 1½ tbsps. of salt
flour (groats) 2 cents' worth of yeast.
1 qt. of water

Preparation: Sift 4 cups of flour and mix it to a smooth batter with lukewarm water and yeast that is dissolved in ¼ cup of water, then set the sponge to rise. After this mix in the salt and knead the rest of the flour in and continue kneading 20 minutes. Form two loaves and put them into greased pans, then set them to rise again to twice their size. Bake ¾ to 1 hour in medium hot oven.

No. 6—BREAD STICKS.
Quantity for 6 Persons.

Ingredients and preparation are given under Chapter 1, Soups, No. 16, Bread Sticks.

No. 7—BISCUIT.
Quantity for 10 Persons.

4½ cups of flour ¼ lb. of butter
1 pt. of milk 1 egg
1½ cents' worth of yeast ½ tsp. of salt

Preparation: Mix 2 cups of flour to a smooth batter with the lukewarm milk and the yeast dissolved in ¼ cup of the lukewarm milk, then set to rise in a warm place. Mix in the melted butter, egg and salt and beat the batter 20 minutes, then add the rest of the flour. Roll out the dough to about ¾ inch thickness, cut out biscuits with a tumbler, fold them half over or leave them round, put them into floured or greased tins, set to rise and bake them to a nice color.

Remarks: If you wish sweet biscuits, stir in ½ cup of sugar. The dough must be beaten 20 minutes.

No. 8—COFFEE CAKE.
Enough for 2 Cakes.

3½—4 cups of flour
1 pt. of milk
¼ lb. of butter
¼ lb. of sugar
3 eggs
1 cent yeast
½ grated lemon rind

Preparation: The milk is made lukewarm and stirred to a smooth batter with 2¼ cups of flour, then the yeast dissolved in ¼ cup of lukewarm milk is mixed in quickly and put in a warm place to rise. After the sponge has risen well, mix in the melted butter, sugar, grated lemon rind, the eggs and the rest of the flour, stir the dough thoroughly with a spoon. Butter 2 tins and put in the dough about 1 inch thick, then set to rise; after this strew on sugar, cinnamon and put on small pieces of butter and some chopped almonds. Bake in medium hot oven

---

No. 9—STREUSEL COFFEE CAKE.
Preparation of the Streusel.

A piece of butter the size of an egg
½ cup of flour
1¼ cups of sugar
½ cup of ground almonds
Yeast dough like No. 8
1 tsp. of cinnamon

Preparation: The dough is prepared as given under No. 8, Coffee Cake. Instead of strewing on sugar, cinnamon and pieces of butter, you make sugar crumbs as follows: Melt the butter, mix flour, sugar, cinnamon and almonds with it and rub to crumbs with the hands. Sprinkle over the cakes before baking.

No. 10—SCHNECKEN (SNAILS).
Yeast dough like No. 8
For the Filling.

⅛ lb. of butter
1 cup of sugar
½ cup of blanched, ground almonds
1 cup of currants

Preparation: The preparation is the same as given under No. 8, Coffee Cake. Stir in 1 cup of flour more than given in No. 8, roll out the dough to 1 inch thickness, strew it with sugar, cinnamon, currants, almonds, sprinkle with melted butter, roll it up carefully and cut slices off to make the snails. Place these into a buttered tin and set to rise about ½ hour. Then bake them in a medium hot oven, brush them while hot with melted butter and sprinkle with sugar.

No. 11—FILLED BERLINER PANCAKES OR STUFFED DOUGHNUTS.

Yeast dough according to No. 8　　Lard for baking
　　　　　　　　　　Jelly for filling

Preparation: The dough is prepared like No. 8, Coffee Cake, but 1 cup of flour more is kneaded in than given under No. 8. Roll out the dough ½ inch thick, cut out small disks with a tumbler, put on one disk some jelly or thick apple sauce, place another disk on top and fasten the two by pressing the dough together all around, leave them on a floured board or tin and set to rise. Heat the lard in an iron kettle and put in a few Berliners at a time and bake them golden yellow. They must be fried in deep fat. Prick them with a knitting needle to see whether the dough is baked enough. While hot, roll them in sugar.

No. 12—WREATH CAKE.

1 lb. of flour　　　　　　1½ cents yeast
¾ cup of butter　　　　　2 tbsps. of vanilla
4 eggs　　　　　　　　　½ cup of milk　　　¼ lb. of sugar

Preparation: Cream the butter, stir in the eggs, sugar vanilla, the yeast which has been dissolved in ½ cup of lukewarm milk and the flour. Roll out the dough quite thick, cut three strips of it and braid it. Then make a wreath of this braid and put it into a buttered pan to rise in a warm place. Brush it with yolks of eggs, strew sugar on and bake in a hot oven to a nice color.

No. 13—ROUND COFFEE CAKE No. 1.

1 lb. of flour　　　　　　½ lemon peel
½ lb. of butter　　　　　1½ cents yeast
½ lb. of sugar　　　　　3 eggs　　　　　1 cup of milk

Preparation: Cream the butter with sugar and eggs. The yeast is dissolved in 1 cup of lukewarm milk and mixed in, also the grated ½ lemon peel; then stir in the flour and beat the dough well for 20 minutes. Butter a round cake pan with tube, fill in the dough to half full and let it rise in a warm place to the top of the pan. Then bake it 1 hour.

No. 14—ROUND COFFEE CAKE WITH RAISINS.

4 cups of flour　　　　　½ lemon peel
1 pt. of milk　　　　　　1 cup of sugar
3 eggs　　　　　　　　　1 cup of raisins
Scant ½ lb. of butter　　2 cents yeast

Preparation: Let the milk get lukewarm and stir to a smooth batter with 2¼ cups of flour, mix with the yeast dissolved in ¼ cup of lukewarm milk. Set the sponge to rise in a warm place, then stir in the melted butter, eggs, sugar, grated lemon peel, raisins and the rest of the flour, beat this dough well for 10 minutes. Butter a round cake pan with tube, fill it half full and set to rise in a warm place until the pan is full, then bake to a nice color for ¾ to 1 hour.

No. 15—STOLLEN.
Sufficient for 2—3 Cakes.

1 qt. of milk
6 cents yeast
12 to 15 cups of flour
1 lb. of sugar
1 lb. of butter
6 eggs
¼ lb. of blanched, ground almonds
⅛ lb. of bitter, blanched, ground almonds
¼ cup of brandy
1½ lbs. of raisins   ¼ lb. of cut citron

Preparation: Warm the milk and stir into a smooth batter with 4½ cups of flour, add the yeast dissolved in ½ cup of lukewarm milk and set the sponge to rise. Stir in the melted butter, sugar, eggs, raisins, citron, sweet and bitter almonds, brandy and the rest of the flour to make a pretty stiff dough. Knead it until it will not adhere to the hands. Cut the dough into 2 or 3 parts, as many "stollen" as you wish to have, and shape them nice and round, then set to rise in a warm place. Butter a pan for each cake, double up the dough, place it into the pan and set to rise again. Bake in a medium oven. If the cakes are large, bake them 2 hours, if small, 1½ hours. As soon as you take them out of the oven, brush them with butter and strew them with sugar. These cakes must be prepared in a warm place.

No. 16—APPLE CAKE.

Yeast dough like No. 8
Sweet-sour apples
Sugar
Cinnamon

For Frosting.

½ cup of cream   2 eggs   ¼ cup of sugar

Preparation: The dough is prepared like No. 8, Coffee Cake. Butter some pans and spread the dough out in them ¼ inch thick, then set to rise in a warm place.

Peel and slice the apples, place them on the dough in rows, sprinkle with sugar and cinnamon, then bake. After the cake is baked, spread the frosting on. The frosting is made by mixing cream, yolks of eggs, sugar and beaten whites of eggs; spread it on the cakes and bake them 10 minutes longer.

Remarks: The frosting is sufficient for 1 small cake. The dough will make 4 to 5 cakes, according to size.

No. 17—CHERRY CAKE.

Yeast dough like No. 8
Stoned sweet-sour cherries
Sugar
Frosting like No. 16

Preparation: The dough is prepared like No. 8, Coffee Cake. Put the dough, about ½ inch thick, into buttered pans and set to rise in a warm place. The cherries and the sugar are put on thick, then the cake is baked in a hot oven. After taking it out, spread on the frosting which has been prepared according to No. 16, Apple Cake, and bake 10 minutes longer. This cake may be prepared without the frosting.

No. 18—PLUM CAKE.

Yeast dough like No. 8
Stoned plums
Sugar
Frosting like No. 16

The preparation is the same as given under No. 17.

No. 19—CHEESE CAKE.

Yeast dough like No. 8
1½ lbs. cottage cheese
½ pt. of cream
¼ lb. of sugar
3 eggs
½ tsp. of vanilla
1 pinch of salt
⅛ lb. of butter

Preparation: The dough is prepared according to No. 8. Butter some pans, spread the dough out in them ¼ inch thick and set to rise. During this time prepare the cheese. The cottage cheese, cream, sugar, eggs, salt and vanilla are mixed well and spread over the dough quite thick. The butter is melted and sprinkled over the cheese. then the cake is baked to a nice color.

Remarks: You may mix into the cheese ½ cup of currants.

No. 20—CURRANT CAKE.

Yeast dough like No. 8
Currants
Sugar
Frosting like No. 16

The preparation and baking are just the same as given under No. 17, Cherry Cake.

No. 21—POPPY SEED CAKE.

Yeast dough like No. 8
2 lbs. of poppy seed
3 juicy pears
¼ lb. of sugar
3 eggs
⅛ lb. of butter

Preparation: The dough is prepared according to No. 8 and spread out in buttered pans about ¼ inch thick, then set to rise in a warm place. The poppy seed is scalded and the water drained off. The pears are peeled and grated into the poppy seed, sugar and eggs are mixed in. Spread the poppy seed mixture thick on the dough, sprinkle melted butter on and bake ¾ hour.

No. 22—HUCKLEBERRY CAKE.

Yeast dough like No. 8
Huckleberries
Sugar
Frosting according to No. 16

Preparation: The dough is prepared as given under No. 8, spread out in buttered pans about ¼ inch thick, then set to rise in a warm place. The berries are strewn on thick and sprinkled with sugar. Bake it and if you wish, spread the frosting on according to No. 16.

No. 23—ONION CAKE.

Yeast dough like No. 8
6 peeled onions
2 sweet-sour apples
¼ lb. of butter
¼ lb. of sugar

Preparation: The dough is prepared as given under No. 8, spread out in buttered pans about ¼ inch thick and set to rise in a warm place. The onions are peeled, sliced and stewed a little in ⅛ lb. of butter, to which the peeled and finely chopped apples are added. Strew sugar on the dough and spread on the onions mixed with apples ¼ inch thick, sprinkle with sugar, then with the melted butter and bake to a nice golden color.

Remarks: The apples may be omitted.

No. 24—COFFEE CAKE WITH EGG CREAM.

Yeast dough like No. 8
½ lb. of butter
11 eggs
¾ lb. of sugar

Preparation: The dough is prepared as given under No. 8, rolled out to ¼ inch thickness and put into buttered pans to rise in a warm place. Melt the butter and stir with the eggs to a thick cream. This cream is spread thickly on the dough and the cake baked quickly in a hot oven. When the cake is done, put on quite a little butter and sprinkle with plenty of sugar.

Baking Powder Cakes.

No. 25—COFFEE CAKE WITH ALMOND FROSTING.

½ cup of butter
1½ cups of sugar
1 cup of milk
3 cups of flour
4 eggs
Juice and rind of 1 lemon
2 heaping tsps. of baking powder

For the Frosting.

1 cup of almonds
¼ cup of melted butter
1 cup of sugar
1 tsp. of cinnamon

Preparation: Cream the butter, stir in sugar, lemon juice and rind, gradually mix in yolks of eggs, milk and flour. Lastly add the baking powder and the beaten whites of eggs.

Spread this batter out 1 inch thick into buttered pans, sprinkle with sugar, cinnamon and blanched almonds cut into narrow strips, sprinkle butter over and bake to a nice color.

No. 26—COFFÉE CAKE WITH CHOCOLATE FROSTING.

The batter according to No. 25
¼ lb. of chocolate
⅛ lb. of sugar
1 tsp. of vanilla
3 tbsps. of cold water
1 white of egg

Preparation: The batter is prepared and baked as in No. 25. Dissolve the chocolate over the fire in the water, add sugar and vanilla and stir until it becomes stringy. Now mix the beaten whites of eggs with it and spread on the cake when it is baked.

No. 27—ROUND COFFEE CAKE No. 2.

Ingredients and preparation are given under No. 25. Put the batter into a round cake pan with tube and bake it ½ hour.

No. 28—STIRRED CAKE.

¾ cup of butter
1¼ cups of powdered sugar
2 cups of flour
Juice of ½ lemon
1½ tsps. of baking powder
6 whites of eggs

Preparation: Cream the butter and mix with sugar, lemon juice and flour, add 1½ teaspoonfuls of baking powder and the beaten whites of eggs. Put in a buttered pan and bake ½ to ¾ hour.

No. 29—LAYER CAKE WITH CHOCOLATE.

½ lb. of butter
½ lb. of sugar
6 eggs
½ lb. of flour
2 heaping tsps. of baking powder
¼ lb. of chocolate

For the Filling.

½ cup of cream
3 eggs
1½ tsps. of vanilla
4 tbsps. of sugar

Preparation: Cream the butter, then mix with sugar, yolks of eggs, flour, and lastly the baking powder and beaten whites of eggs. The chocolate is grated and mixed with one-half of the batter. Bake in four layers, 2 light or yellow ones and 2 dark ones containing chocolate.

The filling is made by mixing well: cream, yolks of eggs, vanilla and sugar and cooking it in a double boiler to a thick cream, stirring constantly. Let it get cold, mix with the beaten whites of eggs and spread it between the layers, putting them together light and dark alternately. The cake may be covered with a chocolate frosting.

No. 30—LAYER CAKE WITH JELLY FILLING.

½ lb. of butter
½ lb. of sugar
5 eggs
½ lb. of flour
2 heaping tsps. of baking powder
Jelly for the filling

Preparation: Cream the butter with sugar, add the yolks of eggs, then gradually work in the flour, baking powder and beaten whites of eggs. Bake in three layers and when these are cooled off, spread jelly over them and place one on the other. If you like, cover the cake with a white frosting.

No. 31—LAYER CAKE WITH BANANA FILLING.

1 cup of butter
2 cups of sugar
2½ cups of flour
6 eggs
½ cup of milk
2 heaping tsps. of baking powder

For the Filling.
4—5 peeled and sliced bananas   ¼ cup of sugar

Preparation: Cream the butter with the sugar and yolks of eggs; gradually add the milk and the flour, and lastly the baking powder and beaten whites of eggs. Bake in 4 layers and when these are cooled, spread the sugared, sliced bananas between the layers and cover the cake with white frosting.

No. 32—LAYER CAKE WITH COCOANUT FILLING. No. 1.

1 cup of butter
2 cups of sugar
4 yolks of eggs
2 whites of eggs
1 cup of milk
2½ cups of flour
2 heaping tsps. of baking powder

For the Filling.
¼ lb. of cocoanut
2 whites of eggs
½ cup of sugar
1 tsp. of vanilla

Preparation: Cream the butter with the sugar, add yolks of eggs and the milk and gradually stir in the flour. Lastly add the baking powder and beaten whites of eggs. Bake in three layers and prepare the filling in the meantime. Mix the beaten whites of eggs with sugar, cocoanut and vanilla and spread between the layers as well as on and over the whole cake.

No. 33—SPONGE CAKE.

4 eggs
1 pinch of salt
1 cup of sugar
1 tsp. of vanilla or lemon juice
1 heaping tsp. of baking powder
1 cup of flour
5 tsps. of milk

For the Filling.
½ cup of milk
4 tbsps. of sugar
1 tsp. of vanilla or essence of lemon
2 eggs
1 tsp. of flour

Preparation: Cream the sugar and yolks of eggs and add

milk, vanilla and ½ cup of flour. To the beaten whites of eggs stir ½ cup of flour and mix it with the rest, then add salt and baking powder. Bake in two layers and prepare the filling in the meantime. Milk, yolks of eggs, sugar and vanilla are mixed well and cooked to a thick cream in a double boiler, stirring constantly. When this is cooled off, mix in the beaten whites of eggs and spread the filling between the layers. Put a cocoanut frosting on the cake.

No. 34—GOLD CAKE.

1 cup of butter
2 cups of sugar
6 yolks of eggs
1 cup of milk
3½ cups of flour
1½ heaping tsps. of baking powder
1 tsp. of vanilla to taste

Preparation: Cream the butter and mix with sugar, yolks of eggs and vanilla, then add milk and gradually the flour and lastly the baking powder. Butter a cake pan, fill in the dough and bake 1 hour.

No. 35—SILVER CAKE.

½ cup of butter
1½ cups of sugar
1 cup of milk
1½ cups of flour
½ cup of corn starch
1 tbsp. of vanilla
2 heaping tsps. of baking powder
6 whites of eggs

Preparation: Cream the butter and sugar, add vanilla, milk, gradually the corn starch, then baking powder and lastly the beaten whites of eggs. Put into a buttered pan and bake 1 hour.

No. 36—THEATER CAKE.

1 tbsp. of butter
2 cups of sugar
1 egg
1½ tsps. of baking powder
1 tsp. of lemon essence or vanilla
1 cup of milk
1¾ cups of flour

Preparation: Cream the butter with sugar, yolks of eggs and vanilla; add the milk, then flour, baking powder and the beaten whites of eggs. Put into a buttered pan and bake ½ hour.

No. 37—FLAT CAKE.

1 lb. of butter
1 lb. of sugar
8 eggs
Juice of 2 lemons
1½ lemon peels
2 lbs. of flour
1 heaping tsp. of salt of hartshorn
A little cardamom

Preparation: The butter is melted, yolks of eggs and sugar are put in and stirred to a cream. Add the grated lemon peel and juice, cardamom and gradually work in the flour. Mix the salt of hartshorn with a little flour and stir it in. Lastly mix in the well beaten whites of eggs and spread the dough out in buttered pans about 2 inches thick. Sprinkle with sugar, cinnamon and ground almonds and bake to a nice color.

No. 38—POTATO CAKE OR TART.

| 1 lb. boiled, peeled, grated potatoes | ½ lb. blanched, ground almonds |
| 14 eggs 1 lb. of sugar | Juice and rind of 2 lemons |

Preparation: The yolks of eggs and sugar are beaten to a cream; then grated lemon rind and juice, the ground almonds, potatoes and beaten whites of eggs mixed in. Butter a round, loose bottom pan and strew with bread crumbs, put the batter in and bake slowly for 1 to 1½ hours.

Remarks: Tarts, so-called in Europe, differ very much from the dainties similarly designated in this country. The former are more like our American pies, but without an upper crust. Sometimes they have narrow strips of crust laid in the form of lattice work across the top.

No. 39—RICE CAKE OR TART.

1 lb. of rice
2½ qts. of milk
12 eggs
½ lb. of butter
½ lb. of sugar
1 lb. of raisins 1 tsp. of cinnamon

Preparation: The rice is washed and partly cooked in milk, but do not stir it, for the kernels must stay whole. Cool the rice. Cream the butter and sugar, add raisins and cinnamon, then the rice and lastly the beaten whites of eggs. Butter a round, loose bottom cake pan, strew with bread crumbs, put the batter in and bake slowly.

No. 40—STRAWBERRY SHORT CAKE.

½ cup of butter
½ cup of sugar
½ cup of milk
3 eggs
2 cups of flour
2 heaping tsps. of baking powder

For the Filling.

2—3 qts. of strawberries
1 pt. of whipped cream
Sugar to taste
1 tsp. of vanilla

Preparation: Cream the butter with sugar, yolks of eggs and milk, gradually work in the flour and baking powder and lastly the beaten whites of eggs. The dough is baked in 2 layers, each being 1½ inches thick. When they are cool, spread between the layers and on top crushed strawberries mixed with sugar and on this the whipped cream mixed with sugar and vanilla.

Remarks: After the whipped cream is on the strawberry short cake, it must be served at once.

No. 41—DEVIL'S FOOD.
For the First Half.

½ cup of butter
½ cup of milk
1 cup of brown sugar
2 cups of flour
1 egg
2 yolks of eggs
1 tsp. of soda

For the Second Half.

1 cup of brown sugar   ½ cup of milk
1 cup of grated bitter chocolate

For the Filling.
The cream prepared according to No. 29

Preparation: The first half is prepared by creaming the butter, mixing with sugar, egg and yolks of eggs. Dissolve the soda in milk and stir it into the mixture, then measure and sift the flour and add it gradually.

The second half is prepared by putting the brown sugar, the bitter chocolate and milk into a double boiler, to stew to a smooth cream which is set to cool. Now the first and second half are put together, mixed and baked in three layers. When these are cooled, make the cream according to No. 29, see Layer Cake with Chocolate, and spread between the layers. Cover the cake with a chocolate frosting.

No. 42—ANGEL'S FOOD.

9 whites of eggs
1 tsp. of cream of tartar
1 cup of sugar
1 cup of the finest flour
1 tsp. of vanilla

Preparation: The whites of eggs are beaten to a stiff froth, the cream of tartar stirred in and also the sugar and vanilla. The flour is sifted 7 times and at last mixed with the other ingredients. Put into a buttered pan and bake slowly ½ hour.

No. 43—YELLOW ANGEL'S FOOD.

12 ounces of sugar
5 ounces of fine flour
1 tsp. of cream of tartar
11 whites of eggs
6 yolks of eggs
1 tsp. of vanilla

Preparation: The sugar is sifted 4 times and stirred to a cream with yolks of eggs; add the beaten whites of eggs, cream of tartar and vanilla. Sift the flour 5 times and work it in. Put the batter into a buttered pan and bake slowly ¾ to 1 hour.

No. 44—FIG CAKE.

¾ cup of butter
2 cups of sugar
6 whites of eggs
1 cup of milk
2 cups of flour

½ cup of corn starch
12 figs
3 heaping tsps. of baking powder
1 tsp. of cinnamon
1 tsp. of cloves

For the Frosting.

3 whites of eggs
1 tbsp. of sugar

4 tbsps. of water
½ lb. finely chopped almonds

Preparation: Cream the butter, add the sugar, milk, flour, baking powder and lastly the beaten whites of eggs. Divide the batter into 3 parts. Into the first part mix the cinnamon, cloves and chopped figs. Bake two light and one dark layer and arrange them with the dark layer in the middle. Prepare the frosting by beating the whites of eggs to a stiff froth and mixing it with 1 tablespoonful of sugar and 4 tablespoonfuls of water which have been boiled 5 minutes. The mixture is stirred until cool, the almonds are added and the frosting spread over the cake.

No. 45—LAYER CAKE WITH COCOANUT. No. 2.

2/3 cup of butter
2 cups of sugar

1 cup of corn starch
2 heaping tsps. of baking powder
7 whites of eggs

For the Filling.

Cream according to No. 29.

For the Frosting.

4 whites of eggs   ½ cup of sugar   ¼ lb. of cocoanut

Preparation: Cream the butter with sugar, then add flour and baking powder and the beaten whites of eggs. Bake in 4 layers. Make the filling according to No. 29, Layer Cake With Chocolate, and when the layers are cool, spread the cream between them. Make the frosting from the beaten whites of eggs mixed with sugar, spread it on the cake and sprinkle with grated cocoanut.

No. 46—TEA CAKE.

½ lb. of sugar
10 eggs
½ lb. of fine flour

¼ lb. of blanched, grated almonds
Juice and rind of 1 lemon
2 heaping tsps. of baking powder

Preparation: The sugar and yolks of eggs are stirred 20 minutes, the ground almonds added and the mixture stirred again 20 minutes. Now add lemon juice and grated lemon rind, the whites of eggs beaten to a froth, and then quickly stir in the flour. Lastly add the baking powder mixed with some of the flour. Put the batter into a buttered pan and bake 1 hour.

Remarks: In the beginning, the heat may be greater in the bottom of the oven than in the top.

No. 47—SUNSHINE CAKE.

5 eggs
1 cup of sugar
¼ tsp. of salt
½ tsp. of cream of tartar
1 tsp. of lemon juice
¾ cup of flour   1 tsp. of orange juice

Preparation: The yolks of eggs are stirred with sugar ½ hour. The flour mixed with the cream of tartar is sifted 4 times. Add salt, lemon and orange juice, the sifted flour and the whites of eggs beaten to a froth. Butter a pan and strew it with roll crumbs, put the batter in and bake 40 minutes in medium hot oven.

No. 48—FRUIT CAKE.

1 lb. of butter
1 lb. of brown sugar
12 eggs
1½ lbs. of flour
6 tbsps. of molasses
2 tsps. of soda
4 lbs. of Sultana raisins
3 lbs. of small raisins
1 lb. of chopped citron
1 chopped orange rind
½ lb. of chopped figs
½ pt. of brandy
¼ pt. of white wine
¼ pt. of rose water
½ tsp. ground cloves
¼ tsp. mace and nutmeg

Preparation: Cream the butter with sugar and yolks of eggs. Dissolve soda in molasses and mix it into the batter, add the brandy, white wine, rose water, ground cloves, mace, nutmeg, flour and lastly the beaten whites of eggs. Mix in the Sultana and the small raisins, citron, orange rind and figs. Line a pan with buttered paper, put the batter in and bake slowly for 2 hours.

No. 49—BREMER BLOCK.

1 lb. washed butter
¾ lb. of sugar
1 lb. of seeded raisins
¾ lb. of currants
¼ lb. blanched, chopped almonds
¼ lb. of chopped citron
¾ qt. warm milk
5 cents yeast
3 tsps. of salt
3 lbs. of sifted flour

Preparation: Cream the butter and sugar. Wash the raisins and currants and put them in a warm place; when real warm, mix them with the butter. Almonds and citron are next stirred in, then the warm milk, the yeast dissolved in ½ cup of warm milk, salt and flour. Put the dough into buttered pans, set to rise and bake 1½ to 2 hours.

No. 50—PLAIN FRUIT CAKE.

1 cup of butter
1 cup of brown sugar
1 cup of white sugar
1 cup of raisins
1 cup of currants
½ cup of molasses
1½ cups of black coffee
3 eggs
4 cups of flour
3 tsps. of saleratus

Preparation: Cream the butter with sugar and yolks of

eggs, add raisins, currants and saleratus dissolved in molasses; then coffee, flour and lastly whites of eggs beaten to a stiff froth. Put the batter into a pan lined with buttered paper and bake in a moderate oven 1 to 1½ hours.

No. 51—BROWN SPICE CAKE No. 1.

2 eggs
2 heaping tbsps. of lard
1 lb. best molasses
1 lb. of brown sugar
1 tsp. of ground cloves
1 tsp. of cinnamon

1 cup of raisins
1 pinch of salt
1 level tsp. baking soda
1 heaping tsp. of cream of tartar
1 cup of sour milk or black coffee
4 cups of flour
½ grated nutmeg

Preparation: The eggs are beaten thoroughly, lard heated a little, sugar, molasses, cloves, cinnamon, nutmeg, raisins and salt mixed in. The soda is dissolved in the milk or coffee and added. The cream of tartar is mixed into the flour, and this added gradually. Line a pan with buttered paper, put the batter in and bake 1 to 1½ hours in medium hot oven.

No. 52—NATRON OR CARBONATE OF SODA CAKE.

¼ lb. of butter
2 cups of sugar
1 cup milk
5 eggs
Juice and rind of 1 lemon

10 bitter almonds
1 lb. of flour
1½ tsps. of cream of tartar
1 tsp. of natron, (carbonate of soda)
⅛ lb. of sweet almonds

Preparation: Cream the butter, sugar and yolks of eggs, then add lemon juice and grated rind and the blanched, ground sweet and bitter almonds. The carbonate of soda and cream of tartar are mixed into the flour and this is gradually worked into the batter; and lastly, stir in lightly the stiffly beaten whites of eggs. Put into a buttered pan and bake 1 hour.

No. 53—LIGHTNING CAKE.

½ lb. of sugar
4 eggs
½ lb. of butter

1 grated lemon rind
½ lb. of flour
2 tsps. of baking powder

For Sprinkling on the Cake.

¼ lb. blanched, ground almonds
1 tsp. of cinnamon
½ cup of sugar

Preparation: Cream the butter, sugar and yolks of eggs, add the lemon rind, flour mixed with baking powder and lastly the stiffly beaten whites of eggs. Butter some pans, spread the dough out in them about ⅛ inch thick, sprinkle with almonds, sugar and cinnamon. Bake in medium oven and while still warm, cut into nice pieces and serve warm.

No. 54—CARAWAY CAKE.

½ lb. of butter
¾ cup of sugar
1 lb. of flour
¼ lb. of raisins
3 eggs
½ pt. of milk
1 tbsp. of caraway
1 tsp. of natron or soda

Preparation: The butter and flour are rubbed together, raisins, sugar and caraway and the well beaten eggs stirred in. Boil the milk and dissolve the soda in it, let it get cold and stir into the dough. Put the batter into a buttered pan and bake ¾ to 1 hour.

No. 55—WIT CAKE.

6 eggs
¾ lb. of sugar
½ lb. of flour
Juice of ½ lemon
2 tbsps. of arrack
1½ tsps. of baking powder ¼ lb. of butter

For Sprinkling.
¼ lb. of chopped, blanched almonds

Preparation: Stir the yolks of eggs and sugar to a cream, work in the flour. Add the melted butter, arrack, lemon juice, baking powder and beaten whites of eggs. Butter some pans, spread the batter in 1 inch thick, sprinkle the almonds over and bake the cake ½ hour.

No. 56——ENGLISH CAKE.

¼ lb. of butter
¾ lb. of flour
Scarce ½ lb. of sugar
⅛ lb. of raisins
2 tbsps. of chopped orange rind
4 eggs
½ pt. of milk
4 grams of ammonium
2 tbsps. of chopped citron

Preparation: Butter, flour and sugar are rubbed together with the hands. Add to this the raisins, citron, grated orange rind; beat the 4 eggs to a froth, boil the milk and mix it with the eggs, then stir into the batter and lastly mix in the ammonium. Butter a pan, strew it with roll crumbs, fill in the batter and bake in medium hot oven 1 hour.

No. 57—WALNUT CAKE.

½ cup of butter
1 cup of brown sugar
2 eggs
1 cup of sour milk
½ cup of chopped walnuts
½ cup of chopped raisins
2 cups of flour
2 tsps. of baking powder ½ tsp. of soda

Preparation: Cream the butter, add sugar and eggs and beat 10 minutes. Soda is dissolved in sour milk and mixed into the batter, the walnuts, raisins, flour and lastly the baking powder added. Put the batter into buttered pans and bake to a nice color.

No. 58—SPICE CAKE No. 2.

1 cup of butter
1½ cups of sugar
1 cup of sour milk
1 tsp. of soda
3 eggs

2 cups of raisins
2 tsps. of cinnamon
1 tsp. of cloves
½ tsp. of nutmeg
2 cups of flour

Preparation: Cream the butter with sugar and yolks of eggs, then add soda, dissolved in sour milk, and raisins, cinnamon, ground cloves, nutmeg and flour, and lastly the whites of eggs beaten to a stiff froth. Butter a pan, put in the batter and bake 1 hour.

No. 59—SOUR CREAM CAKE.

1 cup of sugar
1 cup of sour cream
1 egg

1 pinch of salt
1 pinch of nutmeg
1 tsp. of soda   1 cup of flour

Preparation: The soda is mixed with sour milk and to it are added in the order named, sugar, yolk of egg, salt, nutmeg, flour and the stiffly beaten white of egg. Bake the batter in two layers and spread on the lower layer the sour cream filling. This is made by mixing well ¼ cup of sour cream, 1 yolk of egg, 2 tablespoonfuls of sugar, ½ teaspoonful of flour, ½ teaspoonful of lemon juice and cook it ½ minute, stirring continually. When this has cooled, stir in the beaten white of egg.

No. 60—THOUSAND PUFF TART.

1 lb. of fresh washed butter
1 lb. fine flour
½ pt. cold water
Whites of 2 eggs

2 tbsps. of rum
½ tsp. of baking powder
½ lb. of apricot or raspberry
   marmalade

Preparation: Mix the flour, water, egg, rum and baking powder. Cut the cold butter into bits and spread it over the dough, fold the dough over and roll out, repeat 3 to 4 times, then roll out thin. Now cut out 6 to 8 disks the size of the tart you wish to make, turn up the edge, brush over with yolks of eggs and bake light brown or yellow. Dust with sugar when done, fill in apricot or raspberry marmalade, place the disks one on top of the other. The top one should have no marmalade, but be dusted with powdered sugar.

Remarks: This tart dough can be prepared like Good Tart dough in No. 93, a very good recipe.

No. 61—CHEESE TART.

¼ lb. of butter
¼ lb. of sugar
½ lb. of flour

2 eggs
½ tsp. of baking powder

For the Filling.

2 lbs. of cheese
¼ lb. of butter
¼ lb. of sugar

1 tbsp. of vanilla
2 tbsps. of flour
3 eggs

Preparation: Cream the butter, add sugar, eggs, flour and baking powder. Butter a pan, roll out the dough and put in, turning up a high rim. Cheese, butter, sugar, vanilla, flour, yolks of eggs and beaten whites are mixed well, filled into the tart and baked until of a yellow color.

No. 62—APPLE TART.

½ lb. of washed butter
½ lb. of flour
¼ pt. of water

White of 1 egg
1 tbsp. of rum
¼ tsp. of baking powder

For the Filling.

1 qt. of thick apple sauce or
½ peck of apples, stewed soft in

1½ glasses of white wine and sugar

For the Frosting.

6 whites of eggs
1¼ cups of sugar

½ lb. blanched, ground almonds

Preparation: The preparation of the dough is the same as given under No. 60. The dough is rolled out, put into a buttered, round, loose bottom pan with a high rim, partly baked and spread thick with apple sauce. The 6 whites of eggs are beaten to a stiff froth, sugar and ground almonds mixed in and this frosting spread on the sauce. Now the tart is baked again to a nice light brown color.

Remarks: This tart dough can be made like Good Tart dough, in No. 93, a very good recipe.

No. 63—ORANGE TART.

8 yolks of eggs
¼ lb. of sugar
Juice of 2 large oranges

¾ lb. unblanched, ground almonds
2 tsps. of baking powder

Preparation: Yolks of eggs and sugar are stirred ½ hour, almonds and orange juice mixed in, then the baking powder and beaten whites of eggs. This dough is put into a buttered, round, loose bottom pan, strewn with bread crumbs and baked ¾ hour in medium hot oven.

No. 64—RICE TART WITH ORANGES.

¼ lb. of washed butter
½ lb. of flour
2 eggs
¼ lb. of sugar
¼ tsp. of baking powder

For the Filling.

½ lb. of rice
1 lb. of sugar
Juice and rind of 1 orange
½ pt. of white wine
Juice of 1 lemon
4 eggs

Preparation: The preparation of the dough is the same as No. 61. The dough is rolled out and put into the pan, making a high rim, and baked. The rice is cooked done but not mushy in 3 qts. of water. Then pour off the water, add white wine, lemon juice, orange juice, grated rind of ½ orange and sugar mixed with the rice to simmer ¼ hour. The yolks of eggs and the beaten whites are added and this mixture spread thick on the tart which is baked 20 minutes more in a medium hot oven. Instead of baking this dough, the batter may be prepared for the tart according to No. 93.

No. 65—BREAD TART.

12 eggs
1 lb. powdered sugar
1 pt. grated rye bread
1 tbsp. of cinnamon
1½ cups of blanched, ground almonds
1 tbsp. of citron
¼ tsp. of cardamom
1½ tsps. of baking powder

Preparation: Yolks of eggs and sugar are stirred 20 minutes, then bread, cinnamon, almonds, citron, cardamom, baking powder and beaten whites of eggs mixed in. A round, loose bottom pan is buttered, the batter filled in and the tart baked in a slow oven. You can cover the tart with a chocolate frosting.

No. 66—PUFF-PASTE TART WITH CREAM.

½ lb. of washed butter
½ lb. of flour
¼ pt. of water
White of 1 egg
1 tbsp. of rum
¼ tsp. of baking powder

For the Cream.

1 pt. of cream
1½ tbsps. of flour
6 yolks of eggs
2 tbsps. of butter
Rind of ½ lemon
¼ lb. of sugar
½ cup of blanched, ground almonds

Preparation: Flour, water, egg, rum and baking powder are mixed into a dough, the butter cut into bits and spread on, the dough folded over, rolled out and this repeated several times. Cut out 3 round layers and bake them each in a round baking pan to a golden color. Meanwhile mix the cream, flour, butter, sugar, yolks of eggs, grated lemon rind and cook in double boiler to a thick cream, add the ½ cup of ground almonds, spread this cream between the layers and cover with the frosting. To make this, beat the whites of 4 eggs to a stiff froth, add 12 tablespoonfuls of sugar. After the frosting is on, put the tart into the oven again and bake to a golden yellow.

No. 67—CHERRY TART.

½ lb. of fresh butter
½ lb. of flour
¼ pt. of water

White of 1 egg
1 tbsp. of rum
¼ tsp. baking powder

For the Filling.

2 qts. of stoned cherries   1 cup of sugar

For the Frosting.

¼ lb. blanched, ground almonds   Sugar to taste
5 eggs   3 tbsps. of lemon juice

Preparation: Flour, water, egg, rum and baking powder are stirred to a dough and rolled out. The butter is cut into bits and spread on and the dough folded over and rolled out again; repeat this process 3 to 4 times and lastly put the dough into a round baking pan shaping it with a high rim. Now fill in the cherries and partly bake the cake. In the meantime prepare the frosting by mixing well 5 yolks of eggs, ground almonds, sugar, lemon juice and beaten whites of eggs. Bake the tart again to a nice color.

Remarks: This tart dough can also be made like Good Tart dough, in No. 93.

No. 68—STRAWBERRY OR RASPBERRY PUFF-TART.

½ lb. of washed butter
½ lb. of flour
¼ pt. of water

White of 1 egg
1 tbsp. of rum
¼ tsp. baking powder

For the Filling.

2 qts. of strawberries   1 cup of sugar
1 qt. whipped cream

Preparation: Butter, flour, water, egg, rum and baking powder are stirred into a dough, rolled out and butter cut into bits and spread on, then folded up and rolled out again. Repeat this 3 to 4 times, cut out 3 layers which are baked to a nice color. The strawberries or raspberries are picked over, washed, mixed with sugar and whipped cream and spread between the layers. Cover with whipped cream.

No. 69—EMPEROR TART.

½ lb. blanched, roasted hazelnuts
10 eggs
½ lb. sugar
1 tsp. vanilla
2½ ozs. fine flour

For the Filling.
1 glass apricot marmalade

Preparation: The nuts are ground and stirred for ½ hour with yolks of eggs and sugar, then vanilla and flour are added and lastly the beaten whites of eggs. Bake in two layers, cool them, spread apricot marmalade between them and cover the cake with pineapple frosting.

No. 70—MOUTH POCKETS.

½ lb. of washed butter
½ lb. of flour
¼ pt. of water
¼ tsp. of baking powder
White of 1 egg
1 tbsp. of rum   Fruit marmalade

Preparation: The preparation of the dough is the same as given under No. 68. Roll out the dough very thin, cut out little tarts, put in the center of each some kind of marmalade, either raspberry, apple sauce, cherry or plum, and bake the tarts after folding one half of each over the fruit.

No. 71—PUFF-PASTE STRIPS.

½ lb. of washed butter
½ lb. of sugar
¼ pt. of water
White of 1 egg
1 tbsp. of rum
¼ tsp. baking powder
Sugar
Fruit marmalade

Preparation: The preparation of the dough is the same as given under No. 68. When the dough is rolled out thin, cut strips 3 inches long and 1½ inches wide, bake them until done, dust with sugar and finish baking. When done, spread with fruit marmalade and place two and two together.

No. 72—ALMOND TART FILLED WITH CREAM.

6 eggs
1 large cup of powdered sugar
½ lb. of unblanched, ground almonds
1½ tsps. baking powder

For the Filling.
1 pt. of whipped cream   ½ cup of sugar   1 tsp. of vanilla

Preparation: Yolks of eggs and powdered sugar are beaten for 15 minutes, the ground almonds added, then the baking powder and the beaten whites of eggs.

Bake in 3 layers, cool them, then spread on whipped cream mixed with sugar and vanilla, place the layers one on the other and cover the whole cake with whipped cream. The cake may be filled with fruit marmalade.

No. 73—HUNTER'S TART.

6 eggs 1 grated lemon rind
½ lb. of sugar 1½ tsps. of baking powder ¼ lb. of fine flour

For the Filling.
Fruit marmalade or jelly

For the Frosting.
2 whites of eggs 2 tbsps. of lemon juice
¼ cup of sugar ¼ lb. blanched, ground almonds

Preparation: 4 yolks of eggs and 2 whole eggs are stirred with sugar 15 minutes, add 1 grated lemon rind, flour, baking powder, the beaten whites of 4 eggs. Butter a round, loose bottom pan, sprinkle with roll crumbs, put the batter in, and bake it in medium hot oven. When baked, spread it with marmalade and then with the frosting. This is made by beating the whites of eggs to a stiff froth and mixing it with sugar, lemon juice and almonds. Then bake the cake again in a medium hot oven until the frosting is yellow.

No. 74—FIRE TART.

7 hard boiled eggs ½ lb. sugar
½ lb. blanched, ground almonds Flour enough to make stiff dough

For the Filling.
Jelly or marmalade

For Sprinkling.
¼ lb. blanched, ground almonds ¼ cup of sugar

Preparation: Stir the yolks of the hard boiled eggs well with sugar, add the almonds, then the flour, enough to make a stiff dough. Butter a pan and cover the bottom of it with dough. Leave enough for strips. Then bake the tart in a slow oven, cool it and spread it with jelly or marmalade. Mix the ground almonds with sugar and sprinkle over the jelly, then arrange the strips of dough nicely over the top and bake again. Place something under the pan that the bottom of the tart will not get dark.

No. 75—WHITE ALMOND TART.

½ lb. of butter ½ lb. of blanched, ground
½ lb. of sugar almonds
3 eggs 2½ tbsps. of baking powder ½ lb. of flour

For the Frosting.
¼ cup of rum Powdered sugar

Preparation: Cream the butter, sugar and yolks of eggs, then add the ground almonds, the flour, the baking powder and lastly the beaten whites of eggs. Butter a round, loose bottom pan, put the batter in and bake to a nice color. The rum is mixed with enough powdered sugar to make a creamy frosting and when the tart has cooled off, spread it with this frosting.

No. 76—HEAVEN'S TART.

1 cup of fresh butter
1 cup of powdered sugar
1 egg
1 tsp. of vanilla
2 scant cups of flour
2 heaping tsps. of baking powder
3 yolks of eggs

For the Filling. No. 1.

3 whites of eggs
4 tbsps. of powdered sugar
6 bitter, ground almonds
½ tsp. of cinnamon
¼ lb. blanched, ground almonds

No. 2.

1 glass raspberry jelly

No. 3.

1 cup of cream
2 yolks of eggs
Juice of 1 lemon
1 tbsp. of flour
2 tbsps. of sugar
1 tsp. vanilla

Preparation: Cream the butter, add the sugar, egg, yolks of eggs, flour and baking powder, mix well and bake in three layers.

Beat the 3 whites of eggs to a stiff froth, add 4 tablespoonfuls of powdered sugar, ¼ lb. sweet and 6 bitter, ground almonds and vanilla, and spread on the baked layers. Put them back into the oven to bake light yellow. On two of the layers put jelly. The cup of cream, 2 yolks of eggs, lemon juice, flour, 2 tablespoonfuls of sugar and 1 teaspoonful of vanilla are mixed well and boiled to a cream, stirring constantly. Let it get cold, spread it over the two layers covered with jelly and place one on the other. Place the layers covered with the beaten whites of eggs on top.

No. 77—HEAVEN'S FOOD.

2 eggs
1 cup of sugar
2 heaping tbsps. of flour
1 tsp. of baking powder
½ cup of ground walnuts
½ cup of chopped dates

For the Filling.

3 oranges   1 pt. of whipped cream   2 bananas

Preparation: The eggs are well beaten and stirred with sugar for 10 minutes; add flour and baking powder, ground walnuts and chopped dates and bake the cake to a nice color. When it is done, break it in desirable pieces, place them close together again, put the sliced oranges and bananas on and cover the whole with whipped cream mixed with sugar and vanilla. Serve at once.

No. 78—MERINGUE TART.

6 whites of eggs 1 tsp. of vanilla
2 cups of sugar ¼ tsp. of cream of tartar 1 tbsp. of vinegar

Preparation: The whites of eggs must be beaten very stiff, the cream of tartar, sugar and vanilla added and beaten or stirred 1 hour. Rinse a round cake pan with water, put the mixture in and bake in a slow oven 1 hour. When cold, fill it with whipped cream.

No. 79—SPONGE CAKE.

4 eggs 1 cup of sifted flour
1 cup of sugar 1 pinch of salt
3 tbsps. of water 1 tsp. of vanilla or lemon
1 tsp. of baking powder

Preparation: Cream the yolks of eggs and sugar, add the flour, water, salt and vanilla, then add baking powder and beaten whites of eggs. Butter a pan, put the batter in and bake slowly.

No. 80—WALNUT TART.

7 eggs ½ cup of dates
2 cups of powdered sugar 2½ tsps. of baking powder
Juice of 1 lemon ½ cup of sifted cracker crumbs
¾ lb. of blanched walnuts

Preparation: Rub yolks of eggs to a cream with sugar, add the ground walnuts, chopped dates, lemon juice, cracker crumbs, baking powder and beaten whites of eggs. Butter a round, loose bottom cake pan, put the batter in, bake it to a nice color, and cover with a chocolate frosting.

No. 81—BISCUIT TART.

12 eggs 1¼ tsps. baking powder
1 lb. of sugar 1 tsp. of vanilla or lemon rind 11 ozs. of flour

Preparation: Cream the yolks of eggs and sugar, add vanilla or grated ½ lemon rind, flour, baking powder and the beaten whites of eggs. Butter a round, loose bottom pan, put the batter in and bake in a slow oven. A glass of fine wine poured over the baked tart makes it very nice.

No. 82—SAND TART.

1 lb. of butter 2 tbsps. of good brandy
10 eggs 1 lb. corn starch or half corn
1 lb. of sugar starch and half flour
The juice and rind of 1 lemon 1 tsp. of baking powder

Preparation: The butter is washed to take the salt out, then creamed; add gradually the sugar and yolks of eggs, lemon juice, grated lemon rind and brandy. Then add the flour in spoonfuls. All in all the batter must have been stirred 1 hour. Now add the baking powder and beaten whites of eggs. Butter a round, loose bottom pan, put the batter in and bake slowly 1½ hours.

No. 83—FILLED BISCUIT ROLLS.

4 eggs
¼ lb. of sugar
1 tsp. grated lemon rind
¼ lb. of flour
1 tbsp. of butter
1 cup of fruit marmalade

Preparation: The yolks of eggs and sugar are stirred ½ hour, then the grated lemon rind, flour and beaten whites of eggs mixed in. A pan is buttered with the 1 tablespoonful of butter, the batter spread in ¼ inch thick and baked in a medium hot oven to a light brown color. When still warm, spread with the marmalade, roll it up and cut slices of it which may be baked or dried a little in the oven. If you wish, cover them with frosting.

No. 84—DATE CAKE WITH WHIPPED CREAM.

6 eggs
½ lb. of sugar
½ lb. of chopped walnuts
1 lb. chopped dates
½ cup of wheat bread crumbs
2 tsps. of baking powder

For the Filling.
1 pt. of whipped cream

Preparation: The yolks of eggs are creamed with sugar, then add the chopped or ground walnuts and dates, bread crumbs, baking powder and beaten whites of eggs. Bake in 2 layers. Mix the whipped cream with sugar and ½ teaspoonful of vanilla, spread on the layers and arrange these one on the other. Serve at once.

No. 85—FARINA TART.

7 eggs
¾ cup of sugar
½ cup blanched, ground, sweet almonds
15 bitter, blanched, ground almonds
1 grated lemon peel
¼ lb. of farina, good measure

Preparation: The yolks of eggs, sugar, lemon peel and almonds are stirred 1 hour, the farina mixed in dry and lastly the beaten whites of eggs. Butter a round, loose bottom pan, put the batter in and bake slowly 1 hour.

No. 86—BROWN SPICE CAKE No. 3.

2 cups of brown sugar
1 cup of butter
3 eggs
1 cup of milk
3 cups of flour
1 tsp. of cloves
½ tsp. of nutmeg
1 cup of chopped raisins
1 cup of chopped hickory nuts
3 tsps. of baking powder
1 tsp. of cinnamon

Preparation: Cream the butter with sugar and yolks of

eggs, add the milk, cloves, cinnamon, nutmeg, raisins, nuts, flour, baking powder and whites of eggs. Butter a pan, put the batter in and bake 1¼ to 1½ hours in medium hot oven.

No. 87—SPICE CAKE No. 4.

½ cup of butter
½ cup of lard
1½ cups of dark brown sugar
2 eggs
½ cup of cold coffee
½ cup of sour milk
1 tsp. of soda
¾ tsp. of cinnamon
½ tsp. cloves
3½—4 cups of flour

Preparation: The butter, lard, yolks of eggs and sugar are stirred to a cream, add the coffee, sour milk in which the soda has been dissolved, cinnamon, cloves, flour and beaten whites of eggs. Butter a pan, put the batter in and bake 1 hour or bake in 3 layers.

No. 88—SCOTCH TART.

¾ lb. of butter
1 lb. of sugar
½ lb. of finely cut raisins   9 eggs   1 lb. of flour
2 heaping tsps. of baking powder
Juice and rind of 1 lemon

Preparation: The butter is stirred to a cream, with yolks of eggs, sugar, lemon juice and rind; add the flour and lastly the baking powder and beaten whites of eggs. Butter a pan, put the batter in and bake to a light brown color.

No. 89—LARD CAKE.

½ lb. pork lard
6 eggs
½ lb. of sugar
¼ lb. of corn starch
¼ lb. of flour
⅛ lb. blanched, ground, sweet almonds
20 blanched, ground, bitter almonds
1 heaping tsp. of baking powder

Preparation: Stir the yolks of eggs and sugar to a cream; cream the lard and mix with the eggs and sugar. Now add flour and almonds in spoonfuls and lastly the baking powder and beaten whites of eggs. Butter a pan, put the batter in and bake to a nice brown color.

No. 90—SEXTON'S CAKE.

½ lb. of butter
¼ lb. of sugar
½ lb. of extra fine flour
¼ lb. blanched, ground, sweet almonds
½ tsp. baking powder

Preparation: The butter is stirred to a cream; add the sugar, ground almonds, flour and baking powder and stir 45 minutes. Spread the batter ½ inch thick in small square muffin pans or in a large square buttered cake pan, bake it to a light brown color and leave it to cool a little before taking out of the pan, because it breaks easily. After it has cooled off completely, dust with sugar or spread frosting on.

No. 91—CHOCOLATE TART.

¼ lb. sweet chocolate
1 cup of water
¼ lb. ground almonds
¼ lb. of butter

3 eggs
1¼ cups of sugar
1½ tsps. of baking powder
2 cups of flour

For Filling.
1 pt. of whipped cream

Preparation: Stir the butter, sugar and yolks of eggs to a cream. Add the chocolate dissolved in water, unblanched, ground almonds, flour and baking powder and the beaten whites of eggs. Butter a round, loose bottom pan, put the batter in and bake in a slow oven. Mix the whipped cream with sugar and vanilla and fill or cover the tart with it before serving.

No. 92—ENGLISH BRIDE'S CAKE (FRUIT CAKE).

1 lb. of butter
1 lb. brown sugar
10 eggs
1 lb. of flour
1 pt. of brandy
1 tbsp. ground cinnamon
2 lbs. finely cut citron

½ tbsp. of ground cloves
4 ground nutmegs
1 tsp. of baking soda
1 cup of molasses
10 lbs. of raisins
4 lbs. of currants
1 tbsp. of ground bark of nutmeg tree

Preparation: The butter is stirred to a cream with sugar and yolks of eggs. Then work in ½ lb. of flour, the brandy mixed with the spices and the molasses in which the soda is dissolved, the beaten whites of eggs, then raisins, currants, citron and the other ½ lb. of flour. The cake is baked 3 to 4 hours.

Remarks: This cake may be kept 20 years and longer and will still be palatable. Wine is served with it.

No. 93—GOOD TART DOUGH.

¼ lb. of butter
2 yolks of eggs
¼ lb. of blanched, ground almonds

¼ lb. of sugar
1 tbsp. of brandy
2 cups of flour
½ cup of cracker crumbs

Preparation: Cream the butter with sugar, egg yolks and brandy, and add the flour. Roll out the dough and line a round, loose bottom pan with it. Strew with ½ cup of cracker crumbs and ¼ lb. blanched, ground almonds. Spread the fruit on the almonds. This dough is very good for any kind of Fruit Tart.

No. 94—CHOCOLATE TART No. 2.

6 eggs
1 cup sugar
⅛ lb. chopped bitter chocolate
20 chopped almonds
½ cup of flour
1 heaping tsp. of baking powder

For Filling.
1 pt. of whipped cream

Preparation: Beat the whites of eggs to a stiff froth, add the chopped bitter chocolate and almonds, then yolks of eggs and sugar, and lastly the flour and baking powder. Bake in two layers. A little before serving, spread whipped cream between the layers.

No. 95—FILLED SAND TART.
Sand tart batter as in No. 82.

For Filling.
1 glass of fine fruit marmalade

For Frosting.
Rum frosting according to Chapter 20, No. 22

Preparation: The sand tart batter should be baked in 3 layers; when cold, spread the fruit marmalade between the layers. Then cover with rum frosting.

No. 96—TREE TART.

7 eggs
1 cup sugar
1 cup finest flour
Chocolate or sour filling

Preparation: Beat the yolks with a rotary egg beater, add ½ cup sugar and beat well again, then set aside. Beat whites to stiff froth, add other ½ cup sugar. Mix both and add 1 cup flour measured before sifting. Butter pans, dredge them with flour and put the batter in. Bake in 8 layers in a slow oven. Spread chocolate or sour cream filling as in No. 76. between the layers. You may also cover with a frosting if you wish.

No. 97—FENCE TART.

First Layer.

4 whites of eggs
3 yolks of eggs
1 pinch of salt
1/3 tsp. cream of tartar
1¼ cups of sugar
1 cup flour

Second Layer.

1/3 of ¼ lb. bitter chocolate dissolved in ¼ cup hot water
1 cup of powdered sugar
1 tsp. of vanilla
½ package Knox gelatine dissolved in ¼ cup of water
1½ cups of cream ½ pt. whipped cream

Third Layer.

½ package Knox gelatine with pink coloring dissolved in ¼ cup of water
½ pt. whipped cream
1 cup of powdered sugar
1½ cups of cream
1 tsp. of vanilla

For the Covering.
1 pt. whipped cream

For the Fencing.
1½ doz. ladyfingers or macaroons

Preparation: The first layer. Whip whites of eggs to thin froth, add salt and cream of tartar, then whip to a stiff froth, mix in the sugar and then the yolks of eggs whipped to a cream. Mix the flour in lightly and bake this batter in a buttered, round, loose bottom pan. Loosen edge of layer and arrange ladyfingers or macaroons around in circle. For the second layer. The dissolved bitter chocolate, sugar, cream and vanilla are boiled for 2 minutes, stirring constantly; stir in the dissolved gelatine, set the mixture in cold water and continue stirring until it begins to thicken, then add the ½ pint of whipped cream and spread the mixture over the baked layer. The third layer is made exactly like the second layer only using the pink coloring instead of the bitter chocolate; after the whipped cream is added, spread the mixture over the chocolate layer.

Before serving, spread the 1 pint of whipped cream, to which has been added a little sugar and vanilla, over the cake.

No. 98—FRUIT TART.

Apricot, Peach, Plum, Blueberry, Raspberry or Strawberry Tart.

Prepare the batter according to No. 93, Good Tart Dough. Cover with the desired fruit, either fresh or canned, sprinkle with sufficient sugar, bake for 25 minutes. Before serving the cake, cover with beaten cream or almond frosting, prepared according to No. 23, Chapter 20 and then bake.

No. 99—SUNSHINE CAKE.

6 eggs
1 cup sugar
1 cup flour
1 even tsp. cream of tartar
Pinch of salt
½ tsp. vanilla

Preparation: Beat the yolks of eggs first and add half the sugar; beat the whites of eggs very dry and add remaining sugar; beat well and add the vanilla, salt and the yolks of eggs; lastly, add the flour and cream of tartar. Bake in a moderate oven one hour.

No. 100—LOVE CHOCOLATE CAKE.

¼ cup butter ½ tsp. soda
1 cup sugar 1 large cup flour
1 egg 2 squares bitter chocolate
½ cup hot water ½ cup sour milk 1 tsp. vanilla

Preparation: Cream butter and sugar; add the egg and vanilla; add the milk in which the soda is dissolved; dissolve the chocolate in a half cup boiling water, let cool and add; lastly, add the flour. Bake in flat cake tin about 45 minutes.

No. 101—ANGEL FOOD.

Whites of 9 eggs 1 tsp. vanilla
1 cup sugar 1 cup flour 1 tsp. cream of tartar

Preparation: Beat the whites of eggs to a stiff froth; boil the sugar with 4 tablespoons of water until all the sugar is dissolved; beat the sugar syrup into the whites of the eggs; add vanilla and the flour and cream of tartar. Bake slowly one hour.

No. 102—FRUIT CAKE.

1¼ cups sugar 1½ cups flour
½ cup butter ½ tsp. cloves
Yolks of 2 eggs ½ tsp. cinnamon
1 cup sour milk ½ cup dates, raisins and citron
1 tsp. baking soda 1 cup walnuts

Preparation: Cream the sugar and butter, add yolks of eggs, cloves and cinnamon; dissolve the soda in the sour milk and add to the rest; add the flour and mix well; lastly add the raisins, dates, citron and walnuts. Bake about 45 minutes.

No. 103—CREAM PUFFS.

1 large teacup hot water 1 teacup flour
½ tsp. butter 4 eggs

Preparation: Stir the flour into the boiling water and butter. Set aside to cool and, when cold, stir in the unbeaten eggs one at a time. Drop in muffin tins and bake in a fairly hot oven. When baked, fill with beaten cream, sweetened to taste and flavored with vanilla.

No. 104—CREAM PUFFS.

1 cup boiling water 3 eggs, beaten
½ cup butter 1 cup pastry flour Small pinch of soda

Preparation; Pour the water over the butter. As soon as it boils and the butter is melted, stir in the flour and keep stirring until it leaves the sides of the pan. Let cool, stir in the eggs and soda, drop on the buttered pans and bake thirty minutes. Do not open the oven door for twenty minutes for fear they will fall. Fill with whipped cream, sweetened and flavored.

No. 105—YEAST DOUGHNUTS.

1 cup sugar
3 cups milk
Flour to make soft sponge
1 yeast cake Mix and let stand over night

In the Morning Add:

1 cup sugar
½ cup butter
3 eggs
½ a nutmeg
½ tsp. soda
Flour to mix stiff

Preparation: Let rise, then roll and cut in shape desired, or roll into long strips and twist into shape. Let rise again while the lard is heating and then fry. Raised doughnuts require longer cooking.

No. 106—SOUR CREAM DOUGHNUTS.

5 tbsps. sour cream
1 cup milk
½ cup butter
1 cup sugar
2 eggs
Little salt
1 tsp. soda
1¼ pts. of flour
¼ tsp. cinnamon
¼ tsp. nutmeg
1 tsp. baking powder

Preparation: Stir butter, eggs and cream well, add all other ingredients, roll and cut the dough, bake in hot lard to golden-brown color and sprinkle powdered sugar over.

No. 107—BLITZ-KUCHEN.

1 lb. sugar
½ lb. butter
8 eggs
1 lb. flour

Preparation: Stir sugar, butter and yolks of eggs together well, add the stiffly beaten whites of eggs and flour. Bake in a long tin and cover with sugar, cinnamon and chopped almonds. Cut and serve while warm.

No. 108—SPICE CAKE.

2 cups brown sugar
½ cup butter
2 eggs
2 egg yolks
½ cup sour milk
1 tsp. nutmeg
2 cups flour
1 tsp. cloves
1 tsp. cinnamon
1 tsp. soda

Preparation: Beat the sugar, butter and eggs together until smooth; add the remaining ingredients. Bake in three layers and put together with white frosting.

No. 109—WHIPPED CREAM CAKE.

Make a good sponge cake dough (see No. 29), and omit the chocolate

Filling.

1 pint whipped, sweet cream
Vanilla
1 pound blanched, chopped almonds
Sugar

Preparation: After the layers are baked, beat the cream stiff, add sugar, vanilla and almonds; sweeten the cream and spread between the layers and on top. This is the queen of all cakes.

No. 110—WALNUT CAKE.

1 lb. walnuts (leave out 14 halves for the top)
1 cup powdered sugar
¾ cup crackers (rolled fine)
8 eggs
1 tsp. baking powder
1 cup powdered sugar

Filling.

2 cups milk
Corn starch to thicken
½ cup sugar
Vanilla
Yolks of 2 eggs

Preparation: Cream the yolks of eggs and the sugar; add the beaten whites of the eggs; mix the rolled crackers, finely chopped nuts and baking powder and add. Bake in three layers in a slow oven.

Stir powdered sugar with a little water, spread on top of cake and put on the walnut halves.

No. 111—ANGEL CAKE.

1 scant cup flour
1 scant cup sugar
1 tsp. baking powder
1 cup walnuts (cut)
1 cup dates (cut)
4 eggs

Preparation: Cream the eggs separately, add sugar, walnuts, dates, baking powder and flour. Bake in a buttered pan.

CHAPTER 20.

Fillings and Frostings for Cakes.

No. 1—VANILLA FILLING.

½ cup of sweet cream
3 eggs
1½ tsps. of vanilla
4 tbsps. of sugar

The preparation of the vanilla filling is the same as given in Chapter 19, No. 29, Layer Cake with Chocolate.

No. 2—NUT FILLING No. 1.

1 tsp. of butter
½ cup of milk
2 tbsps. of flour
1 cup of sugar
½ cup of chopped nuts
1 egg

Preparation: The ingredients, excepting the white of egg, are all mixed well. The mixture is cooked one minute, stirring constantly, then cooled and the beaten white of egg mixed in.

No. 3—RAISIN FILLING.

1 cup of sugar
¼ cup of water
1 cup of seedless chopped raisins
1 white of egg

Preparation: Water and sugar are stirred well, then boiled for one minute and taken from the stove. The raisins and beaten white of egg are mixed in and the filling spread on the cake, while still warm.

No. 4—NUT FILLING No. 2.

1 cup of sugar
1 cup of finely chopped nuts
1 cup of sour cream

Preparation: The ingredients are mixed and cooked for several minutes, stirring constantly.

No. 5—ALMOND FILLING.

2½ tbsps. of sugar
1 tbsp. of water
½ tsp. of vanilla
1 cup of blanched, ground almonds
Whipped cream, to taste

Preparation: The sugar, water and vanilla are boiled 1 minute and spread on the cake while warm. The almonds are strewn on immediately, then cover with the sweetened whipped cream.

No. 6—LEMON FILLING.

½ cup of milk
4 tbsps. of sugar
1 tsp. of lemon extract
2 eggs
1 tsp. of flour

Preparation: This is given in Chapter 19, No. 33, Sponge Cake.

No. 7—WALNUT FILLING.

½ cup of chopped walnuts
½ cup of chopped seedless or seeded raisins
1 cup of sugar
¼ tsp. of vanilla
¼ cup of water

Preparation: The ingredients are mixed and boiled, stirring constantly, then spread on the cake while still warm.

No. 8—CHOCOLATE FILLING.

¼ lb. of sweet chocolate
½ cup of sugar
1 tsp. of vanilla
2 tbsps. of water
3 whites of eggs

Preparation: The chocolate is dissolved in the water, vanilla and sugar added and boiled 3 minutes while stirring constantly. Mix in the beaten whites of eggs while the chocolate is still warm.

No. 9—COCOANUT FILLING.

¼ lb. of cocoanut
2 whites of eggs
½ cup of sugar
1 tsp. of vanilla

Preparation: The whites of eggs are beaten to a stiff froth, the cocoanut mixed in, then sugar and vanilla.

No. 10—BANANA FILLING.

4—5 bananas
¼ cup of sugar

Preparation: The bananas are peeled and sliced, mixed with sugar and spread between the layers of the cake.

No. 11—DATE FILLING.

1 cup of dates
Juice and rind of 1 orange
2 tbsps. of water
½ cup of sugar

Preparation: The dates are chopped fine and mixed with orange juice and grated orange rind, water and sugar and spread on the cake.

No. 12—CHOCOLATE FROSTING No. 1.

⅛ lb. of sweet chocolate
¼ lb. of sugar
4 tbsps. of water
1 tsp. of vanilla

Preparation: Chocolate and sugar are dissolved in the water and vanilla and cooked until it threads. Stir it a little while longer and spread on the cake quickly, then put the cake into the oven again for 1 minute.

No. 13—CHOCOLATE FROSTING No. 2.

½ cup of butter
⅛ lb. of chocolate
2 cups of sugar
1 cup of boiling water
½ tsp. of vanilla

Preparation: The chocolate is grated, mixed with the other ingredients, and boiled a few minutes, stirring constantly, until quite stiff. Take off the fire, stir until nearly cold and spread on the cake immediately.

No. 14—CHOCOLATE FROSTING No. 3.

½ lb. of confectionery sugar
2 heaping tbsps. of cocoa
1 tsp. of vanilla
3—5 tbsps. of water

Preparation: Sugar, cocoa and vanilla are mixed and the cold water gradually stirred in, being careful not to take too much water because the mixture must be thick. Spread on the cake at once. If you wish, add ½ cup of blanched and chopped almonds.

No. 15—VANILLA FROSTING.

1 lb. of confectionery sugar
1 tbsp. of vanilla
Sufficient cream to make the frosting of proper consistency

Preparation: Vanilla is added to the sugar and the cream in ½ teaspoonfuls. Take only sufficient cream to make the frosting of consistency to spread.

No. 16—LEMON FROSTING.

1 lb. confectionery sugar
Juice of 1 lemon
Cream, if necessary

Preparation: The lemon juice is mixed with the sugar and stirred a while. If the frosting is too thick, add more cream.

No. 17—TUTTI-FRUTTI FROSTING No. 1.

1½ cups of sugar
1 tbsp. of cocoa or chocolate
1 tbsp. of butter
¼ cup of cocoanut
¼ cup of chopped walnuts
½ cup of milk
¼ cup of finely chopped raisins

The ingredients are mixed well and cooked until the mixture may be spread on the cake while still warm.

No. 18—TUTTI-FRUTTI FROSTING No. 2.

3 tbsps. hot milk
½ cup of confectionery sugar
½ lb. of ground peanuts
1 cup of finely chopped seedless or seeded raisins
¼ cup of chopped citron

Preparation: The sugar and hot milk are stirred a while, then the other ingredients are added and the frosting spread on the cake immediately

No. 19—PLAIN FROSTING.

½ cup of confectionery sugar
1 tsp. of vanilla or lemon
1 white of egg

Preparation: White of egg and sugar are stirred well and vanilla or lemon essence added; white of egg is not beaten to a froth.

No. 20—CARAMEL FROSTING.

1 cup of brown sugar   1 tsp. of butter
¼ cup of milk   1 tsp. of vanilla

Preparation: Sugar and milk are boiled until the mixture draws threads; take off the fire, add butter and vanilla and stir continually until you spread it on the cake while still warm.

No. 21—GLAZE FROSTING FOR HONEY CAKES.

¼ lb. of confectionery sugar   3 tbsps. of rose water   1 white of egg

Preparation: All ingredients are stirred to a cream and spread on the cake.

No. 22—RUM FROSTING.

¾ cup of confectionery sugar   1½ tbsps. of rum   ¼ pt. of water

Preparation: The sugar is dissolved in water and cooked until it threads. Then cool it a little, add the rum and stir until the frosting begins to get white, then spread on the cake.

No. 23—ALMOND FROSTING FOR FRUIT TART No. 1.

6 whites of eggs   Scant ½ lb. blanched almonds
1¼ cups of sugar   cut in long thin strips

Preparation: The whites of eggs are beaten to a stiff froth, mixed with sugar and almonds and spread on the cake. This is then put into a medium oven and baked lightly to harden the frosting.

No. 24—ALMOND FROSTING No. 2.

5 eggs   ¾ cup of sugar
¼ lb. blanched, ground almonds   3 tbsps. of lemon juice

The preparation is the same as given in Chapter 19, No. 67, Cherry Tart.

No. 25—FRUIT FROSTING.

1/3 lb. of powdered sugar   2 tbsps. of fruit marmalade
1 white of egg

Preparation: The ingredients are mixed well, stirred 25 minutes until thick and foamy, then spread on the cake immediately.

No. 26—CREAM FROSTING FOR FRUIT CAKE.

½ cup of sweet or sour cream   2 eggs   ¼ cup of sugar

Preparation: Cream, sugar and yolks of eggs are mixed well and the beaten whites of eggs added. This frosting is spread on the cake and baked 10 minutes until the frosting is a nice yellow color.

No. 27—PLAIN ALMOND FROSTING.

½ lb. of confectionery sugar
¼ cup of cream or milk
1 cup of blanched, ground or chopped almonds

Preparation: The cream and the almonds are stirred into the sugar. The frosting must be quite thick, then spread on the cake immediately.

CHAPTER 21.
COOKIES.

Directions for Preparing Christmas Cookies.

No. 1—BUTTER COOKIES.

1 lb. of butter	½ lb. of sugar
1½ lbs. of flour	¼ lb. of blanched, ground almonds
2 yolks of eggs	
1 tbsp. of arrack or brandy	¼ cup of chopped citron

Preparation: The butter is washed to take the salt out. Then butter, flour and sugar are mixed, yolks of eggs, arrack and almonds added and the dough rolled out to ¼ inch thick. Cut out with cooky cutters and bake to a light yellow color.

Remarks: These cookies may be brushed with whites of eggs and dusted with sugar, cinnamon and almonds before they are baked.

No. 2—HAZELNUT COOKIES.

¾ lb. of sugar	1 lb. of flour
4 eggs	1½ tsps. of vanilla
½ lb. of ground hazelnuts	

Preparation: The ingredients are mixed into a smooth batter, rolled out thin, cut out in various designs and baked a nice yellow color. When done, spread with vanilla frosting.

No. 3—KISSES.

½ lb. of sugar mixed with vanilla   4 whites of eggs

Preparation: The sugar and whites of eggs are whipped to a stiff froth. The pan is spread with wax, little heaps of froth are put on and baked in a very moderate oven.

No. 4—SAND COOKIES.

1 cup of butter	½ tsp. of baking powder
1½ cups of sugar	Flour enough to make a stiff dough
3 eggs	
1 tbsp. of water	Sugar and cinnamon

Preparation: Butter, sugar, yolks of eggs and 1 tablespoonful of water are stirred well, then the beaten whites of eggs and baking powder are added and flour mixed in to make the dough stiff enough to roll out. Cut it into squares, dust with sugar and cinnamon and bake.

No. 5—ALMOND HEAPS.

½ lb. of sugar
3 whites of eggs
¼ tsp. of cinnamon
½ lb. unblanched almonds, cut into long strips
¼ tsp. of corn starch

Preparation: Stir the beaten whites of eggs with sugar ½ hour, add almonds, cinnamon and corn starch. Rinse the cake pans with water, put little heaps of the batter on and bake 20 minutes in a medium oven.

No. 6—ALMOND MACAROONS.

½ lb. of sugar
3 whites of eggs
½ lb. blanched, ground almonds
1 tsp. of corn starch

Preparation: The beaten whites of eggs and sugar are stirred ½ hour, then the almonds and corn starch are added. The cake tins are rinsed with cold water; put little heaps of the mixture on and bake in a medium oven to a golden yellow.

No. 7—CHOCOLATE MACAROONS WITH ALMONDS.

½ lb. unblanched almonds, cut into long strips
¾ cup of sugar
¼ lb. of grated sweet chocolate
3 whites of eggs
2 tbsps. of water

Preparation: The almonds are blanched and cut into long strips, then they are stirred in the sugar and water over the fire until they become sugared. When this has cooled, stir in the chocolate and beaten whites of eggs. Grease the pans with a bacon rind, put little heaps of the batter on and bake in a medium oven.

No. 8—CHOCOLATE MACAROONS WITH COCOANUT.

1 lb. of sugar
4 eggs
¼ lb. of sweet, grated chocolate
¼ lb. of cocoanut
1 tsp. of cinnamon
1 lb. of flour
2 tsps. of baking powder

Preparation: Sugar and eggs are stirred well, then chocolate, cocoanut, cinnamon, lastly flour and baking powder added. Grease the pans with a bacon rind. Put little heaps of the batter on and bake in a slow oven.

No. 9—WALNUT MACAROONS.

½ lb. of ground walnuts
½ lb. of sugar
3 whites of eggs
½ tsp. of vanilla

Preparation: The whites of eggs are beaten to a stiff froth, sugar is mixed in and stirred ½ hour, then walnuts and vanilla are added. Rinse the pans with cold water, place little heaps of the mixture on and bake in a medium oven.

No. 10—FLAWNS.

½ lb. of butter
3 eggs
1 lb. of flour
1 tsp. of baking powder
½ lb. of sugar

For Sprinkling.
Sugar, almonds and cinnamon

Preparation: The butter is stirred to a cream with sugar and the eggs, then work in flour and baking powder. Roll out the dough to the thickness of a knife, cut out designs, sprinkle with sugar, blanched and cut or ground almonds and cinnamon and bake in medium hot oven.

The butter must be washed to take out the salt.

No. 11—ALMOND PUFFS.

3 whites of eggs
½ lb. of sugar
1 grated lemon rind
½ lb. blanched almonds, cut in long strips
2 tsps. of corn starch

Preparation: The whites of eggs are beaten to a froth and stirred ½ hour with the sugar, grated lemon rind, almonds and corn starch. Rinse the pans with cold water, put on small heaps of the mixture and bake in medium oven.

No. 12—ALMOND STRAWS No. 1.

6 eggs
1 lb. of sugar
¾ lb. blanched, grated almonds
1 grated lemon rind

Preparation: Eggs, sugar, almonds and lemon rind are mixed well and stirred until the dough rolls from the spoon with which you stir it. The bread board is floured, the dough rolled out to ½ inch thickness and cut into strips 3 inches long and 2 inches wide. Leave them on the board over night, turn them in the morning and leave them 6 hours longer, then bake in a medium hot oven to a golden yellow color.

No. 13—VANILLA STRAWS.

½ lb. of butter
½ lb. of sugar
5 eggs
1½ tbsps. of vanilla
½ tsp. of baking powder
½ lb. of flour

Preparation: The butter is washed to take out the salt, creamed and mixed with sugar, eggs and vanilla. Add the baking powder mixed with the flour. Roll out the dough on a well floured board to ¼ inch thickness, cut out oblong strips and bake them in buttered pans to a dark yellow color.

No. 14—ANISE COOKIES.

1 lb. of sugar
4 large eggs
Butter, the size of a nut
1 level tsp. of ammonium
1½ lbs. of flour
Anise to taste

Preparation: Sugar, eggs, butter, anise and ammonium dissolved in a little milk are mixed well and stirred ¼ hour, then gradually add the flour. Roll out the dough on a floured board, cut out designs, leave them on the board for 24 hours and bake to a yellow color.

No. 15—VANILLA FLAWNS.

4 eggs   ½ lb. of sugar   1 tbsp. of vanilla   ½ lb. of flour

Preparation: The eggs and sugar are stirred on the stove for ½ hour, then vanilla and flour are added. With a coffee spoon put little heaps of the batter on a pan, let them stand 4 to 5 hours, put in the oven and bake to a nice color.

No. 16—OATMEAL COOKIES No. 1.

2 cups of sugar
½ cup of lard
½ cup of hot water
2½ cups of dry oatmeal
1 tsp. of soda dissolved in water
Spices to taste

Preparation: The lard and sugar are stirred well; oatmeal, hot water and the dissolved soda mixed in; 1 pinch of salt and some nutmeg, cloves and cinnamon added. Put little heaps on a buttered pan and bake to a light brown color.

No. 17—OATMEAL COOKIES No. 2.

¾ lb. of butter
1 cup of brown sugar
2 eggs
½ tsp. of salt
1 tsp. of cinnamon   ½ tsp. of cloves
¼ tsp. of nutmeg
2 cups of dry rolled oatmeal
½ tsp. of saleratus, dissolved in 1 tbsp. of milk
2 cups of flour

Preparation: The butter is rubbed to a cream; mix well with sugar, eggs, salt, cinnamon, cloves, nutmeg, oatmeal, then add the dissolved saleratus and flour. Roll out the dough, cut out cookies with a cutter and bake to a light brown color.

No. 18—BROWN COOKIES No. 1.

½ pt. of molasses 1 pt. of syrup 1 tsp. of cloves 1 tsp. of cinnamon
½ lb. of maple sugar
½ lb. of butter
⅛ lb. of lard
¼ lb. of chopped almonds
1½ grated lemon rind
2 tsps. of potash
½ tsp. of hartshorn salt
2½ lbs. of flour
¼ cup of chopped citron

Preparation: Rub the butter and lard to a cream with sugar, add molasses, syrup, chopped almonds and citron, cloves, cinnamon, grated lemon rind, potash, hartshorn salt and flour. Roll the dough, cut out cookies and bake to a light brown color.

No. 19—BUTTER COOKIES.

¾ cup of butter
2 cups of sugar
4 eggs
5 tbsps. of sour cream
1 tsp. of saleratus
4—5 cups of flour
½ tsp. of nutmeg

Preparation: The butter, sugar and eggs must be stirred to a cream, then add cream, saleratus, nutmeg, and lastly the flour. Roll out the dough, cut out cookies and bake to a golden yellow color.

No. 20—BROWN COOKIES No. 2.

½ lb. of butter
2 lbs. of syrup
¼ lb. of sweet, chopped almonds
⅛ lb. of bitter, ground almonds
½ oz. potash, dissolved in ¼ cup of rose water
½ tsp. of cloves
1½ tsps. of cinnamon
1 tsp. of cardamom
1 grated lemon rind
⅛ lb. of finely chopped citron
2 lbs. of flour
1½ lbs. of sugar

Preparation: Rub the butter to a cream with syrup, sweet and bitter almonds, potash, cloves, cinnamon, cardamom, lemon rind and citron. Lastly mix in the flour and sugar. Roll out the dough, cut out and bake in medium hot oven.

No. 21—BROWN COOKIES No. 3.

1 qt. of syrup
2 cups of sugar
1½ cups of melted lard
1 cup of hot water
1 tsp. of baking soda
½ tsp. of allspice
1 tsp. of cinnamon
¼ tsp. of ginger
½ tsp. of nutmeg
¼ tsp. of salt
½ tsp. of pepper
Flour enough to make a stiff dough

Preparation: Mix the ingredients well, put in enough flour to make a stiff dough, roll it out, cut out cookies and bake.

No. 22—BROWN COOKIES No. 4.

1 qt. of syrup
1 lb. of brown sugar
1 lb. of lard
1 cup of sour milk
2 tsps. of baking soda
1 tsp. of cinnamon
1 pinch of salt
Flour enough to make a stiff dough

Preparation: Mix well the melted lard, sugar, syrup, cinnamon, salt and sour milk in which the soda is dissolved; then work in enough flour to make a stiff dough. Roll out the dough, cut out cookies and bake.

No. 23—BROWN COOKIES No. 5.

1 cup of sugar
1 cup of lard
2 cups of molasses
2 tsps. of baking soda
1 tsp. of cloves
1 tsp. of cinnamon
¼ tsp. of ginger
1 tsp. of salt
2 eggs
Flour enough to make a stiff dough

Preparation: Melt the lard and add sugar, molasses, baking soda, cloves, cinnamon, ginger, salt, eggs and enough flour to make a stiff dough. Roll out the dough, cut out cookies and bake.

No. 24—WHITE COOKIES No. 1.

¼ lb. of butter
½ lb. of sugar
¼ lb. of blanched, ground almonds
2 yolks of eggs
½ cup of sweet cream
1 tbsp. of cardamom
½ lemon rind, grated
2 tsps. of hartshorn salt, dissolved in ¼ cup of rose water
1¼—1½ lbs. of flour

Preparation: Cream the butter with sugar and yolks of eggs, then add almonds, cream, cardamom, lemon rind, dissolved hartshorn salt and flour enough to make a stiff dough. Roll it out, cut out cookies and bake.

No. 25—WHITE COOKIES No. 2.

4 lbs. of fine sugar
1 bottle of rose water
4 yolks of eggs
1 cup of butter
½ oz. hartshorn salt
⅛ lb. of grated orange rind
1 grated lemon rind
½ lb. of blanched, chopped almonds
4 lbs. of flour
¼ lb. of finely chopped citron

Preparation: The sugar is dissolved in the rose water and brought to boil. Yolks of eggs and hartshorn salt are mixed and stirred into the sweetened rose water while still warm, (not hot), then all the other ingredients are quickly mixed in and lastly the flour. Roll out the dough, cut out cookies and bake to a golden yellow color.

Remarks: Let the dough stand for a day before baking.

No. 26—WHITE COOKIES No. 3.

¾ lb. of butter
3 eggs
1 tsp. of hartshorn salt, dissolved in ¼ cup of rose water
1 lb. of sugar
½ cup of blanched, ground almonds
2 grated lemon rinds
2 lbs. of flour

Preparation: The butter is washed to remove the salt. The cold butter is cut into the flour and mixed with the hands, then eggs, dissolved hartshorn salt, sugar, almonds and lemon rind are added. The dough is now rolled out and cut out with a tumbler or cooky cutter. Bake in pans to a golden yellow color.

No. 27—BUTTER STRAWS WITH ALMONDS.

½ lb. of butter
½ lb. of sugar
½ lb. of blanched, ground almonds
2 eggs
½ lb. of flour
1 grated lemon rind
1 tsp. of baking powder

Preparation: Rub the butter to a cream with yolks of eggs. Then add the beaten whites of eggs, lemon rind and baking powder mixed with flour. The dough is rolled out, cut into strips and baked to a golden yellow color.

No. 28—CHOCOLATE COOKIES.

½ lb. of grated, sweet chocolate
¼ lb. of butter
1 lb. of sugar
½ lb. of blanched, ground almonds
3 eggs
1 tsp. of vanilla
1 lb. of flour
1 tsp. of baking powder

Preparation: Rub the butter and sugar to a cream, add chocolate, almonds, eggs and vanilla, then baking powder mixed with flour and roll out the dough. Cut out the cookies with a tumbler or cutter and bake in a slow oven.

Remarks: Cookies containing chocolate take more time for baking.

No. 29—NUT CHOCOLATE COOKIES.

1 cup of grated, sweet chocolate
1½ cups of sugar
4 eggs
12 tbsps. of ground walnuts
1 tsp. of cinnamon
1½ cups of flour

Preparation: The ingredients are mixed well and stirred, the flour added last, then this dough is rolled out and cut into strips or into disks with a tumbler and baked slowly.

No. 30—MOLASSES COOKIES.

1 cup of lard
1 cup of sugar
2 eggs
2 cups of good or best molasses
2/3 cup of hot water
2 tsps. of soda
1 tsp. of cream of tartar
½ tsp. of cinnamon
½ tsp. of ginger
½ tsp. of salt
Flour enough to make a stiff dough

Preparation: The lard is melted and mixed with sugar, molasses, water, the soda dissolved in a little water, the cream of tartar, cinnamon, ginger, salt and enough flour added to make a stiff dough. Roll out, cut out cookies and bake.

No. 31—COCOANUT DROP CAKES.

5 eggs
2 cups of sugar
2 tsps. of baking powder
3 cups of flour
½ lb. of cocoanut

Preparation: The ingredients are mixed well and the flour stirred in last. With a teaspoon drop on well buttered pans and bake until light brown.

No. 32—HICKORYNUT DROP CAKES.

1½ cups of sugar
1 cup of butter
2 eggs
1 cup of sour cream
1 tsp. of vanilla
1 cup of hickory nuts
2 tsps. of baking powder
3½ cups of flour
1 tsp. of soda

Preparation: The butter is stirred to a cream and mixed with sugar and eggs. The soda is dissolved in the sour milk and added, also the vanilla, the nuts and the baking powder mixed with the flour. Little heaps of dough are placed on well buttered pans and baked in a slow oven.

No. 33—SMALL HERMIT CAKES No. 1.

1½ cups of brown sugar
1 cup of butter
3 eggs
1 cup of ground nuts
1 cup of finely chopped raisins
1 tsp. of cloves
1 tsp. of cinnamon
1 tsp. of baking soda
1 tbsp. of good molasses
3 cups of flour
1 cup of finely chopped dates

Preparation: Butter, sugar and eggs are stirred well. The soda dissolved in the molasses and mixed in; then add nuts, raisins, dates, cloves, cinnamon and flour. Grease the pans with a bacon rind, make little cakes the size of a walnut and bake in a slow oven.

No. 34—SMALL HERMIT CAKES No. 2.

1 cup of butter
2 eggs
2 cups of sugar
1 cup of currants
1 tbsp. of molasses
1 tsp. of cinnamon
1 tsp. of cloves
1 tsp. of nutmeg
Flour enough to make a stiff dough
1 tsp. of soda

Preparation: The butter, eggs, sugar and currants are mixed well, soda dissolved in the molasses added, also cinnamon, cloves, nutmeg and enough flour to roll out the dough, being careful not to make it too stiff. Roll out thin, cut out with a cooky cutter or in strips and bake in a hot oven.

No. 35—MOTHER'S COOKIES.

1½ cups of butter 3 tsps. of baking powder
3 eggs 6 cups of flour
3 cups of sugar ½ grated lemon rind ¾ cup of milk

Preparation: Cream the butter with eggs and sugar, add the milk, lemon rind and baking powder mixed with the flour. Roll out quite thin, cut out cookies and bake to a golden yellow color.

No. 36—PEANUT DROP CAKES.

2 tbsps. of butter 1 tsp. of salt
2 eggs 4 tbsps. of milk
4 tbsps. of sugar 1 tsp. of baking powder
1 cup of ground peanuts 1 cup of flour

Preparation: The butter, sugar and yolks of eggs are stirred to a cream; add the milk, nuts, salt, the beaten whites of eggs and baking powder mixed with the flour. With a teaspoon drop on well buttered pans, place a peanut on each and bake in a slow oven.

No. 37—PEANUT STRAWS.

¾ cup of butter 1 large cup of flour
1 large cup of sugar Some chopped or cut peanuts 4 whites of eggs

Preparation: The very cold butter is cut into the flour, sugar is added and quickly mixed with the hands. Beat the whites of eggs to a stiff froth and add it to the dough. Spread the dough into buttered pans, strew the peanuts on and bake the cake. When it has cooled, cut it into small equal strips.

No. 38—SMALL PLAIN COOKIES.

½ cup of butter ½ tsp. of salt
½ cup of lard 1½ cups of sugar
3 eggs Flour enough to make a stiff dough
1 tsp. of baking soda 3 tsps. of boiling water

Preparation: Butter, lard, eggs and sugar are stirred well. The soda is dissolved in the hot water and added, then salt and not too much flour. The dough should be rather soft; roll it out, cut out cookies, sprinkle with sugar and bake to a golden yellow color.

No. 39—RAISIN CAKE.

1 cup of butter · 1½ cups of chopped English
3 eggs walnuts
1½ cups of sugar 1 tsp. of cinnamon
1½ cups of finely chopped 1 tsp. of baking soda
  raisins ¼ cup of hot water
6 tbsps. of strong coffee 3 cups of flour

Preparation: The butter, eggs and sugar are stirred well, raisins, walnuts, coffee, cinnamon, soda dissolved in the hot water and flour mixed in. The pans are buttered well and the dough put on in teaspoonfuls, flattened a little and baked slowly.

No. 40—GINGER SNAPS.

1 cup of butter and lard
1 cup of brown sugar
3 eggs
1 cup of molasses
½ cup of sour milk
2 tsps. of baking soda
1 tbsp. of ginger
1 tbsp. of cinnamon
1 tsp. of cloves
Flour enough to make a stiff dough.

Preparation: Butter, lard, sugar and eggs are stirred well; baking soda dissolved in the sour milk, coffee, ginger, cinnamon, cloves added and flour to make a stiff dough. Roll it out, cut out the cookies with a tumbler and bake.

No. 41—BROWN PEPPERNUTS No. 1.

1½ lbs. of sugar
2 lbs of butter
1½ lbs. of syrup
¼ oz. of cardamom
¼ oz. of cinnamon
3 grated lemon rinds
½ lb. ground almonds
¼ lb. of finely chopped citron
5 lbs. of flour
1¼ ozs. of potash, dissolved in ¼ cup of rose water

Preparation: Sugar and butter are stirred to a cream, then all ingredients mixed in and lastly the flour. Make little heaps or nuts on buttered pans and bake them.

No. 42—BROWN PEPPERNUTS No. 2.

1½ lbs. of butter
1 lb. of sugar
1 lb. of syrup
1 cup of rose water
2 tsps. of hartshorn salt
½ cup of finely chopped citron
¼ lb. of ground almonds
1 tbsp. of cardamom
1 grated lemon rind
3 lbs. of flour

Preparation: Preparation is the same as the one before, No. 41, Brown Peppernuts. The hartshorn salt is dissolved in the given quantity of rose water.

No. 43—SUGAR PEPPERNUTS.

1 lb. of butter
1½ lbs. of sugar
¼ lb. of blanched, ground almonds
¾ cup of sweet cream
½ cup of finely cut citron
1 tbsp. of cardamom
2 tbsps. of brandy
1½ tsps. of hartshorn salt dissolved in 1 cup of rose water
3 lbs. of flour

Preparation is the same as given under No. 41.

No. 44—VANILLA STARS.

1 lb blanched, ground almonds 1 lb. of sugar
5 eggs 2 vanilla beans

Preparation: The vanilla is crushed with the sugar, then yolks of eggs, almonds, beaten whites of eggs mixed in and stirred 1 hour. Roll out the dough, make little stars and bake in medium hot oven. The board must be well floured when rolling out the dough.

No. 45—EGG CRACKNELS.

1 lb. of butter ½ cup of arrack or rum.
¼ lb. of sugar 6 hard boiled yolks of eggs 1 lb. of flour

Preparation: The ingredients are mixed well with the hands, and the dough formed into small rings; these are dipped into beaten egg, then rolled in sugar and cinnamon and baked to a golden yellow color.

Remarks: The eggs must be boiled 20 minutes. The yolks are chopped fine before working into the dough. The whites may be chopped, mixed with salt, pepper, oil and vinegar and used for garnishing green lettuce.

No. 46—ALMOND BREAD.

1 lb. of brown sugar ½ tsp. of ground cinnamon
4 eggs ½ tsp. of ground nutmeg
¼ lb. of grated, sweet chocolate 1½ tsps. of baking powder
½ lb. of chopped almonds 2 cups of flour ½ tsp. of ground cloves

Preparation: Sugar and eggs are stirred well, the other ingredients mixed in and lastly the baking powder mixed with the flour. Roll out the dough and bake. When done and still warm, cut into strips.

No. 47—SPRINGELE.

1 lb. powdered sugar ¼ tsp. of ammonia or
4—5 eggs 1 tsp. of baking powder 1 lb. of flour

Preparation: The sugar and eggs are beaten well. The ammonia is pulverized with a knifeblade and added, then the flour. Roll out the dough and cut out small cookies, then bake in medium oven to a nice color.

No. 48—PLAIN PEPPERNUTS.

½ lb. of sugar ½ tsp. of ammonia
2 eggs Flour enough to make a stiff
1½ tsps. of cinnamon dough
1 tsp. of cloves ¼ tsp. of pepper ½ cup of brandy

Preparation: The sugar is stirred ½ hour with the eggs, then add cinnamon, cloves, pepper and the ammonia, pulverized with a knifeblade. Stir in enough flour to make a stiff dough, roll it out and cut out small cookies. Leave these for 2 to 3 days, turning them over and dipping in brandy and bake slightly in a medium oven.

No. 49—ALMOND STRIPS No. 2.

½ lb. of sugar 3 eggs ½ lb. of almonds, sliced fine and roasted
Flour enough to make a stiff dough

Preparation: Sugar and eggs are stirred well, the almonds mixed in after they are cold, then flour to make a stiff dough. Roll it out and cut into small strips and bake.

No. 50—HONEY CAKES.

2 lbs. of honey
1 lb. of sugar
5 cents worth of refined potash
3 tbsps. of rum
¼ lb. of unblanched, chopped almonds
2 tbsps. of sugared orange rind
¼ lb. of butter
4 eggs
1 tsp. of cinnamon
½ tsp. of ground cloves
3 lbs. of flour
⅛ lb. of finely cut citron

Preparation: Melt the honey. Dissolve the potash in the rum and cover the dish. Then mix all the other ingredients with the honey, add the rum with the dissolved potash, and lastly the flour. Knead the dough 1 hour and set it in a warm place for 5 days. Then roll it out and bake it. When it is still warm, cut it into squares, oblongs or triangles. If you wish, you may cover them with a frosting, or with almonds and citron before baking.

No. 51—COCOANUT KISSES.

Whites of 4 eggs 1 tsp. cream of tartar
2 cups sugar ¾ lb. cocoanut 1 tsp. vanilla

Preparation: Beat the whites of eggs very stiff; add the sugar and beat well; add cream of tartar and vanilla and lastly the cocoanut. Drop from a spoon on a buttered tin and bake in a moderate oven one-half hour.

No. 52—CINNAMON STARS.

Whites of 8 eggs 1 lb. almonds 1 lb. sugar 1 tbsp. cinnamon

Preparation: Stir the sugar, eggs and cinnamon together one hour; put six tablespoonfuls in a separate dish for frosting. To the remainder, add the grated, unblanched almonds; mix well; roll out upon a molding board strewn with flour and sugar; form with a star; frost; bake on buttered tins.

No. 53—LADY FINGERS.

8 eggs ¾ lb. flour Flavoring and salt ¾ lb. sugar

Preparation: Beat eggs and sugar stiff, add salt and flour; put the dough in a form 3 inches long and 2 inches wide, bake rapidly. It will also make a fine cake if baked in a buttered pan.

CHAPTER 22.

CONFECTIONERY.

No. 1—MOLASSES CANDY.

1 qt. of good molasses
½ cup of sugar
1 tbsp. of butter
1 tbsp. of vinegar
1 tsp. of baking soda
1 tbsp. of lemon extract or vanilla

Preparation: Boil the molasses, sugar, butter and vinegar, stirring constantly. Test it by dropping a few drops into cold water; if it hardens it has been boiled sufficiently. Then add soda dissolved in 1 tablespoonful of hot water and lemon essence or vanilla. Pour the candy into a buttered pan and when cool, pull it with your hands well buttered until it is a light color. See candy pulling.

No. 2—VINEGAR TAFFY.

6 tbsps. of sugar   4 tbsps. of water   2 tbsps. of vinegar

Preparation: Mix the ingredients and boil 20 minutes, then pour into a buttered pan and pull.

No. 3—CHOCOLATE FUDGES.

½ cup of molasses
2 cups of sugar
½ cup of milk
½ cup of butter
2 tbsps. of finely chopped figs
2 tbsps. of finely chopped raisins
½ cup of ground English walnuts
1 tbsp. vanilla
½ cup of grated, sweet chocolate

Preparation: Mix the molasses, sugar, milk and butter and cook 7 minutes, add the chocolate and cook 7 minutes more, then add the other ingredients. Pour into a buttered pan and when cold, cut into squares.

No. 4—BUTTER SCOTCH.

1 cup of corn-syrup
2 cups of sugar
¼ cup of water
¼ lb. of butter
1 tbsp. of vinegar
1 tbsp. of vanilla

Preparation: Boil the syrup, sugar, water and butter until it hardens when testing in cold water. Add the vinegar and vanilla and pour into a buttered pan. When cold, cut into squares.

No. 5—LEMON CANDY.

1 lb. of sugar
½ pt. of water
1/3 tsp. of tartaric essence
1/3 tsp. of lemon extract
1 tsp. of cream of tartar

Preparation: Mix the sugar, water and cream of tartar and boil until it cracks and breaks when tried in cold water. Pour into a deep buttered dish and when cool, mix in the tartaric essence and lemon extract, and shape into any desired form.

No. 6—CHOCOLATE CARAMELS No. 1.

2 cups of sugar
1 cup of syrup
½ cup of grated, sweet chocolate
1 cup of milk
1 tbsp. of butter
1 tbsp. of vanilla

Preparation: Mix the sugar and syrup and boil 5 minutes, add the other ingredients and boil until it stiffens. Pour into a buttered pan and cut into squares.

No. 7—BON-BONS.

2 lbs. of sugar
1 pt. of water
1 vanilla bean or
2 tbsps. of vanilla extract

Preparation: Mix the sugar, water and vanilla and boil until it cracks when tried in cold water. Pour into an oiled pan or porcelain platter, spread it out and cut into cubes.

Remarks: You can also flavor with rosewater, orange or lemon instead of vanilla.

No. 8—CHOCOLATE CANDY.

3 pieces of sweet chocolate or
2½ tbsps. of cocoa
2 cups of sugar
½ cup of milk
½ tbsp. of vanilla
½ tbsp. of butter

Preparation: Mix the ingredients and boil 3 minutes, then pour into buttered pans and cut into cubes when cold.

No. 9—NUT CANDY.

3 cups of brown sugar
¾ cup of milk
¼ cup of cream
1 pinch of salt
1 tsp. of vanilla
1 lb. of chopped walnuts   1 tbsp. of butter

Preparation: Mix the sugar, milk and cream and boil until, when trying a few drops in cold water, it holds together and forms a soft mass. Then add butter and salt, take from the stove, mix in vanilla and nuts and stir the mixture until it gets creamy. Pour it to 1 inch thickness into buttered pans and cut it into cubes when cold.

No. 10—POPCORN CANDY.

1 cup of sugar 1 pinch of salt
1 tbsp. of butter 3 tbsps. of water 4 qts. of popped corn

Preparation: Pour enough popped corn into a pan to cover the bottom of the pan, put it on the stove to get very hot, being careful not to burn it. Mix the sugar, butter, water and salt and boil until it hardens when tried in cold water. Now mix it with the hot corn, add the rest of the popped corn and stir until it rolls from the spoon, then spread it out in buttered tins.

Remarks: It is best to use old popcorn.

No. 11—COCOANUT DROPS.

1 cocoanut About 2 cups of sugar 1 white of egg

Preparation: Grate the cocoanut and weigh it, add to it ½ of its weight in sugar, mix this with the beaten white of egg, drop on buttered paper and bake in oven 15 minutes.

No. 12—CHOCOLATE CARAMELS No. 2.

1 cup of sugar 1 cup of molasses
½ cup of butter 1 cup of milk
¼ cup of grated, sweet chocolate

Preparation: Cream the sugar and butter, add chocolate, molasses and milk and boil until it hardens when tried in cold water. Pour it about 1 inch thick into buttered pans and when cold, cut into squares with a buttered knife.

No. 13—PEANUT CANDY.

2 cups sugar 1 cup chopped peanuts

Preparation: Put two cups white sugar into a porcelain kettle; stir constantly until dissolved. Add one cup chopped peanuts. Turn at once into a buttered dish and cut in squares.

No. 14—PULLED TAFFY.

3 cups granulated sugar ½ cup water
½ cup mild vinegar Butter, size of a walnut

Preparation: If vinegar is strong, use two-thirds water and one-third vinegar. Boil the sugar, water and vinegar together until half done; then add the butter and stir until mixed well. When it snaps when tested in cold water, it is done. Pour on buttered tins, let cool, flavor and pull.

No. 15—ICE CREAM CANDY.

2 cups sugar
½ cup vinegar
½ cup water
Butter, size of an egg

Preparation: Boil sugar, vinegar and water together about ten minutes; add butter and let it boil another five minutes. Try a few drops in a glass of cold water. If hard, pour the mass into a buttered tin and set in a cool place until cool enough to pull. Pull it until it becomes white. Cut in pieces as desired.

No. 16—CRACKER JACK.

3 qts. popped corn
½ tsp. soda
½ tsp. vinegar
½ cup sugar
¼ cup syrup
½ cup peanuts

Preparation: Boil syrup, sugar and vinegar until it will crack when tried in cold water. Add the soda, stir well and pour the foamy mixture over the corn.

No. 17—POP CORN BALLS.

2 cups granulated sugar
1 cup water
8 qts. popped corn
Flavoring to taste

Preparation: Pop the corn and remove all the hard kernels. Boil the sugar and water until it hairs, add the flavor, pour over the corn and form into balls.

No. 18—CHOCOLATE FUDGE.

1 cup granulated sugar
1 cup brown sugar
1 cup milk
2 squares chocolate
2 tbsps. butter
1 tsp. vanilla

Preparation: Put sugar, chocolate and milk on to boil and stir occasionally to prevent burning. Remove from fire as soon as a soft ball can be formed when mixture is tested in cold water. Add butter; stir vigorously until creamy. Pour into buttered shallow pan and mark in squares.

No. 19—CARAMELS.

1 cup milk
1 cup syrup
1 cup sugar
1 cup brown sugar
¼ lb. sweet chocolate
1 tbsp. flour
1 tbsp. butter
1 tsp. vanilla

Preparation: Mix everything together. Boil until it hardens in cold water. The last quarter hour stir well. Put in buttered tins. When cold, cut in squares.

No. 20—FUDGE.

2 cups sugar
1 cup grated chocolate
1 cup chopped walnuts
1 tsp. vanilla
1½ cups milk or 1 cup cream
Butter, size of walnut

Preparation: Boil together sugar, chocolate and milk or cream until it hardens in water. Add the butter; take off the fire; add the vanilla and walnuts. Stir until it thickens. Pour in a greased tin and put in a cool place to harden.

CHAPTER 23.
PRESERVES.

Preserving Fruits and Vegetables.

Only the best quality of fruit should be used for preserving, and the preserves must be kept in a cool dry place.

Glass jars are the best to put up preserves; tin cans must be soldered and this cannot very well be done at home.

The kettle in which the preserves are cooked should be clean and kept for this purpose only. The spoon or ladle used for stirring is best of silver or new wood.

The jars should be clean and scalded before using. They must have good rubbers and be closed so tightly that not a drop will come out when turned upside down.

No. 1—STRAWBERRIES.
1 lb. of strawberries   ½ lb. of sugar

Preparation: The strawberries must be dry and sound. Clean them, pour water on and let stand for a few minutes, then drain in a colander. Now weigh the fruit and take ½ lb. of sugar to every pound of fruit. Boil the fruit and sugar a few minutes over a slow fire, then fill it at once into the jars. Close these tightly and set them upside down to test the covers. When they are cold, store them in a cool, dry place.

Can also be made according to No. 13, but cook only 20 minutes instead of 2 hours.

No. 2—RASPBERRIES.
1 lb. of raspberries   ½ lb. of sugar

Preparation: The preparation of the raspberries is the same as that of strawberries. See No. 1, Strawberries.

No. 3—PINEAPPLE.
1 lb. of pineapple   ¼ cup of water, scant   ¾ lb. of sugar

Preparation: Pare and slice the pineapple, which is best done with a silver knife. Weigh the fruit after it is sliced and take to every pound of fruit ¾ lb. of sugar and ¼ small cupful of water. Boil the sugar and water 5 minutes, skim it and put in the fruit to boil 20 minutes until it is transparent, skim it again and put it hot into the jars; then treat the jars as in No. 1 and store them in a cool, dry place.

No. 4—PEACHES AND APRICOTS.

1 lb. of peaches or apricots ¼ cup of water
½ lb. of sugar 4 peach stones

Preparation: Peel the peaches or apricots very thin, cut in halves and stone them. To one pound of fruit take ½ lb. of sugar and ¼ cup of water. Boil the sugar, water and 4 crushed stones 5 minutes, skim and add the fruit and boil a few minutes longer until it is soft. Do not let it get mushy. Skim the fruit again and fill it hot into the jars. Then treat the jars again as in No. 1 to test the covers. Store them in a cool, dry place.

Remarks: The peelings may be used for jelly. See Preparation of Jelly.

No. 5—PEACHES IN JELLY.

2 lbs. of nice, large peaches 1 pt. of water
1 lb. small peaches 3 lbs. of sugar Brandy paper

Preparation: Cut the small peaches into pieces, stone them, weigh them, boil until tender in the water and drain in a colander. Now put the sugar into the fruit syrup and boil until thick, skim it and put the large peeled peaches into it whole. Boil until the fruit is tender but not mushy, then put it carefully into the jars, pour the thick syrup on, place a brandy paper over and close the jars up tightly.

No. 6—APRICOTS IN JELLY.

2 lbs. of nice, large apricots 1 pt. of water
1 lb. of small apricots Brandy paper 3 lbs. of sugar

Preparation: The preparation of apricots is the same as that of peaches. See No. 5, Peaches in Jelly.

No. 7—PICKLED PEACHES.

1 lb. of peaches ¼ cup of water
¼ lb. of sugar 3 cloves
¼ cup of vinegar 1 small stick of cinnamon

Preparation: Peel the peaches, leave them whole and weigh them. Boil the given quantity of water with sugar, vinegar, cloves and cinnamon 5 minutes, skim and add the peaches. When the fruit is soft, put it into the cans or jars and pour the syrup over. If there is too much syrup, boil it down to fill the cans or jars. Cover with a brandy paper and close them up tightly. The stone jars may be tied up with parchment paper.

No. 8—PICKLED APRICOTS.

1 lb. of apricots
¼ lb. of sugar
¼ cup of vinegar
¼ cup of water
3 cloves
1 small stick of cinnamon

Preparation: The preparation of pickled apricots is the same as that of pickled peaches. See No. 7, Pickled Peaches.

No. 9—APRICOTS OR PEACHES IN BRANDY.

1 lb. of apricots or peaches
¾ lb. of sugar
¼ cup of water
1 wineglassfull of French brandy

Preparation: Peel and weigh the apricots or peaches. Boil the sugar and water 5 minutes and skim, then put in the fruit, boil a few minutes and put into the jars. Let the syrup boil down and pour it onto the fruit hot, then pour the brandy on top, close the jars tightly and treat them as in No. 1.

Remarks: To every pound of fruit use 1 glass of brandy.

No. 10—STRAWBERRIES IN JELLY.

1½ lbs. of nice, large strawberries
1 lb. of small strawberries
2 lbs. of sugar
Juice of ½ lemon
Brandy paper

Preparation: Prepare the large strawberries as in No. 1, and drain off the water. Treat the small berries the same way, put the latter on the stove with the sugar, boil until soft, then rub through a sieve or a white, clean cloth so the juice will run into a dish. Put this juice back into the kettle, add to this the lemon juice and boil it down to jelly. Then add the large strawberries and boil 3 to 4 minutes. Put carefully into the jars, boil down the syrup if it is too much and pour it on the fruit hot. Cover with brandy paper and close the jars tightly. Treat them as in No. 1, to test the covers and when cold, store them in a cool, dry place. Melted paraffine is often used to make jars air-tight.

No. 11—RASPBERRIES IN JELLY.

1½ lbs. of raspberries
2 lbs. of sugar
Juice of ½ lemon
Brandy paper

Preparation: The preparation of raspberries is the same as that of strawberries. See No. 10, Strawberries in Jelly.

No. 12—STONED SOUR CHERRIES.

1 lb. of nice cherries   ¾ lb. of sugar   Brandy paper

Preparation: Wash the cherries, stone them and weigh them. To every pound of cherries take ¾ lb. of sugar, boil 5 minutes and fill hot into the jars. Cover with a brandy paper and treat the jars as in No. 1.

No. 13—LARGE SWEET CHERRIES.

1 lb. of cherries Brandy paper
1 lb. of sugar ¼ cup of water

Preparation: Wipe the cherries with a cloth and place them into the jars. Boil the sugar and water 5 minutes, skim it and pour over the cherries. Close the jars, but not tightly. Put the jars into a boiler with water reaching nearly to the top of the jars. Cover the boiler, boil for 2 hours, take out the jars, close them tightly and treat them as in No. 1.

Remarks: The cherries may be stoned. Put a tray or several thicknesses of cloth on the bottom of the boiler, also hay or cloth between the jars.

No. 14—COGNAC CHERRIES.

1 lb. of large, sweet cherries 1 cup of water
1¾ lbs. of sugar 1½ pts. of corn brandy

Preparation: Wash and dry the cherries, prick them with a needle, and trim the stems with a pair of scissors. Fill a jar half full with them. Boil down the sugar and water to one-third of the quantity and add the brandy. When this syrup is cold, pour it into the jars, close them tightly and treat them as in No. 1.

No. 15—MIRABELLE PLUMS, No. 1.

1 lb. of mirabelles ½ lb. of sugar ¼ cup of water

Preparation: Mirabelles are the small, round, yellow plums; they must be firm and sound when preserved. Rub them with a cloth and prick them with a needle a few times. Boil sugar and water 5 minutes, skim, add the plums, boil a few minutes and put into the jars. Boil down the syrup and pour it over the plums hot. Treat the jars as in No. 1 and store in a cool, dry place.

No. 16—MIRABELLE PLUMS, No. 2.

1 lb. of Mirabelle Plums Brandy paper
¾ lb. of sugar ¼ cup of water

Preparation: Treat the plums as before. After they have been rubbed with a cloth and pricked, fill a jar half full. Boil the sugar and water 10 minutes and pour over the plums hot. Close the jars, but not tightly, then place into a boiler with water to boil 2 hours. After that time take out the jars, close them tightly and treat them as in No. 1.

Remarks: Put a piece of brandy paper inside before closing them up tightly.

No. 17—PLUMS.

1 lb. of plums   ¾ lb. of sugar   ¼ cup of water

Preparation: Wipe the plums with a cloth. Boil the sugar and water for 5 minutes, skim and add the plums. Let them boil up a few times; as soon as they begin to crack, skim and put them carefully into the jars. Boil the syrup down and fill into the cans hot. Then close the jars tightly and treat them as in No. 1.

No. 18—PEELED PLUMS.

1 lb. of plums   1 small stick of cinnamon
¾ lb. of sugar   1 tbsp. of wine vinegar   ¼ cup of water

Preparation: Put the large, blue plums into hot water for a minute and skin them. With a sharp knife make a slit into the side of each plum and take out the stone; place them into the jars in layers. Boil the sugar and water with cinnamon and vinegar for 5 minutes, skim and pour it hot over the plums. Close the jars and boil them in a boiler for 45 minutes. Then take them out, close them tightly and treat the jars as in No. 1.

Remarks: Plums must be prepared quickly, as they will easily turn brown. To avoid this, one may sprinkle some of the sugar over as soon as they are skinned.

No. 19—PLUMS IN RED WINE.

1 lb. of plums   ¼ cup of wine vinegar
½ lb. of sugar   1 clove
½ cup of red wine   1 small stick of cinnamon

Preparation: Wipe the ripe, blue plums with a cloth. Boil the sugar, red wine, vinegar, cloves and cinnamon 5 minutes, skim, add the plums and boil a few minutes. Take them out as soon as the skins begin to crack and put them into the jars. Boil down the syrup and fill it hot into the jars. Close the jars tightly and treat them as in No. 1.

No. 20—PICKLED PLUMS.

3 lbs. of plums   Several small sticks of cinnamon
1 lb. of sugar   ½ pt. of vinegar   6 cloves

Preparation: Wipe the plums with a cloth, prick with a toothpick several times and place carefully into a stone jar. Boil the sugar, vinegar, cinnamon and cloves a few minutes, skim and pour over the plums boiling hot. This process is repeated 3 times. When the juice boils for the third time, the plums are put in, let boil up a few times, then all is put back into the stone jar or cans and tightly closed or tied up. These pickled plums are nice to serve with meat.

No. 21—GOOSEBERRIES.

3 lbs. of gooseberries A few sticks of cinnamon
2½ lbs. of sugar 1½ cups of water

Preparation: Clean, wash and drain nice, large gooseberries, which are not overripe. Boil the sugar, water and cinnamon until clear and jelly like, then add the berries, boil a few minutes and put into jars. Boil down the syrup and pour it into the jars. Close tightly and treat them as in No. 1.

Remarks: If after 1 day the syrup is too thin, pour it off and boil it once more.

No. 22—PICKLED PEARS.

2 lbs. of pears ⅛ cup of wine vinegar
1 lb. of sugar Several sticks of cinnamon
1 cup of water 2 cloves

Preparation: Peel the pears, cut them into halves and core them, then put into cold water or rub with lemon juice to keep them white. Boil the sugar, water and vinegar 5 minutes with the cloves and cinnamon tied into a white cloth, skim, add the pears and boil until soft but not mushy. Fill the fruit into jars and close them tightly, then treat them as in No. 1.

No. 23—PICKLED CRAB-APPLES.

1 lb. of crab-apples ⅛ cup of vinegar
½ lb. of sugar 1 cup of water 1 stick of cinnamon

Preparation: Wipe the little red crab-apples with a cloth, leave the stems on. Boil the sugar, water, vinegar and cinnamon 5 minutes, skim, add the apples and boil 10 minutes. They must not cook to pieces and the skin must stay whole if possible. Place the apples carefully into the jars, boil down the syrup and pour it on hot. Then close the jars tightly and treat them as in No. 1.

No. 24—BLUEBERRIES, HUCKLEBERRIES.

1 lb. of blueberries ⅛ cup of vinegar or
½ lb. of sugar Juice of ½ lemon

Preparation: Pick the berries over, wash and drain them, then boil in sugar and vinegar or lemon juice a little while. When still hot, pour them into jars, close tightly and treat them as in No. 1.

No. 25—GREEN GAGES.

1 lb. of green gages ¾ lb. of sugar ½ cup of water

Preparation: The genuine green gages which have red dots are the best for preserving. Wipe them with a cloth, shorten the stem and prick the plum to the stone several times with a darning needle. Then boil the sugar and water 5 minutes, put in 8 to 10 plums, boil them until the skin begins to burst, take them out immediately and put them into the jars. Continue this until all plums are cooked. Pour the syrup over, close the jars and put them into a boiler with water to cook for 45 minutes. Then take them out, close the covers tightly and when cold, store them in a cool place.

No. 26—PEELED GREEN GAGES.

1 lb. of green gages   ¾ lb. of sugar   ½ cup of water

Preparation: Peel and stone the plums. Boil the sugar and water 5 minutes, add the plums and boil until tender, then skim and put them into the jars. If there is too much syrup, boil it down and pour it over the plums hot, then close the jars tightly and treat them as in No. 1.

No. 27—CRANBERRIES.

1 lb. of cranberries   Brandy paper
½ lb. of sugar   ¼ cup of water

Preparation: The American cranberries are in the market in winter to be used fresh, while the German cranberries are in the market in summer to be preserved for the winter. Pick them over and wash them in much water, then drain in a colander. Boil the sugar and water 1 minute, add the berries and boil until they are light red and transparent, skim and fill into cans or stone jars. Boil syrup 15 to 20 minutes longer and pour boiling hot over the berries. Cover with a piece of brandy paper and close the cans or tie up the jars tightly. If you put them into jars, let the fruit cool off before you put on the brandy paper and tie up the jars.

No. 28—CURRANTS.

1 lb. of currants   1 lb. of sugar

Preparation: Only the largest currants are used for preserves. Strip them from the stems, wash in cold water, drain well and weigh them. Boil the sugar and berries slowly for 10 minutes, skim and put into jars hot. Close the jars tightly and treat them as in No. 1.

No. 29—BLACKBERRIES.

1 lb. of blackberries   ¾ lb. of sugar

The Preparation is the same as that of currants, but let them boil only a few minutes instead of 10 minutes.

No. 30—MELONS.

3 lbs. of melon
3 lbs. of sugar
1 pt. of water
4 cloves
Some sticks of cinnamon
¼ pt. of wine vinegar   Brandy paper

Preparation: Peel ripe but firm melons, cut them in halves and scoop out the seeds with a silver spoon, then cut into small pieces and weigh. Boil the sugar, water, vinegar, cloves and cinnamon 5 minutes, add the melon and boil until transparent and soft. Now fill them into jars, boil down the syrup and pour it on the fruit hot. Close the jars tightly and treat them as in No. 1.

No. 31—QUINCES.

5 lbs. of quinces
3 lbs. of sugar
10 cloves
2 finely chopped lemon rinds
Several sticks of cinnamon
Water

Preparation: Pare the quinces, slice them very thin and boil in water. When partly done, take them out and drain on a cloth. Boil the sugar, 2 cups of water, cinnamon, lemon rind and cloves 5 minutes, skim, add the partly boiled quinces and boil until soft. Then put them into jars with the syrup, close the jars tightly and treat as in No. 1.

No. 32—QUINCES IN COGNAC.

1 lb. of quinces
½ cup of water
¾ lb. of sugar
3 sticks of cinnamon
½ lemon rind cut fine
3 cloves   1 wineglassful of cognac

Preparation: Pare the quinces, cut them into small pieces and put at once into cold water. When they are all cut up, put them into boiling water and boil until tender. Boil the sugar, water, cloves, cinnamon and lemon rind 1 minute, add the quinces and boil slowly for 5 minutes. Put the quince into jars, boil down the syrup until it gets thick, add the cognac and pour it hot over the fruit. Close the jars tightly and treat them as in No. 1.

No. 33—PUMPKIN.

3 lbs. of pumpkin flesh
2½ lbs. of sugar
1 qt. of vinegar
3 qts. of water
5 cloves
2 sticks of cinnamon
1 piece of ginger
½ lemon rind ·   Brandy paper

Preparation: Peel the pumpkin, cut in halves, scoop out the seeds and all juicy or thready matter. Cut the flesh into slices ¼ inch thick and put into 1 qt. of cold vinegar mixed with 2½ qts. of cold water. Let it stand 12 hours. Then boil the sugar, ½ qt. of water and the spices tied into a white cloth 1 minute. Add the sliced pumpkin after draining it well, and boil until tender and transparent. Put into jars, boil down the syrup until it thickens, fill up the jars with it while boiling hot, cover with a brandy paper, close and treat them as in No. 1.

No. 34—GREEN OR SMALL YELLOW ORANGES.

60 small oranges   3 lbs. of sugar   ¾ qt. of water

Preparation: Prick the oranges with a fork and blanch them in water for 5 minutes. Then cover them with water and let them stand 10 days, changing the water twice daily. On the eleventh day boil the sugar and ¾ qt. of water 5 minutes, skim and pour cold on the well drained oranges. On the twelfth day pour off the sugar water and boil it until it gets thick. Put in the oranges, let them boil a few minutes and then fill the jars. If necessary, boil the sugar water a little more, pour it over the oranges, close the jars tightly and treat them as in No. 1.

No. 35—PICKLED WALNUTS.

1 lb. of green walnuts   20 grams of whole cinnamon
1 lb. of sugar   1 cup of water

Preparation: The walnuts must be picked before they form a hard shell. Clean the walnuts well and let stand in water 14 days, changing the water once a day. Then drain well and boil until tender in fresh water. Boil the sugar, water and cinnamon 1 minute, add the nuts and boil a few minutes, pour into a porcelain dish and let stand 3 days, then boil again a few minutes and fill the nuts into jars. Boil the syrup if it is not thick enough and pour it over the nuts cold, then close the jars well.

No. 36—GREEN ALMONDS.

60 green almonds   1½ lbs. of sugar   4 qts. of water
¼ lb. of wood ashes   1 pt. of water   ¼ tsp. of bishop extract

Preparation: The almonds must be green, but soft enough to be easily pierced with a fork. Mix the wood ashes and 4 qts. of water and boil until the mixture feels greasy. Now put in the almonds and boil them until the skin can be pulled off. After skinning them, put them into fresh water, pierce them with a fork, put into hot water, set them on the stove and let them simmer, but not boil, until they are soft. Pour off the water, put on fresh cold water and let stand until the next day. Now boil the sugar in 1 pt. of water until it gets thick and pour it cold over the well drained almonds. The next day pour off the sugar water, boil it again, and when cold, pour over the nuts and let stand another day. The third day repeat the cooking again, add the bishop extract, when cold, pour it over the almonds in the jars and close them tightly.

No. 37—GRAPES.

3 lbs. of grapes　　　¾ lb. of sugar　　　½ cup of water

Preparation: Boil the sugar and water 5 minutes, pour over the grapes and let stand for 12 hours. After this time pour off the sugar water, bring it to boil, add the grapes, let them boil a few minutes and put into jars. Boil the syrup down thick, pour over the grapes hot, close the jars tightly and treat them as in No. 1.

Remarks: The little seeds are taken out with a skimmer.

How to Make Jelly, Marmalade and Jam.
No. 38—STRAWBERRY MARMALADE.

1 lb. of strawberries　　　¾ lb. of sugar　　　Brandy paper

Preparation: Rub the prepared strawberries through a sieve, then mix with sugar and boil down to a thick marmalade, stirring constantly. Fill it into jars, let it get cold, put on a piece of brandy paper and close the jars well, or tie them up with parchment paper.

No. 39—RASPBERRY JELLY.

4 lbs. of raspberries　　　1 pt. of water
2 lbs. of currants　　　2½ lbs. of sugar　　　Brandy paper

Preparation: Clean and wash the currants and raspberries, then put on the stove with the water and boil until the berries burst and are soft; then pour them through a thin white cloth and let the juice drain off into another dish. Weigh this juice and to 1 pound of juice take ¾ pound of sugar or to 1 pt. of juice take 1 lb. of sugar and boil 5 minutes or until it jellies when a little of it is cooled in a dish. Put into jars or glasses and when cold, cover with the brandy paper and tie up well with parchment paper.

No. 40—CURRANT JELLY.

Currants　　　　　　　　Brandy paper
1 pt. of currant juice　　　1 lb. of sugar

Preparation: Clean and wash the ripe, red currants, press through a white cloth, squeezing out all juice. This juice is left to stand over night. The next day slowly pour off the clear juice from the settlings. To each pint of juice take 1 pound of sugar, boil it until it jellies when cold. Put it hot into glasses or jars, let it get cold, cover with brandy paper and tie it up or close the jars well.

No. 41—BLACK CURRANT JELLY.

Black currants 1½ cups of sugar
1 pt. currant juice Brandy paper

The preparation of black currants is the same as that of red currants. See Currant Jelly, No. 40.

No. 42—ROSE JELLY.

2 lbs. of green apples 1 pt. of rose water
3 pts. of water 1 drop of oil of roses
1 lb. of red currants 3 lbs. of sugar

Preparation: Wash the unpeeled apples, cut them up and boil without stirring, in a covered kettle with 3 pts. of water until they are soft. When nearly done, put in the currants and boil a while until the berries burst. Now pour the whole mass into a white muslin bag and let the juice run into a dish. Let it stand for a while, then carefully pour it off the settlings into the preserve kettle. Add the sugar and rosewater and boil until it jellies when cold. Stir in the drop of rose oil, fill the jelly into glasses, let it get cold, cover them with paraffine or tie them up.

No. 43—BLUEBERRY JELLY.

1 lb. of blueberry juice 1 lb. of sugar Juice of 1 lemon

Preparation: The preparation of blueberry jelly is the same as that of Currant Jelly, see No. 40.

No. 44—APPLE JELLY.

8 lbs. of sweet-sour apples 4 tbsps. of lemon juice
4 qts. of water ½ vanilla bean or 1 tbsp. of
4 lbs. of sugar vanilla essence
½ pt. of white wine Brandy paper

Preparation: Wash and quarter the unpeeled apples and boil slowly in 4 qts. of water until tender, but do not stir them. Then pour the mass into a muslin bag and let the juice run into a dish. When settled, pour the juice into the kettle and boil down to one-half the quantity. Then add sugar, wine, lemon juice and vanilla and cook until it jellies; fill it into glasses, when cold, cover with a piece of brandy paper and tie them tightly.

No. 45—CRAB-APPLE JELLY.

1 cup of crab-apple juice Vanilla to taste
1 cup of sugar Water Brandy paper

Preparation: Wash and quarter the crab-apples, put on with water to barely cover the apples, then cover the kettle and cook until tender. When they are done, pour them into a white muslin bag and let the juice run into a dish. Carefully pour the juice off the settlings, add to each cup of juice one cup of sugar, put in vanilla as much as you like and boil the whole to jelly, which will take about 10 minutes. Pour it into glasses or jars, when cold, cover with a brandy paper and close up tightly.

No. 46—QUINCE JELLY.

8 lbs. of quinces   4 tbsps. of lemon juice
4 qts. of water   4 lbs. of sugar   Brandy paper

Preparation: The preparation is the same as that of apple jelly. See No. 44, Apple Jelly.

No. 47—PEACH MARMALADE.

1 lb. of peaches   ¾ cup of water
¾ lb. of sugar   Brandy paper

Preparation: The peaches are peeled very thin, cut into pieces and boiled in the water until soft. Rub through a sieve. Moisten the sugar with water and boil 5 minutes, skim it, add the fruit and boil 20 minutes, stirring constantly. Pour it into glasses or jars, cover with a brandy paper when cold and close up the glasses or jars tightly.

Remarks: You can add to the marmalade some kernels of peaches and cut the peaches into very small pieces without rubbing them through a sieve. Through the long cooking much of the fruit flavor is lost.

No. 48—APRICOT MARMALADE.

1 lb. of apricots   ¾ cup of water
¾ lb. of sugar   Brandy paper

The preparation is the same as that of peach marmalade. See No. 47, Peach Marmalade.

No. 49—PLUM MARMALADE.

1 lb. of large, blue plums   ½ lb. of sugar, scant   ½ cup of water

Preparation: Peel and stone the plums, then slice into narrow strips. Boil the sugar and water 1 minute, skim, add the sliced plums and boil until soft and thick but not mushy. Then fill them into glasses or jars, cover with a brandy paper and close them up tightly.

No. 50—RASPBERRY MARMALADE.

1 lb. of raspberries   ¾ cup of sugar   Brandy paper

The preparation of raspberry marmalade is the same as that of strawberry marmalade. See No. 38, Strawberry Marmalade.

No. 51—PLUM JAM.

30 lbs. of plums
2 tsps. of ground cloves
1 small piece of ginger
1 lemon rind
2 tsps. of ground cinnamon
10 green nuts

Preparation: Wipe the plums with a cloth, stone them and boil 4 hours while stirring constantly with a wooden ladle. After this time put in the spices and boil the jam until it is thick, then pour it into stone jars, put these into the oven to dry a little over the top and tie them up with paper, or strew cinnamon on thickly before tying them up. Store the jam in a cool, airy place but never in the cellar; this way it will keep for years.

No. 52—PEAR JAM.

5 lbs. of pears 2 lbs. of sugar 1 qt. of water 1 tsp. of cinnamon

Preparation: Quarter the pears and boil in the water until tender. When you preserve pears, you may use the peelings for jam by boiling them with the pears and rubbing them through a sieve. Then put the jam back on the stove and boil it until it gets thick, stirring constantly. While it is boiling, add sugar and cinnamon; fill it into stone jars, cover with ground cinnamon when cold, tie up the jars well and keep them in a dry, airy place.

No. 53—MIXED MARMALADE.

1 lb. of apples 1 lb. of quinces 1 lb. of pears 1 lb. of melon
1 lb. of yellow plums 1 stick of cinnamon
1 lb. of peaches 2 qts. of water 3 lbs of sugar Brandy paper

Preparation: Wipe the fruit with a cloth, slice it and boil with the water and cinnamon until very soft. Then rub through a fine sieve, add the sugar and boil until it thickens, stirring constantly. Fill it into jars or glasses; when cold, cover with a brandy paper and close them up tightly.

No. 54—GRAPE JELLY.

1 cup of grape juice 1 cup of sugar Brandy paper

Preparation: Wash the grapes, boil with a little water until they burst, then pour them into a muslin bag and let the juice run into a dish. After it has settled, pour the clear juice off carefully from the settlings and to every cup of juice take one cup of sugar. Now boil it down until it jellies, skim it and fill into glasses, cover with a brandy paper when cold and close up tightly.

The Preparation of Fruit Juices or Syrups.

No. 55—RASPBERRY SYRUP.

1 lb. of raspberries　　　　　1 lb. of sugar

Preparation: Put the berries into a deep dish or jar in alternating layers with sugar and let it stand for 2 days. Strain the juice into clean bottles through a white muslin or linen bag, cork tightly and then boil ½ hour in water, being careful that the bottles stand upright and do not touch. Put a tray or cloth on the bottom of the boiler or kettle and pack hay between the bottles. Put a cover on the boiler or kettle.

No. 56—STRAWBERRY SYRUP.

1 lb. of strawberries　　　　　1 lb. of sugar

The preparation of this syrup is the same as that of raspberry syrup. See No. 55, Raspberry Syrup.

No. 57—CHERRY SYRUP.

1 pt. of cherries　　　　　A little fine oil
½ lb. of sugar　　　　　1 stick of cinnamon

Preparation: Take nice, sour cherries, pick off the stems and crush the cherries with the stones in a mortar or in a fruit press. The next day pour off the clear juice from the settlings and boil 15 minutes with sugar and cinnamon, skimming it frequently. When cold, strain it and fill into bottles; into each bottle of syrup pour 1 teaspoonful of fine oil, cork the bottles well and seal them with sealing wax. Before using the syrup, dip off the oil with cotton batting.

No. 58—RASPBERRY WINE.

2 lbs. of raspberries　　　　　25 grams of tartaric acid
1 pt. of water　　　　　2½ lbs. of sugar

Preparation: Dissolve the tartaric acid with the water in a stone jar, add the raspberries and let stand for 30 hours. Press through a white muslin or linen bag and let it stand a while, then carefully pour it off from the settlings, add the sugar and stir the syrup for ½ hour. Fill it into clean, dry bottles, cork them loosely or put cotton batting on top of the bottles. Let stand 8 weeks before using and then strain the juice because the impurities have come to the top.

No. 59—WILD STRAWBERRY WINE.

2 lbs. of strawberries　　　　　25 grams of tartaric acid
1 pt. of water　　　　　2½ lbs. of sugar

The preparation is the same as that of raspberry wine, see No. 58, Raspberry Wine.

No. 60—BLUEBERRY JUICE.

1 qt. of juice   1 lb. of sugar   1 stick of cinnamon

Preparation: Crush the berries and press through a white muslin bag. Put the juice into a cool place to clarify. Carefully pour the clear juice off from the settlings and boil it 10 minutes with the sugar and cinnamon. When cold, strain it, fill it into bottles and cork well.

No. 61—ORANGE JUICE.

8 large oranges   10 pieces of lump sugar
1 lemon   1 lb. of sugar   ¼ pt. of water

Preparation: Clean the oranges and the lemon with a cloth and grate off the rind with the lump sugar. Mix the sugar, water, grated rind of oranges and lemon and boil 1 minute, then add orange and lemon juice, boil another minute, strain through a cloth, fill into bottles and cork well.

No. 62—QUINCE JUICE.

1 pt. of quince juice   1 lb. of sugar

Preparation: Take nice, yellow quinces, clean them with a cloth, grate them down to the granular part, press out and put into glasses or jars over night to clarify or settle. The next day carefully pour off the clear juice, boil 3 minutes with the sugar and when cold, fill it into bottles, and cork well.

No. 63—CURRANT JUICE.

1 pt. of juice   ¾ lb. of sugar   Oil   ¼ cup of water

Preparation: Clean the currants, press through the fruit press and let stand for a few hours to clarify. Then carefully pour off the settlings, boil sugar and water 5 minutes, skim and put in the juice. Boil 10 minutes, skim and when cold, fill into bottles. Into each bottle pour 1 teaspoonful of fine oil; cork well, seal the bottles and keep them in the cellar. Before using, dip off the oil with cotton batting.

No. 64—BLACKBERRY JUICE.

1 pt. of juice   ¾ lb. of sugar   Oil   ¼ cup of water

Preparation: The preparation is the same as that of currant juice. See No. 63, Currant Juice.

No. 65—TUTTI-FRUTTI IN ARRACK.

1 qt. of arrack or rum
1 lb. of strawberries
1 lb. of raspberries
½ lb. of large, red, stoned cherries
6 lbs. of sugar
½ lb. of large, black, stoned cherries
½ lb. of blue, peeled plums
10 medium sized peaches
10 apricots
10 good preserving pears

Preparation: The fruit must be ripe but not soft. Take each fruit as it appears in the market, clean it and put into a large jar. For instance, if strawberries are in the market, prepare these, wash and drain them, put them first into the jar with ½ lb. of sugar and ½ pt. of arrack. Close the jar well and if it is a stone jar, tie it up well. Continue to put in the rest of the fruit as it comes and use the rest of the sugar and arrack, closing the jar or can well every time. Peaches, pears and apricots must be peeled and quartered before they are put in and pears should be boiled partly done in sugar and water.

Remarks: After the fruit has all been used, the juice may be used for pudding sauce.

Preserved Vegetables.
No. 66—ASPARAGUS.

Asparagus   To 1 qt. of water 1 tsp. of salt

Preparation: Take nice, white, thick stalks of asparagus, peel carefully and cut into small pieces that will fit into a jar. Economy jars may be used for asparagus. Pack the asparagus with heads downward into the jars. Mix 1 teaspoonful of salt into each qt. of water and fill up the jars with this salt water. Close the jars and place them into a wash boiler with cold water enough to cover the jars by 1 inch. Place a cloth on the bottom of the boiler, if it has no tray, cover the boiler and boil for 3 hours. After that, take out the jars, dry them and keep them in a cool, airy place.

No. 67—WAX BEANS No. 1.

Wax beans   1 qt. of water   1 stick of cinnamon   3 cloves
    Salt water   ½ cup of sugar   ¾ cup of vinegar

Preparation: Wash the beans, string and slice them, and boil until tender in boiling salt water. Drain the water off and pack them into the jars. Boil the water, vinegar, sugar, cinnamon and cloves a few minutes, skim and pour it over the beans boiling hot. Close the jars tightly and place them upside down to test the covers and rubbers.

Remarks: The syrup should have quite a sweet-sour taste. The jars must be well filled with the beans.

No. 68—WAX BEANS No. 2.

Young wax beans   To 1 qt. of water 1 tsp. of salt

Preparation: The beans must be very tender. String the beans and leave them whole. Wash them and fill the jars with them. Mix the salt water and pour over the beans, close them and boil them in a covered wash boiler as before, for 3 hours. Then take out the jars, which may be Economy jars, and test the covers. If some of them are not tight, put on others and place the jars into the boiler to boil 15 minutes longer.

No. 69—GREEN BEANS.

Very young, green beans   To every qt. of cold water, 1 tsp. of salt.

Preparation: The preparation of these beans is the same as that of wax beans No. 2, see No. 68, Wax Beans No. 2.

No. 70—SALTED GREEN BEANS.

Green beans   Salt

Preparation: Wash, string, and slice the beans, and pack in layers with salt into stone jars. Each layer of beans must be stamped down with a wooden pestle. Through this process some juice will collect on the beans when they are all in. Now place a white piece of muslin on them, a little board weighted with a stone on top of that and keep them cool. When using, soak them in water to take out some of the salt. Look to it that there is no mould forming on them. The cloth, board and stone must be cleaned occasionally.

No. 71—YOUNG CARROTS.

Young carrots   For pickling, to each qt. of water,
Salt water for cooking   1 tsp. of salt

Preparation: The young carrots should be of a uniform size. Clean and wash them, put them into boiling salt water until they are partly done, pour them into a colander and drain off the water. Place them in Economy jars, the first layer must have the points up and the second layer the points down. Make the jars ¾ full and pour on the cooled salt water in the proportions given above, close the jars tightly and boil them for 1½ hours in a boiler, as stated before.

No. 72—RED BEETS.

2 tbsps. of caraway seeds   3 tbsps. of horseradish pieces
1 pt. of vinegar   ¼ cup of sugar   2 tsps. of salt   5 lbs. of red beets

Preparation: Clean the beets, boil until tender in boiling water, skin them and slice them about $\frac{1}{10}$ inch thick into a stone jar. Strew caraway seeds on every layer and place the pieces or slices of horse radish between each layer. Boil the vinegar with salt and sugar and when cold, pour it over the beets to well cover them, tie up the jar or close the can well.

No. 73—GREEN PEAS.

Green peas   To every qt. of cold water, 1 tsp. of salt

Preparation: Shell the peas, wash them and put into Economy jars. Boil the salt water, cool it and fill the jars with it. Close the jars and boil in a covered wash boiler for 3 hours. Then take them out, dry them and test the jar covers. If these are not tight, put on other covers and boil the jars for ½ hour longer. The peas must not be yellow but tender and sound. If there are bad ones among them, they must be carefully selected or the preserves will not keep.

No. 74—CORN.

Very fresh corn   Juice from the corn cobs

Preparation: Cut the kernels from the cobs and put into the jars, press the juice out of the cobs and pour it over the corn. Close the jars and boil in a covered washboiler for 5 hours. After cooling, take out the jars, test them as to the rubbers and covers, close them up tightly and treat them as in No. 1. Covers that are not tight must be replaced by others and the jars put back into the boiler to cook another 15 minutes. **Remarks:** Everything must be very clean.

No. 75—WHOLE TOMATOES.

Nice, medium sized tomatoes   To every qt. jar full of tomatoes
Fresh water   1 tsp. of salt

Preparation: Dip the tomatoes into boiling water for 1 minute and skin them, put into Economy jars. Strew the salt into the jar and fill it with cold water. Close the jars and boil them in a covered boiler for 1 hour. The water in the boiler must be ½ inch above the jars.

No. 76—PICCALILLI.

Vinegar water   4 cups of sugar   7 cups of vinegar
1 pk. of green tomatoes   About 1 cup of salt
10 cents worth of small onions   5 cents worth of mixed spices

Preparation: Slice the tomatoes and strew with 1 cup of salt. Peel the onions and put into salt water. Let both tomatoes and onions stand until the next day. Now take both out of the salt water and bring them to boil in weak vinegar water. When that turns yellow, strain it, put the tomatoes and onions back into the kettle, add sugar, 7 cups of vinegar and spices and boil until nearly done. Fill into cans or stone jars and close them tightly.

No. 77—TOMATO MARMALADE.

Tomatoes   Sugar

Preparation: Put the tomatoes into boiling water for one minute, skin them, slice thin and bring slowly to a boil. Boil to a marmalade, stirring constantly. When you think it is thick enough, mix in the sugar and boil 15 minutes more. Put into jelly glasses and tie them up well.

Remarks: If you like, the tomatoes may be pressed through a sieve before the sugar is added.

No. 78—PLAIN TOMATOES FOR SOUP.

Tomatoes

Preparation: Peel the tomatoes, boil until tender and fill into jars. Close tightly and put in a dry, cool place.

No. 79—SWEET TOMATOES.

1 lb. of tomatoes	¼ slice of lemon	3 cloves
½ lb. of sugar	⅛ cup of water	1 stick of cinnamon
	2 pieces of ginger	

Preparation: Put the medium sized, red tomatoes into boiling water for a minute and skin them. Boil the sugar, water, cloves, cinnamon and ginger 1 minute, skim, add the tomatoes and boil slowly until they are tender but not too soft. Fill them carefully into the jars. Boil the syrup thick, pour it over the fruit and close the jars tightly. Treat the jars as in No. 1 and store them in a cool, dry place.

No. 80—TOMATO CATSUP.

1 pk. of tomatoes	½ tsp. of ground allspice
1 tsp. of ground, black pepper	3 large onions
¼ tsp. of red pepper	2 tbsps. of sugar
½ tsp. of ground cloves	Salt to taste

Preparation: Peel and slice nice, ripe tomatoes, add the spices and boil until thick. Strain thru a fine sieve, put it back into the kettle, boil until of the consistency of thick cream, fill into bottles and when cold, cork them well.

No. 81—RHUBARB.

Rhubarb

Preparation: Skin the rhubarb, cut into small pieces and pack into jars or bottles. Close them well and boil in a covered wash boiler with a tray or cloth on the bottom for 45 minutes. The water is put into the boiler cold and must be ½ inch above the jars or bottles. When they are cooled off, take them out, test the covers, treat them as in No. 1. Before using the contents, put sugar in and boil it a little, then serve cold.

No. 82—RHUBARB MARMALADE.

Sugar   Rhubarb

Preparation: Skin the rhubarb, cut into small pieces, bring slowly to boil in a little water, stirring constantly until it thickens. Add sugar, fill it into jars and close them up tightly.

No. 83—SAUERKRAUT.

Firm, white cabbage heads   Salt   Pepper-corns

Preparation: Remove the bad outer leaves, cut the cabbage in halves, cut out the heart, slice the cabbage in fine shreds and put into a clean barrel or stone jar. First place whole cabbage leaves over the bottom of the jar or barrel, pack on a layer of sliced cabbage, strew it with salt and pepper-corns, pack on another layer and so on until the cabbage is all used up. Stamp it down firmly so the liquor will cover the cabbage, then cover it with a clean piece of white muslin, a board and a stone to hold it down. Look after it occasionally and clean the cloth, board and stone. After the cabbage has fermented enough, which you will know by its sour odor, put it into a cool place.

No. 84—PARSLEY.

Green parsley   Salt

Preparation: Wash the parsley, cut off the stems and wipe dry. Pack in layers with salt into jars, close the jars tightly and keep them like preserves.

Remarks: When using, soak in water to take out some of the salt and close the jar well every time.

No. 85—TO KEEP RED AND WHITE CABBAGE.

Cabbage heads   Paper   Twine

Preparation: The cabbage heads must be firm. Remove all bad leaves, tie the heads in paper and hang them up in the cellar. They will keep all winter.

No. 86—PARSLEY, CARROTS, CELERY AND BORAGE FOR THE WINTER.

Firm parsley roots   Firm borage
Firm carrots   Firm celery roots   Fine, dry sand

Preparation: The sand must be fine and dry. Pour it into the cellar on the cement floor or into a box. Cover each vegetable with it. In this way they will keep all winter.

No. 87—TO PRESERVE PEARL ONIONS.

  Onions   Salt   Vinegar

Preparation: Salt the onions well and leave in the salt for 8 to 10 days, peel and partly cook them in vinegar. Put them into jars with sufficient salt to cover them and close the jars well.

No. 88—CHAMPIGNONS OR MUSHROOMS.

3 lbs. of champignons	1 qt. of water
2 qts. of water	2 tbsps. of salt	2 tbsps. of vinegar

Preparation: There are forest champignons and manure champignons. The former are whiter and easily turn soft. They grow wild while the latter are cultivated.

The champignons to be preserved must be firm; if they have been exposed to the air too long, they are not good for preserving. Wash them in 2 qts. of water mixed with 2 tablespoonfuls of vinegar. Cut off the stems and brush both the stems and caps of the champignons in the vinegar water until they are white. Rinse them in 1 qt. of fresh water mixed with 1 tablespoonful of vinegar. The quart of water mixed with 2 tablespoonfuls of salt is brought to boil. As soon as you have prepared a handful of champignons, throw them into the boiling salt water and let them boil until the second handful is prepared. Now take the boiled champignons out with a skimmer, put them into the jars and continue the boiling until the jars are ¾ full, pour on the liquor to fill the jars completely. Close up the jars or if you are using tin cans, solder them, and boil them in a boiler ¾ to 1 hour.

Remarks: Only in this careful manner, white champignons are obtained and preserved.

No. 89—CHAMPIGNONS IN VINEGAR.

1 lb. of small champignons	¼ tsp. of white pepper
1 tbsp. of salt	1 tbsp. of salt
1 tbsp. of vinegar	1 qt. of wine-vinegar

Preparation: The champignons must be firm and small. Clean them by rubbing each one with salt and brushing them with a brush, rinse them in cold water mixed with 1 tablespoonful of vinegar. Bring the one quart of vinegar to boil with 1 tablespoonful of salt and pepper, and add the champignons. As soon as they begin to get tender, fill them into the jars and when cold, close tightly.

No. 90—TRUFFLES.

1 lb. of truffles 1 tbsp. of salt 1 pt. of water

Preparation: Put the truffles in water for 1 hour and brush them until they are perfectly black and clean. Then put them immediately into boiling water for ½ hour and put into jars. Boil 1 pt. of water mixed with 1 tablespoonful of salt, let it get cold and fill the jars with it, close them and boil in water in a covered boiler for 1 hour.

No. 91—SALT PICKLES No. 1.

Medium sized pickles Minced dill In 6 qts. of water, ½ lb. of salt
Cherry leaves from sour cherry trees

Preparation: Brush the pickles in fresh water, pack into a stone jar in alternate layers with cherry leaves and chopped dill, the uppermost layer being leaves and dill. Boil the water and salt, let it get cold and pour it on the pickles to cover them by 1 to 2 inches. Leave them in a warm place for about a week until they have fermented sufficiently, then set them into a cool place. They can soon be used.

Remarks: If you want these pickles for the winter, pack them into a cask, pour the brine over to completely fill the cask and close the cask tightly, except for a bung-hole in the cover through which it can work off. Put the cask into the sun for a while and when the pickles have fermented sufficiently, put a new cork into the bung-hole and carry the cask into the cellar. Examine the cask from time to time to see if there is sufficient brine on it. If there is not enough, add fresh cold brine and close up the bung-hole.

No. 92—SALT PICKLES No. 2.

Medium sized pickles   Half water and half vinegar
Salt   Dill   Herbs   Mustard seeds
Pepper-corns   Cloves   1 piece of ginger

Preparation: Wash the pickles and pack them into a stone jar with salt about ⅜ inch thick. Pour cold water over to cover them well and place a weight on them. After 3 weeks the pickles are taken out, washed and the water drained off. Then put them back into the jar in layers with dill, herbs, cloves, pepper-corns, and a small piece of ginger, the uppermost layer being herbs. Now boil one-half the quantity that the jar would hold of equal parts water and vinegar and a handful of salt and pour it warm over the pickles. The liquid should cover the pickles by 2 inches. Cover with a round, white muslin bag in which you put yellow and green mustard flour and place a weight on them.

No. 93—VINEGAR PICKLES No. 1.
Small pickles about 3 to 4 inches long

| Salt | Tarragon | Dill | Summer savory |
| Pepper-corns | Bay-leaves | Cloves | Wine vinegar |

Some green or red peppers

Preparation: Cut the blossoms and stems off and put the pickles in fresh water for several hours, drain through a colander, strew thickly with salt and let stand over night. The next morning rub the salt off, pack them closely into a stone jar. Make layers of pickles, herbs and spices, the latter on top. Boil enough wine vinegar to cover them by 2 inches and pour it hot over them. After 4 days, pour it off again, boil and skim it, let it get cold, then pour it over again. If there is not enough to cover them, boil some more. Put a weight on the pickles, and set in a cool place.

No. 94—VINEGAR PICKLES No. 2.
Medium sized, firm cucumbers or pickles

| Vinegar | Tarragon | | Green or red peppers |
| Summer savory | Thyme | Cloves | Pepper-corns | Bay-leaves |

Preparation: Wash the cucumbers and put on to boil with the vinegar. As soon as they begin to boil, take them off, drain them and let them get cold. Put in layers in a stone jar with herbs and spices, the latter on top. Then cook fresh wine vinegar and pour on sufficient to cover the pickles by 1½ inches. The vinegar must be hot. After 8 days, drain off the vinegar, cook it again and pour it hot over the pickles. When it is cold, cover them, put a weight on and keep them in a cool place.

No. 95—MUSTARD PICKLES.
Large, full grown cucumbers — Salt

Tarragon	Pearl onions	Some cloves
Mustard seeds	Horse radish	Spanish peppers
Basil	Pepper-corns	Wine vinegar

Preparation: Peel the cucumbers, cut in halves, scoop out the seeds and cut the vegetable into desirable pieces. Cover thickly with salt and let stand over night. The next morning rub the salt off, pack the cucumbers into stone jars or cans and put all herbs and spices named between them. To every quart of vinegar take one tablespoonful of salt, boil it, and when cold, pour it over the cucumbers. The next day pour it off and cook it again and pour on cold. Repeat this process for the third time. The vinegar should cover the cucumbers by 1 to 2 inches. Tie up the jars or close the cans tightly. After three weeks they will be ready to serve.

No. 96—SPICED PICKLES.

Large, full-grown cucumbers
Pearl onions   Water   Some cloves   Mustard seeds
Wine vinegar   Sugar   Pepper-corns   Salt

Preparation: Peel the cucumbers, cut in halves, scoop out the seeds and cut the vegetable into desirable pieces. Over every 3 lbs. of cucumbers, sprinkle 1 oz. of salt and leave them over night. The next day rub off the salt well and boil them in a pickle of 1 pint of vinegar, ½ pint of water, 1 lb. of sugar, 1 stick of cinnamon 3 inches long, 6 cloves, 10 pepper-corns and 1 tablespoonful of mustard seeds. When it boils, put in the cucumbers and boil them until they are transparent. Fill them into jars and close up tightly.

No. 97—MIXED PICKLES.

Very white cauliflower   Lemon slices
Small salad beans   Whole white pepper-corns
Pearl onions   Tarragon leaves
Red radishes   Bay-leaves
Cucumbers 2 to 3 inches long   Nutmeg
Red and green Spanish peppers Pieces of horse radish
Very small carrots   Salt   Good wine vinegar

Preparation:. Prepare each vegetable in the proper way. Break the cauliflower into little roses. Cauliflower, beans, onions and carrots should be separately cooked in salt water and drained. Put salt on the cucumbers and radishes and let stand over night, the next day rub off the salt. When all is prepared, arrange nicely according to color in jars and strew the pepper-corns, tarragon and bay-leaves, nutmeg, slices of lemon, cubes of horse radish over each layer. Then boil the vinegar, cool it and pour it over to cover well. After a few days, repeat this process with the vinegar and close the jars tightly.

No. 98—DRIED PEARS.

Pears

Preparation: Peel the pears, cut them in halves or quarters and place on very clean baking pans. Cover the bottom of the oven with bricks and start a fire to produce moderate heat. Then place the pans on the bricks and dry the pears, turning them occasionally. This will require fully one day. Store the dried pears away in bags.

No. 99—DRIED APPLES.

Apples

Preparation: The process of drying apples is the same as that of drying pears. See No. 98, Dried Pears. Air the apples for a few days.

No. 100—SUGARED LEMON AND ORANGE RIND.

1 lb. of lemon or orange rind   2 lbs. of sugar

Preparation: Peel the oranges or lemons very thin and cut the rind, pack into jars and cover thickly with sugar. Close the jars well.

No. 101—GREEN COLOR FOR COLORING ICES OR OTHER FOOD.

White of an egg   20 coffee beans, (raw)

Preparation: Rinse the coffee beans, and set aside in the beaten white of an egg for 12 hours in a covered dish; the nicely colored white of egg will then be found convenient to color ices or other sweetmeats.

No. 102—GLAZED CHESTNUTS.

Good chestnuts   1 lb. of sugar
Boiling salt water   ½ cup of water

Preparation: Boil the chestnuts in salt water until they can be easily pierced with a pin or needle. Drain the water off and take off the brown thick shell and then the thin white skin underneath. String 4 to 5 chestnuts on a toothpick or thin stick so they do not touch. Boil the water and sugar until it is jelly-like, dip the stick with chestnuts in and turn them around in the sugar, take them out and dip and turn them once more, then hand them to a second person who will turn them until the sugar is cooled. Place them in an upright position into a dish and put in a dry place until you strip them from the stick to serve.

No. 103—ROASTED ALMONDS.

1 lb. of sweet almonds ½ vanilla bean   ½ pt. of water
1 lb. of sugar   A few drops of oil

Preparation: Boil the sugar, water and vanilla for 15 minutes and add the blanched almonds. Stir them until they pop, then pour them into oiled dishes.

No. 104—SALTED ALMONDS.

Almonds   Fine salt   Hot lard

Preparation: Put blanched, sweet almonds into clean, boiling lard for 1 minute. Then take them out with a skimmer and place on pans lined with blotting paper to drain off the lard. Dust them with very fine salt and dry them in the oven.

No. 105—CANNED SPRING CHICKEN.

Chicken cut into desirable pieces   Salt and pepper to taste

Preparation: Dress the chickens, cut into desirable pieces, wash and pack into Economy jars. Salt and pepper to taste, pour on cold water to fill the jars, close them and boil in a wash boiler with cold water enough to cover the jars by 1 inch. Cover the bottom of the boiler with several thicknesses of cloth. Put the cover on the boiler and boil for 3 hours. When cold, take out the jars and store them in a cool place.

No. 106—CANNED SALMON OR OTHER LARGE FISH.

Preparation: Dress and wash the fish and remove the backbone. Cut it into pieces that will go into a jar, sprinkle with salt and pepper and fill the jars with cold water. Close the jars and boil them in a boiler as before for 3 hours. When cold, store them in a cool place.

No. 107—CANNED FRIED CHICKEN, DUCK OR WILD GAME.

Chicken   Water   Butter for frying   Salt and pepper

Preparation: Carefully dress and prepare the fowl, bake quickly in the oven for 20 minutes, then cut into desirable pieces, leaving the bones in. Sprinkle with salt and pepper, and fill the jars with the hot meat. Make a gravy from the drippings and pour it on hot to cover the meat well. Close the jars and boil in a covered boiler as before for 3 hours. The water in the boiler must cover the jars by 1 inch. When they are cold, put them into a cool place.

No. 108—MINCE MEAT.

For About 22 Pint Glasses.

1 pk. green tomatoes   2 cans syrup   1 tsp. nutmeg
1 cup cold water   1 cup vinegar   1 tbsp. allspice
3 lbs. brown sugar   2 tsps. salt   1¼ tbsps. cloves
1¼ tbsps. cinnamon   1 lb. raisins   2 lbs. currants
2½ lbs. finely chopped apples   2 finely chopped oranges
1 lb. finely chopped plums   1 finely chopped lemon
½ lb. finely chopped suet

Preparation: Chop tomatoes fine, let boil 5 minutes, run through a sieve, and add the other ingredients. Let boil 45 minutes and stir or let steam 30 minutes. While hot, put in glasses and screw covers on tightly. Very good.

No. 109—SPICED GREEN TOMATOES.
For About 12 Pint Glasses.

1 pk. green tomatoes ½ cup salt 2 cups ground onions
5 cups vinegar 2 cups sugar ½ cup mustard seed
2 cups ground table celery 6 ground red peppers (empty inside)

Preparation: Put the tomatoes through a meat grinder, add salt and let stand all night. Drain and squeeze out the juice. Mix well and pack cold into jars, closed tight.

No. 110—SWEET-SOUR SLICED CUCUMBER PICKLES.
For About 15 Pint Glasses.

18 large cucumbers 1½ cups brown sugar 2 tsps. mustard seed
9 onions 2 tsps. celery salt 1½ tsps. pepper
1½ pts. vinegar 1½ tsps. ginger 1½ tsps. salt
1½ tsps. turmeric powder 1½ tsps. cinnamon buds

Preparation: Peel and slice fine cucumbers and onions, sprinkle with salt and let stand one hour. Drain and add remaining ingredients; let come to a boil and seal while hot.

No. 111—CHILI SAUCE.
For About 6 Pint Bottles.

1 onion 12 medium sized ripe tomatoes 3 red peppers
2 cups vinegar 1 tbsp. salt 2 tsps. allspice
3 tbsps. sugar 2 tsps. cloves 2 tsps. grated nutmeg

Preparation: Peel and slice tomatoes; add peppers and onion, cut very fine. Boil one-half hour, and add the rest of the ingredients and boil two hours. Put in jars while hot and seal well.

No. 112—ENGLISH CHOW CHOW.
For About 24 Pint Glasses.

1 qt. young cucumbers 2 qts. small white onions
2 qts. string beans 2/3 cup mustard 2 tbsps. celery seed
3 qts. green tomatoes 1 oz. turmeric powder 2 tbsps. allspice
2 heads cauliflower 6 red peppers 2 tbsps. whole cloves
2 heads cabbage 4 tbsps. mustard seed Vinegar

Preparation: Put cucumbers, onions, tomatoes, cauliflower, and cabbage through the food chopper. Mix all together and put into stone jars with a sprinkling of salt. Let stand 24 hours and drain off the brine. Put the vegetables in a kettle over the fire and stir in the turmeric, red pepper chopped fine, mustard seeds, allspice and ground mustard.

Pour over enough vinegar to cover. Cover tightly and let simmer until thoroughly cooked, stirring often. Put into glass jars and seal while hot.

No. 113—CHILI SAUCE.
For About 18 Pint Glasses.

1 pk. ripe tomatoes	1 cup sugar
2 cups chopped celery	1 qt. vinegar
3 green peppers	½ cup salt
3 onions	2 ozs. mustard seed

Preparation: Chop tomatoes fine and strain, add all other ingredients, boil about two hours, fill glasses while hot and close up tight.

No. 114—DILL PICKLES.
For About 14 Pint Glasses.

To 6 qts. of water, add 2 qts. vinegar	Cloves
1 lb. of salt	Allspice
5 cents worth of Weinstein-saeure (tartaric acid)	A good quantity of dill
Pepper	Horse radish
	Grape leaves
	Bay-leaves

Preparation: Place a layer of cucumbers in a stone jar and sprinkle over some of the spices; continue until all are used, laying the dill and leaves between each layer. Put a tight, well-weighted cover over them.

No. 115—MUSTARD PICKLES.
For About 20 Pint Glasses.

2 qts. green tomatoes	1 lb. Coleman's mustard
2 qts. small onions	1 tbsp. turmeric
2 qts. string beans	1 gal. vinegar
2 heads cauliflower 20 small cucumbers	2 cups sugar

Preparation: Slice the tomatoes, cut the cauliflower in small pieces, and salt vegetables over night. In the morning drain thoroughly. Mix mustard with vinegar. When the vinegar boils, put all in and boil one-half hour. Bottle while hot.

SANDWICHES.

No. 1—EGG SANDWICHES.

Preparation: Slice white or brown bread into thin slices. Spread with butter, mayonnaise and finely chopped eggs; press two slices together and trim into desired shapes.

This is a wonderful improvement over the ordinary rather tasteless sandwiches made with butter alone.

No. 2—CELERY SANDWICHES.

Preparation: Chop celery fine and add mayonnaise to taste. Spread on buttered bread and remove crusts. Cut in narrow strips and serve garnished with celery tips.

No. 3—OLIVE SANDWICHES.

Preparation: Mix cream cheese smooth with mayonnaise dressing, add a dozen chopped olives and use as a filling for bread and butter sandwiches.

No. 4—CHICKEN SANDWICHES.

Preparation: Made the same as veal sandwiches. Always remember to prepare the bread as for bread and butter sandwiches. Put finely chopped cucumbers on top.

No. 5—VEAL SANDWICHES.

Preparation: Spread bread with butter and mayonnaise. Place a layer of chopped meat and a layer of chopped cucumbers or olives between the slices.

No. 6—EGG SANDWICHES.

Preparation: Use hard boiled eggs. Chop finely and mix with mayonnaise dressing. To this may be added a finely chopped pickle, a little ham, sardines mashed to a paste or shredded lettuce. Spread on bread and butter sandwiches.

No. 7—PEANUT SANDWICHES.

Preparation: Spread butter on bread and add peanut butter; put a lettuce leaf between.

No. 8—CORNED BEEF SANDWICHES.

Preparation: Chop cold corned beef to a fine paste; mix with a little mayonnaise dressing. Beat the mixture until smooth and well blended and spread evenly on buttered bread.

CHAPTER 24.
THE MENU.

Family Dinner. A Menu for one day in a Month.

JANUARY. — Oxtail soup. — Fried whitefish. — Small potato balls. — Head lettuce. — Fillet with champignons. — Asparagus. — Riced potatoes. — Mixed salad. — Vanilla ice cream with hot chocolate dressing. — Coffee and cake.

FEBRUARY. — Grape fruit. — Chicken soup. — Meat patties. — Tongue ragout with dumplings and puff-paste scallops. — Tomato salad with boiled mayonnaise dressing. — Rabbit roast with apple sauce and red cabbage. — Orange cream. — Coffee.

MARCH. — Oyster soup. — Fine ragout in shells. — Asparagus with tongue. — Lamb crown roast with turnips and mashed potatoes. — Chocolate pudding with vanilla sauce. — Coffee.

APRIL. — Bouillon in cups. — Bread sticks. — Fish in red wine sauce. — Fried potatoes. — Chicken salad. — Fillet beefsteak with sliced goose liver. — Macaroni with tomato sauce. — Cold rice pudding with peaches and whipped cream.

MAY. — Vegetable soup. — Lamb roast. — Stuffed potatoes. — Spinage. — Green asparagus with salmon. — Fried pigeons with gooseberry jam. — Cheese tart and coffee.

JUNE. — Tomato soup. — Ham noodles. — Roast beef with fried potatoes and cauliflower. — Asparagus salad. — Strawberry ice with macaroons. — Bread and butter and cheese. — Coffee.

JULY. — Bouillon with marrow dumplings. — Fish ragout in shells. — Baked ham with Burgundy sauce. — Stuffed tomatoes. — Potato chips. — Red farina pudding with cream. — Coffee.

AUGUST. — Green pea soup. — Lobster with remoulade sauce. — Veal chops with apple sauce. — Head lettuce. — Broiled spring chicken. — Fried potatoes. — Fruit salad. — Coffee and cake or tart.

SEPTEMBER. — Bouillon with egg sponge dumplings. — Chicken fricassee with dumplings and puff-paste scallops. — Hamburg steak with green beans and creamed potatoes. — Champignon salad. — Chocolate cream. — Bread and butter. — Cheese. — Coffee.

OCTOBER. — Brown bouillon with rice pudding. — Lobster ragout in shells. — Fried duck with cranberries and baked cauliflower. — Mixed salad. — Strawberry cream with almond heaps.

NOVEMBER. — Green corn soup. — Duck ragout. — Lamb cutlet with kohlrabi. — Potato pudding. — Mixed jam or marmalade. — Apple strudel.

DECEMBER. — Fish soup. — Roasted chestnuts with sliced goose liver. — Turkey with jam and potatoes. — Mixed salad. — Plum pudding with vanilla sauce.

A FINE SUPPER OR BREAKFAST.

A Menu for each Season.

JANUARY to MARCH. — Bouillon with cheese wafers. — Lobster with remoulade sauce. — Caviar on toast. — Mutton chops with chestnut puree. — Truffle salad. — Spring chicken with jam. — Tutti-Frutti ice.

APRIL to JUNE. — Crab soup. — Asparagus and cutlets. — Pigeons and salad. — Strawberry cream and cake.

JULY to SEPTEMBER. — Bouillon in cups with bread sticks. — Fish with Bearnaise dressing. — Small potato balls. — Sweetbread ragout with peas. — Venison. — Tomato salad. — Fine wine ice cream.

OCTOBER to DECEMBER. — Grape fruit. — Oysters. — Fillets of sole with mushroom sauce. — Turkey with apple sauce. — Mixed salad. — Chocolate ice.

FINE DINNER.

A Menu for Each Season.

JANUARY to MARCH. — Asparagus soup, meat patties. — Venison with jam. — Trout with horse radish and mustard butter. — Pineapple ice. — Young roast goose with small potato balls. — Partridge with cucumber and tomato salad. — Asparagus with creamed butter. — Strawberry cream with almond heaps. — Crackers. — Butter. — Various kinds of cheese. — Coffee.

APRIL to JUNE. — Vegetable soup. — Timbale of crabs with herb sauce. — Lamb roast with champignons. — Whitefish with beaten egg sauce. — Chicken souffle with puff-paste scallops. — Venison with vegetable salad. — Asparagus with tongue. — Strawberries and vanilla ice cream. — Coffee. — Fruit.

JULY to SEPTEMBER. — Crawfish soup. — Chicken patties with lobster, mayonnaise dressing. — Saddle of veal garnished with beef tongue and riced potatoes. — Broiled spring chicken with Bearnaise dressing. — Champignons and stuffed tomatoes. — Salmon with cucumber salad and browned butter. — Baked sweetbreads with toast. — Snipe with jam. — Truffle and artichoke salad. — Cold rice pudding with peaches and whipped cream. — Coffee.

OCTOBER to DECEMBER. — Turtle soup. — Caviar pie. — Venison with artichokes, garnished with gooseliver and Madeira sauce. — Fine fish with small potato balls. — Brown champignons. — Crawfish. — Turkey with cranberries, salad. — Chocolate ice with cake.

A LARGE BUFFET.

For 30 Persons.

1 salmon with lobsters and mayonnaise dressing
1 venison roast
1 roast beef
1 saddle of veal or veal roast
1 ham
1 chicken, asparagus and crawfish jelly with herb sauce
2 chicken pies with champignons
1 macaroni pudding with tomato sauce
1 goose liver pie garnished with aspic
Fine fish salad
Lobster salad
2 dishes of vegetables, (asparagus, peas, morels with crab-tails
12 deviled eggs
6 qts. assorted ices
2 wine jellies with fruit
4 portions of cake

EVERY DAY DINNER.

No. 1. — Soup with mushrooms. — Roast stuffed chicken. — Potatoes. — Apple sauce. — Orange cream.

No. 2. — Bread soup. — Boiled fish with beaten egg gravy. — Small potato balls. — Head lettuce. — Filled pancakes.

No. 3. — Bouillon with rice. — Veal roast, sauerkraut. — Mashed potatoes. — Chocolate pudding with vanilla sauce.

No. 4. — Pea soup. — Hamburg steak, spinage. — Stuffed potatoes. — Lemon souffle.

No. 5. — Marrow dumpling soup. — Lamb crown roast with cauliflower. — Potatoes. — Apple strudel.

No. 6. — Tomato soup. — Meat pie with rice. — Tomato salad. — Omelet.

No. 7. — Pea soup. — Roast beef. — Stuffed tomatoes. — Fried potatoes. — Vanilla ice cream.

No. 8. — Wine soup. — Fish in red wine sauce, potatoes. — Macaroni with tomato sauce. — Apple sauce with cake.

No. 9. — Soup with bread sticks. — Stuffed duck. — Red cabbage. — Potato pudding. — Strawberry ice cream.

No. 10. — Asparagus soup. — Chicken pie with cold slaw. — Potatoes. — Apple strudel.

No. 11. — Vegetable soup. — Veal chops. — Kohlrabi. — Mashed potatoes. — Stuffed apples with rice pudding.

No. 12. — Oyster soup. — Goose stuffed with chestnuts. — Cranberries. — Potatoes. — Vanilla ice cream with hot chocolate sauce.

No. 13. — Potato soup. — Mock rabbit. — Mashed potatoes. — Green beans. — Wine jelly.

No. 14. — Blueberry soup. — Chicken fricassee with rice and potatoes. — Potato pancakes with apple sauce.

No. 15. — Red wine soup. — Stuffed lamb crown roast. — Turnips. — Mashed potatoes. — Rice pudding with cherry syrup.

No. 16. — Cauliflower soup. — Fried sausage. — Beets. — Potatoes. — Bread pudding with cream.

No. 17. — Lentil soup with Wieners. — Fried fish. — Head lettuce. — Fried potatoes. — Filled omelet.

No. 18. — Bouillon with farina dumplings. — Stuffed veal breast. — Asparagus. — Stuffed potatoes. — Coffee with thousand puff tart.

No. 19. — Bean soup. — Stuffed cabbage head. — Potatoes with cracker sauce. — Apple fritters.

No. 20. — Celery soup. — Sour roast. — Potato dumplings. — Noodles. — Fruit salad with whipped cream.

CHAPTER 25.

Cookery for Invalids.

While the directions found throughout this book will be generally adequate for the preparation of food for invalids or convalescents, always carefully regulating and limiting the quantities of fats, spices, condiments, etc., used, it is nevertheless deemed best to add a separate chapter especially devoted to the enumeration of recipes and directions intended for the sickroom. A majority of the sick and invalids, are usually nervous and irritable, and as it is quite essential that they receive the food prepared for them with all possible readiness and pleasure, it becomes necessary that the manner of presenting the meals to them should obtain great attention; even this detail, if properly carried out, being of assistance to the physician in successfully handling the case.

Invalids should seldom be consulted regarding their wishes as to food; as a usual thing they are quite unable to make a decision, or at the moment they lack the desire to determine upon anything they would like to eat, and yet it is often observable that properly prepared and appetizingly served dishes are eagerly received by them.

All the ingredients used in the preparation of dishes for invalids must be faultlessly good. Meats, fish, poultry, vegetables and fruits must be absolutely fresh and untainted. The natural fats of fleshfoods should not be used, and the very best butter only must be taken when preparing food for invalids.

Water for cold beverages must always be boiled and artificially cooled. Meals should never be prepared in the sickroom, because the air becomes vitiated, the noise and activity inseparable from the work itself is annoying to the patient, and is apt to diminish whatever appetite he may happen to have. Never bring more victuals into the sickroom than are necessary to supply present needs, because the air in the room and the exhalations from the patient act deleteriously upon the food, and may prove dangerous. All cooking utensils, particularly in cases of contagious and severe illness, should be used for that patient only; the most scrupulous cleanliness must, it is perhaps needless to say, always be observed. The quality of many dishes is impaired when they are cooked in utensils too large for the purpose. Sick people are usually very sensitive in their taste, and the slightest taint in an article of food prepared for them will at once destroy all desire for it. The utensils should, as much as possible, consist of small earthenware and enameled pots, kettles, pans, spiders, etc.; a small bouillon pot with tightly-fitting cover should also be provided. The dishes in which the food is served should be adapted to the small portions given, because neatness in everything connected with giving invalids their sustenance is certain to sharpen the appetite; furthermore, the victuals are likely to cool too rapidly when contained in large receptacles. For invalids who can only take their food and beverages slowly, vessels provided with hot water heaters are the best.

No. 1—STRONG BEEF TEA.
Ingredients for 1 pint.
½ lb. lean beef   1 old pigeon   1 tsp. of salt
½ lb. breast of veal   1 qt. of water   Small piece of carrot

Preparation: Cut the beef and veal into small pieces, clean the pigeon carefully, remove the breast and cut up into small pieces, crush drumsticks and bones, put everything into a very clean kettle, pour over the required quantity of cold water and set aside for one hour; then add salt and carrot, and cook slowly for 3 hours, rub through a very fine sieve, take off the fat and pour the soup carefully from the settlings. This bouillon can be served in cups, or be used in any kind of soup, as desired.

No. 2—WEAK VEAL BOUILLON.
Ingredients for 1 pint.
½ lb. breast of veal   1 qt. of water   1 small carrot   1 tsp. of salt

Preparation: Wash the veal, cut into very small pieces, put it into the cold water and boil very slowly for 2 hours with the carrot and 1 teaspoonful of salt, then pass through a sieve and use in soups as desired.

No. 3—BEEF BOUILLON.
Ingredients for 1 pint.
1½ lbs. of lean beef 1 qt. of water   1 tsp. of salt   ¼ small carrot

Preparation: Cut the beef into dice, put them into the required quantity of cold water, add carrot and salt and boil in a small covered kettle or double boiler for 3 hours; pour through a sieve and remove all of the fat. This bouillon may be mixed with the yolk of 1 egg and served in cups.

No. 4—BEEF TEA.
Ingredients for ½ cup.
½ lb. fresh beef steak ¼ pt. boiled water, cold 1/10 tsp. of salt

Preparation: Chop the meat, put into a fruit jar together with the water and salt, close top lightly, put in a kettle with water, cover and boil very slowly for 2 hours, then pour the tea through a fine sieve. Administer a teaspoonful at a time. Beef tea must be freshly prepared every day.

No. 5—BEEF TEA WITH COGNAC.
Ingredients and preparation same as in No. 4. Add 1 tablespoonful of cognac to the beef tea; the beverage must be served cold.

No. 6—POULTRY BOUILLON.
Ingredients for 1 quart.
1 chicken, either young or old
2 qts. of water 1 tsp. of salt A piece of carrot

Preparation: Clean chicken carefully, remove breast and cut it into small pieces. Chop drumsticks and bones, put into the water together with carrot and salt, boil very slowly for 2 hours and strain through a fine sieve. The pieces of the breast are added to the bouillon at the last hour of the boiling, and the cooking finished over a very slow fire.

The bouillon is served with the meat in it.

No. 7—PIGEON OR PARTRIDGE BOUILLON.
Prepare same as in No. 6.

No. 8—LAMB BOUILLON.
Ingredients for 1 pint.
2 qts. of water 1 lb. of lamb's trotters 1 tsp. of salt
½ lb. of lean mutton

Preparation: The lamb's trotters are carefully cleaned, and then chopped into small pieces; the meat is cut up very fine, salt added and boiled slowly in a small, tightly covered kettle for 3½ hours. Strain through a fine sieve and take off the fat carefully. This bouillon can be used for rice or barley soups.

No. 9—BOUILLON OF GAME.
Ingredients for 1 pint.
1½ lbs. of fresh game ½ lb. of bones 1 small fresh tomato
1 tsp. of salt 1 tsp. of finely chopped celery 1¼ qts. of water

Preparation: The meat is cut into small pieces and the bones crushed, put into a small, tightly covered kettle with the tomato, celery, salt and water and boiled very slowly for 2 hours; it may also be cooked for 3 hours in a slow oven.

No. 10—NOODLE OR GRITS SOUP MADE OF CLEAR BOUILLON.

Ingredients for 1 pint.

Bouillon made as in No. 3.   1 pt. of bouillon
½ cup of finely cut noodles   3 tbsps. of grits

Preparation: Slowly boil the noodles or the grits in the hot bouillon for 15 minutes. Before adding the grits to the bouillon, rinse same in cold water, stir it in 4 tablespoonfuls of the bouillon, then put it into the rest of the bouillon and boil.

No. 11—SAGO SOUP WITH GAME BOUILLON.

Ingredients for 1 pint.

Game bouillon as in No. 9   1—3 tbsps. of sherry
¼ cupful of French sago

Preparation: Mix the sherry with the sago, add the hot bouillon and boil for 12 minutes.

No. 12—ROLL SOUP WITH BOUILLON.

Ingredients for 1 pint.

Bouillon as in No. 1, 2, 3 or 6   1 tsp. of butter
½ cup of grated wheat flour   Yolk of 1 egg
rolls   1 tsp. of cream

Preparation: Rolls must be stale, grate them, heat with the butter on the stove, but do not get them yellow or brown in color, then add the bouillon and boil slowly for 20 minutes. Stir yolk of egg and the cream into the soup and rub through a sieve.

No. 13—BARLEY GRUEL.

Ingredients for 1 pint.

¼ cup of barley   Bouillon as in No. 1, 2, 3, 6 or 8   ¾ pt. of water

Preparation: Rinse the barley with 1 cupful of boiling water, put over the fire in ¾ pint of water and boil slowly for 1½ hours; then add the bouillon, and boil slowly for another hour, rub through a sieve, heat again and serve.

Remarks: The yolk of an egg may be stirred into this soup.

No. 14—RICE GRUEL.

Bouillon according to No. 1, 2,   ¾ pt. of water
3, 6 or 8   ¼ cupful of rice

Preparation: Same as No. 13, Barley Gruel.

No. 15—BARLEY SOUP WITH SWEETBREADS AND ASPARAGUS.
Ingredients for 1 pint.

Yolk of an egg
Bouillon according to No. 1, 2, 3 or 6
¼ cup of rice
1 tsp. of butter
4 tbsps. of sweetbreads cut in small pieces
1 tbsp. of flour
½ cup of asparagus cut in small pieces
1½ pts. of water

Preparation: Put the rice on the stove with 1 cup of cold water, heat it and strain and add the required quantity of water. Boil slowly for 1 hour, add bouillon, then boil for another ½ hour. During this time, boil the asparagus in a small quantity of salt water until tender; the sweetbreads should also simmer in salt water for about 5 minutes. Strain the soup, add the parsley and sweetbreads, stir the yolk of an egg with some asparagus liquor until smooth, heat the soup again and stir into it the yolk of the egg.

No. 16—PLAIN BARLEY GRUEL.
Ingredients for 1 pint.

Preparation and ingredients same as in No. 15, but instead of rice use pearl barley.

No. 17—CHICKEN PUREE SOUP.
Ingredients for 1 pint.

Chicken bouillon according to No. 6
½ cup of roll crumbs
⅛ lb. of stewed breast of chicken
1 tsp. of cream

Preparation: Boil the roll crumbs in the bouillon for 10 minutes; chop the breast of chicken very fine, rub through a sieve and add ¼ cup of soup into which 1 tablespoonful of cream has been stirred, stir into the soup and let it come to a boil; serve immediately.

No. 18—VEAL PUREE SOUP.
Ingredients for 1 pint.

Ingredients and preparation the same as in No. 17, but instead of the meat of a chicken and chicken bouillon take veal, and bouillon according to No. 1 or 2.

No. 19—PIGEON OR PARTRIDGE PUREE SOUP.

Ingredients and preparation the same as in No. 17, but instead of the meat of a chicken and chicken bouillon, take pigeon or partridge puree and bouillon; cook as explained in No. 6.

No. 20—PLAIN SOUP FOR INVALIDS.
Ingredients for 1 plateful.
½ lb. of potatoes, scant   1 pt. of water
½ tsp. of salt   1 tsp. of butter   Yolk of 1 egg

Preparation: Peel and wash potatoes and cut them into small pieces, boil until done, rub through a fine sieve, add salt, butter and the yolk of an egg, heat the soup quickly, stirring vigorously all the time and serve at once.

No. 21—THIN RICE SOUP.
Ingredients for 1 plateful.
1/6 cupful of rice   1 pt. of water   1 pinch of salt
2 tbsps. of sugar   1 tbsp. of lemon juice

Preparation: Put the rice over the fire in cold water, when the water is hot pour it off, then boil the rice in 1 pint of water until it is well done and add salt, sugar and lemon juice.

No. 22—PEARL BARLEY SOUP.
Ingredients for 1 plateful.
½ cupful of pearl barley   ¼ tsp. extract of beef
1 tsp. of butter   1 pint of water   1 pinch of salt

Preparation according to Chapter 1, No. 32, Soups.

No. 23—RYEBREAD SOUP.
Ingredients for 1 plateful.
½ cupful of grated rye bread   ½ pt. of water
½ pt. of boiling milk   2 tbsps. of sugar   1 pinch of salt
Yolk of an egg   2 tbsps. of cream

Preparation: Heat the bread crumbs in a clean spider until crisp, pour over them the required quantity of water, and let it stand to one side of the hot stove for 1 hour, but do not boil; add the hot milk, salt, sugar and the yolk of the egg and pass the soup through a sieve.

No. 24—FRUIT SOUP.
Blueberry, Cherry, Raspberry or Strawberry Soups.
Ingredients for 1 pint.
½ lb. of fruit   1½ pts. of water   1/3 cupful of sugar
½ tbsp. of lemon juice   1 tbsp. of corn starch

Preparation: Prepare and wash the fruit thoroughly and crush it with a potato masher, add the water and boil the soup for half an hour, put in sugar, lemon juice and corn starch stirred up with a tablespoonful of water, then boil the soup until it is quite smooth.

No. 25—RED WINE SOUP.

Preparation is designated in Chapter 1, No. 29, Soups; take only ⅙ of the quantities given.

No. 26—RYEFLOUR SOUP AND MILK SOUP.

Are described in Chapter 1, Nos. 53 and 54.

No. 27—MEAT PUREE FOR THE SERIOUSLY ILL.
No. 1.
Quantity for 1 Person.

⅛ lb. of veal or beef roast, medium well done
5 tbsps. of stock from the roast
2 yolks of eggs
1 pinch of salt, if necessary

Preparation: Chop the meat very finely, pass through a sieve on a porcelain dish, stir with the yolks of eggs and the stock, from which all fat has been removed, then put in a double boiler, and boil until quite thick, stirring occasionally.

No. 28—PUREE OF GAME ROAST.
For a Seriously Ill Patient.
Quantity for 1 Person.

1 tbsp. of red wine
⅛ lb. game roast
3 tbsps. of bouillon or stock
Yolk of an egg
1 tbsp. of Madeira

Preparation: Chop the meat very fine, rub through a sieve, and heat in a small porcelain dish with the Madeira, red wine, meat stock and yolk of egg in a double boiler, stirring until it thickens.

No. 29—MINCED BEEF, VEAL OR LAMB STEAK.
Quantity for 1 Person.

1/3 lb. of good meat, free from bones or fat
Yolk of an egg
½ tsp. of salt
1 tbsp. of butter

For the Gravy.

⅛ tsp. of extract of meat
Yolk of an egg
¼ pt. of bouillon or water
1 drop of extract of lemon
1 tsp. of cream

Preparation: Chop the meat very finely and rub it through a fine sieve, stir into it the yolk of an egg and the salt, form into a steak about an inch thick, which is fried with brown butter in a small pan for about 5 minutes, turning frequently, then serve on a hot plate. Yolk of an egg, extract of meat, lemon juice, cream and bouillon are stirred in a double boiler, boiled until thick and this gravy poured over the steak.

No. 30—FRIED CALF'S BRAIN.
Quantity for 1 Person.

½ of a calf's brain   Yolk of an egg   1½ tbsps. of milk
1 tbsp. of flour   White of 1 egg   1 pinch of salt   1 tbsp. of sugar

Preparation: Rinse the calf's brain and then pour hot water over it; drain off the water and remove all veins or blood vessels, then cut up the brain into small pieces. Stir together yolk of egg, milk, flour and salt, add the brain and the beaten white of egg. This mixture is fried in the butter in two pancakes, and served on a hot dish with a little spinage.

No. 31—CALF'S TONGUE.
Quantity for 1 Person.

1 calf's tongue   1 tbsp. of Madeira, if permitted
1½ pts. of water   by physician
½ tsp. of extract of meat   1 tsp. of flour
¼ tsp. of lemon juice

Preparation: Clean the tongue and boil slowly in the water for 1¼ hours until tender, then remove the skin and all fat. After this, stew the tongue, gradually adding the bouillon which should be boiled down by this time to ¾ of a pint, also add the lemon juice, extract of beef and flour, which has been stirred with 2 tablespoonfuls of cold bouillon and the Madeira, then stew the tongue for half an hour. It must be very tender when given to the invalid. Tongue and gravy should be served together.

No. 32—BREAST OF CHICKEN WITH WHITE GRAVY.
Quantity for 1 Person.

1 young chicken, weighing   1 qt. of bouillon
about 1½ lbs.   1 tsp. of salt

For the Gravy.

1 tbsp. of butter   Yolks of 2 eggs   1 pinch of salt
1 tbsp. of white wine or ¼ tbsp. of lemon juice

Preparation: Clean the chicken carefully and stew slowly in a small kettle for a little while, then pour enough hot water over it to just cover; add a little salt, put cover on tightly and cook slowly for ½ hour. Yolk of egg, white wine or lemon juice, and ½ cup of chicken bouillon are stirred in double boiler until thick. The chicken is taken out and its breast cut away, skin removed and then served on a hot plate with the hot gravy poured over it. If permitted by the physician, serve a few asparagus tips with it.

No. 33—BREAST OF PIGEON WITH WHITE GRAVY.
Quantity for 1 Person.

Ingredients and preparation same as for No. 32, but instead of a chicken take a young pigeon.

No. 34—BREAST OF PARTRIDGE WITH MADEIRA SAUCE.
Quantity for 1 Person.

Preparation same as in No. 32; use 2 tablespoonfuls of Madeira and ¼ teaspoonful of meat extract for the gravy.

No. 35—RAW HAM WITH EGG.
Quantity for 1 Person.

⅛ lb. of raw ham   Yolks of 2 eggs   1 tsp. of butter

Preparation: Rub the lean ham through a sieve, mix with butter and the yolks of eggs, and then heat in a double boiler, stirring constantly. Serve with wheat bread toast.

No. 36—FISH FOR INVALIDS.
Boiled fish for 1 Person.

½ lb. of fish

Preparation is given in Chapter 8, No. 8. However, skin and bones are carefully removed, and a trifle of egg or butter sauce is served with it.

No. 37—FISH CUTLET.
Quantity for 1 Person.

½ lb. of fish   1 tsp. of salt
½ of a roll   ½ tsp. of finely chopped parsley
1 tbsp. of butter   1 tsp. of lemon juice
Yolks of 2 eggs   ¼ cupful of roll crumbs

Preparation: Chop up the fish, remove skin and bones, mix well with yolks of eggs, salt and soaked ½ roll. Form 2 cutlets, dredge with crumbs and bake in the butter slowly for 8 minutes. Add some parsley and lemon juice to the butter.

No. 38—VEGETABLES FOR INVALIDS.

Cauliflower, scorzonera, spinage, purees of young carrots, artichokes, green peas, and macaroni may also be served to invalids. These vegetables are listed in Chapter 12; prepare them as there described, but for 1 person take only one-sixth the quantity of ingredients specified in those recipes.

Sweet Dishes for Invalids.

No. 39—RICE IN MILK.
Quantity for 1 Person.

¼ cupful of good rice   1 pinch of salt
¾ pt. of milk   1 tbsp. of sugar

Preparation: Heat the rice twice in cold water, pour off the water, add salt and milk and boil in a double boiler until very tender. Sprinkle the sugar over the rice when serving.

Remarks: If desired, the yolk of an egg can be stirred into this dish.

No. 40—MILK JELLY.
Quantity for 1 Person.

¼ pt. of thin cream   2½ layers or 1 tsp. of gelatine
¼ cupful of sugar   dissolved in 5 tbsps. of
¼ grated lemon rind   water
¼ pt. of Madeira   1 tsp. of lemon juice

Preparation: The cream, sugar and lemon juice are boiled together, then add the dissolved gelatine and let it cool. Add the wine and the lemon juice, fill into glasses and let it get stiff.

No. 41—CHOCOLATE CREAM WITH RED WINE.
Quantity for 1 Person.

⅛ lb. of chocolate   3 layers or 1 tsp. of white
1/5 pt. of red wine   gelatine
1/5 cupful of sugar   Whites of 2 eggs
½ cupful of water   ¼ tsp. of vanilla

Preparation: Chocolate and sugar are dissolved in the red wine, and the gelatine in the ½ cupful of water; pass the chocolate and gelatine through a sieve, and mix. Beat the whites of eggs to a stiff froth, and quickly add to the first mixture, spread a drop of good oil over the bottom of a mold, sprinkle with a teaspoonful of sugar, fill in the cream, and when stiff, turn it out.

No. 42—RHUBARB JELLY.
Quantity for 1 Person.

½ lb. of rhubarb   ¼ pt. of water   ¼ lb. of sugar
2 layers or 1 tsp. of gelatine   ¼ pt. of cream

Preparation: Rinse the rhubarb carefully and cut it into small pieces, then boil in the water with the sugar until tender, and rub through a sieve. When this is cool, dissolve the gelatine in it, mix in the cream, and then heat the mixture, stirring constantly. Oil the mold with a drop of oil and sprinkle it with a teaspoonful of sugar, fill in the jelly and after it stiffens, turn it out.

No. 43—RICE WITH RED WINE.
Quantity for 1 Person.
¼ cupful of rice   ½ pt. of red wine   1 small stick of cinnamon
¼ cupful of sugar   1 pinch of salt

Preparation: Bring the rice to boil in 1 cupful of water, drain, then take another cupful of water and boil the rice until it is about half done; add the wine, cinnamon, salt and sugar and boil the rice until quite tender, shaking frequently. Rinse a mold with a little wine, sprinkle with sugar, fill in the rice and turn it out when cold. Serve with a little cream as a sauce.

No. 44—BAKED APPLES.
Quantity for 1 Person.
2 medium sized sweet-sour apples   2 tbsps. of sugar
4 tbsps. of water

Preparation: Take the cores out of the apples very carefully, leaving the bottom intact to hold the filling, which is made of the sugar and water; bake the apples in the oven for ½ hour.

No. 45—EGG FOAM.
Quantity for 1 Person.
White of an egg   1 tbsp. of cream
1 tbsp. of California brandy   1½ tsps. of sugar

Preparation: Beat the white of an egg to a stiff foam, gradually beat in the cream, mix in the brandy and sugar and serve to the patient, a spoonful at a time.

No. 46—BEATEN EGG.
Quantity for 1 Person.
1 fresh egg   1 pinch of salt

Preparation: Beat the egg with the salt in a tumbler until the glass is half full of foam. The egg should be beaten in a well ventilated room only, because the air in the room influences the nourishment served to the invalid.

No. 47—BEATEN YOLK OF EGG.
Quantity for 1 Person.
Yolk of an egg   1 tsp. of powdered sugar

Preparation: With a teaspoon beat the yolk of egg and the sugar in a tumbler for about 20 minutes and pour it into a clean glass, or else wipe the first glass with a damp towel before using it to serve the egg.

Remarks: A tablespoonful of brandy or Malaga or orange juice may be mixed with the egg, if desired.

No. 48—RED WINE FOAM.
Quantity for 1 Person.

¼ pt. of red wine   ¼ cupful of sugar
2 eggs   1 tbsp. of raspberry jelly

Preparation: Beat all ingredients to a froth over the fire with an egg beater; serve in a tumbler.

No. 49—ICE CREAM.

Ices, for instance vanilla or chocolate ice cream can often be given to invalids without harm. Their preparation is given in Chapter 17.

No. 50—FIG SAUCE.
Quantity for 1 Person.

⅛ lb. of figs   ½ wineglassful of Malaga
½ pt. of water   1 tbsp. of sugar

Preparation: Rinse the figs and cut them into small pieces, add the water, and set them aside for 12 hours. At the expiration of this time boil until very tender, add the other ingredients, rub through a sieve; to those not seriously ill it can be served without straining.

No. 51—ZWIEBACK (SWEET TOAST).
Ingredients.

½ lb. of flour   1 pinch of salt
¼ lb. of butter   2 cents yeast
⅛ lb. of sugar   ⅛ pt. of milk and water
2 eggs

Preparation: Take 2 parts of water and 1 part of milk to make ⅛ pint, heat until lukewarm and dissolve the yeast in it; the mixture is stirred to a smooth batter with part of the flour, then let it rise in a warm place for about an hour. Butter, sugar, eggs, salt and the remainder of the flour are mixed well and added to the yeast mixture. Wrap the dough in a cloth sprinkled with flour and set aside in a warm place over night; the next day the dough is put into oblong bread pans, and baked in a medium hot oven. After the baking is done and cold, cut it into strips that are of a uniform thickness of ¼ inch, place them into a buttered pan and brown them slightly. The Zwieback can be sprinkled with sugar before browning.

No. 52—TEAS PREPARED FROM VARIOUS MEDICINAL HERBS.

Camomile, Peppermint, Fennel, Elderberry Blossoms, Basswood Blossoms, Sage, etc.

Quantity for 1 Person.

1 tsp. of tea   ½ pt. of water

Preparation: Put the herbs into a porcelain jar, pour the boiling water over them and after 5 minutes strain through a sieve.

No. 53—LUNG TEA WITH MALT SUGAR.

Quantity for 1 Person.

1 tbsp. of lung tea   ¾ pt. of boiling water
1 tbsp. of malt sugar

Preparation: Cover all of the ingredients, boil slowly for 5 minutes and strain through a sieve.

No. 54—IRON AND WINE.

Ingredients.

1 bottle of white wine   1/10 lb. of horse radish
1/20 lb. of iron filings   ¼ tsp. of ginger

Preparation: Mix the ingredients and set aside for about 12 hours in a warm place, strain through a sieve and fill into a bottle. The iron filings must be rinsed in water before using. Take ½ wineglassful twice every day. As a remedy in anaemia or stomach troubles, this preparation will be found efficacious.

No. 55—WHEY.

Ingredients.

1 qt. of milk   1½ tsps. of lemon juice   2 tbsps. of sugar

Preparation: Put the lemon juice into the milk, warm up slowly and when curdled, pour through a thin cloth and sweeten with sugar.

No. 56—WARM MILK WITH COGNAC.

Quantity for 1 tumblerful.

½ pt. of milk   Yolk of an egg   Rind of ¼ of a lemon
3 tbsps. of cognac   2½ tbsps. of sugar

Preparation: Warm the milk with the lemon rind, pour through a sieve, add the yolk of an egg, sugar and cognac, put on the stove and beat to a froth; serve while hot.

No. 57—YOLK OF EGG AND WINE.
Ingredients.
Yolk of an egg
3 tbsps. of sugar
2 tbsps. of Tokay wine
1 tbsp. of cognac

Preparation: Beat the yolk of an egg and the sugar to a foam, and mix with the Tokay wine and the cognac.

No. 58—CREAM OF ALMONDS AS A BEVERAGE.
Ingredients.
¼ lb. of sweet almonds
1 qt. of water or milk
1/10 lb. of sugar
1 tbsp. of orange-flower water

Preparation: Blanch the almonds and let them lie in cold water for 24 hours, then crush them very finely and mix with the water or milk; at the expiration of about 4 hours, pour through a fine cloth and mix with the sugar and the orange-flower water; the latter can be omitted.

No. 59—MILK LEMONADE.
Ingredients.
½ pt. of water   ¼ lb. of sugar   ½ qt. of milk
3 tbsps. of lemon juice   ¼ pt. of white wine

Preparation: Boil the water with the sugar, add milk, lemon juice and white wine, bring the lemonade to a boil, then pass through a fine sieve or cloth and set in a cold place.

No. 60—TOAST AND WATER.
Quantity for 1 Quart.
¼ lb. of rye bread   1 qt. of water   1 tbsp. of lemon juice
3 tbsps. of sugar   1 pinch of salt

Preparation: Hold the bread over the fire with a toasting fork until thoroughly toasted, cut into small cubes and pour boiling water over it. When cool, pour the water through a sieve and season with lemon juice and sugar.

No. 61—BARLEY WATER.
Ingredients.
¼ lb. of barley   1 qt. of water   1 pinch of salt

Preparation: Rinse the barley carefully, dry it thoroughly with a cloth and put it in the oven to roast. Grind the barley after it is roasted, put it into the water and boil for 2 hours until smooth and thick, using an earthenware utensil for this purpose; then rub through a fine sieve. Add a little sugar when serving. Can be mixed with any kind of wine or fruit juice.

No. 62—APPLE DRINK.
Quantity for 1 Quart.

1½ lbs. of sweet-sour apples 1 tbsp. of lemon juice
¾ qt. of water ⅛ lb. of sugar
¾ pt. of white wine

Preparation: Clean away the bud-end of the apples, cut the fruit into pieces and boil slowly in the ¾ quart of water until quite soft; after cooking, rub through a thin cloth, add the white wine, sugar and lemon juice. Serve this beverage either hot or cold.

No. 63—WATER WITH LEMON JUICE.
Quantity for 1 Quart.

1 qt. of water 1 cupful of sugar
Rind of 1 lemon 4 tbsps. of sherry wine

Preparation: Put the thinly pared rind of a lemon into boiling water and cover. When cold, pass through a sieve and mix into it the sugar and sherry.

The following Recipe belongs under Chapter 8 and is an omission from page 151:

No. 61—SALMON STEAK.
Quantity for 6 Persons.

2½—3 lbs. of salmon in 6 slices 2 medium sized onions
9 tsps. of lemon juice 1 bunch of parsley
Pepper 12 tbsps. of fine oil Salt

Preparation: The steaks should be cut in 6 neat medium sized pieces from the middle of the fish, sprinkle with salt and pepper, pour 1½ tablespoonfuls of lemon juice on each steak, the onion must be thinly sliced, and the slices put on the steaks, also the parsley; then spread 1 tablespoonful of oil on each steak and let them lie for 1½ hours; get cooking utensil very hot, then remove the onions and parsley from each slice of fish, spread another tablespoonful of oil on each and broil for 5 minutes. Serve on a hot platter and garnish with lemon slices and parsley. An olive sauce should be served with this dish.

CHAPTER 26.

MISCELLANEOUS.

Treatment of Burns. — Meat Carving. — Carving of Poultry in the Kitchen. — Time Required for Broiling, or for Frying in a Pan with Butter, Fat or Both, Small Cuts of Meat. — Time Required for Meats on the Stove or in the Oven. — Roasting. — Roasting in the pan — Frying. — Broiling. — Roasting in the Oven. — Flour. — Yeast. — Table of Comparison.

TREATMENT OF BURNS.

Since it often happens that you burn yourself while cooking and baking, I shall give some methods of treating the wounds.

There are various kinds of burns:

1. When the surface is burned and a burning pain sets in, make cold water applications or compresses of raw grated potatoes or lime water.

2. When the burn causes swelling and blisters, put on cotton batting dipped in olive oil or the following mixture: equal parts of lime water and linseed oil and a little thymol. Shake it well before using.

3. When the heat has destroyed the lower skin and the epidermis rises in large blisters filled with a dark, bloody fluid. When the patient has fever and nervous symptoms.

4. When the skin is completely destroyed and black, and the patient has fever.

As a remedy for the last two cases use a mixture of carbolic acid and water and apply it with cotton batting. For healing use white vaseline, 20 grams; provence oil, 10 grams; glycerine, 50 grams; mix well and spread on the wounds.

MEAT CARVING.

In order to carve meat properly it is necessary to know something about the anatomy of meat, muscles, tendons and the skeleton.

The simplest carving is on meat without bones, as beef steak and roast meat. Hold the meat with a large fork and cut across the grain or fiber in not too thin slices. The knife must be held a little on the slant.

Fricandeau of veal or fillet both have all the fibers running in the same direction, so find out how they run and cut against the grain or across the fiber.

For roast beef without bones the same must be observed. Mark carefully that the vertebrae in the roast are chopped in two. Cut thin slices from the whole width of the roast, fat and all, and pour a little of the drippings over to make them juicy.

Leg of veal, mutton or game is carved on one side, first beginning at the chump end of loin. Perpendicular and rather thick slices are carved.

The English way is to cut horizontal and very thin slices.

Venison is carved in slanting slices to keep the larded pieces together.

In carving ham you begin at the middle and cut around the bone.

To carve a saddle of lamb or veal or other meat requires some skill. Hold the meat with the fork and make deep cuts along the backbone, then place the knife in from below and shove it forward. In this way you carve the meat from the ribs. Make slanting slices.

It is advisable to carve poultry in the kitchen.

CARVING OF POULTRY IN THE KITCHEN.

When poultry is the main course you cut larger pieces than if it were served in ragout, or with vegetables or as a side dish.

Small birds, like quail or larks are served whole on toast and are not carved.

Partridges, hazelhens, spring chickens and pigeons are cut in half when they are the main course. With a poultry shears they are cut lengthwise and the two halves placed together again and covered with a hot gravy. When they are a side dish, they are quartered and the backbones cut out. When they are fried, the breast is carved into 3 parts.

Turkeys, ducks, geese, chickens, pheasants and woodcocks when fried are carved in the same way. The drumsticks or legs are cut around the hip joint and then the joint separated. The wings with some breastmeat are cut off. The meat on the breast is carved from either side of the breastbone and cut into desirable pieces. When serving, place them together again to make the breast appear whole. The legs are also cut into two or three pieces and replaced before serving.

TIME REQUIRED FOR BROILING, OR FOR FRYING IN A PAN WITH BUTTER, FAT OR BOTH, SMALL CUTS OF MEAT.

	Time minutes.	Turn times.
1 loin beef steak, ½ lb.	6	4
1 chopped beef steak, ¼ lb.	6	5
1 round steak, ¼ inch slices	2	2
1 round steak, 1 inch slices	7	6
1 veal steak from leg, 1 lb. in ¾ inch slices	12	6
1 Vienna schnitzel, ¼ lb., breaded	6	2
1 breaded veal cutlet, ¼ lb.	6	2
1 lamb chop, 1/5 lb.	2	2
1 breaded pork chop, ¼ lb.	8	4
1 cutlet from leg of venison, ⅛ lb.	4	4
1 breaded oyster	1	1
1 meat ball, ⅛ lb., 1 inch thick	6	4

TIME REQUIRED FOR MEATS ON THE STOVE OR IN THE OVEN.

	Pounds.	Hours.
Beef rib roast	4	1¼
Roast beef, rolled	4	1½
Pot roast	5	2½
Sour roast (Sauerbraten)	5	2½—3
Leg of veal	5	2
Filled breast of veal	4	1½—2
Saddle of veal	4	1
Leg of lamb	3½	1¾
Saddle of lamb	4	1
Young chicken	2	½
Young chicken	3—4	¾
Older chicken	4	1½
Young turkey	10	2
Older turkey	10	3
Young capon	5½	1½
Older capon	5½	2
Ham	10	4
Roast pork	5	3
Pork tenderloin	1	2/3
1 squab filled	..	1
1 duck	5	2
1 fat goose filled	10	2¼—2½
1 young goose	8	1½

ROASTING.

Roasting means the rapid confining of the meat's juices by coagulating the albumen in the surface tissues, the slow changing of the outer layers into a brown palatable crust, dissolving of the natural fats of the meat, changing the albumen gradually to a semi-fluid form and loosening and breaking up the fibers by steam generated in the mass of the meat. Roasting may be done on a stove in a pan, or over the open fire on a spit, or in an oven.

ROASTING IN THE PAN—FRYING.

Heat a clean pan, put in the fat of the meat or butter and heat it; the fat must be steaming and the butter have a light brown color before the meat is put into the pan. Fat and butter mixed may also be used.

Beef steak, veal, mutton or pork chops, liver, pork or veal steak, etc., are cut into uniformly thick slices; the time for frying is estimated according to the average weight of the pieces. Do not salt too soon as this will draw out the juice. Breading must be done immediately before frying, otherwise the juices of the meat will be drawn out and the breading will not hold.

Do not leave meat on boards, as the juices will be absorbed by the wood; it is better to put meat on china. The pieces of meat, the largest first are placed in the hot fat with a cake turner, not with a fork, and take note of the time when beginning. Never put so much meat into the pan at one time as to cool the fat and stop its sizzling. After every three pieces stop long enough to give the fat a chance to heat up.

When several pieces of meat are in the pan, they must be turned in the order in which they were put in, baste frequently with the fat or butter in the pan and turn often.

When done, the meat must be well browned but not hard on the outside, and be reddish and tender inside. Stabbing the meat with a fork is not advisable for two reasons. In the first place the juice will run out and the meat will be dry, and then the meat will begin to stew in the juice and the temperature of the fat will be reduced, the meat will not turn brown; breaded meat loses the breading or this will be soft. Washed meat must be well dried with a clean cloth before breading. When fried meat is pale and colorless, it has been either fried in too low a temperature or was stabbed with a fork or was not well dried before frying.

BROILING.

Flat pieces of meat only are suitable for broiling, the fire must be a fairly hot one, all coals aglowing. The broiler is greased with a bit of bacon or suet and heated over the fire. Lay on the pounded slices of meat and as soon as the same begins to blister, turn with a cake turner. The meat must be rich and not too lean. The meat is seasoned after broiling and hot butter may be poured over it before serving.

ROASTING IN THE OVEN.

In Germany roasts made in the oven are preferred on account of the desired gravies.

Roast beef, fillet of beef, mutton, game and small birds require comparatively little time for roasting, but a uniformly hot oven.

Veal, lamb, turkey and goose roasts require a longer time but only a moderate heat. For roasting use only meats from full grown, but not old, animals. The cellular walls of the muscle tissues must be still tender and filled with juice. In older animals the tissues become harder and less juicy and such meat is better suited for stewing than for roasting. Meats for roasting should be 2 to 3 days old and ought to be slightly pounded.

FLOUR.

Good nutritive flour has a yellowish tinge on account of the nutritive gluten contained therein; flour must not be gray, for this color denotes impurities. The whiter the flour the larger is the proportion of starch and smaller the proportion of albuminous substances. To test flour, put some of it on a bluish white sheet of paper, where color, finish and grain can be distinguished.

The finest brands of flour have less albumen than others, because this is distributed near the outer shell, which is removed. Good flour possesses a certain degree of cohesiveness which can be observed when pressing some of it in the hand; poor flour acts like dust.

Flour made of grain not thoroughly seasoned is not well adapted for gravies and baking. Adulterations and mixtures of good and poor flour are easily detected in cooking and baking as the gravies are thinner and cakes are liable to fall.

To keep large quantities of flour, the same must be placed high in a covered wooden box in an airy place, so that the moisture of the floor and air, which is deleterious, may not affect it. Flour must be turned and sifted often.

YEAST.

Compressed yeast is the best to use; it must be fresh and to obtain the best results in baking, the same must have an odor of fine brandy or fruit and not smell cheesy or sour. Yeast must have a yellowish white color, must be moist and break up in lumps, not like dust. To retain activity, yeast must not be subjected to heat or great cold.

To obtain the best results in baking, the yeast needs careful attention, drafts must be avoided and the baking room must be warm.

NOTICE.

Wherever the use of wine in recipes is prescribed and cannot be obtained, take Ginger Ale.

Weights and Measures Most Commonly Used in the Art of Cooking.

EUROPE AND THE UNITED STATES.

COPYRIGHT 1922, BY C N. CASPAR CO, MILWAUKEE, WIS.

NOTE—*The Metric System is used in all civilized countries except the United States and Great Britain and has also in the Art of Cooking great advantages compared with the out-of-date Weights and Measures used in the United States.*

For practical purposes, consider one kilogram 2 Pounds U. S. and one liter = Quart U. S.

The following conversion tables present a practical selection of Weights and Measures most commonly used in Europe and the United States.

```
1 Kilogram (kg.).. = 1000 Gram = *2 Pounds (United States)
½ Kilogram........ =  500 Gram = *1 Pound   (    "       "    )
1 German Pound..  =  500 Gram = *1 Pound   (    "       "    )
1 Liter      (l.).... =  1 Quart (qt.) = *8 Jelly glasses (medium)
½ Liter............. =  1 Pint  (pt.)
1 Deciliter (dl.).... =  1 Gill  (gi.) = Vol. of 1¾ Diam. by 3 in. high.
```

THEREFORE:

```
1 Kilogram or Kilo . = * 2 Pounds (United States)
500 Gram............ = * 1 Pound   (    "       "    )
250 Gram............ = * ½ Pound   (    "       "    )
125 Gram............ = * ¼ Pound   (    "       "    )
```

POPULAR MEASURES

```
 2 Gram............ = *1 Thimble   full        ⎫
 4 Gram............ = *1 Teaspoon  struck      │ Rice, Farina, Barley
 6 Gram............ = *1    "      heaped      ⎬ Starch, Sugar
25 Gram............ = *1 Tablespoon struck     │
30 Gram............ = *1    "      heaped      ⎭
```
50 to 60 Gram butter = *1 Tablespoon well rounded (*Eidick* = size of an egg)

¼ Pound { Metric or / Unit. States } Flour........ = *2 Teacups (small cups)

¼ Pound { Metric or / Unit. States } { Raisins / Almonds } = *1½ Teacups

1 German Pound (Metric) = *1 Pound 1½ Ounces (United States)
1 German Pound......... = *1⅛ U. S. Pounds
1 United States Pound.... = * ⅞ German Pounds = 16 Ounces

The sign * means approximately

GRAM AND OUNCES COMPARED

United States	Metric	United States	Metric
1 Ounce	28 Grams	9 Ounces	255 Grams
2 Ounces	57 Grams	10 Ounces	283 Grams
3 Ounces	85 Grams	11 Ounces	312 Grams
4 Ounces	113 Grams	12 Ounces	340 Grams
5 Ounces	142 Grams	13 Ounces	369 Grams
6 Ounces	170 Grams	14 Ounces	397 Grams
7 Ounces	198 Grams	15 Ounces	425 Grams
8 Ounces	227 Grams	16 Ounces	454 Grams

Gram	Ounces	Dram	kilogram	Pounds	Ounces
1	1/32	1/2	1	2	3
2	1/16	1	..	..	..
3	3/32	1½	2	4	7
4	1/8	2	..	..	..
5	5/32	2½	3	6	10
6	3/16	3	..	..	..
7	7/32	3½	4	8	13
8	1/4	4	..	..	..
9	9/32	4½	5	11	..
10	5/16	5			
			10	22	..

WEIGHTS (old and new) USED PARTICULARLY IN SOUTHERN GERMANY (INCLUDING AUSTRIA)

1 Vienna Pound = 32 *Loth*   1 Vienna Pound ... = 56 *Deka* = 560 Gram
1 Vienna *Loth* .. = 17½ Gram   1 *Deka* (Dekagram) .... = 10 Gram
1 Vienna *Loth* .. = 5/8 Ounce   1 *Deka* .... = *3/8 Ounce

1 Kilogram (kg.) .... = 1000 Gram = 2 German Pounds (Metric)
 = *1¼ Vienna Pounds
1 Vienna Pound .... = 560 Gram = 1⅛ German Pounds @ 500 Gram
 = *1¼ Pounds (United States)
1 German Pound (Metric). = 500 Gram = 7/8 Vienna Pounds...........
 = *1⅛ United States Pounds

1 Kilogram or Kilo .... = 100 *Deka* (Dekagram)
1 Liter .... (l.) = 10 Deciliter
1 Deciliter .... (dl.) = 10 Centiliter = ¼ Pint

1 Tablespoon struck .... = 1 Centiliter

1 *Deka* .... = *10   Gram = * 3/8 Ounces = 6 Dram
1 *Loth* .... = * 17½ Gram = * 5/8 Ounces = 10 Dram
1 Gram .... = ... = *1/32 Ounce = ½ Dram

The sign * means approximately.

GRAM AND OUNCES COMPARED

OLD Loth	METRIC Deka & Gram		Gram	United States Lb.	Ounces	OLD Loth	METRIC Deka & Gram		Gram	United States Lb.	Ounces
1	1	7½	17½	..	⅝	17	29	7½	297½	..	10⅝
2	3	5	35	..	1¼	18	31	5	315	..	11¼
3	5	2½	52½	..	1⅞	19	33	2½	332½	..	11⅞
4	7	...	70	..	2½	20	35	...	350	..	12½
5	8	7½	87½	..	3⅛	21	36	7½	367½	..	13⅛
6	10	5	105	..	3¾	22	38	5	385	..	13¾
7	12	2½	122½	..	4⅜	23	40	2½	402½	..	14⅜
9	15	7½	157½	..	5⅝	24	42	...	420	..	15
9	15	7½	157	..	5⅝	25	43	7½	437½	..	15⅝
10	17	5	175	..	6¼	26	45	5	455	1	...
11	19	1½	191½	..	6⅞	27	47	2½	472½	1	⅞
12	21	...	210	..	7½	28	49	...	490	1	1½
13	22	7½	227½	..	8⅛	29	50	7½	507½	1	2⅛
14	24	5	245	..	8¾	30	52	5	525	1	2¾
15	26	2½	262½	..	9⅜	31	54	2½	542½	1	3⅜
16	28	...	280	..	10	32	56	...	560	1	4

GRAM AND OUNCES COMPARED

U.S. Ounces	Metric Gram	U.S. Ounces	Metric Gram
⅛	4	⅝	18
¼	7	¾	22
⅜	11	⅞	25
½	14	1	28

DRY MEASURES

TEASPOON and TABLESPOON

1 Teaspoon Sugar—heaped .... =* 1 Ounce

1 Tablespoon { Rice, Farina, Sugar / Flour, Starch } heaped .... =* 1 Ounce

1 Tablespoon Butter—well rounded .... =* 1¾ Ounces

CUP OR GLASS (medium)

1	Cup or Glass (medium)			Sugar	=* 1 Pound
2½	"	"	"	" Sugar—pulverized	=* 1 Pound
3	"	"	"	" Farina	=* 1 Pound
3½	"	"	"	" Flour (wheat)	=* 1 Pound
2	"	"	"	" Butter	=* 1 Pound

PINT:

1 Pint Sugar .... =* 1 Pound
1½ " Flour (wheat) .... =* 1 Pound

The sign * means approximately.

UNITED STATES MEASURES

1 Gill (gil.)	= ¼ Pint	= 8⅖	cubic inches	= 0.1376 Liter
1 Pint (pt.)	= ½ Quart	= 33⅗	" "	= 0.5506 Liter
1 Quart (qt.)	= 2 Pints	= 67⅕	" "	= 1.1012 Liter
1 Peck (pk.)	= 8 Quarts	= 537⅝	" "	= 8.810 Liter
1 Bushel (bu.)	= 4 Pecks	= 2150 7/16	" "	= 36.3477 Liter
1 Gallon (gal.)	=	= 268⅘	" "	

NOTE:—Dry Measures are about ⅙ larger than liquid measures.

1 Bushel=4 Pk.; 1 Bushel, heaped=5 Pk.; 4 Bushel, heaped=5 Bu., struck

LIQUID MEASURES

UNITED STATES MEASURES

1 Gill (gi.)	= ¼ Pint	= 7 7/32 cu. in.		= 0.1183 Liter
1 Pint (pt.)	= ½ Quart	= 4 Gills	= 28⅞ cu. in.	= 0.473 Liter
1 Quart (qt.)	= 2 Pints	= 8 Gills	= 57¾ " "	= 0.946 Liter
1 Gallon (gal.)	= 4 Quarts	= 8 Pints	= 231 " "	= 3.785 Liter

1 Liter = 10 Deciliter = 100 Centiliter = 1000 Milliliter

1 Liter = 0.908 Dry Quart = 1.0567 Liquid Quart
1 Dry Quart = 1⅛ Liquid Quart
1 Liquid Quart = ⅞ Dry Quart

OLD GERMAN WEIGHTS AND MEASURES (After 1834)

1 *Zollpfund* (German Pound) = 30 *Loth* = 500 Gram
= * 17½ Ounces = * 1 Pound 1½ oz.

1 *Loth*...................... = 10 *Quentchen* = 16.66 Gram
= * ½ Ounce

1 *Quentchen*.................................. = 1.66 Gram
= * 1/20 Ounce

1 *Quentchen* = 1 Thimblefull

Southern Germany, including Austria:

1 Vienna Pound. = 32 *Loth* = 560 Gram = * 1¼ Pound (U. S.)
1 *Loth* (Vienna) = ... = 17½ Gram = * ⅝ Ounce (U. S.)

1 Vienna Pound........... = 56 *Deka*
1 *Deka* (Dekagram)....... = 10 Gram

1 *Neuloth*.. = 4 Vienna *Loth* = 7 *Deka* = * 2½ Ounces (U. S.)

1 *Unze* (German Ounce) — 1/16 German Pound (Metric)
= * 1/12 Troy Pound = * 30 Gram = * 1 Ounce (U. S.)

1 German Pound (*Zollpfund*) = ⅞ Vienna Pound
1 Vienna Pound............ = 1⅛ German Pound

1 *Scheffel* = { 16 *Metzen* (Prussia, Saxony) / 6 *Metzen* (Bavaria) } = 53 Liter = * 1½ Bushels (U. S.)

1 *Metze* .... = * .... = * 3½ Liter = 3 Quarts (U. S.)

1 *Mass*
1 *Quart*, *Quartier*
1 *Kanne*
.... = * 15/16 Liter = 1 Quart (U. S.)

1 *Schoppen* .... = ½ Liter = * 1 Pint (U. S.)

1 *Nössel*
1 *Töpfchen*
.... = ½ *Kanne* .... = ½ Liter = * 1 Pint (U. S.)

The sign * means approximately.

INDEX.

	Page.
Preface	3
Reliable Weights and Measures	4

Chapter 1, Nos. 1—68.
SOUPS.

	No.	Page.
Apple Soup	50	19
Asparagus Soup with Bouillon.	38	15
Barley Gruel Soup	26	12
" Soup with Bouillon	25	11
" Soup with Bouillon.	24	11
Bean-Puree Soup with Crab or Lobster Butter	34	14
Bean Soup with Bouillon	33	13
Beer Soup	49	19
Bouillon	1—2	5
" made of Roast Bones or Meat Remnants	6	6
Bouillon	1—6	5
" of Meat Extract	4	5
" Rice Soup with Tomatoes	21	10
Breadsticks for Bouillon	16	9
Butter-Dumpling Soup	8	6
Buttermilk Soup or Sour Milk Soup	67	25
Cauliflower Soup with Bouillon	39	15
Celery Soup with Milk	41	16
Cheesesticks for Bouillon	17	9
Cheese Pastry	18	9
Chicken Bouillon to drink	59	22
" Soup	62	23
Chocolate Soup	55	21
Cold Rice Soup with Apples	23	11
Crawfish or Crab Soup with Marrow-Dumplings or Liver-Dumplings	57	22
Curdle Soup	14	8
Dumplings for Bouillon, Marrow-Dumpling Soup	7	6
Farina-Dumpling Soup	12	7
" Soup with Bouillon	30	13
Fish Soup with Fish-Dumplings	56	21
Flour Dumplings	19	10
" Soup (Wheat)	52	20
Fresh Vegetable Soup with Bouillon	37	15
Green Corn Soup with Bouillon	31	13
Lentil Soup	36	14
Liver-Dumpling Soup	9	7
Marrowstrips for Soup	15	8
Meat-Dumpling Soup	10	7
Milk Soup	54	21
Mock-Turtle Soup	44	17
Oatmeal Soup	32	13
Ox-tail Bouillon	3	5
Oyster Soup	58	22
Oysterplant Soup	68	26
Partridge Soup	63	24
Pea Soup with Bouillon	35	14
Pigeon Bouillon to drink	60	23
" Soup	61	23
Potato Soup	46	18
" " with Bouillon	45	18
Red Wine Soup	48	19
" " " with Sago	65	24

	No.	Page.
Rice Soup with Bouillon	20	10
" " with Milk	22	10
Rye Bread Soup	51	20
" Flour Soup	53	20
Sago Soup with Bouillon	28	12
" " with Red Wine or Raspberry Juice	29	12
Sorrel Soup with Bouillon	40	16
Sponge-Dumpling Soup	11	7
Stirred Sponge-Dumplings	13	8
Sweet Barley Gruel Soup	27	12
Tomato Soup	42	16
" " with Milk	43	17
" " with Small Meat or Potato-Dumplings	66	25
White Wine Soup	47	18
Wild Game or Poultry Soup	64	24

Chapter 2, Nos. 1—36.
BEEF.

	No.	Page.
Beef Cutlets of Roastbeef	18	36
" Fillet Beefsteak	4	29
" " Roast	3	29
" " Steaks with Champignons and fried Gooseliver	5	30
Beef Gulash	16	35
" Hash	20	37
" Pot Roast	11	33
" Roulade	15	35
" Salad	24	38
" with Onions	22	37
Boiled Beef	19	36
Boiled Beef Slices fried with Eggs and Onions	23	37
Braised Beef Slices	12	33
Broiled Steak of Roast Beef	6	30
Chopped German Steak or Hamburg Steak	8	31
Chop Suey	36	43
Corned Beef	30	40
" " for Cooking	31	40
Cow Udder	29	40
Croquettes	25	38
Fillet Beefsteak for Breakfast	10	32
Fried Beef Liver with Breakfast Bacon	28	39
Hash with Potatoes	21	37
Königsberger Klops	27	39
Meat Pudding— How to Utilize Roast Beef. Roastbeef with Rice Covering	2	28
Meat Pudding No. 2	26	39
Pickled Beef Tongue	33	41
Ragout of Ox Tongue	35	42
Raw Beefsteak a la Tartare	9	32
Roast Beef	1	28
Roasted Rib-Piece	13	33
Smoked Corned Beef	32	41
" Pickled or Fresh Beef for Cooking and Frying	34	41
Sour Roast	14	34
Steak from the Beef Round	7	31
Steamed Beef-Brisket	17	35

Chapter 3, Nos. 1—42.

VEAL.

	No.	Page.
Breaded Veal Chops	22	55
" " Cutlets	19	53
Breast of Veal with Beer	12	50
Calf's Brains	15	51
" Head Ragout	13	50
" Tongue	14	51
Chopped Veal Cutlets	21	54
Croquettes from Veal Remnants	31	59
" of Sweetbreads	30	58
Stuffed Breast of Veal	11	49
Larded and Baked Calf's Liver	36	61
" Braised Calf's Liver	37	61
Leg of Veal	1	45
Liver Dumplings	34	60
Meat Balls from Veal Remnants	32	59
Puff-Paste Patties filled with Sweetbread Ragout	29	58
Roasted Fricandeau of Veal	10	49
Roast Veal Loin with Kidney	9	49
Saddle of Veal	8	48
Shells filled with Veal Roast	5	47
Stewed Veal or Calf's Tongue with Raisins	41	63
Stuffed Veal Crown Roast	42	63
Sweetbreads	27	57
" in Shells or other Small Molds	28	57
Unbreaded Veal Cutlets (Chops)	18	53
Veal Cutlets as a fine Side-Dish	20	54
" " in White Wine	25	56
" " or Schnitzel a la Holstein	24	55
Veal Fricassee	16	52
" Gulash	17	52
" Hash from Remnants	33	60
Veal Kidneys	38	62
" " with Bread or Rolls	39	62
" or Calf's Liver with Breakfast Bacon	35	60
Veal or Calf's Tripe	40	62
" Roast Pudding	6	47
" " Ragout — Brown	4	46
" " Salad	7	48
" " with Potatoes	3	46
" Steak from the Leg	26	56
Vienna Veal-Schnitzel (Veal Cutlets)	23	55
Warmed up Veal Roast	2	45

Chapter 4, Nos. 1—32.

MUTTON.

	No.	Page.
Baked Mutton Kidneys	19	71
Breaded Lamb Roast	28	75
Broiled Breaded Mutton Chops	15	70
Irish Stew. Mutton Cutlets in all kinds of Vegetables and Potatoes	18	71
Lamb Crown Roast	32	76
" Roast	27	74
" Stew	30	76
Larded Saddle of Mutton, Mock Venison	7	67
Leg of Mutton, English Style	1	65
" " " in Milk	2	65
" " " with Red Wine	3	66
Mutton Chops with Potatoes	16	70
" Cutlets Broiled	14	69
" " or Chops	13	69
" Kidney Pudding	20	72
" or Lamb Ragout	29	75
" Pie	25	73
" " Prepared Simply	26	74
" Ragout	21	72
" Roast Salad	24	73
" Steak	12	69
" Stew	6	67
" Stew with White Cabbage	11	69
" Tenderloin	9	68
" with Pickles	23	73
" with Potatoes	22	72
Plain Ragout of Mutton or Lamb	31	76
Roasted Leg of Mutton with Champignons	4	66
Saddle of Mutton a la English Style	8	68
Stewed Mutton Cutlets	17	70
" Rack of Mutton	10	68
Stuffed Roasted Leg of Mutton	5	67

Chapter 5, Nos. 1—35.

PORK.

	No.	Page.
Boiled Ham with Macaroni	13	82
" " " Noodles	12	82
Braised Pork Roast	4	79
Breaded Ham	14	82
" Leg of Pork	3	79
Cabbage Sausages	30	89
Chopped Pork Cutlets	18	84
Fresh Young Leg of Pork for Roast	2	78
Fried Ham with Eggs	11	81
" Sausage	26	87
" Sausages	28	88
Ham in Burgundy Wine	10	81
Meat Salting and Pickling	34	90
Mock-Rabbit	22	85
Pickled Ham	35	90
Pork Kidneys	20	85
" Ragout or Pork Pepper	21	85
" Ribs and Sauerkraut	24	87
" Stew	6	80
" Roast	1	78
Roasted Pork Cutlets	17	84
" Pork-Fillet	15	83
Sausage	25	87
Sausages	27	88
Salt Pork or Hip-bone for stew	7	80
Smoked Ham Boiled, Breaded with Rye Bread Crumbs	9	80
Smoked Ham for Cooking	8	80
Sour Pork Roast	5	79
Spanferkel or Roast Little Pig	31	89
" a la French Style	33	90
Stewed Pork Cutlets	19	84
Stuffed Hog's Head	23	86
" Pork-Fillet called Mock Duck	16	83
Stuffed Spanferkel or Roast Little Pig	32	89
White Cabbage Pie with Pork	29	88

Chapter 6, Nos. 1—56.
POULTRY AND GAME BIRDS.

	No.	Page.
Blackbirds	43	110
Chicken Croquettes	9	95
" or Pigeon Cutlet	12	90
" Pie	6	94
" " English Style	13	97
" Ragout in Shells or other small Molds	8	95
Duck Ragout	56	115
Fat Goose Stuffed with Apples	21	100
" " " " Chestnuts	22	101
Fine Chicken Fricassee	10	95
" Ragout of Partridge	42	109
Fried Capon Ragout	51	113
" Duck Liver	31	105
" Goose Liver	23	101
" Old Pheasant	34	106
" Partridge	40	109
" Pheasant	33	105
" Pigeon	15	98
" Pigeons with Sweet Stuffing	17	98
Fried Snipes	45	111
" Woodcock	47	112
" Woodcock, Another Form of	48	112
Goose and Duck Schwartz-sauer	32	105
" Giblets	24	101
" Liver Pie	25	102
" Liver Pudding	26	102
Grouse Pie	39	108
Leipzig Larks	44	111
Old or Young Chicken with Rice	5	93
Partridge with Sauerkraut	41	109
Pheasant Patties in Shells or other Small Molds	35	106
Pheasant Pie	37	107
Pigeon Pie, English Style	14	97
Poulard Fricassee	55	115
Puff-Paste Patties, Filled with Chicken Ragout	7	94
Red Grouse and Guinea Hen	38	108
" " Cutlets	53	114
Roast Capons	50	113
" Duck	29	104
" Poulard	54	114
" Spring Chicken	1	91
" Turkey	18	99
" Wild Duck	49	112
Roasted and Stuffed Turkey	19	99
" Wild Goose	27	103
" Young Goose	20	100
Smoked Goose Breast	28	103
Snipe on Toast	46	111
Stewed Capon	52	113
" Chicken with Champignons	4	93
" Pheasant	36	107
Stuffed Chicken, Another Form of	3	92
Stuffed Duck, Another Form of	30	104
" Roasted Chickens	2	92
" Fried Pigeons	16	98
Vienna Baked Chicken	11	96

Chapter 7, Nos. 1—25.
GAME.

	No.	Page.
Chopped Steak of Game. Deer, Doe, Boar or Wild Rabbit Meat is used	10	120
Cold Game Pie. Made from Deer, Doe, Boar or Rabbit Meat	11	120
Deer or Doe Liver	4	118
Domestic Rabbit Roast	23	126
Game Ragout made from Remnants	12	121
Hasenpfeffer (Rabbit Pepper)	19	124
How to Skin a Rabbit	14	122
Lapins	25	127
Leg or Saddle of Wild Boar	13	121
" of Venison	2	117
" " "	8	119
" " " Another Form of	9	119
Rabbit Cutlets	18	123
" Liver	20	125
" Pie	22	125
" Roast	15	122
" Salad	21	125
Roast Saddle of Venison	1	116
Saddle of Venison	7	119
Stuffed Domestic Rabbit Roast	24	126
Stewed Rabbit	16	123
" " Another Form of	17	123
To Carve a Leg of Venison	6	118
Venison Cutlets	3	117
" Ragout	5	118

Chapter 8, Nos. 1—61.
FISH.

	No.	Page.
Baked Eel	12	133
" Gurnet	36	143
" Lobster	52	148
" Red Snapper	22	138
" Sole	35	143
Boiled Codfish	32	142
" Crawfish or Crabs	53	149
" Lobster	48	147
" Red Snapper	26	139
" Salmon	5	131
" " Trout	9	132
" Turbot	24	139
Codfish Hash	42	145
" Ragout	33	142
Cold Eel Roulade	15	134
" Lobster	49	148
Crab Cutlets with Vegetables	54	149
" Ragout	55	150
Eel, Blue	11	133
" in Beer	13	133
" with Rice (Fricassee)	14	134
Fillet of Shellfish, Whitefish, Cabeljou, Sole, with Dressing	29	140
Fish, Boiled	1	129
" Broiled or Roasted	4	130
" Baked	2	129
" Steamed or Stewed	3	130
" and Potato Pudding	40	144
" Croquettes	38	144
" Cutlets	39	144
" Fricassee from Pickerel or Whitefish	19	136

	No.	Page.
Fried Fresh Herring	43	145
" Mackerel	30	141
" Oysters or Clams	58	150
" Smelt or Sparling	28	140
" Sole	34	142
" Trout	10	132
Herring Salad	47	147
Larded and Stuffed Pickerel	17	136
" Pickerel	16	135
Lobster Croquettes or Cutlets.	50	148
" Ragout in Shells or on Toast	51	148
Marinated Salt Herring	45	146
" " " a Simple Way	46	146
Oysters	56	150
Oyster or Clam Pudding with Rice	60	151
Oyster or Clam Salad	59	151
" Patties	57	150
Pickerel or Codfish Salad	21	138
" or Whitefish with Sauerkrant	23	138
Pickerel with Tomato Sauce	20	137
Red Snapper with Red Wine Dressing	27	140
Rolled, Stuffed Fish Fillets	31	141
Salmon, Blue	6	131
" Salad	7	131
" Steak	61	385
Salted Codfish Croquettes	41	145
Sliced Salmon Broiled	8	132
Small Fish Ragouts in Shells or Small Molds; Utilizing Remnants of Fish	37	143
Stuffed and Larded Pike	18	136
To Marinate or Pickle Herring	44	146
Turbot Fricassee	25	139

Chapter 9, Nos. 1—12.

HEAD-CHEESE AND GELATINES.

Eel in Jelly	9	156
Fish in Jelly	8	155
Gelatine or Head-Cheese from Poultry Bouillon	3	153
Goose-Liver in Jelly	12	157
Head-Cheese from Goose or Duck	6	154
Head-Cheese from Ox-Tongue	5	154
" " " Partridge	7	155
" " " Pigs' Feet and Calf's Tongue	4	153
How to Prepare Gelatine	1	152
Meat Gelatine for Patients	2	152
Oysters and Caviar in Jelly	11	157
Salmon in Jelly	10	156

Chapter 10, Nos. 1—58.

DRESSINGS OR GRAVIES.

	No.	Page.
Apricot Sauce	54	174
Arrack Sauce	46	173
Asparagus Gravy	7	161
Bacon Gravy	26	167
Brown Champignon Sauce	28	167
Burgundy or Madeira Sauce for Ham, Fish or Tongue	25	166
Cocoa Sauce	48	173
Caper Sauce	17	164
Cauliflower Gravy	6	161
Cherry, Currant, Blueberry Sauce	57	175
Cherry Sauce	52	174
Chocolate Sauce	49	173
Cold Caviar Dressing	40	171
" Chive Dressing for Beef	39	171
" Herb Dressing	37	170
" Mustard Dressing for Cold Lamb or Veal Roast	35	170
Cold Remoulade Dressing, very fine	38	171
Cooked Mayonnaise Dressing, very good with Lobster or Chicken Salad	43	172
Crab or Lobster Gravy for Fish, Chicken and Fricassee	19	164
Dill, Chive or Tarragon Gravy.	32	169
Dutch Gravy	2	159
Fine Bearnaise Sauce, for Fillets, Saddle of Mutton, Mutton Cutlets	10	162
Fine Dutch Gravy for Fish or Veal	3	160
Fine Gravy, for Poultry, Meat and Fish	13	163
Fine Mustard Gravy, for Beef and Fish	8	161
Fine Tomato Dressing	12	162
Fruit Puree Sauce	58	175
Good Fish Gravy	5	160
Herb Gravy	27	167
Horse Radish Dressing, Raw	15	163
" " Gravy	14	163
Lemon Sauce	50	174
Maraschino Sauce	51	174
Mayonnaise Dressing No. 1 (Cold)	41	171
Mayonnaise Dressing No. 2	42	172
Mayonnaise Dressing No. 3 for Poultry Salad	44	172
Morel Sauce	30	168
Oil Dressing a la Tartare, for Hard Boiled Eggs, Cold Beef and Head-Cheese	34	169
Onion Gravy, for Boiled Beef	22	165
Oyster Dressing	18	164
Parsley Gravy	31	168
Pearl Onion Gravy	23	166
Pickle Gravy	24	166
Plain Mustard Dressing, for Fish and Beef	9	161
Prune Sauce	53	174
Raspberry Sauce	56	175
Remoulade Sauce	20	165
Sardine Gravy, for Meat and Fish	16	163
Sorrel Gravy	33	169
Strawberry Sauce	55	174
Whipped Dutch Gravy, for Fish, Asparagus, Cauliflower, Oyster Plants and Scorzonera	4	183
Tartare Dressing	36	170
Tomato Gravy	11	162
Truffle Sauce	29	168
Vanilla Sauce	47	173

—399—

	No.	Page.
Whipped Dutch Gravy, for Fish Asparagus, Cauliflower, Oyster Plants and Scorzonera	4	160
White Fricassee Sauce, for Chicken or Veal Fricassee	21	165
White Gravy	1	159
White Wine Sauce	45	172

Chapter 11, Nos. 1—26.

POTATOES.

	No.	Page.
Baked Potatoes	3	176
" Potato Pudding	15	180
Bouillon Potatoes	18	181
Creamed Potatoes	14	180
French Fried Potatoes, Pomme Souffle	8	178
Fried Raw Potatoes	21	182
New Potatoes in their Jackets.	2	176
Parsley Potatoes	7	177
Peeled Potatoes	4	177
Potato Balls, Fried	12	179
" Chips	9	178
" Croquettes	11	179
" Dumplings from Boiled Potatoes	23	182
Potato Dumplings, Another kind of	24	183
Potatoes in their Skins or Jackets	1	176
Potato Pancakes	17	180
Potatoes with Crackers	20	182
Raw Potato-Dumplings	25	183
Sardine or Herring Potatoes..	19	181
Small Potato Balls, for Fish...	5	177
Sour Potatoes	13	179
Steamed Potato Pudding	16	180
Stuffed Potatoes	10	178
Sweet Potatoes	22	182
Utilizing Remnants of Potato-Dumplings	26	184
Utilizing Remnants of Potato Balls, Mashed Potatoes	6	177

Chapter 12, Nos. 1—74.

VEGETABLES.

	No.	Page.
Asparagus	8	187
" and Cauliflower Omelet	23	192
" with Brown Butter..	1	185
" with Cream Dressing	3	186
" with Creamed Butter	2	185
Artichokes with Butter	13	189
Beets	51	200
Brussels Sprouts	32	194
" " Another Way of Preparing	33	194
Canned Artichokes	15	189
" Asparagus	4	186
" Green Beans	47	199
" Sweet-sour Beans	50	199
" Wax Beans	48	199
Cauliflower	9	187
" with Butter Sauce..	10	188
" with Crab or Lobster Dressing	11	188
Champignon Puree	63	204
Champignons	62	203
Chanterelles, Another Species of Mushrooms	68	205
Chestnut Puree	73	207
Filled or Stuffed Olives with Champignons	71	206
Fried Chestnuts	74	207
French Asparagus with Cream Dressing	5	186
Fresh Green Peas	19	191
" " " Another Way	20	191
" " " and Carrots.	26	192
" " " with Crab Meat	21	192
" Wax Beans	49	199
Gardi and Finocci as Vegetables.	60	203
Green Asparagus	7	187
" String Beans, Prepared Another Way	45	198
Kale or Borecole	34	195
Kohlrabi	41	197
Lettuce	29	193
Marrow Peas	24	192
Mixed or Leipzig Vegetables..	61	203
Morels	66	205
Mushrooms	67	205
Olives as Vegetables	69	206
Oyster Plants, Salsify	17	190
Pea Omelet	22	192
Preserved Asparagus with Cream	6	187
Roasted Chestnuts	72	206
Salted Green Beans	46	198
Savoy Cabbage	31	194
Scalloped Artichokes with Cheese	16	190
" Cauliflower, au gratin.	12	188
Scorzonera	18	190
Sorrel	28	193
Spinach	27	193
" in Individual Molds...	30	193
Stewed Artichokes	14	189
" Cucumbers	58	202
" Green String Beans ..	44	198
" Red Cabbage	35	195
" White Cabbage	37	196
Stuffed Root Celery or Celeriac au jus	59	202
" Cucumbers	57	201
" Olives	70	206
" Onions	53	200
" Tomatoes	55	201
Teltow Turnips	43	197
Tomatoes	54	201
" Filled with Meat	56	201
Truffle Puree	65	204
Truffles in Brown Dressing	64	234
Turnips	42	197
White Cabbage	36	195
" " Prepared like Cauliflower	38	196
" " Sausages	39	196
" " with Lamb	40	197
Young Carrots	25	192
" Onions	52	200

Chapter 13, Nos. 1—47.

SALADS.

	No.	Page.
Asparagus Salad	17	212
" " with Mayonnaise	18	212
Bean Salad	22	213
" "	26	214
Beef Salad	33	216
Carrot Salad	21	212
Cauliflower Salad	19	212
" " with Cooked Mayonnaise	20	212
Celeriac or Root Celery Salad.	23	213
Celery Salad mixed with Potato Salad with Mayonnaise Dressing	24	213
Celery Salad with Mayonnaise Dressing	25	213
Champignon Salad	30	215
Chicken Salad	35	217
Cold Slaw	32	216
Cucumber Salad	10	210
" " with Sour Cream	12	210
Cucumbers and Head Lettuce Mixed	13	211
Fine Mixed Vegetable Salad...	28	214
Fruit Salad No. 1	44	219
" " " 2	45	219
" " " 3	46	219
" " " 4	47	219
" " Dressing	43	219
" " as Dessert	41	218
Green Lettuce	1	208
" " Prepared Sweet, Head Lettuce	5	209
Green Lettuce with Bacon, Head, Endive Lettuce	4	209
Green Lettuce with Egg Dressing	2	208
Green Lettuce with Mayonnaise Dressing, Head, Endive, Escariol Lettuce	3	208
Herring Salad	36	217
Lettuce Combination Salad	42	218
Lobster Salad	40	218
Mixed Salad	27	214
" " with Meat	29	215
Oyster or Clam Salad	39	218
Pike Salad	38	217
Potato Salad	6	209
" " with Bacon	9	210
" " with Sour Cream	8	210
" " with Spiced Dressing	7	209
Rabbit Roast Salad	34	216
Salmon Salad	37	217
Sweet Cucumber Salad	11	210
Tomato Salad	14	211
" " with Cooked Mayonnaise	16	211
Tomato Salad with Mayonnaise Dressing	15	211
Truffle Salad	31	216

Chapter 14, Nos. 1—15.

EGGS.

	No.	Page.
Boiled Eggs in Brine	7	221
Brine Eggs in Cream Sauce	8	221
Fried Eggs	4	220
" " in Tomato Sauce	6	221
Hard Boiled Eggs	2	220
" " " for Garnishing	3	220
Poached Eggs	5	221
Scrambled Egg Pancake	10	222
" " Eggs	9	222
" " " English Style	11	222
" " " with Chives	13	222
" " " with Red Herring	12	222
Soft Boiled Eggs	1	220
Stuffed Eggs, (Deviled Eggs)	14	223
" " Another Form of	15	223

Chapter 15, Nos. 1—58.

Omelets, Pancakes, Waffles, Noodles and Pie.

	No.	Page.
Apple Fritters	51	236
" Pie	17	228
" " Another kind of	18	229
" Strudel	49	235
Asparagus Omelet	3	224
Baked Macaroni	53	237
Chicken Patties	36	234
" Pie	30	232
Chocolate Pie with Whipped Cream	58	238
Cold Game Pie, Venison, Doe, Boar, Rabbit	41	234
Cooked Noodles	45	235
Filled Pancakes	11	227
Fish Macaroni	55	237
Goose Liver Pie	38	234
Grape Pie	27	232
Ham Noodles	47	235
Lemon Pie	16	228
Macaroni Pudding	56	237
" " with Ham	54	237
" " with Parmesan Cheese	52	236
Mince Pie	24	231
" " Another Kind of	25	231
Muffins	57	238
Noodle Pudding with Apples as Dessert	48	235
Noodles	44	234
Omelet for Breakfast	1	224
" " with Meat or Champignons	6	225
Omelet with Parmesan Cheese or Oysters	5	225
Oyster Patties	43	234
Pancakes	10	226
Patty Paste	31	233
Peach Pie	21	230
Pea Omelet	4	225
Pheasant Pie	39	234
Pie made from Grouse, Hazelhen, Snowhen, Snipe, Quail, Partridge	40	234

	No.	Page.
Pieplant Pie, Rhubarb	26	231
Pigeon Pie, English Style	37	234
Potato Pancakes		226
Puff Paste Scallops	33	233
" " Tarts	34	233
Pumpkin Pie	23	230
Rabbit Pie	42	234
Rolled up Apples	50	236
Sand Cake Waffles	14	227
Soup Noodles	46	235
Sour Cream Pie	28	232
Squash Pie	22	230
Strawberry or Huckleberry Pie	19	229
" Pie with Whipped Cream	20	229
Sweetbread Patties	35	233
Sweet Omelet as Dessert	2	224
" Pnff Paste	32	233
Vanilla Cream Pie	29	232
Waffles	12	227
" Another Form of	13	227
Whipped Cream Omelet	7	225
" " " as Dessert	8	226
Whipped Cream Omelet with Frosting	9	226
Yeast Waffles	15	228

Chapter 16, Nos. 1—23.

SAUCES.

	No.	Page.
Apple Sauce	1	239
Apricot Sauce	12	241
Stewed Sliced Apples for Sauce	18	243
Black Mulberry Sauce	7	240
Blueberry Sauce	10	241
Cherry Sauce	2	239
Currant Sauce	5	240
Dried Apples for Sauce	19	243
Fresh Plum Sauce	8	240
Gooseberry Sauce	9	241
Greengage Sauce	14	242
Melon Sauce	16	242
Orange and Apple Sauce	17	242
Peach Sauce	11	241
Pear Sauce	22	244
Pineapple Sauce	15	242
Plum Sauce	13	241
Prunes for Sauce	20	243
Raspberry Sauce	4	240
Rhubarb Sauce	21	243
Strawberry Sauce	3	239
Tomato Sauce	23	244
Whortleberry or Huckleberry Sauce	6	240

Chapter 17, Nos. 1—128.

DESSERTS.

	No.	Page.
Apple Fritters or Banana Fritters	54	259
Apple Rice Pudding	2	245
" Strudel	55	259
Apricot Ice	120	275
" Cream	109	273
" Rice Pudding	5	246
Arrack Cream with Whipped Cream	73	265

	No.	Page.
Baked Almond Pudding	36	254
" Apple and Farina Pudding	39	255
" " Stew Pudding	40	255
" Charlotte Pudding	35	254
" Cherry Pudding	31	253
" Chocolate Pudding	38	254
" Cream Pudding	27	252
" " "	43	256
" Farina Pudding with Fruit	30	253
Baked Flour Pudding	44	256
" Lemon Pudding	32	253
" Macaroon Pudding	51	258
" Noodle Pudding	49	257
" Omelet Pudding	42	256
" Potato Pudding	33	253
" " " to be served with Meat	34	254
Baked Quince Pudding	50	258
" Rice Pudding	28	252
" " Pudding with Fruit Layers	29	252
Baked Rye Bread Pudding with Apples	48	257
Baked Sponge Pudding	45	256
" Sweet Pudding with Wine Frosting	47	257
Baked Veal Roast Pudding	46	256
" Yorkshire Pudding	37	254
Biscuit Tortoni, Macaroon Mousse	60	261
Black Pudding	25	251
Cabinet Pudding	8	247
Carthusian Dumplings with Wine Sauce	53	258
Champagne Cream	100	271
" Frappe	124	276
" Sherbet	123	276
Cherry Jelly	70	264
" Pudding	22	250
" "	103	272
" Rice Pudding	3	246
Chocolate Cream	88	268
" " Prepared Cold	87	268
" Ice Cream	112	274
" Mousse	89	268
" Pudding	11	248
" Strudel	56	259
" " with Dressing	57	260
Coffee Cream Prepared Cold	86	268
" Ice Cream	113	274
" Mousse	91	269
Cold Apple Cream	78	266
" " Pudding	79	266
" Chocolate Pudding with Farina	97	270
Cold Lemon Cream	82	267
" " "	85	268
" Rice Pudding with Peaches	98	270
" " Starch Pudding	96	270
Corn Starch Pudding	81	267
Count Pueckler or Layer Mousse	95	269
Currant and Raspberry Pudding	101	271
Farina Pudding No. 1	14	249
" " " 2	23	251
Fine Baked Apple Pudding	41	255
Flour Pudding	12	248
French Toast	52	258
Fried Apple Pockets	59	260
Froth or Foam Pudding	7	247
Gooseberry Pudding	102	272
Goose Liver Pudding	21	250

—402—

	No.	Page.
Hazelnut Mousse	92	269
Hill Cream	104	272
Layer Pudding	13	249
Lemon Ice Cream	110	273
" " Garnished with Fruit	128	277
" Jelly	67	263
Macaroni Pudding	15	250
Maple Syrup Ice	125	276
Meat Pudding with Rice Layers	17	250
" " Another Form of.	18	250
Mutton Kidney Pudding	19	250
Nectar	80	267
Nut Ice Cream	114	274
Orange Cream Prepared Cold	84	267
" Gelatine	72	264
" Jelly	68	263
Peach Ice	119	275
" Cream	108	273
" Rice Pudding	4	246
Pineapple Cream	76	265
" Ice	121	275
" Cream	111	274
" Jelly	69	264
" Mousse	93	269
Plain Cold Rice Pudding	99	271
" Rice Pudding	6	247
Plum Pudding	10	248
Potato Pudding	16	250
Pudding a la Brandenburg	26	252
Raspberry Cream	75	265
" Ice	118	275
" " Cream	107	273
Rice Pudding	1	245
Roll Dumplings	126	277
" " Better Kind of	127	277
Rum Cream with Cherry Sauce	61	261
" or Cognac Mousse	94	269
Russian Cream	83	267
Sour Cream Pudding	24	251
Steam Noodles	58	260
Strawberry Cream	74	265
" Ice	117	275
" " Cream	106	272
" Jelly	71	264
Tea Ice Cream	115	274
Tutti-Frutti Ice	122	276
Vanilla Cream	77	266
" Ice Cream	105	273
" " " with Fruit	116	275
" Mousse	90	269
Veal Roast Pudding	20	250
Wheat Bread Pudding	9	247
Whipped Cream Pudding	62	261
White Wine Jelly with Fruit Layers	66	263
Wine Cream	64	262
" Jelly with Rice Layers	65	262
" Pudding	63	261

Chapter 18, Nos. 1—29.

BEVERAGES.

	No.	Page.
Almond Milk	21	281
Bishop	9	279
Cardinal, (Cold)	10	279
Chocolate	22	282
" Iced	23	282
Cocoa	24	282
Coffee	28	283
Cold Lemonade	19	281
" Punch	1	278
Cream Punch	11	279
Currant Wine	17	281
Egg Punch	5	278
Fine Lemonade	20	281
Gooseberry or Currant Wine	29	283
Grog	8	279
Hot King's Punch	3	278
" Punch	2	278
" Wine	7	279
Iced Tea	27	283
May Bowl or Woodruff Punch.	16	280
Peach Punch	15	280
Pineapple Punch	12	280
President's Punch, cold or warm	4	278
Raspberry Wine	14	280
Strawberry Punch	13	280
Tea	25	282
" with Vanilla	26	282
Warmbeer	18	281
Warm Burgundy Punch	6	279

Chapter 19, Nos. 1—111.

BREAD AND CAKES.

	No.	Page.
Apple Cake	16	288
Biscuit	7	285
Bread Sticks	6	285
Cheese Cake	19	289
Cherry Cake	17	289
Coffee Cake	8	286
" " with Egg Cream	24	290
Currant Cake	20	289
Filled Berliner Pancakes or Stuffed Doughnuts	11	287
Health Bread or Groats Bread.	5	285
Huckleberry Cake	22	290
Onion Cake	23	290
Plum Cake	18	289
Poppy Seed Cake	21	289
Round Coffee Cake No. 1	13	287
" " " " with Raisins	14	287
Rye Bread with Leaven	3	284
" " Yeast	4	285
Schnecken (Snails)	10	286
Stollen	15	288
Streusel Coffee Cake	9	286
Wheat Bread No. 1	1	284
" " " 2	2	284
Wreath Cake	12	287
Baking Powder Cakes.		
Almond Tart Filled with Cream	72	304
Angel Cake	111	315
Angel Food	101	312
Angel's Food	42	295
Apple Tart	62	301
Biscuit Tart	81	307
Blitz-Kuchen	107	314
Bread Tart	65	302
Bremer Block	49	297
Brown Spice Cake No. 1	51	298
" " " " 3	86	308
Caraway Cake	54	299
Cheese Tart	61	301
Cherry Tart	67	303
Chocolate Tart	91	310
" " No. 2	94	311

	No.	Page.
Coffee Cake with Almond Frosting	25	290
Coffee Cake with Chocolate Frosting	26	291
Cream Puffs	103	313
" "	104	313
Date Cake with Whipped Cream	84	308
Devil's Food	41	295
Emperor Tart	69	304
English Cake	56	299
" Bride's Cake (Fruit Cake)	92	310
Farina Tart	85	308
Fence Tart	97	311
Fig Cake	44	296
Filled Biscuit Rolls	83	308
" Sand Tart	95	311
Fire Tart	74	305
Flat Cake	37	293
Fruit Cake	48	297
" "	102	313
" Tart	98	312
Gold Cake	34	293
Good Tart Dough	93	310
Heaven's Food	77	306
" Tart	76	306
Hunter's Tart	73	305
Lard Cake	89	309
Layer Cake with Banana Filling	31	292
" " with Chocolate "	29	291
" " with Cocoanut "	32	292
" " with Cocoanut No. 2	45	296
" " with Jelly Filling.	30	292
Lightning Cake	53	298
Love Chocolate Cake	100	313
Meringue Tart	78	307
Mouth Pockets	70	304
Natron Cake	52	298
Orange Tart	63	301
Plain Fruit Cake	50	297
Potato Tart or Cake	38	294
Puff Paste Strips	71	304
" " Tart with Cream.	66	302
Rice Cake or Tart	39	294
" Tart with Oranges	64	302
Round Coffee Cake No. 2	27	291
Sand Tart	82	307
Scotch Tart	88	309
Sexton's Cake	90	309
Silver Cake	35	293
Sour Cream Cake	59	300
" " Doughnuts	105	314
Spice Cake No. 2	58	300
" " " 4	87	309
" "	108	314
Sponge Cake	33	292
" "	79	307
Stirred Cake	28	291
Strawberry or Raspberry Puff Tart	68	303
Strawberry Short Cake	40	294
Sunshine Cake	47	297
" "	99	312
Tea Cake	46	296
Theater Cake	36	293
Thousand Puff Tart	60	300
Tree Tart	96	311
Walnut Cake	57	299
" "	110	315
" Tart	80	307

	No.	Page.
Whipped Cream Cake	109	315
White Almond Tart	75	305
Wit Cake	55	299
Yellow Angel's Food	43	295

Chapter 20, Nos. 1—27.

Fillings and Frostings for Cakes.

	No.	Page.
Almond Filling	5	316
" Frosting for Fruit Tart No. 1	23	319
Almond Frosting No. 2	24	319
Banana Filling	10	317
Caramel Frosting	20	319
Chocolate Filling	8	317
" Frosting No. 1	12	317
" " " 2	13	317
" " " 3	14	318
Cocoanut Filling	9	317
Cream Frosting for Fruit Cake	26	319
Date Filling	11	317
Fruit Frosting	25	319
Glaze Frosting for Honey Cake	21	319
Lemon Filling	6	316
" Frosting	16	318
Nut Filling No. 1	2	316
" " " 2	4	316
Plain Almond Frosting	27	320
" Frosting	19	318
Raisin Filling	3	316
Rum Frosting	22	319
Tutti-Frutti Frosting No. 1	17	318
" " " 2	18	318
Vanilla Filling	1	316
" Frosting	15	318
Walnut Filling	7	317

Chapter 21, Nos. 1—53.

COOKIES.

	No.	Page.
Almond Bread	46	331
" Heaps	5	322
" Macaroons	6	322
" Puffs	11	323
" Straws No. 1	12	323
" Strips No. 2	49	332
Anise Cookies	14	324
Brown Cookies No. 1	18	324
" " " 2	20	325
" " " 3	21	325
" " " 4	22	325
" " " 5	23	326
" Peppernuts No. 1	41	330
" " " 2	42	330
Butter Cookies	1	321
" "	19	325
" Straws with Almonds	27	327
Chocolate Cookies	28	327
" Macaroons with Almonds	7	322
Chocolate Macaroons with Cocoanut	8	322

	No.	Page.
Cinnamon Stars	52	332
Cocoanut Kisses	51	332
" Drop Cakes	31	328
Egg Cracknels	45	331
Flawns	10	323
Ginger Snaps	40	330
Hazelnut Cookies	2	321
Hickory Drop Cakes	32	328
Honey Cakes	50	332
Kisses	3	321
Lady Fingers	53	332
Molasses Cookies	30	327
Mother's Cookies	35	329
Nut Chocolate Cookies	29	327
Oatmeal Cookies No. 1	16	324
" " " 2	17	324
Peanut Drop Cakes	36	329
" Straws	37	329
Plain Peppernuts	48	331
Raisin Cake	39	329
Sand Cookies	4	321
Small Hermit Cakes No. 1	33	328
" " " " 2	34	328
" Plain Cookies	38	329
Springele	47	331
Sugar Peppernuts	43	330
Vanilla Flawns	15	324
" Stars	44	331
" Straws	13	323
Walnut Macaroons	9	322
White Cookies No. 1	24	326
" " " 2	25	326
" " " 3	26	326

Chapter 22, Nos. 1—20.

CONFECTIONERY.

	No.	Page.
Bon-Bons	7	334
Butter Scotch	4	333
Caramels	19	336
Chocolate Candy	8	334
" Caramels No. 1	6	334
" " " 2	12	335
" Fudge	3	333
" "	18	336
Cocoanut Drops	11	335
Cracker Jack	16	336
Fudge	20	337
Ice Cream Candy	15	336
Lemon Candy	5	334
Molasses Candy	1	333
Nut Candy	9	334
Peanut Candy	13	335
Popcorn Balls	17	336
Popcorn Candy	10	335
Pulled Taffy	14	335
Vinegar Taffy	2	333

Chapter 23, Nos. 1—115.

PRESERVES.

	No.	Page.
Apple Jelly	44	348
Apricot Marmelade	48	349
Apricots in Jelly	6	339
" or Peaches in Brandy	9	340
Asparagus	66	353

	No.	Page.
Blackberries	29	344
Blackberry Juice	64	352
Black Currant Jelly	41	348
Blueberries, Huckleberries	24	343
Blueberry Jelly	43	348
" Juice	60	352
Canned Fried Chicken, Duck or Wild Game	107	363
Canned Salmon or other Large Fish	106	363
Canned Spring Chicken	105	363
Champignons in Vinegar	89	358
" or Mushrooms	88	358
Cherry Syrup	57	351
Chili Sauce	111	364
" "	113	365
Cognac Cherries	14	341
Corn	74	355
Crab Apple Jelly	45	348
Cranberries	27	344
Currants	28	344
Currant Jelly	40	347
" Juice	63	352
Dill Pickles	114	365
Dried Apples	99	362
" Pears	98	361
English Chow Chow	112	364
Glazed Chestnuts	102	362
Gooseberries	21	343
Grapes	37	347
Grape Jelly	54	350
Green Almonds	36	346
" Beans	69	354
" Color for Coloring Ices or Garnished Dishes	101	362
Green Gages	25	343
" or Small Yellow Oranges	34	346
" Peas	73	355
Large Sweet Cherries	13	341
Melons	30	345
Mince Meat	108	363
Mirabelle Plums No. 1	15	341
" " " " 2	16	341
Mustard Pickles	95	360
" "	115	365
Orange Juice	61	352
Parsley	84	357
" Carrots, Celery and Borage for the Winter	86	357
Peaches and Apricots	4	339
" in Jelly	5	339
Peach Marmelade	47	349
Pear Jam	52	350
Pearl Onions	87	358
Peeled Green Gages	26	344
" Plums	18	342
Piccalilli	76	355
Pickled Apricots	8	340
" Crab Apples	23	343
" Peaches	7	339
" Pears	22	343
" Plums	20	342
" Walnuts	35	346
Pine Apple	3	338
Plain Tomatoes for Soup	78	356
Plums	17	342
Plum Jam	51	350
" Marmelade	49	349
Plums in Red Wine	19	342
Pumpkin	33	345
Quinces	31	345
" in Cognac	32	345

	No.	Page.
Quince Jelly	46	349
" Juice	62	352
Raspberries	2	338
" in Jelly	11	340
Raspberry Jelly	39	347
" Marmelade	50	349
" Syrup	55	351
" Wine	58	351
Red Beets	72	354
Rhubarb	81	356
" Marmelade	82	357
Roasted Almonds	103	362
Rose Jelly	42	348
Salted Almonds	104	363
" Green Beans	70	354
Salt Pickles No. 1	91	359
" " " 2	92	359
Sauerkraut	83	357
Spiced Pickles	96	361
" Green Tomatoes	109	364
Stoned Sour Cherries	12	340
Strawberries	1	338
" in Jelly	10	340
Strawberry Marmelade	38	347
" Syrup	56	351
Sugared Lemon and Orange Rind	100	362
Sweet-Sour Sliced Cucumbers	110	364
Sweet Tomatoes	79	356
To keep Red and White Cabbage	85	357
Tomato Catsup	80	356
" Marmelade	77	356
Truffles	90	359
Tutti Frutti in Arrack	65	353
Vinegar Pickles No. 1	93	360
" " " 2	94	360
Wax Beans No. 1	67	353
" " " 2	68	354
Whole Tomatoes	75	355
Wild Strawberry Wine	59	351
Young Carrots	71	354

SANDWICHES.

	No.	Page.
Celery Sandwiches	2	366
Chicken Sandwiches	4	366
Corned Beef Sandwiches	8	366
Egg Sandwiches	1	366
" "	6	366
Olive Sandwiches	3	366
Peanut Sandwiches	7	366
Veal Sandwiches	5	366

Chapter 24.

THE MENU.

	Page.
Everyday Dinner	869
Family Dinner	367
Fine Dinner	368
" Supper	368
Large Buffet	369

Chapter 25, Nos. 1—63.

For Invalids, Convalescents, etc.

	No.	Page.
Apple Drink	62	385
Baked Apples	44	381
Barley Gruel	13	374
" Soup with Sweetbreads and Asparagus	15	375
Barley Water	61	384
Beaten Egg	46	381
" Yolks of Egg	47	381
Beef Bouillon	3	372
" Tea	4	373
" " with Cognac	5	373
Bouillon of Game	9	373
Breast of Chicken with White Gravy	32	378
Breast of Pigeon with White Gravy	33	379
Breast of Partridge with Madeira Sauce	34	379
Calf's Tongue	31	378
Chicken Puree Soup	17	375
Chocolate Cream with Red Wine	41	380
Cream of Almonds as a Beverage	58	384
Egg Foam	45	381
Fig Sauce	50	382
Fish Cutlet	37	379
" for Invalids	36	379
Foam with Red Wine	48	382
Fried Calf's Brain	30	378
Fruit Soup	24	376
Ice Cream	49	382
Iron and Wine	54	383
Lamb Bouillon	8	373
Lung Tea with Malt Sugar	53	383
Meat Puree for the Seriously Ill.	27	377
Milk Jelly	40	380
" Lemonade	59	384
Minced Meat, Veal or Lamb Steak	29	377
Noodle or Grits Soups made of clear Bouillon	10	374
Pearl Barley Soup	22	376
Pigeon or Partridge Bouillon	7	373
" " " Puree Soup	19	375
Plain Barley Gruel	16	375
" Soup for Invalids	20	376
Poultry Bouillon	6	373
Puree of Game Roast; for a severely ill patient	28	377
Raw Ham with Egg	35	379
Red Wine Soup	25	377
Rhubarb Jelly	42	380

	No.	Page.
Rice Gruel	14	374
" in Milk	39	380
" with Red Wine	43	381
Roll Soup with Bouillon	12	374
Ryebread Soup	23	376
Ryeflour Soup and Milk Soup	26	377
Sago Soup with Game Bouillon	11	374
Strong Beef Tea	1	372
Tea from Medicinal Herbs	52	383
Thin Rice Soup	21	376
Toast and Water	60	384
Veal Puree Soup	18	375
Vegetables for Invalids	38	379
Warm Milk with Cognac	56	383
Water with Lemon Juice	63	385
Weak Veal Bouillon	2	372
Whey	55	383
Yolk of Egg and Wine	57	384
Zwieback (Sweet Toast)	51	382

Chapter 26.

MISCELLANEOUS.

	Page.
Broiling	389
Burns, Treatment of	386
Carving Poultry in the Kitchen	387
Comparative Table of Weights and Measures	391
Flour	389
Meat Carving	386
Meats, Time Required for Broiling or Frying	387
Meats, Time Required on the Stove or in the Oven	388
Roasting	388
Roasting in the Pan—Frying	388
Roasting in the Oven	389
Yeast	390

MEMORANDA.

MEMORANDA.

MEMORANDA.

MEMORANDA.

MEMORANDA.

MEMORANDA.

MEMORANDA.

MEMORANDA.

MEMORANDA.

Just a Reminder.

"Lina Meier's Genuine German Cooking and Baking," when first published, appeared in one volume, in English-German combined.

To meet a great demand of the public, the publishers have decided to publish this, the second, revised and enlarged editions, in three different volumes:

*One in the English language,
One in the German language,
One in English-German combined.*

The books are all bound in full cloth and either one or all of the different editions can be secured at any time through book stores or from the publishers, by addressing:

WETZEL BROS. PRINTING CO.,
324-328 Broadway,
Milwaukee, Wis.

Just a Reminder.

"Lina Meier's Genuine German Cooking and Baking," when first published, appeared in one volume, in English-German combined.

To meet a great demand of the public, the publishers have decided to publish this, the second, revised and enlarged editions, in three different volumes:

One in the English language,
One in the German language,
One in English-German combined.

The books are all bound in full cloth and either one or all of the different editions can be secured at any time through book stores or from the publishers, by addressing:

WETZEL BROS. PRINTING CO.,
324-328 Broadway,
Milwaukee, Wis.

Reprint Publishing

FOR PEOPLE WHO GO FOR ORIGINALS.

This book is a facsimile reprint of the original edition. The term refers to the facsimile with an original in size and design exactly matching simulation as photographic or scanned reproduction.

Facsimile editions offer us the chance to join in the library of historical, cultural and scientific history of mankind, and to rediscover.

The books of the facsimile edition may have marks, notations and other marginalia and pages with errors contained in the original volume. These traces of the past refers to the historical journey that has covered the book.

ISBN 978-3-95940-110-4

Facsimile reprint of the original edition
Copyright © 2015 Reprint Publishing
All rights reserved.

www.reprintpublishing.com

www.ingramcontent.com/pod-product-compliance
Lightning Source LLC
Chambersburg PA
CBHW060104170426
43198CB00010B/761